AA

Explorer Mexico

Fiona Dunlop

AA Publishing

Page 3: 17th-century convent in Desierto de los Leones National Park, Mexico City
Page 4: harvest in Oaxaca state
Page 5 (top): Mazatlan fishermen
Page 5 (left): in preparation for the Day of the Dead
Page 5 (right): pyramid of Kukulkan, Chichén Itzá
Pages 6 and 7 (top): near Loreto, Baja California
Page 7: the mountain encircled city of Guanajuato, Guanajuato
Page 8: Mil Cumbres, Sierra Madre Occidental National Park, Michoacán
Page 9 (main picture): copper goods on sale at Lake Chapala, Jalisco
Page 29: stone-carving of Quetzalcoatl
Page 253: public transport, Puebla
Page 269 (top): in the Hotel Cuidad de Mexico
Page 269: Les Moustaches, Mexico City

Los Cabos Westin Regina resort, Baja California

Written by Fiona Dunlop
Original photography by Rick Strange
Revised second edition 1999. Reprinted 1999
First published 1995

Edited, designed, produced and distributed by AA Publishing,
Maps © The Automobile Association 1995, 1999
Distributed in the United Kingdom by AA Publishing, Norfolk House, Priestley Road, Basingstoke, Hampshire, RG24 9NY.

A CIP catalogue record for this book is available from the British Library.

ISBN 0 7495 1887 1

Published by AA Publishing (a trading name of Automobile Association Developments Limited, whose registered office is Norfolk House, Priestley Road, Basingstoke, Hampshire RG24 4NY. Registered number 1878835).

Colour separation by Fotographics Ltd
Printed and bound in Italy by Printer Trento srl

Titles in the Explorer series:
Australia • Boston & New England • Britain • California
Caribbean • China • Costa Rica • Crete • Cuba • Cyprus • Egypt
Florence & Tuscany • Florida • Germany • Greek Islands • Hawaii
India • Indonesia • Ireland • Israel • Italy • Japan • London
Mallorca • Moscow & St Petersburg • New York • New Zealand
Paris • Portugal • Prague • Provence • Rome • San Francisco
Scotland • Singapore & Malaysia • South Africa • Spain
Tenerife • Thailand • Turkey • Turkish Coast • Venice • Vietnam

How to use this book

ORGANISATION

Mexico Is, Mexico Was
Discusses aspects of life and culture in contemporary Mexico and explores significant periods in its history.

A–Z
An alphabetical listing of places to visit. The book begins with a section on Mexico City, and is subsequently divided into geographical regions. Places of interest are listed alphabetically within each section. Suggested walks, drives and Focus On articles, which provide an insight into aspects of life in Mexico, are included in each section.

Travel Facts
Contains the strictly practical information that is vital for a successful trip.

Hotels & Restaurants
An alphabetical listing of places to stay and places to eat. Entries are graded budget, moderate or expensive.

ABOUT THE RATINGS
Most places described in this book have been given a separate rating. These are as follows:

▶▶▶ **Do not miss**

▶▶ **Highly recommended**

▶ **Worth seeing**

MAP REFERENCES
To make the location of a particular place easier to find, every main entry in this book is given a map reference, such as 176B3. The first number (176) indicates the page on which the map can be found, the letter (B) and the second number (3) pinpoint the square in which the main entry is located. The maps on the inside front cover and inside back cover are referred to as IFC and IBC respectively.

Contents

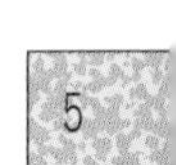

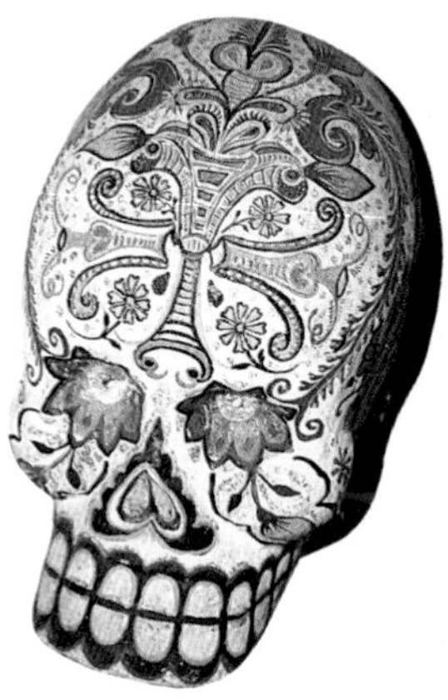

Fiona Dunlop's taste for the tropics and fascination for developing countries have taken her around the world. Between trips, she has written AA Explorer books on Paris, Singapore and Malaysia, Indonesia, Vietnam, Costa Rica and India. For this guide she has scoured Mexico from Baja to the Yucatán, sampled endless tacos and tequilas and revelled in the complexities of Mexican public transport. And she still wants to go back.

My Mexico by Fiona Dunlop

How can I define the countless threads woven through this complex country? Every time I go there, it seems another knot is untied – but then more appear. Ancient ruins are restored to become essential landmarks, a new museum reveals sublime exhibits, yet another glorious beach unfolds, or a threatened indigenous group takes a radical political stand.

Above all, Mexico's terrain is daunting – distances are vast and landscapes are empty. I'll never forget my first visit to the archaeological site of Monte Albán. After enduring a day-long bus journey from Mexico City, winding through endless arid sierra to reach Oaxaca, I headed for this hilltop site – a mere 2,500 years old. The stones didn't exactly speak, but the space above, below and around me did. In its clearly defined form, uninterrupted by vegetation, there was a sense of scale, of light and of majesty that I had never experienced before.

Time, too, takes on new meanings here. There may be no alternative to that knee-stiffening bus journey or to the finger-tapping wait for restaurant service. Then suddenly things speed up, the old *mañana* cliché becomes obsolete, and Mexico moves on, as dynamically and unexpectedly as its turbulent 4,000-year-old history.

Behind the dynamism are the Mexicans themselves. On one occasion, I found myself at the wheel of a car stuck in front of a flash-flooded road in Baja California. I was still two hours away from the airport, where the last flight of the day awaited me. Then along came a gang of boys offering to push me through the fast-moving torrents. As I steered the car, watching the water rise to just below my knees, I did wonder if they really knew what they were doing. Miraculously, we reached the other side, the agreed *pesos* were handed over, and I started the engine. Off it went, and I caught my flight – which, unusually, left on time. Unpredictability is yet another Mexican trait.

Scratch the surface of Mexico and there is an incredible wealth of culture: not just the obvious crafts that fill markets and tourist shops, but contemporary creativity that produces striking architecture, haunting music, moving paintings and thought-provoking literature. Whether rural or urban, mainstream or rebel, passionate beliefs are the hallmarks of this country's extraordinary vitality.

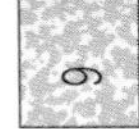

Mexico Is

Throwing off their habitual reserve, Mexicans spring into action for over 4,000 fiestas and festivals every year. Whether taking place in a tiny village or on a national scale, fiestas verge on a sacred institution, offering the opportunity to dance, sing, eat and drink intensively in an outburst of exuberance that mirrors the vibrant colours of this vast land.

From the grand colonial cities of the central highlands to the more modest villages of the south, façades are brilliant pink, dense turquoise, saffron yellow or deep red-ochre. Baroque churches resemble ornate Mexican cream-cakes, ice-cream parlours rival the rainbow and vibrant Indian costumes lend colour to the whole. Yucatán *cenotes* (sinkholes) offer shades of emerald and jade, the Caribbean topaz and aquamarine, and the Pacific a deep cobalt. It is a palette which reflects one aspect of the complex Mexican spirit – exuberance.

Typically colourful houses in Oaxaca

VIVA MEXICO Wherever you are, at whatever time of the year, day or night, you are likely to experience one of Mexico's myriad festivals. Birthdays of patron saints, anniversaries of obscure heroes, political and historical milestones, agricultural rites or Catholic feast days – all are celebrated with equal animation. In the political calendar the most important is Independence Day (15–16 September) when the *zócalo* (main square) of every town and village in the country becomes a heaving mass of humanity gathered to roar *Viva México!* Costumed processions and brass bands transform a formal occasion into an uninhibited communal catharsis – with tacos and tequila and sky-shattering fireworks. The anniversaries of the Mexican revolution (20 November) and the Battle of Puebla (5 May) offer equally intensive revelry.

RELIGIOUS CALENDAR After four centuries of Catholicism, church festivals are now deeply embedded in the Mexican psyche and calendar. Over 90 per cent of the country is Catholic, dedicated to venerating the Virgin of Guadalupe ever since this vision appeared to a local peasant in 1531 (see page 64). On 12 December her feast is heralded in churches all over the country and celebrations are particularly lively in the town of Tequila where two weeks of festivities culminate in bullfights, rodeos, music and dancing. Delirious Mardi Gras carnivals in the ports of Veracruz and Mazatlán announce the approach of Easter Week, highlight of the religious calendar. Candle-lit processions and Passion plays can last over four days, and Taxco's famous week-long *fiesta* is comparable in scale to that of Seville in Spain. Countless other Christian celebrations pepper the calendar and include the inimitable feast of San Antonio, when household pets

Traditional conchero dancers perform in Mexico City's Zócalo

(including pigs, chickens and cows) are decked out in ribbons and flowers and taken to church for a blessing. Far more fervent in their drug-imbued nature are the Easter processions of the Tarahumara, in the northern sierra (see page 101).

PRE-HISPANIC REMNANTS Any excuse to don a mask and brilliantly coloured costume is sufficient. Ordinary people indulge with gusto, along with countless itinerant traditional dance groups who perform pre-Hispanic fertility rites or act out the lives of patron saints at village festivals. *Voladores* (see pages 165 and 170) spin through the air in a breathtaking re-enactment of a Totonac ritual, 'devils' are defeated by 'priests' and 'Christians' by 'Moors'. Vividly coloured Quetzal head-dresses monopolise Puebla's dances while, in Oaxaca, the *Guelaguezta*, two weeks of dance festivities in late July, has its roots in corn-god rituals. In Mexico All Saints' Day becomes the Day of the Dead (see pages 144–5), a unique combination of pagan and Christian customs.

> ❏ 'During these ceremonies ... the Mexican opens himself up. They allow him to reveal himself and dialogue with a god, his homeland, friends or relatives. During these days, the silent Mexican whistles, shouts, sings, lights fireworks, fires his pistol into the air. Fires his soul.' Octavio Paz: *The Labyrinth of Solitude*, 1950. ❏

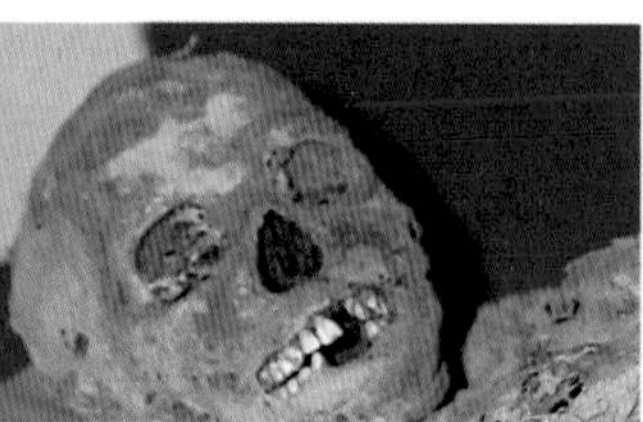

The Mexicans are fervent lovers of myths and legends, assimilating the cult of death into the cult of life. Their fascination with death is revealed in every aspect of their existence, from rattling fiesta *skeletons to the soul-wrenching laments of* mariachi *singers and the often tragic vagaries of Mexican history.*

For the Aztecs life and death were two sides of the same coin – the sun set only to rise again, just as dead souls would be reborn once more. This deeply rooted belief led to their downfall when the Spanish *conquistadores* Hernán Cortés was mistakenly welcomed as the reincarnation of the Aztec god Quetzalcóatl who, according to legend, had sailed towards the horizon of the rising sun, vowing to return. With the arrival of Christianity and its central belief in resurrection, Mexicans could adapt to the new spirituality without totally abandoning the old. Hence Mexico's traditional serenity in the face of death.

MASOCHISM Even the Mayas, previoulsy considered peaceable, are now recognised as having pursued warfare with enthusiasm. Their tattoos, painful in application, were seen as proof of courage. Today, the exploits of the famous divers plunging 40m into the pounding Pacific at La Quebrada, Acapulco may be inextricably linked with macho *bravura*, but they reveal the same fascination with challenging the ultimate – death. And as Papantla's *voladores* (flying dancers) spin headfirst to earth in a ritual that dates from pre-Hispanic days, they too are toying with the infinite; casualties occur in both cases. More widespread is the Mexican propensity for transcending life through alcohol (usually *mezcal* or tequila) or the use, mainly by the Huichols and the Tarahumara, of the hallucinogenic *peyote*, which is an integral part of their spiritual rituals. But then comes the reverse, *fiesta*, an exuberant and chaotic expression of life.

Many pilgrims to Guadalupe take the last few steps on their knees

RELIGION Behind these attitudes lies a unique fusion of two systems of belief which place the afterworld on an equal footing with this life. Human sacrifice was common practice among most Mesoamerican (Mexican and Central American) civilisations, with victims becoming deified at the moment their hearts were torn from their bodies. Election for sacrifice was the ultimate reward as it transported a poor mortal from

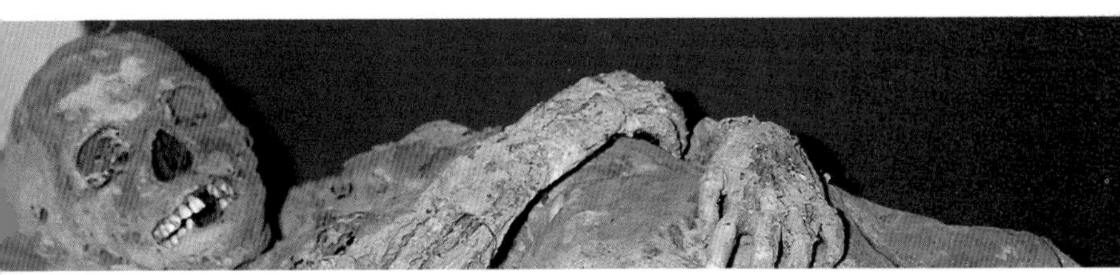

his insignificant place in the universe into a divine realm. The arrival of Spanish friars with their claims that salvation was only attainable through the worship of one Christian god may have changed certain aspects of their rituals and switched images of 'idols' for those of the Virgin Mary and the saints, but it hardly had any impact on the deeply fervent nature and morbid obsessions of the indigenous Mexicans. Incense-choked ceremonies continued and the Christian cross became combined with the Mayan symbol for the *axis mundi* (crossroads of the world). Draped in pine branches – both a Christian and pagan symbol – these crosses still dominate the plazas of certain villages in the Chiapas highlands. And what else is the Day of the Dead but an extension of the Mexican worship of the dead, right down to skull and skeleton imagery and the bone-shaped bread rolls.

CATASTROPHES Natural disasters frequently occur here, perhaps reinforcing the nation's acceptance of death as part of life. Volcanic eruptions, earthquakes, floods and hurricanes hit the country with seemingly inexorable regularity, shattering the structure of daily existence and underlining the fragility of life. Dry inhospitable land, remoteness and inaccessibility have long been the lot of Mexico's *campesinos* (peasant farmers) when they are not fighting battles to reclaim land stripped from them by corrupt administrations. Decimated by disease and appalling working conditions within a century of the Conquest of 1519, the indigenous people are still fighting for their rights, producing extremes of protest that have often provoked a bloody response from the authorities.

These papier-mâché images for the Day of the Dead are on show in Mexico City's Anahuacalli Museum

Folk art, in a bewildering variety of colours, forms and media, is present all over the country, as diverse as the landscapes and peoples from which it originates. Industrialised techniques may be creeping in to replace time-honoured skills passed on down the generations but little can change the imagination and flair of the craftspeople.

Most regions of Mexico have specific craft traditions, whether pottery, woodcarving, basket-making, weaving, metalwork or simple objects made from pine trees, maguey fibre and sisal. The markets of large towns generally offer the best selection for visitors, with the majority concentrated in the states of Michoacán, Jalisco, Puebla, Guerrero, Oaxaca and Chiapas, but Mexico City and Guadalajara offer the most varied selection from every region of the country. Hard to resist, these beautifully crafted objects were once extensions of spiritual beliefs, a rapidly disappearing practice in the face of commercialism and large-scale demand.

METALWORK Silver and gold brought the *conquistadores* to Mexico and their importance is still apparent today in the silver shops of Taxco, teeming with tourists bargaining for hammered, engraved or inlaid jewellery and *objets d'art*. By law all silver items are stamped with 'sterling' or .925 (the minimum silver content) so confusion with alloys is impossible. Gold jewellery, sometimes inlaid with precious or semiprecious stones, is usually crafted from 14- and 18-carat gold. Intricate designs (often cast using the lost-wax method with moulds of clay and beeswax) remain a speciality of the Mixtecs in Oaxaca, while filigree, incorporating local pearls and coral, is a Yucatán tradition. Gleaming copperware has its ancestral home at Santa Clara del Cobre in Michoacán where the Tarascans excel at creating flawless pitchers, pans and platters. Most popular of all Mexican metals is tin, a cheap and malleable alloy that can be beaten or cast into countless quirky *milagros* (votive offerings to saints), ornamental boxes, lanterns, candelabra, mirror frames or trees swarming with fruit and birds.

WOOD Whether in the form of rustic 'colonial' furniture or terrifying ceremonial masks, sleek Seri ironwood carvings or vividly patterned Oaxacan imaginary animals, Mexican wood is cut, carved and coloured into endless shapes and forms. Naively crude Tarahumara animal carvings contrast with Uruapan boxes and chests decorated with sophisticated lacquering techniques. The popular pre-Hispanic *equipale*, a curved-backed chair of leather and slatted wood, is made in Tlaquepaque, while ritual masks – in every macabre and garish form – are a national passion, reaching heights of fantasy in Guerrero and Michoacán. Unfortunately, the quality of these masks has been much affected by tourist demand.

Silversmith at work in Taxco. This fine colonial town is famous for its silverware which is crafted locally and recognised for the originality of its designs

Eclectic display of local crafts in Tzintzuntzán, Michoacán

POTTERY As closely linked to daily needs as to ceremonial purposes, pottery is a continuation of indigenous traditions which were strongly influenced by Hispanic-Moorish techniques. The Valley of Mexico is the main area where *barro* (terracotta) is produced, but these basic kitchen containers are easily surpassed in the elaborate clay *arbol de la vida* ('tree of life') made in Metepec. Puebla and Guanajuato are home to ceramics which are renowned for their sophisticated glazed patterns, whether the *azulejos* (painted tiles) of Dolores Hidalgo, majolica-style objects from Guanajuato, or Puebla's famed *talavera poblana* (considered the *crème de la crème* of decorative *azulejos*) and superb ceramic tableware. Oaxaca is famous for its black pots from San Bartolomé, while the impoverished Tzotzil villages of Chiapas produce whimsical little clay *animalitos* (animals) sold for derisory amounts by child vendors. However, the extremes of fantasy lie in the state of Michoacán where diabolic figures are conjured up by Ocumicho's women potters, and Patambán's green pineapple ceramics vie with the popularity of Tzintzuntzán's subtle cream and black designs.

❑ The most realistic masks are those fashioned out of wax. Their complex fabrication involves starching, moulding and hardening cotton gauze which is painted then coated with thin layers of wax. Before one of the all-male dancers dons a mask he allows the wax to soften in the sun so that it will assume the contours of his own face. ❑

Colourful and exotic, Mexico's indigenous peoples are the most marginalised section of the population. Reflecting a strong continuity with the past, they are the tragic victims of a political system and world view whose economic ends disregard their constitutional rights. Their very existence is now under threat.

Mexico's original inhabitants are an estimated 29 per cent of the total population (94.3 million, of mostly mixed indigenous and Spanish blood). Despite Independence and the 1910 Revolution, their lot has deteriorated with the demands of a rapidly modernising Mexico. Most exist in extreme poverty and earn less than the minimum daily wage as artisans or members of the *campesino* (peasant-farmer) class. Their lands are fast being eroded by changes made to the constitution during President Salinas' term. Titles are no longer binding, tempting many to surrender ownership to liquidate debt. With negligible social assistance, their only recourse is to try for work in the big cities or seek illegal seasonal employment north of the border. For others the last resort is begging.

An illustration in Mexico City's Museum of Anthropology depicting ritual sacrifice

❑ The Nahua, who speak Náhuatl, the ancient Aztec language, are the largest ethnic group. Substantial numbers of Mixtecs and Zapotecs exist in Oaxaca, and Otomis (Nahñu), Mazahua, Totoacs, Purepecha, Huichols and Huastecs in central and coastal areas. The once isolated Tarahumara (Raramuri) are the only people to be found in significant numbers in the north. ❑

SURVIVORS The 1992 Quincentenary of Columbus' 'discovery' of the Americas was commemorated by indigenous pressure groups as '500 years of resistance'. After what writer Octavio Paz has described as 'massive rape' under Spanish colonialism, it is miraculous that 56 languages survive. Local bosses have always treated any bid for autonomy with brutality. Even the foundation of the INI (National Institute for Indigenous Peoples) in 1949 was to acculturate these original inhabitants into the Mexico of the *ladino* (non-indigenous). Such ambiguity is accentuated by the promotion of indigenous culture for touristic purposes.

REVOLT Today *campesino* agrarian uprisings are based on Marxist ideology and Liberation Theology. The most successful has been that of the

EZLN (Zapatista National Liberation Army) in the state of Chiapas, home to an estimated 750,000 indigenous people. On 1 January 1994 they attacked San Cristóbal de las Casas and four other towns, aiming to embarrass the inauguration of NAFTA (North American Free Trade Agreement). Adopting the name and aims of the revolutionary Emiliano Zapata, some 2,000 armed rebels, demanded respect for their land titles, proper health care, education and democracy while denouncing the '70 years of dictatorship' of the ruling PRI (Institutional Revolutionary Party). Some 160 Zapatistas died in the first year of conflict.

❑ Eighty per cent of Mexico's indigenous communities suffer from severe alcohol problems. In the state of Oaxaca, where indigenous people make up 70 per cent of the population, about half the communities are assessed as 'very marginalised' with no sewage disposal or electricity. Inhabitants are often iliterate and undernourished. ❑

WAR ON THE INTERNET Armed confrontation rapidly changed into a war of words fronted by the charismatic *subcomandante* Marcos, who regularly publishes in left-wing newspapers such as *La Jornada*, as well as on the Internet. In 1996, the Accords of San Andrés Larrainzar, offering indigenous autonomy, were made between the government and the EZLN, but so far these have not been honoured. Meanwhile, violent paramilitary attacks on local communities have been seen as a PRI-backed effort to destabilise a region whose rich natural resources are attracting foreign interest. Resistance is not limited to the EZLN. In 1996, the EPR (Popular Revolutionary Army) struck in Guerrero. Their demands have resulted in increased militarisation in the region. In the Yucatán peninsula, alarm bells are also ringing about the comparable plight of its indigenous inhabitants. The army's growing sophistication, combined with the interests of *ladino* landowners, are proving a threat to indigenous rights and survival.

Yautepec, in Morelos state: an old town with great rural charm

Tacos and tortillas...

Mexican cuisine is a combination of traditional Indian dishes and later Spanish influences, often spicy and invariably accompanied by tortillas and red beans. Its famous mole *(sauce), when cooked over three days according to custom, is divine; when prepared in fast-food style it can be tasteless and depressing.*

From north to south the basic ingredients in Mexican food remain much the same. Outside the main towns it is difficult to find restaurants of a high standard, but Pacific and Gulf regions compensate with a wealth of exquisitely fresh seafood (lobster, red snapper, abalone, clams) on often gargantuan scales or integrated into delicious soups. Resort towns have an increasing variety of sophisticated restaurants catering for an international clientèle. Meanwhile, Mexican *nouvelle cuisine* is found above all in the capital, where stylish restaurants revive pre-Hispanic recipes.

Mexican eating habits require a shift from the usual Western pattern, as the main meal of the day is taken between 2 and 5. This is when restaurants offer *comidas corridas* (set menus) of three or four courses which are usually excellent value. Evening meals are lighter, often consisting of *antojitos* ('little whims') or tortilla-based snacks.

TORTILLAS A national passion, the tortilla (a flat, unleavened corn pancake) constitutes the basis of daily Mexican fare. Although traditionally made from distinctively flavoured corn-meal, blander, mass-produced wheat tortillas are making in-roads into Mexican culture. But whatever its composition, the plain tortilla can be quickly transformed into a variety of more interesting dishes.

A taco or *burrito* is a stuffed tortilla. In its wrapping come infinite combinations of vegetables, beans, cheese, chicken or meat seasoned with chilli sauce, freshly prepared and sold on street corners or in markets. *Tamales* are southern euphemisms for tacos wrapped and steamed in corn husks or banana leaves, which sometimes have sweet fillings. The big difference with *enchiladas* is that here the taco is fried or baked in a cheese sauce then served hot. The *quesadilla*, on the other hand, is usually filled with cheese. The ultimate variation is the *tostada*, a flat tortilla piled with meat, cheese, tomatoes and the ubiquitous *frijoles* (red beans). And even the breakfast classic, *huevos rancheros*, consists of fried eggs and chilli in a tomato sauce, placed – where else? – on a tortilla.

❑ Of the 200 or more varieties of chilli, few actually blow the roof of your mouth off (though beware of the Yucatán's *habanero* or the *serrano*) and most merely add spice to your life. However, recent public health studies indicate that frequent consumption can lead to gastric cancer – Mexico has one of the world's highest incidences of this disease. ❑

Give us our daily bread – tortillas have been the staff of life for Mexicans for centuries

INFINITE INGREDIENTS *Mole poblano*, the nearest thing to a national dish, is a rich, dark sauce which comes straight out of Mexico's baroque past. According to legend, it was invented in a Pueblan convent to disguise a rather skinny turkey for an imminent visit from the Viceroy. Recipes vary immensely and a real *mole* is ideally cooked slowly over three days, but it basically incorporates numerous spices, herbs, chillies, cinnamon and almonds with chocolate – a drink inherited from the Aztecs who liked it frothy and spiked with chillies.

Time is an essential ingredient in Mexican cuisine, whether 24-hour marinades in citrus juice (orange being the Yucatán special), Veracruz- and Acapulco-style *ceviche* (raw seafood marinated in lime juice), slow steaming of meat or vegetables wrapped in banana leaves or the stewing of beef in *pulque* (maguey beer). Meat runs the gamut from iguana to suckling pig, lamb, beef, kid goat and venison. The best beef comes from the cattle ranches of Chihuahua, while Monterrey is well-known for its (*cabrito*) roast kid.

❑ They came, they saw and they conquered, but the *conquistadores* also brought with them apples, goats, chickens, pigs, wheat, garlic and sugar. In return, Mexico gave the world chocolate, vanilla, potatoes, corn, pumpkins, avocados and countless other fruits, seeds and nuts. ❑

Deserts, mountains and tropics

The cliché – land of contrasts – is hard to avoid when describing Mexico's variety of climates, altitudes, vegetation and landscapes. In a few hours you can move from cool, dry mountain air to steamy, tropical climes, from pine trees to banana palms, or from a palette of sandy yellows to one of lush greens.

Shaped like a funnel which links the US with Central America, Mexico sweeps down the map from the arid, desert lands of the north to the tropical south, with a final twist as it turns east into the flat Yucatán peninsula. An area of almost 2 million sq km offers a challenge to the most intrepid of travellers: even Baja California extends 1,300km from north to south. But distances are not the end of the story. Mexico is dominated by lofty mountain ranges which offer not only transitional contrasts in vegetation and climate but also spectacular canyons and waterfalls.

THREE LEVELS A common division of this vast land creates three climatic zones: *tierras calientes* (hot lands); *tierras templadas* (temperate lands), and *tierras frías* (cold lands). The last covers the central highlands and plateau (including Mexico City) where altitudes averaging 2,000m are sandwiched between the mighty *cordilleras* of the Sierra Madre. The highest, permanently snowcapped peaks tower to over 5,000m in an east–west volcanic belt and create a fourth level – the *tierra helada* (frozen land). *Tierras calientes* cover the Gulf and Pacific coastal regions, the Isthmus, most of Chiapas and all of the Yucatán peninsula: these are Mexico's humid tropical zones where temperatures rarely drop below 20°C and can hit as high as 40°C. The last pockets of rainforest lie in the extreme south in Chiapas on the Guatemalan border. Between the two extremes lie temperate regions of mountain slopes and the depressions of the central plateau with average altitudes of 1,200m.

In the oven-like northern plains rainfall is minimal and comes mainly in autumn, whereas coastal regions and the south, particularly Tabasco and Chiapas, experience year-round precipitation with heavy summer downfalls.

WHAT GROWS? Little can survive in the arid north and Baja California other than drought-resistant plants such as fast-growing shrubs, thorn bushes and cacti. But move south through the temperate zones to

The rugged peaks of the Sierra de la Giganta, west of Loreto, in Baja California Sur

The prickly pear cactus is cultivated for its fruit and for its leaves, both edible

the humid coastal regions (bordering Mexico's 9,200km of coastline) and you encounter many of the country's 20,000 species of flowering plants: cascading bougainvillaea, fragrant frangipani, jacaranda trees draped in blue flowers, poinsettias, hibiscus, clambering gold cups and vivid clouds of orange flame-trees are interspersed with classic palm trees and feathery casuarinas. Cultivated crops include sugar-cane, cocoa, coffee and fruits such as papayas, bananas, pineapples, limes, guavas, avocados and mangoes. Savanna regions are home to a range of agaves, from the prickly pear to the maguey, often towered over by spindly yuccas. In the wet regions of the *tierra templada* thrives Mexico's national tree, the *ahuehuete*, an imposing giant cypress which has reached mind-boggling proportions in Tule, Oaxaca, while in the mixed forests of higher altitudes Moctezuma pines are joined by oaks, cypresses and an Australian import, the eucalyptus.

❑ Lagoons and mangrove swamps dot Mexico's coasts from the Pacific to the Caribbean. These offer the best birdwatching and are often within easy reach of resorts. Mazatlán has Teacapán and Acapulco the lagoons of Coyuca and Papagayo. Puerto Escondido boasts those of Chacahua, Veracruz the marshes surrrounding the Río Papaloapán, Villahermosa the Usumacinta marshes and the Yucatán peninsula the wetland reserves of Celestún, Río Lagartos and Sian Ka'an. On the Gulf coast virtually the entire coastline from Tampico north to the border is wetland. ❑

Mexico is often cited as an example of untethered environmental disaster. Industrial pollution, deforestation, toxic waste, waste dumping, water depletion and ecologically unfriendly transport have stained the nation, perhaps indelibly. Despite stringent government laws designed to put a brake on Mexico's notoriously bad environmental record, official laxity and general ignorance prevail.

In a country which has experienced an unprecedented industrial boom since the 1960s, together with an average annual population growth of 2.7 per cent (now reduced to 1.6 per cent), little thought, let alone money has been given to preserving the environment. Thus rocketed into the industrial age, Mexico shudders on the brink of ecological disaster.

A CITY IN CRISIS Mexico City is the world's largest metropolis. Thermal inversions aggravate industrial and automobile emissions (particularly in the winter months) with dangerous levels of ozone, carbon dioxide, nitrogen dioxide and sulphur dioxide creating smog and provoking fatal respiratory illnesses.

Numerous factories around the capital pump out thousands of tons of sulphur dioxide, one of the worst air pollutants, but also generate a sizeable part of Mexico's gross national product. Their chimneys were once seen as milestones on the way to the First World; today they are perceived as symbols of environmental degradation.

In 1992 it was announced that government and private industry would invest $5 billion over three years to meet minimum standards of pollution control. Some factories were moved out of the urban area and inspections of pollution-control equipment led to the shut-down of over 100 plants. More serious still is the situation on the US border, where over 32 million tons of toxic waste are produced annually by 150 industrial plants. 'Clean' industries (often owned by multi-national companies) are now setting the example in Monterrey, Guadalajara and the capital. But enforcement of regulations remains lax and officials ignore warning signals: the 1992 gas explosion in Guadalajara which killed 200 people could have been avoided if local complaints had been investigated.

DEPLETED RESOURCES At the beginning of this century Mexico City stood more than 1m above Lake Texcoco; it now lies over 3m below as

Vehicle emissions exacerbate Mexico City's poor air quality. Respiratory diseases are a direct result of atmospheric pollution

❑ 'Mexico City is an omen, that jammed city of toxic air and leafless trees may be the first to know asphyxiation by progress ... Mexico City warns the rest of the species of all that has gone wrong with modernity's promised millennium of happiness.' Carlos Fuentes, contemporary Mexican writer. ❑

its foundations continue to sink. Excessive industrial and domestic water needs (1998 figures registered the capital's consumption at 35,000 litres per second) have so depleted the lakes of the Valley of Mexico that water is now being pumped from 200km away. The surrounding agricultural regions are directly affected by this, along with other problems such as soil erosion which affects about half the territory. Mexico has lost over 95 per cent of its tropical forests to loggers, farming and fires. The number of fires soared in 1998, partly due to the drought engendered by El Niño and partly due to arson. Vast tracts of virgin forest were wiped out on the border of Oaxaca and Chiapas. On a more positive note, there are now over 58 national parks and biosphere reserves, and ecological awareness is growing.

TOO LATE? The side effects of industrial pollution are notorious, and in the north much of the blame has been laid at the door of *maquiladoras* (assembly plants using American imported materials for re-export) which profit from lax environmental controls. In 1995, *maquiladora* plants in Matamoros were ordered to pay US $10 million to settle law suits over birth defects in Texas. The American Medical Association has labelled the border area 'a virtual cesspool and breeding ground for infectious diseases'. Meanwhile, smoke billows out of stacks which, say some American environmentalists, could affect up to 16 US national parks. NAFTA has brought changes including a jointly financed development bank and committee to pay for the clean-up of the border and supervise future projects. These new moves may combine with growing public and government awareness (seen in the creation of biosphere reserves and the gradual replacement of urban bus engines with eco-friendly ones) to create a less polluted nation for the next generation.

Driving restrictions aim to reduce pollution in the capital

The advance propaganda for NAFTA (North American Free Trade Agreement) during President Salinas' sixth year in office promised a radical improvement in standards of living. But in December 1994, a month after incoming President Zedillo took over, the dream shattered with the crash of the peso. *Mexico's erratic history continues, and recent efforts to retrench have had conflicting results.*

In a seemingly inevitable recyling of its past, Mexico is currently licking its wounds after celebrating an apparent change for the better in its political and economical life. At first it welcomed what had superficially seemed a forward-looking presidency, steering the nation towards the First World. During President Salinas' term (1988–94), Mexico joined its economic fate to those of the US and Canada on a 15-year path aiming to abolish all trade barriers between the three countries. NAFTA was greeted with enthusiasm by some, who saw it as a much-needed road to *modernidad* (modernity), and with dark pessimism by others, who predicted a wave of Americanisation and a socio-economic takeover that did not correspond to the complex Mexican soul.

CRISIS Considered today to be one of the world's wealthiest men, Salinas and his coterie profited from the spoils of privatisation while the gap between rich and poor widened. His years in power were marked by corruption and fraudulent elections, both endemic in the structure of the 70-year-old ruling PRI (Institutional Revolutionary Party). Assassinations included those of presidential candidate Luís Donaldo Colosio, party chairman José Ruiz Massieu and some 300 opposition PRD (Democratic Revolutionary Party) sympathisers. Hardly had Salinas left office after the inauguration of NAFTA than the carefully promoted image of Mexico's success story tumbled. The *peso* crash in 'Black December' 1994 led to a US$20 billion US government bail out at interest rates well above market norms.

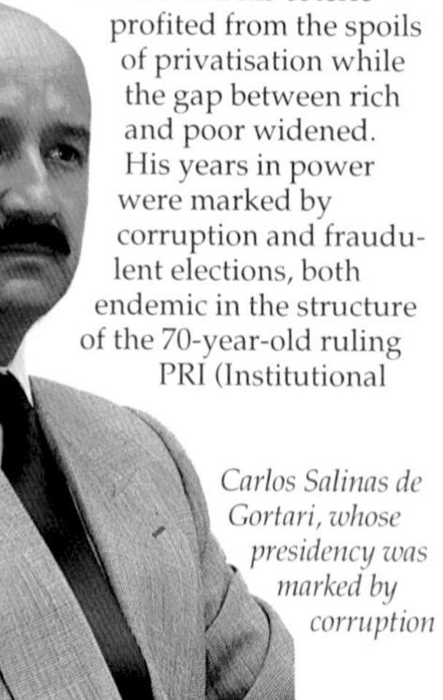

Carlos Salinas de Gortari, whose presidency was marked by corruption

'TEQUILA EFFECT' Initial lack of confidence in Mexico's ability to ride out the storm led to capital flight, with a resultant domino effect on the Latin-American economy, dubbed the 'tequila effect'. Recession bit hard in 1995–6, leading to increased social problems, inflation exceeding 50 per cent and subsequent and repetitive price hikes on basic goods and services (gas, electricity, tortillas, transport, sales tax). Crime has soared, particularly in the capital, while members of the wealthy classes are faced with the constant threat of kidnap for ransom. So the boom went bust with a vengeance. But how is Mexico likely to fare in the next millennium?

A FRESH START? By late 1997 it seemed that the worst was over on the financial front, with Mexico attracting US$8 billion in portfolio investment and generating an annual trade surplus of over US$1 billion. In the wake of the Asian currency crisis, its relative stability and increased privatisation then became attractive to foreign investment. Despite

internal problems, the *peso* has remained steady against the dollar since 1996. Moreover, 'Mexico's democratic opening', helped by Zedillo's apparent sincerity, has created some hope for this corruption-weary country. By 1998 the Catholic PAN (National Action Party), already a considerable voice in the Chamber of Deputies, controlled six states out of a total of 32, and in July 1997 PRD presidential candidate Cuauhtemoc Cardenas won elections for the post of Mexico City's mayor. Economic growth for 1997 hit 7 per cent, inflation dropped to below 20 per cent and, despite the turbulent situation in Chiapas and increasing violence in the streets, economists at least were sanguine. Government reports underlined that Mexico's 1997 figures were the strongest since 1981. However, the nation's dependency on world oil prices, combined with the uncertainties brought by Asian devaluations, make it ever vulnerable.

❑ While the former president, Salinas, hides out in the Republic of Ireland, the only European country without an extradition agreement with Mexico, his brother, Raul Salinas, languishes in jail. He is being held in custody, charged with involvement in the murder of his brother-in-law, Massieu, in addition to a number of other offences: being an intermediary for drug-trafficking Columbian cartels, money-laundering and embezzlement. His secret Swiss bank accounts have been revealed holding over US$120 million. Meanwhile, 45 million Mexicans live in conditions of extreme poverty. ❑

Monterrey's proximity to the US has stimulated rapid growth

Mexico shares a 3,326km border with the United States. This vast strip has long been a testing-ground for two different cultures which meet, clash and join economic forces. But interaction does not stop there. Particularly since the advent of NAFTA in 1994, Mexico's way of life is increasingly dominated by American culture.

There is nothing new about Mexico's fears of a cultural and political takeover: the country has been under invasion by the US in one form or another since the 1846–8 Mexican-American War. This cost Mexico half its territory. Since then, the arrival of each new fad or technology from the north has been denounced by pessimists as heralding the end of Mexican traditions. However, extensive US investment is nothing new: in the late 19th century the policies of dictator Porfirio Diaz led to substantial American participation in profitable oil, mining, lumber and transportation concerns.

Today, with Mexican labour costs far below those in the States, *maquiladoras* (industrial plants that process duty-free American raw materials for re-export), which were once only located along the border, are expanding into the heart of the country.

Tijuana, Mexico's legendary border town, offers a warped and seedy vision of Mexican culture

THE BORDER STORY Fears of invasion are no less strong north of the border. For the last 50 years Mexican workers, legal and illegal, have flooded the labour markets of California and adjoining states in search of decent wages, much of which are sent home to their families. The great border divide traverses north-eastern Mexico by following the course of the Rio Grande/Rio Bravo before zigzagging west across sierra and desert, punctuated by official border-posts. With over a million illegal immigrants apprehended trying to enter the US and another 315,000 succeeding (in 1996), workers north of the border fear for their jobs and politicans stir up nascent xenophobia.

Since 1994 the US has taken stronger measures. Tijuana has a long 'Tortilla Curtain' equipped with night-vision infrared cameras, and in 1996 a wall was erected on the Ciudad Juarez–El Paso crossing. San Diego's 'Operation Gatekeeper' was responsible for the deaths of 80 illegal immigrants in 1997. California has also responded by denying schooling and other public services to undocumented workers. Despite these tough measures, a bi-lateral analysis presented in 1998 pointed out that stepped-up security has not reduced the number of

❑ The US anti-drugs drive, which includes donations of state-of-the-art military equipment and training, has been viewed by some as a covert means of maintaining influence in the area. In February 1997 Mexico was officially recognised as a partner in the anti-drugs campaign, but against a background of scandals that have linked such trafficking to the highest political level. ❑

illegal immigrants. According to this report, an estimated 2.4 million of a total 7.3 million Mexican residents (approximately 3 per cent of the US population) were unauthorised.

AMERICANISATION Eighty per cent of Mexico's exports now go to the States. Tomatoes grown in Sonora and Sinaloa have contributed to the 60 per cent rise in agricultural exports since 1994, and cheap Mexican oranges threaten the growers of Florida and California. But Mexico's US imports have also increased. Billions of dollars' worth of merchandise is carried back over the border on shopping-trips that do not show up in official statistics. Meanwhile, supermarkets increasingly stock American products that are edging out home-grown produce. Highly commercialised Christmas and Hallowe'en are gradually undermining Mexican traditions of Noche Buena (Christmas Eve) and the Day of the Dead. McDonalds, Taco Bell and Domino's Pizza are ubiquitous in the cities. Cellular phones, holidays in Disneyland and aerobics classes are now part of the life-style of upwardly mobile Mexicans. Such changes could be part of globalisation or they could be signs of a radical change in the culture of a nation.

Downtown Tijuana

Mexico owes much of its fate as the recurring victim of natural disasters to the expanding layers deep below the earth. Some of its highest peaks are active volcanoes, constant reminders of the seismic vulnerability of the nation.

The Náhuatl name for the towering, snow-capped peak that looms over Mexico City – Popocatépetl, or 'smoking mountain', is a sign that the Aztecs were only too familiar with its true nature. Craters, too, are an integral part of Mexico's landscape but over the centuries earthquakes have destroyed city centres from Oaxaca to Guadalajara, culminating in the calamitous quake that struck Mexico City in 1985. In June 1997 Popocatépetl started erupting after 67 dormant years, showering ashes down on the capital and in 1998 its slopes were still out of bounds.

VOLCANIC BELT The Sierra Neovolcánica Transversal, which forms the southern boundary of the central plateau, is spiked by Mexico's highest peaks: Cofre de Perote, Pico de Orizaba (or Citlaltépetl – Mountain of the Star), La Malinche, Iztaccíhuatl (Sleeping Woman) and Popocatépetl.

To the west lies the volcanic zone of Michoacán where in 1943 the appearance of the Volcán de Paricutín led to nine years of lava flow that englufed the little village of Parangaricutiro.

The last puffing peak at the Pacific end is that of the active Volcán de Colima, overshadowed by the mighty and now inactive crater of the Nevado de Colima. There are 3,000 volcanoes in Mexcio, and in the south the 1982 eruption of El Chichon (Chiapas) left villages in darkness for two days: even the sky over Hawaii showed the effects.

SEISMIC CHAOS The earthquakes of 19 and 20 September 1985, respectively measured 8.1 and 7.5 on the Richter scale. They succeeded in shattering Latin America's largest hospital, government buildings, hotels and countless homes, and put the final nail in the coffin of the image of municipal and federal organisations, which proved to be hopelessly inadequate in the face of such a calamity. The job of excavating the victims of the quakes from beneath the rubble was almost entirely undertaken by the inhabitants themselves, who worked round the clock in a desperate attempt to uncover survivors among the estimated 6,000 dead.

The Church of San Juan, in Parangaricutiro, rises forlornly from the lava that engulfed it in 1943

Mexico Was

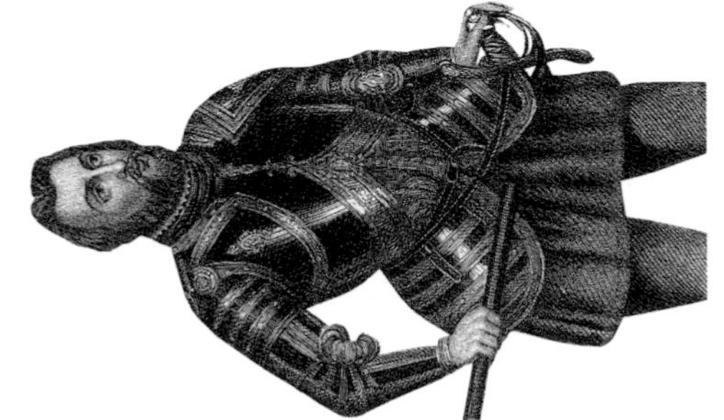

The mysterious Olmecs, analysed through a mere three archaeological sites, have only been recognised as Mexico's ancestral civilisation in the last few decades. Their art, social organisation and astronomical and numerical achievements have profoundly influenced Mesoamerica's subsequent cultures – Zapotecs, Mixtecs, Toltecs and Teotihuacans.

Corn (maize) was the prosaic catalyst of ancient Mexican history. Between 12,000 and 6000 BC, during the last Ice Age, waves of nomadic hunters crossed the Bering Strait via a land-bridge between Siberia and Alaska.They gradually moved south, shifting their base according to the laws of available food.

The earliest evidence of man in Mexico dates from around 20,000 BC, but it was not until about 6000 BC that the peoples of this 'desert culture' took up a more settled existence, cultivating corn, pumpkins, beans and chilli peppers. By the onset of the pre-Classic period (*c*1200 BC) settlements had sprung up all over Mexico and included the mother of all Mesoamerican cultures, the Olmecs, one of the most artistically advanced of Mexico's puzzling and still unresolved network of civilisations.

ORIGINS UNVEILED Scattered across the sweltering, alluvial coastal regions of Veracruz and Tabasco, the vestiges of the Olmecs (meaning 'People from the Land of Rubber') lay shrouded in jungle for over 2,000 years, to be uncovered only in the 1930s. This prompted a remake of the whole historical jigsaw puzzle.

❑ Scarcity of stone in the Veracruz/Tabasco region probably stimulated the Olmecs' inland trade network, which led them through the Valley of Mexico and Morelos to the state of Guerrero. Olmec sites and cave paintings here date from about 1500 BC and their influence even extended through Oaxaca to Izapa on the Guatemalan border. ❑

❑ The Olmecs' greatest achievement was their imposing carved monolithic basalt heads, measuring as much as 3m and weighing over 20 tonnes. Basalt was dragged and rafted up to 100km from its source near Tuxtla. These noble heads, believed to be portraits of Olmec rulers, all wear headgear resembling helmets, probably protection for war and during ball games (*juegos de pelota*). ❑

Olmec head at Mexico City's Museum of Anthropology

Three main Olmec centres came to light: San Lorenzo (*c*1500–900 BC), La Venta (900–400 BC) and the contemporaneous Tres Zapotes. During the heyday of La Venta, Olmec groups increased in number; earth mounds and platforms for houses and temples were arranged around patios to form ceremonial centres, but their architecture was poor in comparison to their advanced sculptural, calendric and mathematical achievements. But their zenith was short-lived and by about 600 BC Olmec prosperity was eclipsed by the economic and political development of Monte Albán.

JAGUAR AND COLOSSUS Jade, serpentine, obsidian, nephrite and basalt were among the Olmecs' favourite materials, which they carved to create fantastic sculptures ranging from delicate jade heads, engraved stelae (stone slabs), figurines, stone masks and votive axes to monolithic altars and astonishing colossal basalt heads. A recurring theme is the jaguar, or were-jaguar (half-human, half-jaguar), the Olmec god of all gods, symbolising day and night and depicted in stelae, masks and figurines as a cleft-headed babe-in-arms or in motifs used on pottery. This motif emerged around 1150 BC at San Lorenzo. They generally wore little or no clothing, and ornamentation ranged from mutilated teeth to earplugs, pendants, headbands, body tattoos and breastplates. The use of wooden or clay masks representing jaguars, ducks and mythological birds was restricted to shamans and priests during agricultural and religious festivities.

STRUCTURE AND REVOLUTION The highly élitist society of the Olmecs reserved the centre of their settlements for priests and rulers while the outlying areas were left to corn-growing farmers, fishermen, tradesmen and lesser craftsmen. Judicial, military and religious power lay firmly in the hands of the first group, they also had the benefit of higher grounds, less subject to floods and more liable to produce bumper crops.

Revolution was ever present and both San Lorenzo (*c*900 BC) and La Venta (*c*400 BC) underwent violent downfalls, their statues smashed and mutilated for as yet unknown reasons.

Monument 19, showing an Olmec in a head-dress enveloped by a plumed serpent, displayed at the open-air museum of La Venta, in Villahermosa

During the Classic period of ad 250–900, central Mexican arts and sciences reached their peak. Each civilisation had its own distinctive cultural traits, but interaction accelerated along with trade networks. Of the many flourishing centres of this prosperous era, three were dominant: Monte Albán, Teotihuacán, and El Tajín.

Mexico's Golden or Classic Age saw an abundance of art and architectural forms that were the result of increasingly wealthy and powerful city states. Although the basic farming economy and elitist social structures remained the same, innovation appeared in architectural techniques and styles, art, and science, resulting in an unprecedented cultural brilliance.

MONTE ALBÁN

Although the Zapotecs traded with and were influenced by the Olmecs, it was not until the decline of the latter that Monte Albán (see pages 198–9), the main Zapotec civic and religious centre, appeared around 500 BC. Some 200 settlements peppered the Valley of Oaxaca but, over the next five centuries, it was the lords of Monte Albán who held sway and extended their military and economic influence. They used calendric calculations, used the bar-and-dot numerical system, wrote the first true literary text in Mexico (found in glyphs on the Danzantes slabs dating from 600–500 BC), and painted stuccoed edifices alongside elaborate subterranean tombs, a testimony to Monte Albán's great wealth. Their frescoes display a strong Teotihuacán influence, and their pantheon included many of the Mesoamerican gods. By 200 BC the Zapotec state had consolidated its power which lasted several centuries until the early 8th century AD. Its decline may have been due to the rising power of smaller-scale states in the Valley of Oaxaca, including that of the Mixtecs (see page 37), who subsequently used Monte Albán as a ceremonial site.

❑ Preclassic: 2000 BC–AD 250
Classic: AD 250–900
Post-classic: AD 900–1521
Monte Albán: *c*500 BC–AD 700
Teotihuacán: *c*200 BC–AD 750
El Tajín: AD 550–1100. ❑

❑ The significance of Teotihuacán is demonstrated by the fact that 500 years after its fall the Aztecs, including Moctezuma himself, worshipped at the ruined site and, even in the early 20th century, local indigenous Mexicans still practised rites at its pyramids. According to the Aztecs, Teotihuacán had given birth to the Fifth Sun, creator of the universe, at a meeting of all the gods (the four earlier ones having met catastrophic ends). Quetzalcóatl was sacrificed in order to create mankind. ❑

TEOTIHUACÁN

This was the first planned metropolis of the Americas, laid out on a precise grid plan according to planetary alignments around 100 BC. At its zenith, in AD 500, Teotihuacán covered over 20sq km and had a population of 120,000 to 200,000. At that time, this was the largest and possibly most powerful city in the Western hemisphere, with some 600 pyramids honouring their gods, artisans brought in from other regions and a vast trade network. Along with their jade, green obsidian, pottery and clay figurines, the cosmospolitan Teotihuacános exported their

architectural styles and cosmology to the Gulf Coast and as far as the Maya lowlands, including Kaminaljuyu and Tikal in present-day Guatemala. Its inexorable expansion in central Mexico meant that Teotihuacán had no rival states, although its military strategy and methods are still a matter for speculation. Writing, books, the bar-and-dot numerical system (already used by the Olmecs and the Zapotecs), and the 260-day sacred year were all part of their achievements (see pages 228–9).

Los Danzantes (The Dancers) – Zapotec carvings at Monte Albán

CLASSIC EL TAJÍN

As Teotihuacán's influence declined – hastened by the destruction of the city centre by fire around AD 750 – so rose the star of the Classic El Tajín civilization on the Gulf Coast. Its founders, possibly of Huastec origin, generated their own artistic techniques, which reached their peak in El Tajín between AD 300 and 900; its administrative and religious importance endured until around 1100. The ball-game, accompanied by human sacrifice, was fervently practised there and was continued by the Totonacs, who later occupied the area. El Tajín's eleven ball-courts, illustrative *bas-reliefs* and numerous related carvings – from the heavy stone *yugos* (yolks) and *hachas* (axes) to the finely chiselled, flat human profiles that were possibly linked to the losers' decapitation – reflect the key role played by the ball-game in El Tajín's way of life.

El Tajín's most striking structure is the Pyramid of the Niches, once painted in red, black and blue

The Maya are best noted for their complex systems of astronomy and mathematics, prolific city-building and advanced artistic styles. This astonishing civilisation flourished for over 1,500 years, its power bases gradually shifting from the southern lowland cities in Chiapas and Central America to the northern Yucatán. Interstate raids and rivalries, together with environmental problems, eventually spelled its decline.

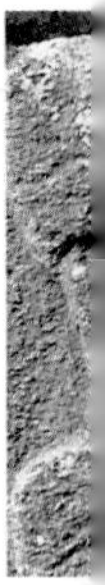

Around 1500 BC pre-Mayan groups started moving south-east from the Olmec heartland along the Gulf Coast, and the first settlements appeared around 1000 BC. By the onset of the Classic period (AD 250–800), the Maya world was experiencing the same development as the Valley of Oaxaca (Monte Albán) and the Valley of Mexico (Teotihuacán). Palenque, Yaxchilán, and Bonampak (as well as sites in Guatemala, Belize, and Honduras) had large populations, and their religious constructions became increasingly ambitious. The building of Calakmul (thought to be the Maya's largest city, with some 60,000 inhabitants), Uxmal, Kabah, Cobá and Chichén Itzá occurred at the zenith of the civilization. By the early 9th century, southern Mayan cities went into decline and were abandoned, probably due to overpopulation, depletion of natural resources and external economic and military pressures.

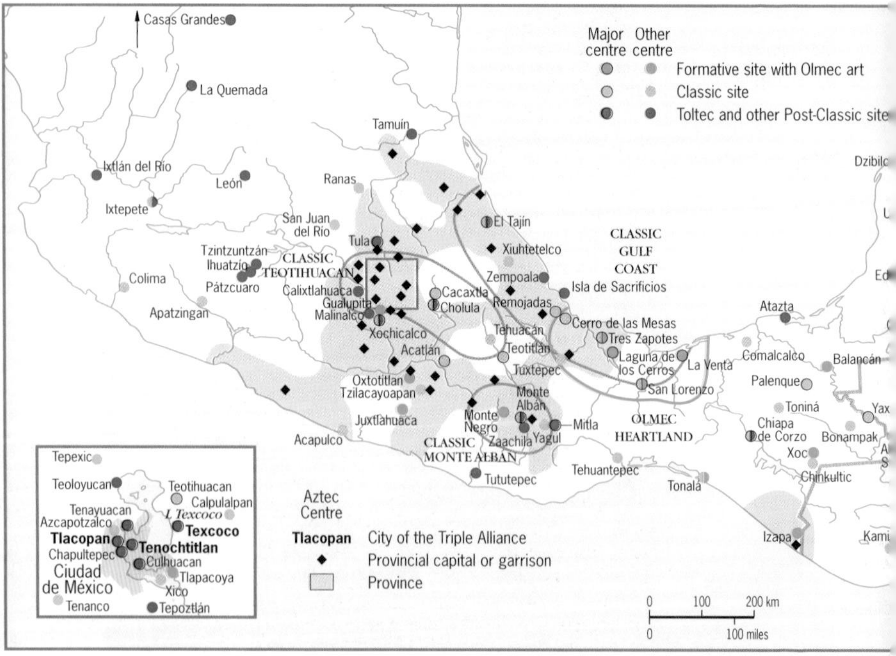

The Postclassic Maya (900–1521), saw the flowering of northern Yucatán cities in and around the Puuc Hills and new influences

brought to Chichén Itzá by the Chontal Maya from the Gulf Coast. Although there was a strong continuity in architecture, religious symbolism and hieroglyphics, this later period also saw a more extensive use of stone mosaic and greater emphasis on death and militaristic themes. Major decline from 900 to 1200, witnessed the collapse of the lesser Puuc sites, then of Chichén Itzá, followed by the rise of the walled city of Mayapan, located near its contemporary, Tulúm. This ascendancy was short-lived, and by the arrival of the *conquistadores*, the Maya had lost any centralised authority.

Mesoamerican civilisations

STRUCTURE The Maya were dependent on agriculture, and the peasant farming class lay at the bottom of a hierarchical social structure. Each city was dominated by noble families (with the king, at the top) who created a network of regional alliances and were supported by warriors and a priestly caste. Architects, scribes, artisans and traders formed the middle class. Long thought to be a peaceful race, the Maya are now recognised as having used torture and human sacrifice for religious celebrations and sporting events, while skirmishes between city states later escalated into full-scale wars.

ACHIEVEMENTS The Mayan fields of excellence were mathematics and astronomy (see pages 228–9), backed up by a hieroglyphic system which has still not been deciphered fully. Their knowledge was recorded on stelae (stone slabs) and codices (of which only four have survived) filled with bar-and-dot numerals – including a glyph for zero. These detail historical and social events as well as planetary movements. Their mythology was encapsulated in sacred books such as *Chilam Balam*, written a few decades before the Spanish Conquest. Nor did the Maya die out with the conquest: Mayan communities still speak the language of their ancestors and observe many of their customs, while the 260-day Sacred Almanac continues to be consulted by remote shamans.

Puuc architecture: stonework detail on the Nuns' Quadrangle, Uxmal

The mysterious fall of Teotihuacán and the dispersal of the Maya, Totonacs and Zapotecs from their respective ceremonial centres was followed by a new Mesoamerican culture – that of the militaristic Toltecs. In Oaxaca, the Mixtec invasion was more peaceful, while Michoacán later saw the arrival of the Purépechas.

The seemingly cataclysmic end of the Classic period between the 9th and 10th centuries is still unexplained, but what is certain is the arrival of strong new forces that conquered earlier races and imposed a new emphasis on war and the sacrificial spilling of human blood. Presumed to be a branch of the barbarian Chichimecs from the north, the Toltecs, by the time they founded their capital at Tula, had forcibly appropriated 'civilised' traits from Teotihuacán. Their controversial influence has been traced from the Veracruz area to Oaxaca and even to the Yucatán.

THE REAL QUETZALCÓATL Led by their ruler Topiltzin, the Toltecs moved their capital to Tollan, present-day Tula ('City of God'), in the 10th century. According to some accounts, Topiltzin was an intellectual priest-king dedicated to the cult of the feathered serpent Quetzalcóatl, whose pacifistic attitude provoked a revolution of more bellicose Toltecs. Forced into exile, he made his way to the Gulf Coast where one of two fates befell him: either he set fire to himself, his ashes rising to become the Morning Star; or he set sail to the east on a raft of serpents, promising to return. He may have actually landed in the Yucatán, where his followers vanquished the Classic Maya and left as part of their legacy, beliefs in Kukulcán (the Toltec name for the Mayan feathered serpent).

Back in Tula, one of Mexico's most violent and bloodthirsty races blossomed into a prosperous civilisation where the arts were so developed that the description *tolteca* came to mean 'skilled, wise, dexterous'. The rise of the warrior class over the priests led to Tula's destruction – by the late 12th century inner conflicts dispersed the Toltecs all over Mexico.

Detail of intricate stone mosaic at Mitla, Oaxaca. This typical Mixtec decorative technique was applied to earlier Zapotec structures

THE MIXTECS Around the 9th century, the Mixtecs emerged from the mountainous, semi-desert region of northwestern Oaxaca, and by a series of astute intermarriages soon brought most of the Zapotec territory under their sway. Eight pre-Conquest codices (ancient scrolls) have survived, facilitating the task of tracing their evolution, although their origins remain as hazy as their name ('Inhabitants of the Land of the Clouds'). They, too, were obsessed with the feathered serpent, claiming direct descent from Quetzalcóatl, and were under direct Toltec influence before the latter's dispersal. Yet their outstanding legacy of architectural detail (notably intricate stone fretwork exemplified at Mitla), their inventive polychrome pottery and above all their advanced metalwork techniques were their own inventions. Allying themselves with the Zapotecs, they were never completely conquered by the Aztecs and their descendants still inhabit the Valley of Oaxaca.

PURÉPECHAS Clustered around Lake Pátzcuaro in Michoacán, the Purépechas (later named Tarascans by the Spanish) were an isolated society that managed to escape Aztec domination. They worshipped the sun and moon (one of several traits which could suggest links with Peru), and their complex social structure was governed by priests; the high priest was the *kasonsi*, who acted as war chief and supreme judge. From their successive bases at Pátzcuaro, Ihuatzio and Tzintzuntzán, the Purépechas dominated most of the fertile region of Michoacán. They left their unique *yácatas* (circular pyramid bases attached to a rectangular body) and advanced craftsmanship (ceramics, complex jewellery, lacquerwork and featherwork) as evidence of their sophisticated culture.

❑ Mixtec accomplishments included their lime-coated deer-skin scrolls (codices) which, when unfolded, measured up to 12m long. Historical events, royal births and marriages, place-names and customs were recorded by superb illustrations and glyphs. Equally remarkable was their jewellery: turquoise mosaics and finely wrought gold pieces cast with the lost-wax method surpass the artistry of any other Mesoamerican ornamentation. ❑

One of the many Mixtec treasures from Monte Albán's Tomb 7, now displayed at Oaxaca's Regional Museum

Hot on the heels of the expansionist Toltecs came the Aztecs, guided by the prophecies of their tribal god of war, Huitzilopóchtli, and set to become the last great Mesoamerican empire. They ably overcame numerous neighbouring city-states with unpopular, sanguinary methods and by the mid-14th century had laid the foundations of their capital.

Although their origins are lost in myth, notably concerning the island town of Aztlán, the Aztecs were controlled in all matters by their god Huitzilopóchtli, whose appetite for human hearts inspired much of their infamous ferocity. Raiding and sacrificing their neighbours, they finally settled on the swampy islands of the 'Lake of the Moon', obeying a tribal prophecy which said their home would be announced by an eagle perched on a cactus with a snake in its mouth. Two adjoining capitals were founded: Tlatelolco and Tenochtitlán (modern-day Mexico City), later united, along with Tacuba, as the Triple Alliance under one king. By 1367 the Aztecs, calling themselves the Méxica, were serving as mercenaries for the Tepanecs, and by 1428 their rapid grasp of political and military strategy left them victorious over this once powerful tribe.

CONSOLIDATION The Aztecs were adept at rewriting history, and set about destroying existing codices to create their own in which they supplanted their squalid past with glorious, cultured Toltec origins imbued with a divine mission. They built canals, paths, dikes and an aqueduct, reclaimed land and adapted agriculture to the soggy terrain with *chinampas*, floating gardens whose plants eventually rooted themselves to the lake bed. At the heart of the city stood the walled administrative and ceremonial centre composed of the Great Pyramid, the Temple of Quetzalcóatl, the ball-court and the skull rack. Beyond the enclosure were the palaces of nobles, schools, market-places, temples and more modest homes and farms.

❑ The Aztecs developed a distinctive, rigid art style, much applied to monumental stone sculptures. An important surviving masterpiece is the statue of Coatlicue, the earth goddess and mother of the moon and stars, who wears a necklace of human hearts and a skirt of serpents. ❑

The Aztec Calendar, unofficial symbol of Mexico, in the capital's National Museum of Anthropology

STRUCTURE AND EXPANSION At the top of the Aztec hierarchy was the king, possessor of military, administrative and judicial powers. Below him was the *cihuacóatl*, a kind of prime minister, followed by the nobles and priests, the free citizens organised into clans, and finally the serfs and porters. Aztec territorial expansion through military and economic subjugation was astounding, and their great market-places became the reflections of this far-reaching

Emperor Moctezuma II

❑ Twenty thousand war captives were said to have been sacrificed for the dedication of the Great Pyramid in 1487, their hearts torn from their bodies by the priests. By thus 'feeding' the gods, the Aztecs ensured the continuity of the cosmos, while both priest and victim were 'entered' by the gods. ❑

dominion. Empire-building boomed, above all under the sixth Aztec king, Ahuítzotl (1486–1502), who conquered lands as far as the Guatemalan border and brought most of central Mexico under Aztec control. Endless problems ensued from this unwieldy empire. The risk of rebellion was constant, and the large appetite of the nobles for tribute spelled the need for further, costly expeditions.

MOCTEZUMA II Greatest of all Aztec emperors was Moctezuma II (who ruled from 1502 to 1520), a philosophically inclined character given more to meditation and learning than to warfare. His semi-divine status was such that nobody was allowed to look him in the face. He was guarded by 200 warriors, carried in a litter beneath a canopy of feathers, gold and pearls, and preceded by lords who laid cloaks on the ground. Moctezuma seemed untouchable. Yet nothing could protect him from his initial conviction that Cortés was the great Quetzalcóatl returning from the east, which led to his tragic downfall. Tormented by indecision, Moctezuma was kidnapped by the Spaniards within his own city and killed (it is not known whether by his frustrated Aztecs or by the *conquistadores*) just before the calamitous Spanish retreat of La Noche Triste (Sad Night) when the majority of Cortés' troops were killed or drowned under the weight of their plunder.

❑ The tributes imposed on conquered peoples, supplied the Aztecs with exotic fruits and animals from tropical zones, gold and silver from Central America, jade from Guerrero, woven cloth from northern Veracruz, tortoise-shell from the Gulf, and *liquidambar*, tobacco, turquoise and copal (resin from tropical trees) from numerous other vassal states. ❑

Thirst for gold was the inspiration for the advance of Cortés and his men on the Aztec capital in 1519. Their destruction of Tenochtitlán laid the foundations of 300 years of Spanish rule which saw the decimation of the indigenous population, the introduction of Christianity and the establishment of a landowning system which has repercussions today.

When Hernán Cortés sailed from Cuba to land at Villa Rica, near Veracruz on 21 April 1519 he was motivated above all by a lust for gold and silver. Bold, single-minded, and not above double-dealing he offered simple glass beads as gifts in exchange for chest-loads of precious jewellery and cloth. Cortés literally burnt his boats to prevent his small army fleeing. During the eventful march on Tenochtitlán he allied himself with various tribes (notably the Zempoalans and Tlaxcalans) who resented the Aztecs' domination, thus vastly multiplying his forces, and acquired the redoubtable La Malinche, a princess from Tabasco who was to become his consort and interpreter. After a prolonged siege, the Aztec capital finally fell on 13 August 1521. The young emperor Cuauhtémoc (Moctezuma's successor) was captured and eventually killed, signalling the final chapter of Mesoamerican civilisation and the beginning of a new colonial era.

❑ At the time of the Conquest the indigenous population was estimated at 4.5 million; by the mid-17th century it had plummeted to 1.2 million, but by Independence in 1820 it had risen again to 3.5 million. The main causes of the decline were European diseases such as smallpox, and exhaustion resulting from forced labour. ❑

Mural by Diego Rivera in the Palace of Cortés, Cuernavaca, depicting the brutality of the Spaniards toward the indígenas

ORDER AND EXCESS The Spanish justified their presence by the need to stamp out human sacrifice, cannibalism and sodomy, and they wasted no time in destroying local temples and idols. Stones taken from the pyramids were used to build cathedrals around which new towns grew, laid out in a grid plan – a pattern repeated in hundreds of towns. Cortés' soldiers were rewarded with vast tracts of land (*encomiendas*) over which they were given total ownership (including animals and local inhabitants). Cortés himself was granted 22 *encomiendas*, and given the title Marqués del Valle de Oaxaca. The seeds were thus sown for the

merciless land-grant system which left native inhabitants virtual slaves working the estates and prolific mines of the great *hacendados* (estate owners). African slaves were even imported to swell the ranks of the workers.

CASTE SYSTEM Fearful of losing control over this profitable new colony, the Spanish Crown appointed an *audiencia*, a 12-man government-cum-court which from 1535 was headed by a Viceroy. A rigid social hierarchy was soon established: high government and church posts were reserved for *gachupines* ('pure' Spanish-born); educated *criollos* (creoles or Mexican-born Spanish) became wealthy landowners; *mestizos* (mixed Spanish and Mexican Indian blood) were restricted to lower middle-class roles while at the bottom the indigenous Mexicans (*indígenas*) formed a diminishing work-force. The viceregal period saw increasing discontent among creoles at their lack of political power and the top-heavy hand of distant Spain.

Mitla's red-domed church was built using stones taken from earlier Zapotec buildings

❑ Among enlightened churchmen who sought to protect the *indígenas* were Bernardino de Sahagún, Bartolomé de Las Casas, Vasco de Quiroga and Eusabio Francisco Kino. ❑

THE CHURCH The priests, who initially worked hand-in-hand with the *conquistadores* and were a brake on their excesses, later became an independently powerful force. Franciscans, Dominicans and Jesuits carved up territory between them, building monasteries and missions in remote sierras and converting the local population. Although the Jesuits were expelled by the Crown in 1769, the rest of the Church amassed so much wealth that it became the greatest landowner and money-lender in the land. In 1804 all Church property was expropriated by the Crown, creating havoc. This, together with Napoléon's invasion of Spain in 1808, the spread of revolutionary ideas from France and the US, and continuing social iniquities set the stage for the next turbulent chapter in Mexican history.

The 19th century, announced by the War of Independence, was to become the most confused period in Mexican history. Political systems veered from republicanism to monarchy and back again, foreign intervention became the norm and the nation was locked in a permanent state of civil war. When Miguel Hidalgo's grito *(cry) of* 'Mexicanos, Viva México!' *rang out on 16 September 1810 it sparked off a popular revolt which succeeded in dividing the Church and set* mestizos *and* indígenas *against the ruling classes.*

Land and social justice were the aims of the impromptu mob of 80,000 insurgents which rampaged across the countryside, massacring and pillaging. Even the capture and execution of a key figure, the Creole priest Hidalgo, could not stop this relentless movement, soon steered by the *mestizo* priest José María Morelos. Inspired by his revolutionary vision of a caste-free republic with all lands restored to the *indígenas*, Morelos' small guerrilla army controlled most of the country by 1813, but he too was captured and the reins next passed to Vicente Guerrero. The crunch came when the powerful creole population, worried by the impact of new Spanish reforms, switched their allegiance to Guerrero, resulting in the former royalist General Agustín de Iturbide siding with the insurgents and marching on Mexico City in 1820. The following year the Plan de Iguala finally gave Mexico independence under a constitutional monarchy.

❑ An estimated 600,000 lives were lost during the 11-year struggle for independence. ❑

The Independence Bell on the Governor's Palace in Guadalajara – from here Hidalgo declared an end to slavery in 1810

MEXICAN–AMERICAN WAR Iturbide declared himself emperor, but this was only short-lived and power passed fitfully and eventfully into the hands of General Antonio López de Santa Ana, at the head of the new federal republic. Times remained troubled, separatist intrigues fermented and in 1836, despite Santa Ana's successful siege of the Alamo, Texas declared itself independent of Mexico. Nine years later US expansionist policy led to the annexation of Texas, provoking a war which soon left Veracruz, Monterrey and Mexico City in American hands. The Treaty of Guadalupe in 1848 ceded most of New Mexico, California and Texas to the US for $15 million, followed by a further territorial cession in 1854 (for another $10 million into the Mexican coffers) which defined present-day

borders. Altogether Mexico lost more than half its former territory.

JUÁREZ VERSUS MAXIMILIAN Santa Ana was ousted by a liberal movement headed by the Zapotec lawyer, Benito Juárez, and Mexico plunged headlong into another bloody civil war between conservatives in Mexico City, backed by the Church, and liberals based in Veracruz. Priests were killed and churches sacked until in 1861 Juárez finally triumphed, imposing judicial reforms and anticlerical legislation that shattered the power of the Church. Exhausted and torn apart, Mexico was not allowed to rest. The next threat came as a direct result of the nation's bankruptcy: payment of all foreign debts was suspended, leading to a concerted reprisal by Spain, France and Britain, who attacked Veracruz. French troops, not content with a mere show of strength, proceeded to invade Mexico and, despite a major defeat at Puebla, had occupied Mexico City by 1863. The hapless Maximilian of Habsburg and his wife Carlota were hand-picked by Napoleon III as puppet Emperor and Empress but their reign proved short-lived. Juárez, a fervent admirer of Abraham Lincoln, astutely obtained US backing under the Monroe Doctrine of 'America for the Americans' and Napoleon III, already threatened on the home front, consented to withdraw most of his troops. Abandoned to his fate, isolated and outnumbered, Maximilian was finally executed in 1867 in Querétaro, leaving Carlota to end her days, insane, in Belgium. Back in power, Juárez set about implementing his Reform Laws, reconstructing the economy and developing public education, but his days, too, were numbered; in 1872 he died of a heart attack while still in office.

❑ For 30 years, between 1821 and 1851, Mexico teetered under more than 40 different governments. ❑

Maximilian of Habsburg, the ill-fated puppet Emperor of Mexico from 1862 to 1867. On his death Benito Juárez resumed office

Crowning the débâcle *of the 19th century was the 34-year-long dictatorship of Porfirio Díaz which brought relative peace and prosperity to the nation, but also a peak of repression and social injustice. Never ones to take things lying down, the Mexicans rebelled in 1910, initiating a decade of anarchy and further decimation of the population.*

Commanding the troops that recaptured Mexico City for Juárez in 1867 was a *mestizo* (mixed Spanish and Indian blood) called Porfirio Díaz who, within 10 years, was sufficiently bitten by the attractions of political power to seize office for himself. Ruthless but efficient, he ruled in true dictatorial style with a hand-picked clique, obliterating any opposition through a newly formed rural police force. Intent on rebuilding the nation, Díaz constructed roads and railways, telephone and telegraph lines and opened up remote towns to the march of modernisation. Ultimate symbol of this progress was the grandiose architectural style, now called Porfiriato, that thrust itself on every city to stress the greatness of the regime. But none of this reconstruction came cheaply, and Díaz's policies included attracting outside investment: oil fields, mines and railways were soon all in foreign hands, provoking a rising xenophobia. More crucial was the fraudulent seizure of common land by voracious *hacendados* (estate owners); whole villages were wiped out to extend plantations and indigenous Mexicans found themselves yet again in a state of slavery, bound by debt to their exploitative employers and unable to escape due to the brutal methods of internal security forces.

ON THE BOIL When the liberal idealist Francisco Madero stood for election against Díaz in 1910, the dictator responded characteristically by throwing him into prison. But Madero escaped to Texas and from here called for a national insurrection. Several existing revolutionary groups responded, including forces led by Pancho Villa in the north and Emiliano Zapata in the south. By 1911 Madero had been elected President and Díaz was on the run to Europe. Reluctant to restore *hacienda* land to the people, Madero lost Zapata's support and soon had to confront a new protagonist, General Victoriano Huerta. After 10 days of vicious fighting in

❑ Zapata's stirring lines included 'I'd rather die enslaved to my principles than to man' and 'Rebels of the South! It is better to die on your feet than live on your knees!' ❑

Dictator Porfirio Díaz governed Mexico with an iron fist, exploiting the middle and lower classes

American aviator Hamilton carries out the first-ever aerial reconnaissance over Juárez, besieged by rebels, 1911

the capital, Huerta was installed as President, backed by American business interests, and soon recognised by foreign powers. Ineffective and unpopular, Huerta did nothing except ferment further conflicts and in March 1913 the Plan of Guadalupe united three powerful revolutionary factions against him: Pancho Villa in Chihuahua, General Alvaro Obregón in Sonora and Venustiano Carranza in Coahuila. Continuing his courageous struggle in the state of Morelos, Zapata also turned his forces against Huerta, and the final *coup de grâce* was given when the new president of the United States, Woodrow Wilson, changed allegiance and sent aid to the revolutionaries. In 1914 American troops occupied Veracruz and Huerta's capitulation became inevitable.

BOILING Against a background of continuing civil war, Carranza formed a new government in alliance with Obregón. By 1916 it had set up a constitutional congress and on 5 February 1917 proclaimed the new constitution, which in theory recognised most of the revolutionary demands. The intervening years had witnessed anarchy on an unheard-of scale with the uncompromising Villa skirmishing away in the north and Zapata even briefly occupying the capital in 1915. Rival factions issued their own currencies, railways were blown up and armed ambushes became a daily occurrence. Millions of people died and the countryside was left in a state of total destruction. In 1919 the cowardly ambush of Zapata by one of Carranza's generals brought an end to Mexico's greatest defender of land rights and, although the 1920 Coahuila Pact marked the end of armed revolution, deadly rivalries did not fully abate until the next decade.

❑ **Revolutionary deaths**

1913 – Madero executed
1919 – Zapata assassinated
1920 – Carranza assassinated
1923 – Villa assassinated
1928 – Obregón assassinated ❑

The chaotic aftermath of the Mexican Revolution settled into political stability in the 1930s, propelling the nation into the 20th century. But a booming economy and greatly developed infrastructure came at the same time as a population explosion and spiralling corruption: the path of progress was a stony one.

When President Plutarco Elías Calles was sworn into office in 1924 he was faced with a nation in social and economic ruins, still fragmented by political allegiances. By the end of his term he had formed the Partido Nacional Revolucionario (the precursor of today's PRI which has monopolised office ever since), a unifying force for the countless splinter groups. Education and land reforms were instigated and, once again, the Church became a target for attack, with the closure of monasteries and convents. Religious processions were forbidden and fanatical anticlerical excesses were committed, while Masses had to be celebrated secretly in private homes. The result was more civil unrest in the prolonged Cristero rebellion which produced sporadic banditry as well as open warfare from 1927 to 1935.

Former President Salinas (in power 1988–94) is still on the run from justice

REFORM It was only under President Lázaro Cárdenas (1934–40) that Mexico finally entered a period of acknowledged prosperity and civil peace. Social injustices were partially addressed by the redistribution of land to peasants under the *ejido*

❑ When Cárdenas left office in 1940 over 20 million hectares of land had been redistributed to two million peasants. ❑

(communal holding) system; this transferred *hacienda* land back into the hands of the *campesinos* (peasant farmers). Being of indigenous stock at last became a plus, promoted by the murals of Rivera, Orozco and Siqueiros which graphically glorified the indigenous role. The union movement was strengthened and the ruling party transformed from a tool of personal power into a corporate organisation. In 1938 Cárdenas crowned this democratic approach by nationalising all foreign oil companies and mines, a move which temporarily slowed growth by discouraging foreign investment but greatly boosted national confidence. At the onset of World War II Mexico was poised for profit. World demand for its natural resources combined with domestic manufacture replacing imported goods gave the economy an unprecedented boost.

CORRUPTION The rapid expansion of the infrastructure and industrial landscape brought with it a new political lobby, that of the industrialists. To integrate this powerful new force, the ruling party was given the self-contradictory label of Partido Revolucionario Institucional (PRI) which remains to this day. Under President Miguel Alemán (1946–52) Mexico saw corruption start to rise again and take root in the economic framework of nationalised companies, a practice which blossomed again under the Díaz Ordáz administration in the late 1960s, and which is still common currency. More visible was a population explosion that came hand in hand with improved social welfare during a period of stabilised growth which lasted from 1954 to 1970. In the two preceding decades the Mexican population had doubled and the chaotic, unregulated growth of industry appeared like a shining light on the horizon to the millions of still-deprived rural inhabitants. The great urban drift had begun.

UNREST AND RECESSION Increasing strains were evident by the late 1960s when inflation seriously started to take off and questioning of the legitimacy of the political system resulted in mounting dissent. Events came to a head in October 1968 when Mexico City staged the Olympic Games: university students descended on the Plaza de las Tres Culturas in Tlatelolco to protest against the injustices of Díaz Ordaz's regime (rigged elections, repression of liberals, corruption). In a merciless and bloody reprisal government troops shot hundreds of students, women and children – the blackest moment in Mexico's post-revolutionary history. The 1970s saw continuing unrest, notably an armed uprising in 1974 in the state of Guerrero, and an economy which veered from an ephemeral, post oil-crisis boom to economic recession by the end of the decade. Accelerating inflation and a crippling foreign debt culminated in a shattering announcement by President José López Portillo in 1982: Mexico was unable to repay its foreign creditors.

▶▶▶ **CITY HIGHLIGHTS**

Catedral Metropolitana *page 52*

Ex-Colegio de San Ildefonso *pages 52–3*

Palacio Nacional *page 53*

Templo Mayor *page 53*

Museo Franz Mayer *page 54*

Palacio de Bellas Artes *page 56*

Museo Nacional de Antropología *pages 60–1*

Museo Anahuacalli *pages 66–7*

Museo Frida Kahlo *page 67*

Museo del Carmen *page 68*

Xochimilco *page 70*

Mexico City (Ciudad de México), the oldest capital in the New World, sprawls across its valley floor. Despite its size, it is still possible to see the mountains from the city centre

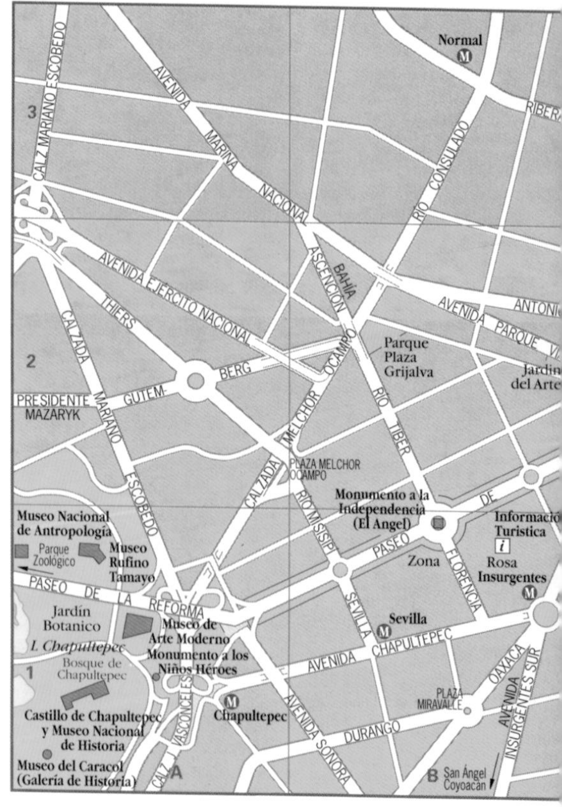

MEXICO CITY At first sight Mexico City's vast expanse is daunting, filling its 2,240m-high valley to the horizon. With a population currently hovering around the 22 million mark, pollution, uncontrollable traffic, severe water shortage, cheap buildings that crack at the slightest seismic shudder, sporadic cholera outbreaks on the outskirts and highly visible imbalances in wealth, the capital's minus points are legion. Built over Lago de Texcoco, its foundations sink 15cm every year while its edges creep inexorably outwards in the form of shanty-towns. A city out of control? In recent years, public safety has become another concern. Assaults on taxi passengers, with the driver a willing accomplice, are not uncommon now and even public buses and private cars are no guarantee of protection. In unexpected contrast, Mexico City boasts one of the world's cheapest, cleanest, and most efficient subway systems. Love it or hate it, this unique metropolis, which somehow seems American to Europeans and European to Americans, is truly Mexican.

Whatever your reaction to it, Mexico City is magnetic, an essential starting point for exploring the rest of a richly diverse country and remains the social, economic, cultural and political pulse of the nation.

EARLY HISTORY It was the shores of Lago de Texcoco that attracted early settlers, forming the focal point for some of Mesoamerica's most powerful dynasties. After the

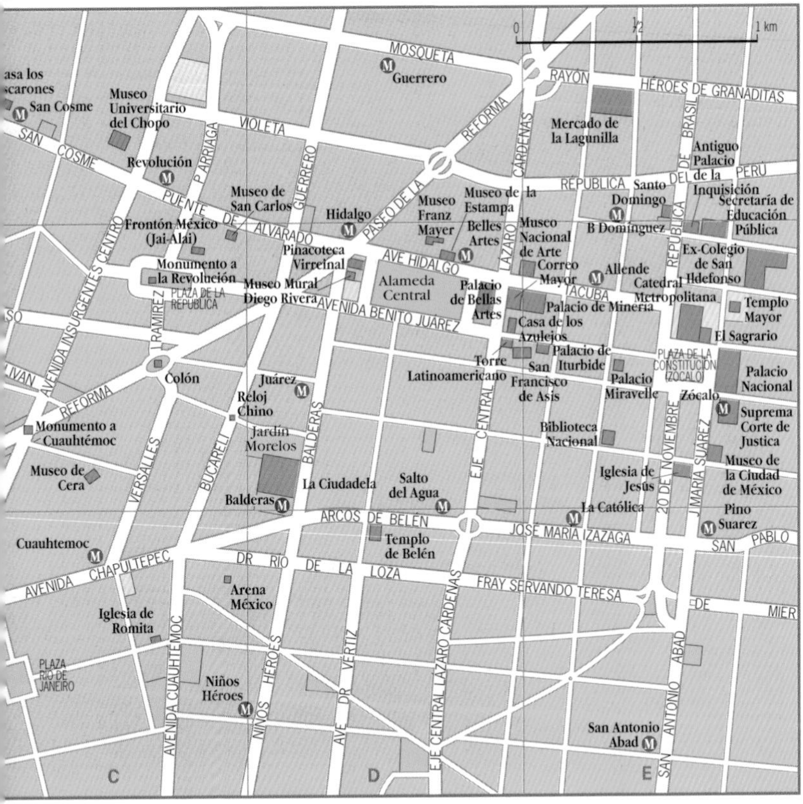

SIXTEENTH-CENTURY ARRIVAL

'Wide though the causeway was, it was so crowded with people that there was hardly room for them all ... For the towers and the cues were full, and they came in canoes from all parts of the lake. No wonder, since they had never seen horses or men like us before!
... With such wonderful sights to gaze on we did not know what to say, or if this was real that we saw before our eyes. On the land side there were great cities and on the lake many more. The lake was crowded with canoes. At intervals along the causeway there were many bridges, and before us was the great city of Mexico.'
Bernal Díaz del Castillo: *The Conquest of New Spain*, 1568.

ancient site of Cuicuilco was buried by volcanic lava around the 1st century AD came Teotihuacán, with its astonishing ceremonial structures and far-reaching influence. On the collapse of this civilisation in 750, power moved to the equally dominant Toltecs at Tula who in the 12th century scattered to the Hill of Chapultepec and throughout Mexico. Then around 1300 came a tribe nourished by the prophecies of their god of war, Huitzilipóchtli: the Aztecs had arrived. They named their settlement Tenochtitlán ('Place of the Cactus'), dominated the neighbouring tribes and, calling themselves the México, occupied the island of Tlatelolco. They also captured Coyoacán and Xochimilco to the south.

By the time Hernán Cortés arrived in 1519, Tenochtitlán's power and wealth had been consolidated and the lake city was deemed the 'Venice of the New World'. The defeat of the Aztecs in 1521 was followed by the deliberate and total destruction of their magnificent city, to make way for the capital of Nueva España.

RECENT DEVELOPMENTS After surviving centuries of adversity, riots inspired by racial divisions, floods, invasion by foreign powers, starvation and homelessness caused by independence, revolutionary chaos, the 1968 bloodbath of Tlatelolco (see page 47), and, more recently the earthquake of 1985, the inhabitants of Mexico City now have to confront severe environmental problems. Thermal inversions trap smog caused by industrial air-pollutants and the exhaust fumes of around 15,000 antiquated buses, over 40,000 taxis and 3 million cars in the valley (a situation that led the government to introduce *Hoy No Circula*, restricting vehicle use). Contaminated water creates severe health problems, and tremors put nerves on edge.

Juan O'Gorman's fine mosaics cover the walls of the university library

Corruption is still widespread with public funds often missing their mark, and crime is on the increase. Wealthier classes move out to the healthier hills beyond the urban sprawl, while a weekly average of 10,000 poor from rural areas continue to be sucked into the city's maelstrom. Despite these negative factors, Mexico City has an extraordinary vitality and staying power that, combined with extensive cultural offerings, make it a captivating destination. The election of Cuauhtémoc Cardenas in 1997 as Mexico City's socialist mayor may herald a change. However, his determination is handicapped by a vast debt left in the City coffers by his PRI predecessor.

ORIENTATION The spruced-up historic heart of Mexico City lies in and around the Zócalo (main square), once the Plaza Mayor of Aztec Tenochtitlán. From here Avenida Madero and Calle Tacuba run parallel, west to Alameda Central, a small park flanked by numerous monuments and cut diagonally to the west by the Paseo de la Reforma. This majestic, broad avenue, more than 12km in length, sweeps south-west between the tourist ghetto of the Zona Rosa and Polanco, the upmarket business and commercial district, then through Bosque de Chapultepec (Chapultepec Park), the green, recreational 'lungs' of the city, to end in the residential hills of Lomas. This entire area is, broadly, the city centre, and a taxi ride from the Zócalo to Chapultepec will take no more than 20 minutes.

Insurgentes, a major north–south axis, starts north of Guadelupe and intersects Paseo de la Reforma at the monument to Cuauhtémoc, the last emperor of Mexico, before continuing south to San Ángel, the University and the Pyramid of Cuicuilco. Parallel to Insurgentes, to the east, is the other north–south axis, Calzada de Tlalpán, which runs south from the Zócalo to Coyoacán, joining up with Insurgentes beyond the *periférico* (ring road).

TWENTIETH-CENTURY DEPARTURE

Mexico City's long-distance bus stations are named according to the points of the compass, and all can be reached by metro. The largest, Terminal Norte (metro: Autobuses del Norte, tel: 587 1552), covers northern and other destinations including Guadalajara, Mazatlán, Pachuca and Papantla. Terminal Oriente (metro: San Lázaro, tel: 762 5977) serves destinations east and south, including Puebla, Veracruz and the states of Oaxaca, Chiapas and the Yucatán. Terminal Sur (metro: Tasqueña, tel: 544 0059) runs buses southeast to Cuernavaca, Taxco, Cuautla and Acapulco. Terminal Poniente (metro: Observatorio, tel: 271 0481) shuttles to Toluca as well as Morelia and Guadalajara. The airport, too, has its metro station, Terminal Aerea, for those travelling light.

View from the Latin America Tower

MURALS
More work by Mexico's muralists can be seen in public buildings round the Zócalo area. The courtyard and upper floor of the 1920s Secretaría de Educación Pública (Ministry of Public Education), 3½ blocks north of the Zócalo on Calle República de Argentina, boasts 235 early mural panels by Rivera which depict social and economic themes. Other muralists represented here include Juan O'Gorman, Carlos Merida and Amado de la Cueva. At the Suprema Corte de Justicia, on the southeastern corner of the Zócalo, are grandiose works by Orozco. Located up the main staircase and along the second-floor walls, they pay homage to workers' rights, to national pride and – naturally enough – to justice.

The Catedral Metropolitana

Zócalo

►► Catedral Metropolitana (Metropolitan Cathedral) 49E2

Metro: Zócalo
Open: daily 8–8

The cathedral, dominating the historic heart of Mexico City, was begun in 1563 to replace an earlier version built by Cortés. It incorporates stones from the ruins of the Temple of Quetzalcóatl, as well as the macabre wall of skulls where the skulls of sacrificial victims were displayed by the Aztecs. Most of the baroque southern façade and tiered columns were completed in 1681, while the asymmetrical twin towers and large central dome were added as late as 1813. The interior is ornate, particularly the **Capilla de Los Reyes►►** and its gilded altar (1718–25), although much of the cathedral's artwork was destroyed or damaged by fire in 1967. Serious structural problems caused by subsidence were aggravated by the 1985 earthquake: there is a 6m difference in level between the entrance and the high altar – you can't miss the heavily employed metal supports. Next door stands **El Sagrario►►** (1760), its gilded interior, now undergoing renovation, designed to house the archbishop's archives.

►► Ex-Colegio de San Ildefonso 49E2

Justo Sierra 16
Metro: Allende
Open: Tue–Sun 11–6

This large college, one block north of the Templo Mayor, was built by the Jesuits in 1588, and boasts a rare display of early murals by Rivera, Orozco and Siqueiros. Between

1923 and 1933 they painted the central courtyard, main staircase and amphitheatre in an effort to create a national muralist movement. The college is now a cultural centre and hosts major temporary exhibitions.

▶ Museo de la Ciudad de México (Mexico City Museum) 49E2

Avenida Pino Suárez 30
Metro: Zócalo
Open: Tue–Sun 10–5.30

Situated three blocks south of the Zócalo, this museum is housed in a magnificent 1528 mansion, rebuilt in the late 18th century for the extravagant counts of Santiago de Calimaya and later redecorated in art-deco style. Displays cover the geological and socio-political history of Mexico City, from volcanic eruptions to the first settlers (8000 BC) and the inspired creators of Teotihuacán and Tenochtitlán. Much of it is currently closed for renovation with rather mediocre art exhibitions replacing the main collection (work is due to be completed in 1999) .

▶▶ Palacio Nacional (National Palace) 49E2

Metro: Zócalo
Open: daily 9–5. Admission: free with identity document

Flanking the eastern side of the Zócalo is Mexico's political powerhouse, home to the offices of the President, the National Archives and the Federal Treasury. Above the entrance is the highly symbolic 'Freedom Bell' which announced independence on 15 September 1810 in the town of Dolores, and which is now rung annually on the eve of Independence Day by the President. The building itself dates from the late 17th century and replaced two previous palaces, the second extensively damaged by the 1692 Indian revolt. Entrance to public areas is through a stately courtyard and up a staircase dominated by Diego Rivera's celebrated mural depicting the history of Mexico. The walls of the first-floor gallery continue his dramatic interpretation. On the second floor is a small museum dedicated to President Benito Juárez, leader of the Reform movement, who died here in 1872.

▶▶▶ Templo Mayor (Great Temple) 49E2

Metro: Zócalo, Allende
Open: Tue–Sun 10–5

The Aztecs' main temple, unearthed quite by chance in 1978, was dedicated to their gods Huitzilopóchtli (war) and Tláloc (rain) before being razed to the ground by Cortés. Today visitors can explore the multiple layers of the site from a raised walkway: serpentine carvings, a giant conch shell, remains of pyramids and a *chacmool* (a reclining statue on which sacrificial offerings were laid) are visible. More illuminating is the modern site museum based on the original temple layout where over 3,000 artefacts reflect the far-reaching significance of the Aztec empire. Pride of place is given to the huge votive stone disc of Coyolxauhqui, goddess of the moon – the first artefact to be discovered. A scale model of Tenochtitlán shows the urban sophistication of the Aztecs.

SHOE-SHINERS AND SCRIBES

Four blocks north of the Zócalo, in the lively Plaza Santo Domingo, a pervasive smell of boot-polish masks the usual traffic fumes as shoe-shiners wait for customers, while under the arcades is a row of printing presses and *evangelistas* (scribes) who, using typewriters, produce words to the wishes of their illiterate clients, creating the ultimate love letter or plea for employment, or, more often, completing tax-returns.

Shoe-shiners can be found on almost every street corner

Alameda

► Alameda Central (Central Park) 49D2

Between Avenida Juárez and Avenida Hidalgo
Metro: Hidalgo, Bellas Artes

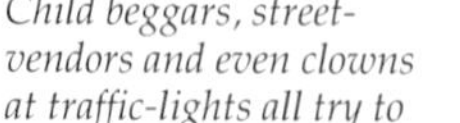

Child beggars, street-vendors and even clowns at traffic-lights all try to eke out a living

Mexico City's neatly tended central park is a focal point for street vendors, dog-walkers and children, all circulating along shady paths past fountains and a central bandstand. Before independence, admission was restricted to the upper classes, a policy instigated when the area was developed in the late 16th century. The western side of the park has a particularly dark past as it was here, on the Plaza del Quemadero, that the Spanish Inquisition set up its stake for burning heretics. During the 19th century the park was relandscaped in formal French style under Emperor Maximilian, and continued by Porfirio Díaz.

►► Casa de los Azulejos (House of Tiles) 49D2

Avenida Madero 4
Metro: Bellas Artes
Open: daily 7am–1am

This extraordinary example of Mexican colonial architecture, entirely faced in blue Talavera tiles (added in the 18th century), was built in 1596 for the Counts of the Valley of Orizaba. The glassed-in courtyard displays an eclectic mix of art-nouveau murals, stained glass, tilework, Moorish-style carved stone and plaster, and a forceful staircase mural by Orozco. The mansion is now home to one of the Sanborn chain of restaurants and shops.

►►► Museo Franz Mayer (Franz Mayer Museum) 49D2

Avenida Hidalgo 45
Metro: Hidalgo, Bellas Artes
Open: Tue–Sun 10–5

If you only visit one art museum in Mexico City, this should be it. Opened in 1986 in a superbly restored 16th-century hospital, the museum contains an extraordinarily rich collection of 16th- to 19th-century European, Asian and Mexican fine and applied arts. The works were collected over several decades by German immigrant and construction magnate, Franz Mayer. Exhibits are carefully arranged to highlight influences and contrasts, whether Chinese or Arab, and the fine workmanship of Mexican artists is also brought to the fore. Inlaid furniture, tapestries, ceramics, carved wood sculptures, silver and gold objects, glass, chests, mirrors and paintings (including works by Ribera, Zurbarán and the school of Velázquez) fill rooms surrounding a delightful open-air courtyard. The Cafeteria del Claustro, also accessible to those not visiting the museum, makes a peaceful retreat from the frenetic streets outside.

AZTEC METRO
Directly south of the Zócalo, at Pino Suárez, stands the city's most extraordinary metro entrance. While the metro was being built in the late 1960s, this important Aztec shrine, dedicated to Quetzalcóatl and dating from the late 14th century, was uncovered and subsequently integrated into the concourse.

►► Museo Mural Diego Rivera (Diego Rivera Mural Museum) 49D2

Plaza Solidaridad
Metro: Hidalgo, Juárez
Open: Tue–Sun 10–6

Devoted to one vast mural, Rivera's *Dream of a Sunday Afternoon in Alameda Central*, this small museum owes its existence to the 1985 earthquake. Rivera's masterpiece had been displayed in the Hotel del Prado since it was completed in 1948, but earthquake damage to the hotel was so great that a complex operation was undertaken to move it. Photographs show how the mural (15.6m by 4.3m) was mounted onto a 40-ton metal frame and transported across the road to its present site. The theme of this work is a lyrical satire of Mexican history in the form of a promenade in Alameda Park in the early 20th century. Benito Juárez, Hernán Cortés, Emiliano Zapata, Emperor Maximilian and Carlota, and Porfirio Díaz all figure, while Rivera himself appears, both as a boy and a man, accompanied by Frida Kahlo. The fresco was considered highly controversial due to the inclusion of the words '*Dios no existe*' (God does not exist), which Rivera finally agreed to substitute with a more moderate statement in 1956. A side room is used for temporary exhibitions of photography and contemporary art.

EARTHQUAKE!
The southern flank of the Alameda still reveals the forlorn ruins of the 1985 earthquake. This was the worst hit sector of central Mexico City when the terrifying quake left 6,000 dead (the official figure, though the toll was probably more) and 30–40,000 injured. About 150,000 people suffered damage to their homes.

►► Museo Nacional de Arte (National Art Museum) 49E2

Calle Tacuba 8
Metro: Bellas Artes
Open: Tue–Mon 10.30–5.30

The national art museum is housed in a Porfiriato extravaganza of great elegance and fronted by an equestrian statue of Carlos IV of Spain (*El Caballito*) which once stood on the Zócalo. The museum displays Mexican painting and sculpture of the 19th and early 20th centuries. One of the highlights is a room devoted to the evocative works of José Maria Velasco, master of turn-of-the-century landscapes of the Valley of Mexico. Similar in theme are the works of Saturnino Herrán and Gerardo Murillo, forefather of the muralists. José Guadalupe Posada's biting political comments and Frida Kahlo's disturbing tortured self-portraits offer other radical visions. Nineteenth-century sculptures and drawings complete the collection. Across Calle Tacuba stands the **Palacio de Minería►**, which was built between 1797 and 1813 and is an outstanding example of neo-classical architecture.

JARDIN DE SOLIDARIDAD
This small square at the western end of the Alameda was built in 1986 on the site of the Hotel Regis, one of the many buildings on the south side of the Alameda which collapsed in the 1985 earthquake, including a modern government health ministry and hospital on the north side. The Jardín de Solidaridad commemorates the tremendous interaction and solidarity among the capital's population, who organised relief and achieved far more success than any official organisation.

► Museo Nacional de la Estampa (National Museum of Engraving) 49D2

Avenida Hidalgo 59
Metro: Bellas Artes
Open: Tue–Sun 10–6

Although the history of engraving in Mexico dates from pre-Hispanic days followed by a prolific production during colonial times, this museum concentrates on 19th- and 20th-century works. Exhibits include prints by Leopoldo Mendez and the powerful etchings of José Guadalupe Posada. One room serves as an introduction to techniques. The neo-classical building opens onto the small Plaza de la Santa Veracruz – home to two 17th-century churches.

The Palace of Fine Arts is also the home of the colourful Ballet Folklórico

JAI ALAI
Take a break from culture and watch a high-action game of *jai alai*. This old Basque sport is played at the Frontón México, Plaza de la República 17, from Tuesday to Saturday at 7pm and on Sunday at 5pm. Professional players hurl fast-moving rubber balls with wicker rackets along a 61m court. Betting is part of the fun, with odds changing as each game progresses. The Frontón México attracts a chic crowd who often combine an evening of *jai alai* with dinner at the adjoining Prendes restaurant.

CORREO CENTRAL
If you need to use a post office in Mexico City, try the one located opposite the Bellas Artes on the corner of Tacuba. This grandiose edifice was completed by Adamo Boari of Bellas Artes fame in 1908 and combines an extraordinary Moorish/Gothic/Renaissance façade with a lofty interior resplendent with marble and fine ironwork from Florence.

►►► Palacio de Bellas Artes (Palace of Fine Arts) 49D2

Avenida Juárez
Metro: Bellas Artes
Open: Tue–Sun 10–6

The extravagant forms of this massive theatre and art gallery, built of Carrara marble, dominate the eastern end of Alameda Central but are sinking fast into the capital's spongy soil. The Palacio was commissioned by Porfirio Díaz and designed by Italian architect Adamo Boari in 1900. Political upheavals – not least the revolution – interrupted its construction, and it was not completed until 1934. It thus presents a curious and delightful blend of neo-classical, art-nouveau and art-deco styles. Some of Mexico's most outstanding murals by Rivera, Orozco, Siqueiros and Tamayo can be seen on the second and third floors. The concert hall, which has a spectacular Tiffany stained-glass stage-curtain depicting the volcanoes of the Valley of Mexico, can be visited outside performances. Completing the offerings are the bookshop and a café, both favourite haunts for the capital's literati.

► Palacio de Iturbide (Iturbide Palace) 49E2

Avenida Madero 17
Metro: Bellas Artes
Open: Mon–Fri 9–5. Admission free

This superb baroque mansion was completed in 1785. Between 1821 and 1823 it was occupied by the notorious independence leader Agustín de Iturbide, whose Napoleonic delusions of grandeur led to his crowning himself Emperor after he had engineered independence. Today, more prosaically, the Palacio houses the cultural foundation of Banamex, Mexico's national bank, and is used for exhibitions of contemporary art.

► Pinacoteca Virreinal (Museum of Colonial Painting) 49D2

Calle Doctor Mora 7
Metro: Hidalgo
Open: Tue–Sun 9–5

This museum, in a former church and Dominican monastery, dating from 1591, houses a collection of Mexican paintings dating from the colonial (viceregal) period of the late 16th to the early 19th centuries. The highlights are works by Miguel Cabrera, an 18th-century

Oaxacan-born painter who produced some of Mexico's finest religious paintings.

► Templo de San Francisco de Asis (Church of St Francis) *49E2*

Avenida Madero
Metro: Bellas Artes
Open: daily 8–8
This church dates back to the early days of Cortés and the first Franciscan monks in 1524. Most of the structure, now sunk well below street-level is early 18th century (when the elaborate, Churrigueresque-style stone portal and façade were built), but fragments of the early construction are visible.

► Torre Latinoamericana (Latin American Tower) *49D2*

Corner Avenida Madero and Lázaro Cárdenas
Metro: Bellas Artes
Open: daily 9:30am–10:30pm. Admission charge
This downtown landmark, the capital's first skyscraper, when it was completed in 1956, was once the tallest building in the city at 181m, but today it is surpassed by others. Views from the bar/restaurant on the 43rd floor, the observation deck on the 42nd floor or the outdoor viewing deck on the 44th, are best at night when the lights of Mexico City extend to the horizons.

BLACKLISTED
A significant exhibit at the Palacio de Bellas Artes is Rivera's famous mural *Man at the Crossing of the Ways*, first commissioned for New York's Rockefeller Center in 1933 when it was entitled *Man in Control of his Universe*. The work was destroyed when Rivera refused to delete the face of Lenin. He painted this subsequent version depicting class struggles and the dehumanising effects of industrialisation with even more fire and venom. Nor did Siqueiros pull his punches: his mural *Cain in the United States* clearly reveals his feelings about racism against blacks in the US, while *The Birth of Fascism* portrays the spread of Fascism and dictatorship worldwide.

The Church of St Francis is a masterpiece of Churrigueresque (Spanish baroque)

Zona Rosa

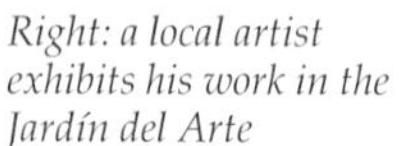

Right: a local artist exhibits his work in the Jardín del Arte

EL ÁNGEL
Mexico City's celebrated gilded angel, symbol of liberty, has a chequered history. It was originally commissioned by Emperor Maximilian in 1864 to be placed in the Zócalo, but it remained unfinished for years, its pedestal forlornly empty – thus the word *zócalo* (meaning pedestal) came to denote the central plaza. Porfirio Díaz relaunched the project and in 1902 commissioned the architect Antonio Rivas Mercado to supervise its erection in the Paseo de la Reforma. On 16 September 1910 the majestic 36m column was officially inaugurated to mark the centenary of Mexican Independence. Toppled by an earthquake in 1957, the statue gleams once more in restored splendour.

▶ Zona Rosa *48B1*

In the 1960s, the triangular Zona Rosa was the city's most fashionable area for restaurants, clubs, boutiques and antiques, though today it has been superseded by more avant-garde venues in Colonia Roma, the Centro Historico and Coyoacán. It lies south-east of the wide artery of Paseo de la Reforma, ending at the Avenida Chapultepec. Despite an improvement programme – involving pedestrian streets – the area has a fast-food and fast-money atmosphere but it makes a convenient sightseeing base.

▶ Paseo de la Reforma *48B2*

This wide boulevard slices through the city from Chapultepec Park, north-east past the Alameda Central to the Plaza de las Tres Culturas. Buzzing with traffic and wandering vendors, dotted with statues and monuments, and lined with some of Mexico City's most daring contemporary architecture, it is often compared to Paris' Champs-Elysées. It is still the address for airline offices, banks, embassies and the impressive buildings of the Lotería Nacional. Major statues at roundabouts (*glorietas*) include the **Monumento a la Independencia**, more commonly known as El Ángel, the **Monumento a Cuauhtémoc**, Mexico's last Aztec Emperor, and the **Monumento a Cristóbal Colón**, by French sculptor Charles Cordier.

▶ Museo de San Carlos (Museum of San Carlos) *49C2*

Puente de Alvarado 50, Colonia Tabacalera
Metro: Revolución
Open: Wed–Mon 10–6

An important fine art collection is housed in this graceful early 19th-century mansion, designed in neo-classical style, with hints of baroque. The origins of the collection date back to the founding of the Royal Academy of San Carlos in 1785, an art school and museum. Both Rivera and Orozco graduated from San Carlos. In 1968 the collection, though not the school, was moved to this site. It offers an impressive overview of 14th- to 19th-century religious painting which includes major works by Lucas Cranach the Elder, Tintoretto, Brueghel, Zurbarán, Rubens, Rembrandt, Goya, Titian, Ingres and Reynolds.

Bosque de Chapultepec

▶▶▶ Bosque de Chapultepec (Chapultepec Park) 65A2

Metro: Chapultepec, Auditorio, Constituyentes

The largest park in Mexico City is west of the centre and incorporates small lakes and woods which are invaded by the capital's inhabitants at weekends. The park, whose name in Náhuatl means 'Grasshopper Hill', was used as a summer residence under Moctezuma, and became public in 1530. Set in over 4sq km of vegetation are several major museums, recreation areas and a zoo. Transport around the park is provided by little trains.

Above: Statue of Morelos, Chapultepec Castle

▶ Castillo de Chapultepec (Chapultepec Castle) 48A1

Metro: Chapultepec
Open: Tue–Sun 9–5

On top of Chapultepec's hill looms a massive, austere construction built in 1785 as the viceroy's residence and converted into a military academy in 1843. It fell into the hands of American troops in 1847, was refurbished by Maximilian and Carlota and finally converted to the **Museo Nacional de Historia▶** in 1944. The museum's exhibits, although unimaginatively displayed, give a solid background to national history from the period of Spanish rule to the independence movement, the Republic, Maximilian and Carlota, dictatorship and the revolution. Several murals enliven the displays and offer incisive comments on Mexican history. **Maximilian and Carlota's apartments▶▶** (later inhabited by Porfirio) can be visited through a separate entrance. To get there, follow the spiral path from the **Monumento a los Niños Héroes▶** (Monument to the Boy Heroes) up to the summit for spectacular views from the spacious terraces.

CHILD HEROES

A massive semi-circular columned sculpture, the Monumento a los Niños Héroes, situated at the base of the hill, has great historic significance. This symbol of Mexican patriotism honours the six young military cadets (the oldest aged 16) who, during the American invasion in 1847, threw themselves from the castle ramparts rather than surrender. They wrapped themselves in the Mexican flag as they jumped from a spot now marked by statues.

▶▶ Museo de Arte Moderno (Museum of Modern Art) 48A1

Metro: Chapultepec
Open: Tue–Sun 10–5.30

This large, airy building, enclosing a circular marble atrium, has temporary exhibitions of contemporary art alongside a permanent collection of modern and contemporary Mexican artists. Exhibits start from the 1920s with some post-Impressionist-style works before moving into what was to become a very distinctive Mexican school. Included are Rivera's portrait of Lupe Marín (1938), a typical Zuñiga sculpture of a swathed indigenous woman, Murillo's apocalyptic rendering of the eruption of the Paricutín volcano (1946), Frida Kahlo's painful autobiographical comment *Las Dos Fridas* (1939), representing her schizophrenic state, and numerous works by Siqueiros, Orozco, Tamayo, Abraham Angel, Cuevas, Carrillo, Echeverría, Toledo and O'Gorman.

TLALOC OR CHALCHIUHTLICUE?
Greeting the visitor outside the Museum of Anthropology entrance is a massive pink stone sculpture, once thought to represent Tláloc, the god of rain. Unearthed in an area south of Texcoco in the Valley of Mexico, this 7.5m-tall, 167-ton stone monolith had to be transported on a specially designed 72-wheel trailer to its present site. Archaeologists now believe the subject of the statue to be Chalchiuhtlicue, the water goddess.

Carving of Chalchiuhtlicue – or is it Tláloc?

▶ Museo del Caracol (Snail Museum) *48A1*

Metro: Chapultepec
Open: Tue–Sun 9–5.30

The Caracol, also called the Galería de Historia, is a short distance downhill from Chapultepec Castle, and is named after its snail-like shape. It was conceived by Pedro Ramírez Vázquez to blend into the wooded slope and opened in 1960. Diagrams, models and reproductions aimed at instructing younger visitors illustrate Mexico's long fight for freedom, culminating in the 1917 Constitution. This is dramatically exhibited in the last room, a conically shaped area of lava brick, skylit by a red dome.

▶▶▶ Museo Nacional de Antropología (National Museum of Anthropology) *48A1*

Metro: Auditorio, Chapultepec
Open: Tue–Sat 9–7, Sun 10–6

The world-renowned Anthropological Museum, once exemplary in its field, is still one of the capital's musts. It was built in the early 1960s to a design by Pedro Ramirez Vázquez, and its lofty proportions and imaginative displays have hardly aged, paying a fitting homage to the sophistication and artistry of Mexico's pre-Hispanic cultures. Nevertheless there is a lack of updating with respect to new archaeological discoveries and an absence of information in English.

Olmec head from San Lorenzo, now in the Museum of Anthropology

The focal point is a large semi-roofed courtyard with an inverted fountain around which lie two floors of exhibition halls, the ground floor devoted to Mesoamerican artefacts, the upper to ethnographic exhibits illustrating *indígena* traditions today. The museum covers a vast field in great depth with an estimated 5km of exhibits. In the foyer is an excellent bookshop and the Sala de Orientación which gives an audio-visual preview of the museum's contents.

The galleries are arranged anti-clockwise around the courtyard, starting in the right wing with an introduction to world anthropology and ethnology and continuing with the origins of Mesoamerican man, before moving into pre-Classic civilisation (1700–200 BC). Then follow rooms devoted to Teotihuacán, Tula (the Toltecs), México (the Aztecs), Oaxaca (Mixtec and Zapotec), the Gulf of Mexico (Olmecs, Huastecs and Totonacs), Maya, northern cultures and finally Occidente (western cultures in Nayarit, Jalisco and Colima).

Particularly remarkable exhibits include a giant Toltec *Atlante* in the Sala de Tula, the Aztec Calendar Stone in the spectacularly laid-out Sala México, and a huge Olmec head from San Lorenzo. Also striking are the muscular *Luchador*, a well-preserved sculpture in the Sala Olmec, the Mayan mask of the God of the Sun, reproductions of Bonampak murals and a re-creation of King Pakal's tomb from Palenque outside the Sala Maya. Countless other equally precious and impressive pieces offer a wealth of discoveries – even more fascinating after visiting any of the archaeological sites in question.

CHARROS

Sunday morning activities in Chapultepec Park include a *charreada*, a Mexican rodeo performed by *charros* (macho gentlemen cowboys) in a colourful spectacle which also features girl riders, singers and *mariachi* bands. They perform remarkable feats, galloping round the ring, lassooing cattle and switching mounts in mid-flight. Performances at 10am at the Rancho del Charro, off Avenida Constituyentes.

►► Museo Rufino Tamayo (Rufino Tamayo Museum) 48A1

Metro: Chapultepec
Open: Tue–Sun 10–6

Rufino Tamayo (1899–1991), one of Mexico's most revered 20th-century artists, left an impressive legacy to his adopted city (he was born in Oaxaca) in the form of this sleekly designed art museum. East of the Anthropology Museum and just across the road from the Museum of Modern Art is the low-lying, multi-planed granite structure, built in 1979 and highly regarded for its avant-garde contemporary art exhibitions, often covering international work. The permanent collection of 20th-century art includes many of Tamayo's contemporaries – Ernst, Masson, Lam, Matta, Léger and Picasso, as well as George Segal, Francis Bacon, Warhol and Botero. A small bookshop and conference facilities complete the scene.

Parque Zoológico (Zoological Park) 65A2

Metro: Auditorio
Open: Wed–Sun 9–4.30

This claims to be the world's first zoo, with a history going back to the Aztecs (*c*1500). The 2,000 species housed here are popular with children. Chinese pandas, lions and tigers, together with pony-rides and a tram, all provide thrills for the young. Rowing-boats can be hired on the lake and there is an adjacent children's amusement park. The zoo is located along with the **Jardín Botanico►**, beside **Lago Chapultepec►** on the south side of Paseo de la Reforma from the Anthropological Museum.

Goddess of fertility at the Museum of Anthropology

Rivera and Kahlo were one of the world's most flamboyant 'art couples'. They lived and worked in Mexico City's Coyoacán and San Ángel districts, surrounded by the intellectual and artistic élite of post-revolutionary Mexico, and were fundamental to Mexico's cultural renaissance.

CULT FIGURE
It is only recently that Frida Kahlo's works have found their place in the art market. An auction price of $1.5 million in 1991 became a record for a Latin-American artist's work. Adopted by feminists as a figurehead, Kahlo has achieved cult status. But it is hard to better the last great exhibition of her paintings in 1953, organised by Lola Alvarez Bravo. Along with the painter and her entourage Alvarez saw the end approaching and transported the dying artist to the gallery to lie in state in her legendary four-poster. Dressed in her richest Zapotec costume and jewellery, Kahlo bravely received admirers and friends all evening in a conscious farewell to life.

Portrait of the flamboyant Rivera

When the couple first met, in 1923, Kahlo was a bright-eyed teenager and Rivera a 37-year-old man-of-the-world. Innocent versus womaniser, 'dove' versus 'elephant' (the words of Kahlo's father), beauty and the beast. Variously described as an ogre, a seducer and a frog (Kahlo's description), Rivera was a provocative, violent character whose physical stamina, black humour and egotism only served to attract more mistresses. By the time they met again, five years later, Kahlo had developed into a mature, arresting-looking but severely traumatised woman. A near fatal tramway accident in 1925 had shattered her spine, pelvis and legs, adding to the traumas of childhood polio, but had also inspired an exorcising passion – painting. Convalescing in a four-poster bed at her family home in Coyoacán, she occupied the hours by transferring her image – reflected in a mirror on the canopy of the bed – on to paper and canvas, thus initiating a lifetime series of agonised self-portraits. 'I've never painted a dream, I've always painted my reality,' she once said.

The ogre Rivera, meanwhile, was at the peak of his career. After a 10-year stay in Paris where he had lived the life of a Montparnasse Bohemian, his return to Mexico in 1921 marked the beginning of 30 years as the uncontested leader of pictorial nationalism. Muralism was in its infancy but by the time he and Kahlo married, in 1929, he had covered hundreds of square metres of government-owned walls with his powerful, stylised depictions of class-struggles and indigenous history. Inspired by the revolution and a meeting with Stalin in 1927 in the USSR, he never lost his socialist spirit, a characteristic which caused, in the case of New York's Rockefeller Center and Detroit's Art Institute, endless scandal and controversy, due to his overt glorification of Communism.

Magnetism Rivera and Kahlo's relationship was a meeting of opposites, eased by a common dedication to Communism that was part of the post-revolutionary political climate and shared by exiles such as the great photographer, Tina Modotti. But their true mutual passion was painting – something which, in later blacker moments of Kahlo's life, saved her from suicide. The 25-year vagaries of their marriage, divorce and remarriage were due as much to Rivera's uncontrollable need to seduce other women (his conquests included Kahlo's younger sister) as to Kahlo's deeply embedded psychological trauma, her obsession with bearing his child (two miscarriages left profound marks) and her long periods of intense physical suffering following numerous operations.

Rivera's career flourished; they spent long periods in the US while he worked on commissions and she floundered in self-imposed linguistic and social isolation.

Truce The couple's confrontations and separations only served to stimulate an increasing flow of pictorial violence from Kahlo's brushes. Her former bitter-sweet world of flowers, birds and animals gave way to increasingly tormented images of blood, laceration, self-mutilation, suicide and death. In the words of surrealist theoretician André Breton they were 'bombs wrapped up in ribbon.' Strong-willed and proud, she also indulged in sexual provocation, managing to seduce the ageing Trotsky, as well as the sculptor Isamu Noguchi and the elegant American photographer Nickolas Muray. After divorce in 1939, their remarriage the following year announced a new basis to the relationship. Rivera lived in his San Ángel studio while Kahlo was entrenched in her newly repainted blue Coyoacán house; although there were no sexual relations, they recognised a profound emotional and spiritual bond. Rivera continued his overt socio-political provocation while Kahlo plunged more deeply into her inner struggle. Her death in 1954 ended years of deterioration and, although Rivera remarried the following year, the absence of her guiding spirit and inspiration contributed to his own death in 1957.

MEXICAN FLAMBOYANCE
Frida Kahlo was a mesmerising woman, whose striking features were part *mestizo* and part Austro-Hungarian, the latter inherited from her Jewish father. Her dark eyes and high forehead were accentuated by heavy, strong eyebrows which she exaggerated in her stiff, frontal self-portraits. Crowned with elaborate hair-styles and exuberant jewellery, she had an inimitable style of dressing which came from the liberated women of Tehuantepec and Juchitán in the Isthmus. Their brilliantly coloured and embroidered costumes were the perfect foil for Kahlo as she retreated increasingly into her disdainful, high-priestess role.

Rivera mural in the Presidential Palace, Mexico City

Frida Kahlo (1907–54)

Children's band outside the basilica

VISION OF THE VIRGIN

On 9 December 1531, Juan Diego, a humble peasant, was walking to church in Tlatelolco when he was stopped by a vision of the Virgin Mary. Speaking in the Náhautl language, she told him to have a church built on the spot. Diego reported back to the local bishop and was treated with some scepticism but on 12 December Mary reappeared, asking him to take roses to the Bishop as proof. This he did, but on opening his cloak to show them to the Bishop found in their place an image of the dark-skinned Virgin imprinted on the cloth. Named after the statue of the black-faced Nuestra Señora de Guadalupe found in 13th-century Spain, said to have been carved by St Luke himself, her image is displayed in thousands of churches all over Mexico and 12 December remains a high point in the religious calendar. The shrine is the object of year-round pilgrimages, peaking with four million visitors in December.

Image of the Virgin of Guadalupe

►► Basilica de Nuestra Señora de Guadalupe (Church of Our Lady of Guadalupe) *65B3*

Metro: Basilica, La Villa
Open: daily 6am–8pm

This should be a priority destination, if only to understand Mexico's obsession with her patron saint, the Virgen de Guadalupe. Two churches bear her name: the first, dating from 1533, though later completely remodelled, stands on Tepeyac hill; the second, built in 1976, is a gigantic, dramatic construction which now houses the much revered cloak imprinted with the Virgin's image. This is displayed over the main altar: closer views are aided by a mechanical walkway which carries visitors under the altar. Set around the enormous stone plaza in gardens and up the hill are numerous other shrines, churches and chapels, thronging with pilgrims and

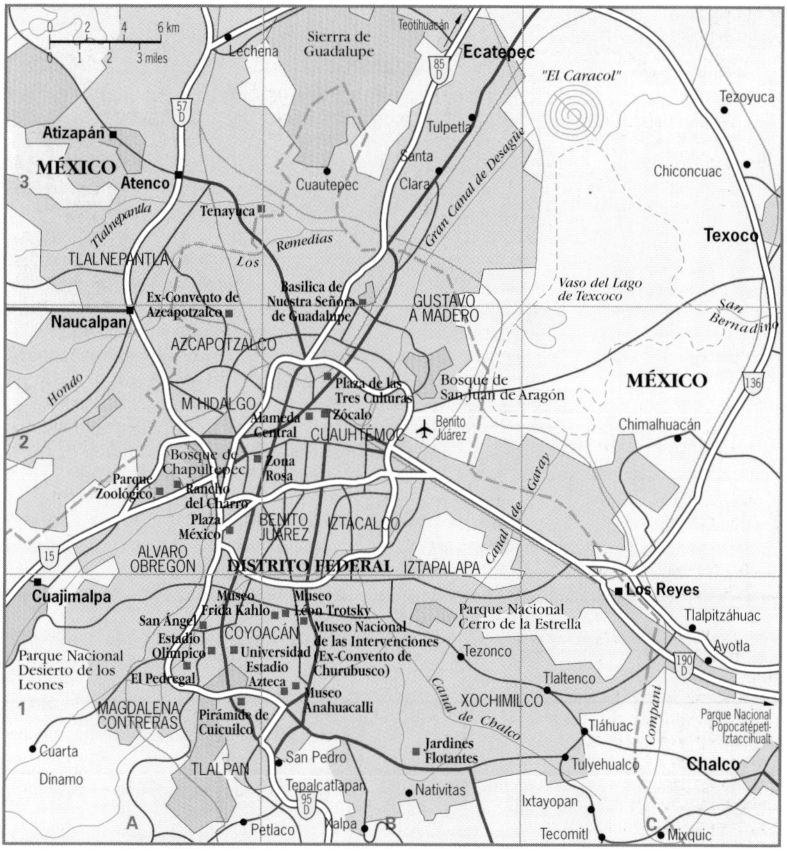

Mexico City environs

vendors of religious souvenirs. The spectacular basilica accomodates 10,000 worshippers and holds hourly mass. It was created by Pedro Ramírez Vázquez, also responsible for the Museum of Anthropology.

► Plaza de las Tres Culturas (Square of the Three Cultures) 65B2

Metro: Tlatelolco

This large square represents the meeting of three cultures – Aztec, Spanish and modern Mexican. It overlies what was once a gigantic Aztec market-place selling goods brought here from all over Mexico. The ruins of Tlatelolco's main pyramid and other temple structures can be seen from a raised walkway, while in the centre of the square a plaque recalls the Aztecs' last stand on 13 August 1521. Sensitive to Tlatelolco's significance, the Spanish built a chapel and Franciscan monastery in the square before erecting the church of San Diego in 1609. Unfortunately the contemporary Mexican aspect of this trio of cultures is less impressive. The buildings lining the plaza are hardly the best examples of modern architecture.

Not to be forgotten in this context are the events of October 1968 (see page 47) when government troops fired on thousands of student demonstrators in the square.

Juan Diego's cloak, framed to reveal the image of Mary in the new basilica

CORTÉS AND CUAUHTÉMOC
Inside the Casa de Cortés are two Rivera murals depicting the conquest, imprisonment and torture of Emperor Cuauhtémoc, the last of the Aztec lineage. It was here that the 25-year-old emperor was held and tortured by Cortés to reveal the hiding-place of the great Aztec treasure, much coveted by the Spaniards. From here Cuauhtémoc was taken to Tabasco, where he was killed.

Coyoacán's Casa de Cortés was Nueva España's first town-hall, built in 1524 and rebuilt in the 18th century

Coyoacán

▶▶▶ Coyoacán 65A1

The pretty suburb of Coyoacán, a leafy retreat 8km south of Mexico City's roaring central hub, was under Aztec domination before the Spanish *conquistadores* oversaw Tenochtitlán's destruction. Many members of Mexico's high society, former presidents and intellectuals live there today, following in the footsteps of Frida Kahlo, Diego Rivera and Leon Trotsky, whose museums constitute three high points. The relaxed atmosphere (the university campus is not far) peaks on Sundays around the central **Plaza Hidalgo▶▶▶** and adjoining Jardín Centenario, which throng with musicians, craftspeople and strolling Mexican families. On the northern side of the square stands the 18th-century Casa de Cortés opposite the Parroquía de San Juan Bautista, which, with its adjoining former Dominican monastery, dates from 1582, but was heavily reconstructed in 1804. The main artery, **Avenida Francisco Sosa▶▶**, runs west from here past the pink domes of the **Centro Cultural Coyoacán▶▶**, numerous beautiful colonial homes, lively local restaurants and the charming **Plaza Santa Caterina▶▶**, to culminate at Avenida Universidad.

▶ Ex-Convento de Churubusco 65B1

Calle 20 de Agosto
Metro: General Anaya
Open: Tue–Fri 10–5, Sat–Sun 10–6

The 17th-century monastery of Churubusco, scene of one of Mexico's most important military defeats at the hands of American forces in 1847, now houses the large Museo Nacional de las Intervenciones, which covers foreign incursions into Mexico (US, Spain, France). The US comes in for strong criticism in the panels and captions here.

▶▶▶ Museo Anahuacalli (House of Anáhuac) 65B1

Calle del Museo 150
Metro: Tasqueña, then taxi
Open: Tue–Sun 10–6

This museum, in a dramatic setting on the southern edge of Coyoacán overlooking the volcanoes beyond, encapsulates Rivera's imagination and identification with Mesoamerican cultures. He designed the labyrinthine lava-stone edifice to house his extensive collection of artefacts, as well as incorporate an open studio where he briefly worked before his death in 1957, leaving some works in progress. Somewhere between a mausoleum and a fortress, the architecture combines dark corridors with onyx windows, staircases with open terraces and apertures, stone ceiling mosaics, arches, niches and stepped altar-like displays. Within this extraordinary structure are 2,000 superb pieces representing most of Mexico's pre-Hispanic cultures, with the top floor devoted to the Aztecs. The name means 'House of Anáhuac', Anáhuac being the Valley of Mexico, and it truly fits this description.

Diego Rivera's studio in San Ángel

▶▶▶ Museo Frida Kahlo (Frida Kahlo Museum) *65B1*

Calle Londres 247
Metro: Coyoacán
Open: Tue–Sun 10–6

Deep indigo and terracotta walls accented with green window-frames announce the former home and studio of tragic, flamboyant and talented Frida Kahlo, wife and muse of Diego Rivera (see pages 62–3). A lifetime of frenetic intellectual and artistic activity is reflected in the paintings and memorabilia of her birthplace and home where brilliant colour covers every wall and shelf, spilling into the deep green foliage of the luxuriant garden. Paintings by friends including Duchamp, Klee and Tanguy hang beside showcases of her eclectic collections of masks, Teotihuacán sculptures, ex-votos (votive offerings), glass, lacquerware and ceramics. Her wheelchair and last unfinished painting (a portrait of Stalin), Rivera's famous hat and overalls and a neat accounts book all contribute to this powerful personal museum.

LIFE ON THE RUN

A first assassination attempt on Leon Trotsky was made in May 1940 by an armed gang, presumed to have been led by the painter David Alfaro Siqueiros. Trotsky and his wife managed to survive this bloody attack by hiding under their beds. A second attempt, this time successful, was engineered by Ramon Mercader del Río, a Spanish Stalinist agent who gained the confidence of the Trotsky household and finally ended Trotsky's life with an ice-pick on 20 August 1940. Mercader was arrested and imprisoned. Trotsky's widow remained in the house until 1961, when she moved to Paris, dying a year later.

▶▶ Museo Leon Trotsky (Leon Trotsky Museum) *65B1*

Calle Viena 45
Metro: Coyoacán
Open: Tue–Sun 10–5

The home of Trotsky, from May 1939 until his assassination in August 1940, offers a fascinating insight in the heart of residential Coyoacán. After fleeing Stalin, Trotsky was offered asylum by Mexico's President Lázaro Cárdenas, and settled here with his wife Natalia, near their friends Rivera and Kahlo. This gloomy, delapidated edifice, much fortified due to his justifiable paranoia about attempted assaults, nevertheless reflects his disciplined existence and interests, ranging from the poultry yard to his study and bedroom pockmarked with bullet-holes. His tomb, designed by Juan O'Gorman and topped by a red flag, hammer and sickle, stands in the garden.

Leon Trotsky's study – just as he left it

The walled garden of 16th-century San Jacinto church

DESIERTO DE LOS LEONES
From the heart of San Ángel the Camino al Desierto de los Leones winds 25km west up into a national park of the same name. Pine-forest trails make it a favourite Sunday picnic destination for the capital's hordes in their desperate search for fresh air. Culture in the form of concerts and exhibitions is offered at a beautiful 17th-century Carmelite monastery, set in pretty gardens within the park.

Ruins of the 17th-century monastery of Desierto de los Leones

San Ángel

►►► San Ángel *65A1*

Bus: San Ángel pesero *(mini-bus) down Insurgentes*

San Ángel is an exclusive residential area and a favourite tourist destination. Like neighbouring Coyoacán, it makes a welcome, slow-paced change from the city centre. It was originally an Aztec town named Chimalistac, later becoming a popular retreat for the city's wealthier classes. Packed with historical buildings, cafés, shops and restaurants, its cobblestone streets and flowery patios wind around and outwards from the central hubs of Plaza de Carmen and Plaza San Jacinto.

►► Museo de Arte Carrillo Gil (Carrillo Gil Art Museum) *69C2*

Avenida Revolución 1608
Metro: Viveros, then bus 43
Open: Tue–Sun 10–6

This pristine art museum and gallery on the north-eastern edge of San Ángel, displays an impressive private collection of contemporary Mexican and international art and Japanese prints, along with a video room, a bookshop and a corner café. Mexico's big three (Rivera, Siqueiros and Orozco) are well represented, including some unusual Cubist-inspired early works by Rivera, and Orozco's powerful *El Muerto* (1925–8). Contemporary works move strongly into conceptual mode.

►►► Museo del Carmen (Carmen Museum) *69C1*

Avenida Revolución 4, corner Monasterio
Bus: San Ángel pesero down Insurgentes
Open: Tue–Sun 10–5

The tile-domed church and adjoining monks' quarters were built as a Carmelite monastery between 1615 and 1617, surrounding a pretty cloister garden. Heavy studded wooden doors, delicate floral friezes on the embrasures, superb wood and gesso ceiling reliefs in the sacristy and Moorish tiles and frescoes in the crypt contribute to the architectural feast. The important collection of religious art is particularly rich in 18th-century baroque sculptures, but for many the highlight is in the crypt where mummified bodies, removed from their tombs by Zapata's troops in 1916, are stored in glass-topped cases.

►► Museo Estudio Diego Rivera (Diego Rivera Studio Museum) *69A2*

Calle Diego Rivera/Altavista
Metro: Viveros, then bus 43
Open: Tue–Sun 10–6

Rivera and Kahlo's studio was designed by Juan O'Gorman in 1930, and this brightly coloured functionalist structure preserves Rivera's jumbled studio and tiny bedroom upstairs, while lower areas are used for temporary exhibitions. The most interesting room is the artist's large studio. Pigments, clippings, photos and masks are randomly exhibited beside his ubiquitous denim jacket and a showcase of pre-Hispanic artefacts, reflecting the eclectic interests of this genius.

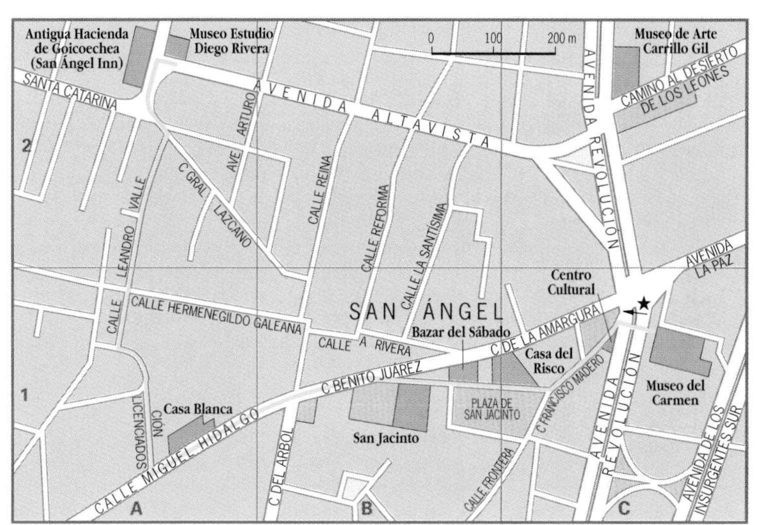

Walk

San Ángel

This exploration of the elegant and historical suburb of San Ángel (see opposite), at its liveliest on a Saturday morning, finishes at the famous old San Ángel Inn. Allow two to three hours to visit monuments on the way.

Start from the domed church and museum of the **Museo del Carmen**, then walk past the Plaza del Carmen along Calle Francisco Madero to the central **Plaza de San Jacinto**, where a hive of indigenous vendors and local painters exhibit their wares on Saturdays. On the right is the 18th-century **Casa del Risco**, whose courtyard fountain is a riot of ceramic tiles, plates and encrusted shells: upstairs rooms house a museum of colonial and European art. A little further is the **Bazar del Sábado**, an indoor crafts market open only on Saturdays and joined by an outdoor market at the north-west end of the plaza. Follow the cobbled Calle Benito Juárez west to the 16th-century church and former monastery of **San Jacinto**, unmistakable with its bougainvillaea-draped walls. This colourful street becomes Calle Miguel Hidalgo as it leads into the heart of residential San Ángel. Walk past the 17th-century **Casa Blanca** on your right, a national monument but not open to the public, and take the next right. Brightly painted fortress-like walls surround many private properties in a patchwork of architectural styles as Calle Leandro Valle leads downhill to the junction with Avenida Altavista. Opposite stands the **Museo Estudio Diego Rivera**. At the 18th-century *hacienda* housing the **San Ángel Inn** you can have a drink or stop for lunch.

San Ángel Inn

EL PEDREGAL
Immediately south of San Ángel, and stretching through the University to Coyoacán, lies an area known as El Pedregal. It came into being about 2,000 years ago when the Xitle volcano erupted in great lava waves which eventually solidified into over 39sq km of craggy crevices and caverns. In 1945 the architect Luís Barragán developed a Utopian project to create a residential area which respected the existing lava formations and extraordinary natural vegetation. After creating three showcase gardens he laid out rigorous building restrictions, but these were ignored and although by 1960 El Pedregal contained more than 900 houses, few of them respected the founding vision.

Flower-seller (above) and colourful punts on the canals at Xochimilco

▶ Universidad Nacional Autonoma de México (UNAM) *65A1*

Metro: Copilco

Latin America's oldest and largest university lies south of Coyoacán on the great lava field of El Pedregal. The University was founded in the 1550s, but its campus (Ciudad Universitaria) dates from the early 1950s. Today over 300,000 students frequent what at the time was a particularly avant-garde complex, its landmark being the library designed by Juan O'Gorman. This 12-storey block is entirely faced with a mural of natural stones, tile and glass illustrating Mexican history. Siqueiros, too, is represented with a vast mosaic frieze on the south wall of the Rectory, near the university arts and science museum.

▶▶ Xochimilco *65B1*

Metro: Tasqueña then tren ligero *(light railway) to Embarcadero*

On the southern edge of Mexico City lies the quintessential weekend destination away from the pollution. Xochimilco's 'floating' nursery gardens and tree-lined canals are a throwback to the Aztecs, who, short of agricultural land, ingeniously developed *chinampas* (rafts of reeds that rooted underwater) to grow fruit, vegetables and flowers. This practice continues today, and the central market is a delight. Capital-dwellers flock here on Sundays and public holidays to cruise the canals in brilliantly decorated *trajineras* (gondolas), usually to exuberant *mariachi* accompaniment. Close behind are vendors in canoes hawking flowers, fresh tortillas or corn-on-the-cob.

Xochimilco's 135 sq km area harbours several churches, notably the beautiful 16th-century church of **San Bernardino**▶▶, the Museo Arqueologico and the Parque Ecologico. This extensive district of grasslands, lagoons and canals has ecological tours (tel: 673 8061/7890). Otherwise, head for the main *embarcadero* (jetty) for a leisurely boat tour.

West of Xochimilco (light railway station: La Noria) is a striking 400-year-old *hacienda* housing the **Museo Dolores Olmedo Patiño**▶▶ (*Open* Tue–Sun 10–6). The museum is set in landscaped grounds inhabited by peacocks, and has an impressive display of Mexican folk art, pre-Hispanic artefacts and the largest collection of paintings by Diego Rivera. Works by his two wives, Angelina Beloff and Frida Kahlo, are interspersed with countless photos of the owner and benefactor, the formidable Dolores Olmedo, who lives on in the *hacienda*.

Accommodation

Visitors arriving in Mexico City will have no trouble finding accommodation, whatever the time of year and whatever their budget. Hotels range from the luxury giants and a few rare colonial beauties, to more basic establishments north, west and south of the Zócalo. For details of hotels see page 270.

Luxury locations Mexico City's most luxurious hotels are clustered just north of Chapultepec Park in the residential area of Polanco. The dramatic 1960s **Camino Real** is still a show-stopper, and its internal facilities include numerous restaurants, discos, pools and tennis courts.

In contrast is the plush, small-scale **Park Villa**, tucked away in a quiet residential street and offering more personalised service. Closer to the historic centre, on the Paseo de la Reforma, is a string of modern international hotels, some at more accessible prices. These include the **Four Seasons** (exorbitant and lacking atmosphere), the **Emporio** and the **Hotel Marquis Reforma**. Those looking for a more personalised setting should aim for **La Casona**, in the increasingly hip **Colonia Roma**, with attractively renovated rooms. In the Zona Rosa, the **Galería Plaza** has tranquillity, good service and a popular nightclub, while the **Marco Polo** maintains consistently high standards.

Middle range At the top of this category are two of Mexico City's best located hotels. The **Howard Johnson Gran Hotel** is a marvel of art-nouveau design with a soaring central lobby, open ironwork lift and stained-glass roof.

On the corner of the Zócalo, the **Majestic** is housed in a former Spanish mansion, with a panoramic rooftop restaurant.

A favourite with regular visitors is the **María Cristina**, just north of Reforma and the Zona Rosa. The delightful patio and garden of this pretty colonial-style hotel make it a welcome retreat from modern urban life. In a similar vein, the **Hotel de Cortés**, on the northern edge of Alameda Park, was built in the 18th century as a hospice for Augustinian monks. Although their cells have been modernised the rooms can still be dark. The **Vasco de Quiroga** is a Spanish-style hotel beyond the tacky section of the Zona Rosa and reasonably priced.

Bottom range Hotels around the Zócalo are good for budget travellers. Those with a historical bent should make for the **Hotel Monte Carlo**, built as a monastery and once home to D H Lawrence.

Just round the corner from the Templo Mayor is the clean, modern **Hotel Catedral**, while a few blocks north is the large, reasonably-priced **Hotel Antillas**.

A cluster of budget hotels, dotted west of the Zócalo along Cinco de Mayo near metro Allende, includes the **Hotel Canada**, the **Hotel New York** and the **Hotel Gillow**.

COST FACTORS
Upper bracket hotel prices in Mexico City usually include a 15 per cent tax and in middle- to top-range hotels tipping is expected. By law, rates are posted either in the lobby or room, or both. In low season you may be able to negotiate a discount or benefit from a special offer, but this is more common outside the capital. Remember to make use of your hotel safe if it has one.

Hotel María Cristina, one of only a handful of hotels that reflect Mexico's colonial past

COMFORT FACTORS
One thing to bear in mind when booking a room is the decibel level. Mexico City's inner streets and boulevards can be very noisy, so always inspect a room before checking in. This goes for other large towns. In middle-range hotels televisions tend to take priority over phones, while showers, rather than baths, are the rule everywhere except in top establishments. Even bottom-range hotels nearly always supply drinking water (*agua purificada*) either in carafes in the room or by access to a corridor demijohn.

Taking a quick snack in a street café

Bars and restaurants

Mexico City offers the widest range of international cuisine in the country, so profit from it before setting off on the taco and tortilla trail. It also has a diverse price range, from street-corner taco-stands to elegant establishments all over the city. Lunch is the main meal, starting around 3pm, and dragging on till dusk at weekends. This is the ideal time to witness Mexican family outings, whether in the southern suburbs of Coyoacán and San Ángel, or in some of the central historical settings. Many typical restaurants close early in the evening, so if you are intent on dinner phone beforehand (see pages 279–80 for details).

Historic hits Plunge into Mexico's *belle époque* past at the **Bar l'Opéra**, a Parisian-style bar and brasserie complete with carved mahogany and mirrors, just behind the Bellas Artes. Popular with the arty crowd for after-theatre drinks, it also offers meals, but these are slow to come and not the city's greatest. Similar in style is **Prendes**, dating back to 1892, whose walls are lined with images of former patrons – from Pancho Villa to Walt Disney – and which still dishes up mountains of paella and hearty Mexican fare. Another institution is the **Café de Tacuba** which opened its doors in 1912 in a former monastery and has hardly changed since, leaving tiled walls and brass lamps intact, with a menu offering typical Mexican dishes. Not far away is the outrageously decorated **Cicero**, now over a century old. Plush decoration veers between a 19th-century brothel and high baroque, *mariachis* roam between the

Café Tacuba is set in an old monastery with original fixtures and fittings still in place

tables, tequila flows in a cosy bar and diners indulge in sophisticated Mexican cuisine in the lofty, elegant upstairs rooms.

For a contemporary facelift of a historic mansion, try **Los Girasoles on Tacuba** for a drink or inspired dinner accompanied by European wines. Helpful service aids a rather pretentious menu – but the end products are imaginative and beautifully presented. Closer to Alameda, the spectacular Moorish patio of the **Casa de Azulejos** houses a branch of Sanborns: tame Mexican cuisine prevails at reasonable prices and there is an upstairs bar.

Zona Rosa International Vegetarian, Japanese, Italian and Chinese cuisines jostle with western fare in the Zona Rosa's haunts. Pedestrian streets and wide pavements allow many restaurants to expand outside. The **Fonda El Refugio** offers Mexican specialities in a lively setting. Those bitten with the *mariachi* bug should head for **Carrousel Internacional**, a relaxed pub/restaurant which serves drinks, snacks and meals to familiar local sounds and is open till 2am. For diners missing *haute cuisine*, try the **Champs-Elysées**: it is the place to be seen in Mexico City, much frequented by politicians, and its food is on a par with top French restaurants. Similarly Gallic in style is the amusing though ostentatious **Les Moustaches**, located across Reforma. Apart from the fact that every waiter sports a moustache, it offers a wide-ranging menu of international cuisine. More reasonable, but equally European, is the design-conscious **Caffé Milano**, which has a pleasant outdoor section and serves good Italian food.

This Mexico City institution is housed in an attractive restored 19th-century mansion

San Ángel and Coyoacán If you are not booked at the elegant **San Ángel Inn**, dine at the more relaxed and cheaper **Fonda San Ángel**, right on the Plaza San Jacinto, popular throughout the day and evening.

Just east of Insurgentes is one of the capital's exclusive establishments, **Los Irabiens**, which serves what could be classed as *nouvelle cuisine Mexicaine* in an up-market setting hung with works of contemporary art.

Moving into Coyoacán, head straight for **Café El Parnaso** between the central squares, a long-standing café with an intellectual reputation and a bookshop.

For more substantial fare head back towards the Jardín Santa Caterina and the bustling **Hostería Santa Caterina**, a popular neighbourhood restaurant serving homely fare.

RESTAURANT WITH A VIEW

Take in the pastoral delights of Chapultepec Park from a restaurant overlooking the fountain of the Lago Mayor in the western section of the park (beyond the wide Anillo Periférico which cuts through the park north–south). The high-standard international menu of the Lago Chapultepec is backed up by good service and a pianist. It opens till late at night, but its delights unfortunately do not come cheap.

CANTINAS* AND *MARIACHIS

On Coyoacán's main square is the lively El Hijo del Cuervo, with its friendly atmosphere. In the historic city centre aim for Plaza Garibaldi which throbs to the tunes of local *mariachis* from nightfall until the early hours. Bars line the square, the most popular being the Tenampa, the ideal place for a shot of tequila. However uproarious the atmosphere, care should be taken with wallets, particularly later in the evening. Tequila also flows at Los Portales, a vast, tiled hall with dusty chandeliers on Calle Bolívar.

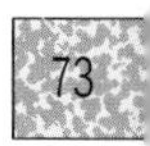

MODERN MEXICO
The Galería Mexicana de Diseño (Calle Anatole France 13, metro: Reforma) is devoted to exhibitions of contemporary Mexican design. Equally 20th century are the items and gadgets on sale at the Centro Cultural Contemporáneo (next to the Stouffer Presidente Hotel in Polanco), where the Mexican TV company Televisa sponsors major exhibitions of contemporary art. The gift shop here has plenty of imaginative items.

Above: the Iron Palace department store
Right: Ciudadela market

ANTIQUE MEXICO
Many of Mexico City's antique dealers trade in the Zona Rosa, in particular in the Plaza del Ángel at Calle Londrés 161. At weekends the interior plaza is filled with expensive antique stands, enticingly eclectic on Saturdays and more specialised on Sundays, particularly for antiquarian books and maps. Calle Estocolmo also harbours a number of antique shops, a good place to gaze at superb Talavera vases.

Shopping

Often optimistically over-priced, Mexico City's markets are not always the best options. Better purchases can sometimes be found in specialised shops where quality is also assured. The obvious buys are handicrafts, a diverse, living tradition that originates from every region of the country and is well represented in the capital.

City centre Just off Alameda at Avenida Juarez 89, Fonart (Fondación Nacional de Artesanía) sells a selection of craftwork including ceramics, toys, textiles and furniture with more choice at its less central showroom (Avenida Patriotismo 691, metro: Mixcoac). More reasonably priced is the sprawling **Mercado de la Ciudadela** on the corner of Calle Balderas and Plaza de la Ciudadela (metro: Balderas). This is the city's best treasure trove of *huipiles* (tunics), *rebozos* (shawls), Taxco silver, papier-mâché, glass and guitars, and on the pavements lining the approach you can take your pick from second-hand books or cheap watches. In the Zona Rosa, the **Mercado Insurgentes** (Calle Londrés 154) mixes handicrafts with gleaming Taxco silver in a labyrinthine covered market. Less frequented by tourists is the smaller **Mercado San Juan** at Plaza de San Juan (metro: Salto del Agua). If

experiencing handicrafts overload, explore the surrounding streets and covered food market across the square.

Further afield Reserve Sunday for **La Lagunilla** market (corner of Comonfort and Rayón, metro: Guerrero), where craftwork and clothes are sold alongside anything remotely ageing. This is also the day when craftspeople sell their wares in Coyoacán's **Plaza Hidalgo**. Saturday is a favourite in San Ángel when the **Bazar Sábado** teems with visitors, indigenous women set up their wares, artists mount their easels and the outdoor market springs into action. For authenticity, go to the **Mercado de Sonora** on Fray Servando Teresa de Mier (metro: La Merced). Here, pottery, toys, miniatures and a selection of medicinal plants sets the tone.

Nightlife

To follow the capital's agenda of nocturnal activities, check the listings in the weekly *Tiempo Libre* or the *Mexico City News*. Hardly the world's wildest city in terms of entertainment, the capital nevertheless has some firm favourites which add greatly to understanding the Mexicans and quite simply to having a good time.

Watching The scurrilous cabaret of **El Habito** in Coyoacán (tel: 659 6305 for reservations) opened in 1990 and is now firmly entrenched in the city agenda. Visitors should have a good grasp of Spanish in order to follow its satirical twists. During the week the cabaret sometimes hosts blues or jazz singers, a rarity elsewhere in town, and also has a dance-floor. The **Ballet Folklórico** performs on Sunday mornings and Wednesday and Sunday nights at the Bellas Artes between opera or concert performances. Colourful swirling skirts and stomping boots create a wonderful panorama of regional folk dances, supported by Mexico's much loved marimbas, guitars, trumpets, flutes and drums. Costumes, choreography, lighting and highly trained dancers provide a sophisticated foretaste of what you may come across in a more authentic form and setting while travelling round the country. Tickets can be bought through Ticketmaster (tel: 325 9000). The

The ever-popular Ballet Folklórico

Teatro de la Ciudad (Donceles 36, tel: 510 2197/2942) stages a rival folk dance company and concerts.

Participating The **Bar León** has great sounds (a Latin-style beat till 5am) and a large dance-hall behind an uninspiring façade on Calle Brasil, while **Bar Mata** on Filomena Mata is legendary. Flashier clubs are found in any of the top hotels, notably the Camino Real's **Cero Cero**. Yuppy crowds head for the Zona Rosa. **Chupachanga** at Florencia 56 is a favourite for its salsa and rock. Near by, **Rock Stock**, at Paseo de la Reforma 260, belts out live rock till 4am. The trendy head for **La Dolce Vita** (Orizaba 146, Col. Roma) where several floors and a garden cater for eclectic tastes, or the avant-garde bar, **Ixchel** (Medellin 65, Col. Roma).

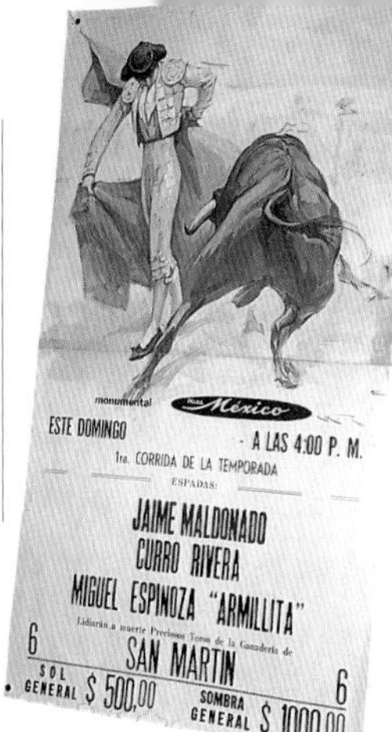

BULLFIGHTS
An alternative to dancing the night away is watching matadors dance with bulls. High season is December to March when top bullfighters perform, but the rest of the year novices display their growing talents in the face of smaller bulls. Bullfights are staged most Sundays from 4pm at the immense Plaza México, just off Insurgentes, halfway to San Ángel – the bullring is the world's largest and holds up to 50,000 spectators! It's easiest to buy tickets in advance through your hotel or an agency.

CINEMA
The city's cinemas show a reasonable range of international films, sometimes subtitled (marked VO – *version original*), but don't expect plush seating conditions. At the Ciudad Universitaria there is a good cine-club which shows avant-garde films, although this is a bit of a trek from the centre in the evening. Equally distant but screening 12 different films is the mega American complex, Cinemark 12 (metro: Taxqueña).

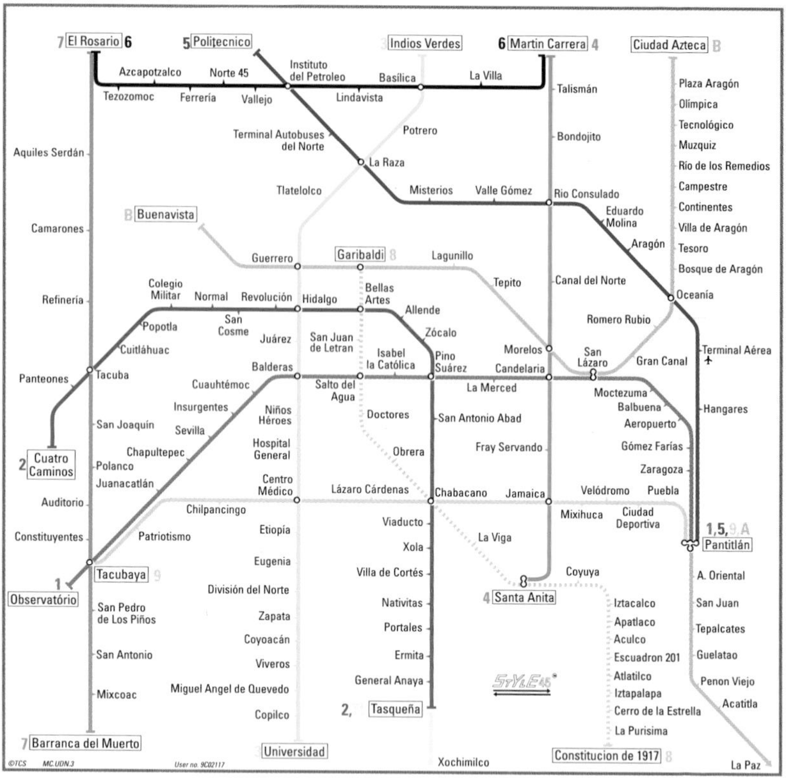

Mexico City – metro

76

Practical points

Transport Public transport is excellent and easy to use. The metro is based on the Parisian system and is eminently user-friendly. Tickets are sold at every metro station: just insert the ticket at the entrance turnstile. Avoid rush-hours (roughly 8 to 9am, 2 to 3pm and 6 to 7pm) as the crush facilitates the work of pickpockets.

White and green mini-buses (*peseros*), often blasting loud rock-music, tear along Mexico City's main arteries, stopping at main street corners. Their routes are identified by destination plaques (usually metro stations), and the fare is paid directly to the driver. Pedicabs also now operate in the Centro Historico, but you need to bargain hard.

Taxis With the recent increase in taxi-muggings, it is not advisable to hail a taxi in the street, especially at night. Only use

One of Mexico City's eco-friendly green taxis

Tourist sight-seeing trams cover the Centro Historico daily 10–5, starting from the Palacio de Bellas Artes

TOURIST HELP
The federal district tourist office is located in the Zona Rosa at Amberes 54 (metro: Insurgentes) and is open between 9am and 9pm. English-speaking staff provide limited maps, brochures and general information. A free phone service, Infotur, is available on 525 9380 for any queries about the city and its sights. A useful 24-hour emergency service (LO.CATEL) can be dialled on 658 1111, or go to their pink offices at Florencia 20, just off El Ángel in the Zona Rosa. Bilingual staff will help with any problem, particularly stolen or lost property, as well as emotional crises.

sitios (radio-taxis) or hotel taxis. *Sitios* can be called on 519 7690 or 516 6020/34. Tips are not essential, but you will find that drivers demand them. Remember, too, that the same street names crop up again and again all over the city, so state what *colonia* or *barrio* your destination is in and, even better, the nearest metro station or large crossroads.

Money and security For changing travellers' cheques or cash, the best rates are available at Casas de Cambio around El Ángel, in the adjoining Zona Rosa or at Madero 60, off the Zócalo. Banks offer marginally higher rates but require long waits. Cash dispensers at Banamex and Bancomer accept VISA, but again, be careful about where you use them.

Avoid carrying large amounts of cash and don't wear jewellery or reveal wads of notes. The more low-key your appearance is, the better. Be especially careful when using the metro or bus stations or wandering around markets.

Long-distance buses at Mexico City's largest bus station, Terminal Norte

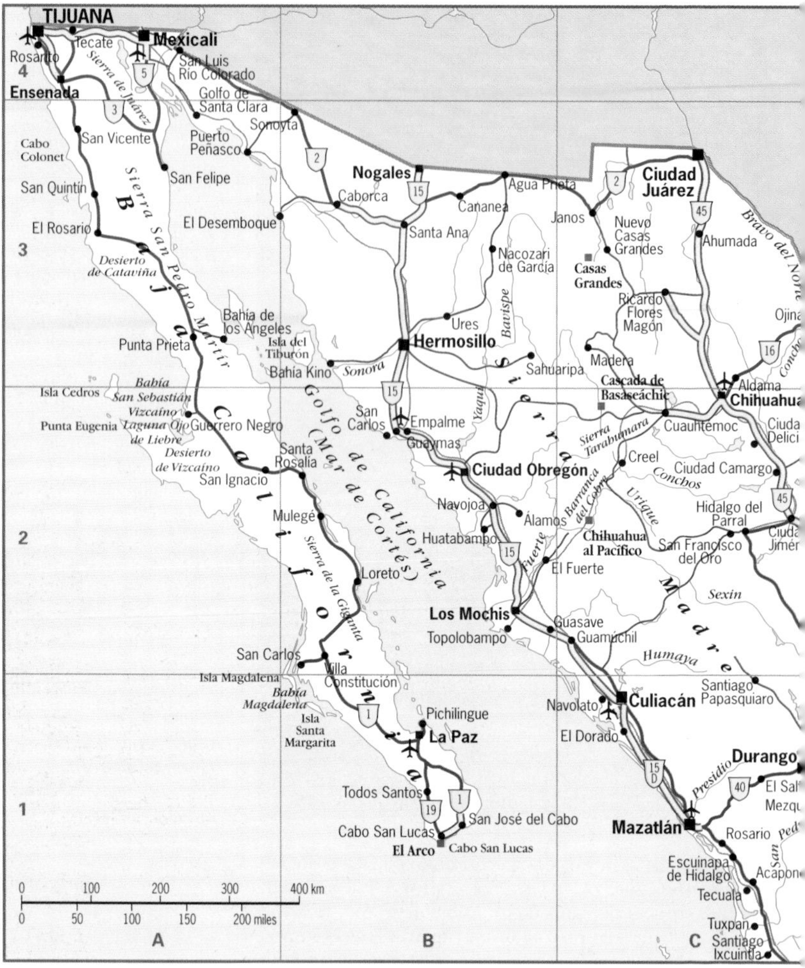

TIJUANA
Tecate
Mexicali
Rosarito
San Luis
Río Colorado
Ensenada
Sierra de Juárez
Golfo de
Santa Clara
Sonoyta
Cabo
Colonet
San Vicente
Puerto
Peñasco
San Felipe
Nogales
Ciudad
Juárez
San Quintín
Caborca
Agua Prieta
Cananea
Janos
Nuevo
Casas
Grandes
Bravo del Norte
El Rosario
El Desemboque
Santa Ana
Ahumada
Desierto
de Cataviña
Sierra San Pedro Mártir
Nacozari
de García
Casas
Grandes
Baja California
Bahía de
los Angeles
Ricardo
Flores
Magón
Ojinaga
Ures
Bavispe
Punta Prieta
Isla del
Tiburón
Hermosillo
Sahuaripa
Madera
Bahía Kino
Sonora
Cascada de
Basaseáchic
Aldama
Chihuahua
Conchos
Isla Cedros
Bahía
San Sebastián
Vizcaíno
Yaqui
Sierra Madre
Punta Eugenia
Laguna Ojo
de Liebre
Guerrero Negro
San
Carlos
Empalme
Guaymas
Sierra
Tarahumara
Cuauhtémoc
Ciudad
Delicias
Desierto
de Vizcaíno
Santa
Rosalía
Golfo de California (Mar de Cortés)
Creel
Ciudad Camargo
San Ignacio
Ciudad Obregón
Barranca
del Cobre
Conchos
Urique
Navojoa
Mulegé
Álamos
Hidalgo del
Parral
Sierra de la Giganta
Huatabampo
Chihuahua
al Pacífico
San Francisco
del Oro
Ciudad
Jiménez
Fuerte
El Fuerte
Loreto
Sexin
Los Mochis
Guasave
Topolobampo
Guamúchil
San Carlos
Villa
Constitución
Humaya
Isla Magdalena
Santiago
Papasquiaro
Bahía
Magdalena
Navolato
Culiacán
Isla
Santa
Margarita
Pichilingue
La Paz
El Dorado
Durango
Presidio
El Salto
Mezquital
Todos Santos
San José del Cabo
Mazatlán
Cabo San Lucas
El Arco
Cabo San Lucas
Rosario
San Pedro
Escuinapa
de Hidalgo
Acaponeta
Tecuala
Tuxpan
Santiago
Ixcuintla
0 100 200 300 400 km
0 50 100 150 200 miles
A
B
C
1
2
3
4
1
2
3
5
15
15
15 D
19
1
1
16
45
45
40

Baja California & the North

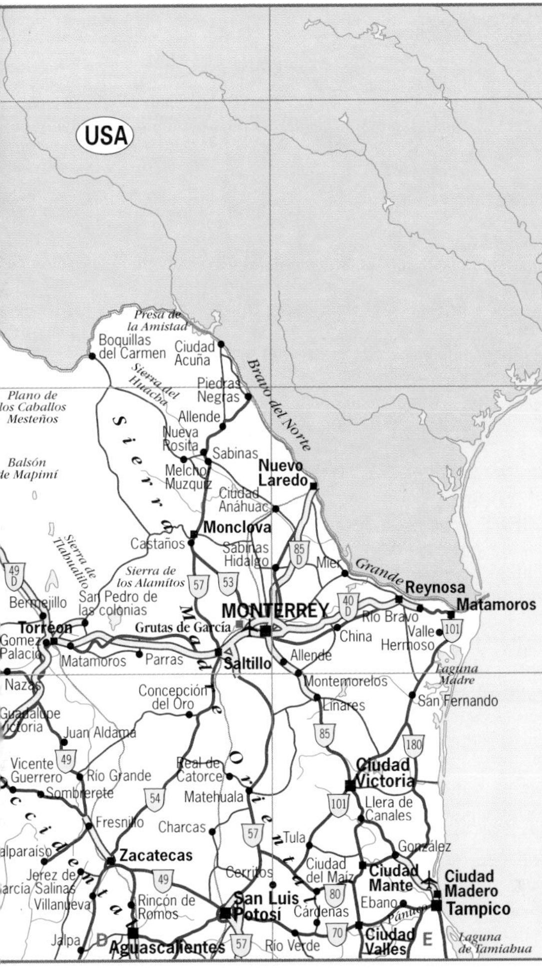

BAJA CALIFORNIA AND THE NORTH The coastline of northern Mexico is washed by the Pacific Ocean, the Gulf of California (Mar de Cortés) and the Gulf of Mexico. Between them lie interminable stretches of desert, plains, lofty mountains and canyons, punctuated by sprawling industrial cities whose proximity to the US ensures growing prosperity.

From the still cave-dwelling people of the Sierra Tarahumara to colonies of American retirees residing on the coasts of Baja, the north matches its climatic extremes with an equally diverse population. But above all, an indelible impression has been left by the empty, eroded landscapes where millions of years of the earth's evolution seem still to be taking shape.

This is the region where visitors can revel in the comforts of resorts such as Los Cabos, watch dolphins and whales, ride out the perilous bends of the Chihuahua–Pacifico railway or delve into Chijuahua's heroic revolutionary past. Distances are great, so plan your itinerary carefully.

Previous page: Sierra San Pedro Martír, which runs down the northern half of Baja California

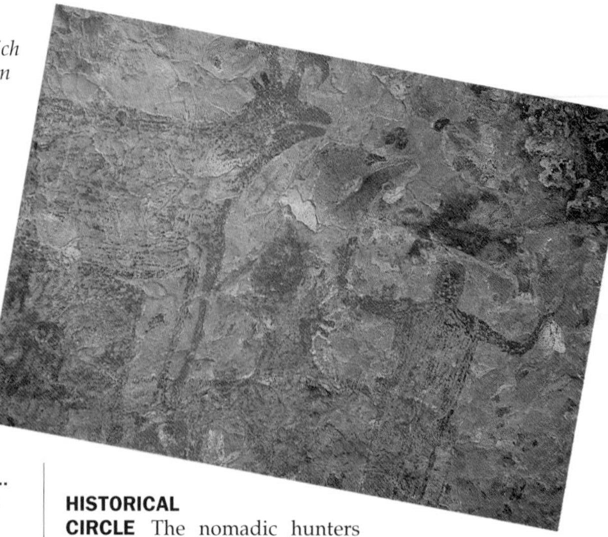

Cave paintings at San Francisco de la Sierra, estimated at over 1,000 years old, depict deer, wolves and the cave-dwellers themselves

HISTORICAL CIRCLE The nomadic hunters roaming the inhospitable north were called the Chichimecs (roughly translated as 'descendants of dogs') although the more diplomatic term 'Desert Culture' has since been coined. At the mercy of droughts, they sporadically forged south to the more fertile central highlands. Many of the ruling dynasties during the post-Classic era were of Chichimec origin, including the Aztecs themselves. It took the Spaniards over 70 years and the added enticement of rich veins of silver to even begin to pacify the forbidding north. Mines and cattle ranches later prospered, but in 1848 the Mexican– American War sliced off today's California, Texas, Arizona and part of New Mexico. The new frontier left Baja out on a limb and the vast *haciendas* of the northern states poised for the ferment of the revolution, led by Pancho Villa in Chihuahua. With the demise of the silver mines and social and political turbulence the region foundered, but World War II's industrial needs provided a new economic boost. Since then, it has become the focal point for American investment. *Maquiladoras* (assembly plants for American products) flourish and thousands of workers head north to try to cross the border into the US.

ROUTES SOUTH Mexican border towns are notorious for their absence of character, seemingly absorbing the worst of both sides of *la frontera*, but for North American travellers there is no option: it's an unenviable toss-up between Tijuana, Nogales, Ciudad Juárez, Nuevo Laredo, Reynosa or Matamoros. However,

HOT, STONY AND DRY...
'The first stop is a town called Saltillo. It is the capital of one of those lonely vast terrritories stretching from the US frontier roughly to the Tropic of Cancer: the States of Coahuila, Chihuahua, Baja California, Sonora and Durango, which are the limbo and ante-room to Mexico ... It is hot, stony, dry country, almost without rivers or rain, part desert, part mountain, part mining district. Innocent of art and architecture, yet innocent also of the amenities, these states are kind of natural poor relations to the Western American ones across the border, and a reminder that a very large portion of the earth's surface is, if not uninhabitable, unattractive to inhabit.'
Sybille Bedford: *A Visit to Don Octavio*, 1953.

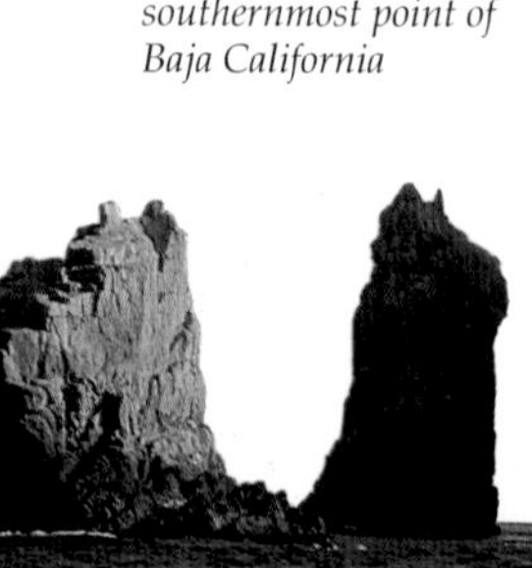

Cabo San Lucas, the southernmost point of Baja California

beyond the urban scars lie some of Mexico's most spectacular landscapes, enticing coastlines and rare colonial towns.

The northern coastline of the Gulf of Mexico, in the state of Tamaulipas, is an undeveloped, sparsely populated region of remote beaches and lagoons, known for its hunting and fishing potential, but offering little else. To the west, Monterrey and Saltillo respectively offer dynamism and relaxation, although both hold historical interest. The former now stands as a model of flourishing business and industrial concerns, matched by ambitious urban design. On the central route south, Chihuahua and Hidalgo del Parral have not forgotten indigenous revolts and revolution and make interesting stops. And between here and the Gulf of California rises the mighty mountain range of the Sierra Madre Occidental, slashed by canyons and boasting the Chihuahua–Pacífico railway.

BAJA PENINSULA Across the Mar de Cortés lies the rugged sierra and desert of Baja, barely four per cent of which is under cultivation. A third of its inhabitants live around Tijuana, although the Los Cabos area and La Paz are catching up fast. Between the two are vast tracts of cactus-strewn desert, shaped by an awesome mountainous spine, a merciless terrain that postponed Spanish settlement until 1697. Few indigenous Mexicans remain as most were wiped out by disease or mistreatment, and the land where Jesuits and Franciscans, whalers and pirates once lived has now been taken over by luxury marinas and trailer parks. Baja is set for the future as the land of nature tourism, its endless bays a prime target for sports fishermen, divers or whale-watchers, while its remote interior offers plenty of riding, hiking and camping. A necessity here is private transport, preferably four-wheel drive, as buses miss the best places. More resorts and a four-lane highway from Ensenada down the west coast to Ciudad Constitución wait on the drawing-board, but most of Baja will long remain virgin territory.

Bahía Concepción's beaches attract crowds of campers

▶▶▶ REGION HIGHLIGHTS

Bahía de los Ángeles *page 82*

Barranca del Cobre *page 83*

Casas Grandes *page 84*

Chihuahua–Pacífico Railway *page 87*

Hidalgo del Parral *page 94*

La Paz *pages 94–5*

Sierra de la Giganta (Loreto) *page 96*

Bahía Concepcíon (Mulegé) *page 98*

Real de Catorce *page 99*

San José del Cabo *pages 102–3*

THE LEGENDS OF BAJA

Baja California was mentioned as early as the 11th century in the Anglo-Norman *Chanson de Roland* (*Song of Roland*) as Califerne, a distant Eldorado. Legend grew over the centuries and it became the 'fabulous island of California', home of Amazonian women ruled by Queen Calafia. From their base, by a lake filled with pearls, silver, gold, diamonds and emeralds, these formidable women lured men to their destruction (allowing only a few to live for breeding purposes). The straits to the north of this so-called island were believed to be the route to the Moluccas (Spice Islands) and it was not until the 17th century that the peninsular theory was accepted.

***HACIENDA* HAVENS**
Several of Álamos's old Spanish mansions have been converted into hotels and these fine examples of colonial architecture should not be missed. The Hotel Los Portales on the main square and the Hotel Casa de los Tesoros, two blocks south on Calle Obregón, occupying an 18th-century monastery are exceptional. Los Portales once belonged to Don José María Aldama, vice-governor of the state in newly independent Mexico, and has a typically Spanish stone-arched central courtyard.

▶▶ Álamos 78B2

A detour 53km inland from the Pacific highway, just south of Ciudad Obregón, leads up through rugged mountains to this small colonial town, once a thriving 18th-century mining town. By the 1920s this casualty of chaotic 19th- and early 20th-century political upheavals had its mines closed and *haciendas* abandoned, thus becoming a virtual ghost town. After World War II it was 'discovered' by enterprising Americans who soon made fortunes in real estate and restored the decrepit buildings to their former glory. Despite the artificial sprucing-up, Álamos has a beautiful central plaza dominated by **La Immaculada Concepción**, built in 1783 on the site of an earlier Jesuit mission. A small regional museum on the eastern side of the plaza is monopolised by mining memorabilia.

▶ Bahía de los Ángeles 78A3

This magnificent bay on the Gulf side of Baja California Norte, makes a welcome change from the dry central desert and lies 68km off the main highway along a good surfaced road. Growing tourist facilities include an airstrip, hotels, campsite and trailer parks. The modest **Museo de Historia Natural** provides a cultural attraction. Faced by the **Isla Ángel de la Guarda**, a large island nature reserve, the bay is alive with dolphins, finback whales and sea-lions, and has great snorkelling and diving in addition to a sandy beach backed by dramatic craggy rocks. Some 24km south, and accessible only by boat, lies the camping and beauty spot of **La Unica**.

Bahía de los Ángeles' only cultural attraction is a museum of natural history, featuring such exhibits as this whale skeleton

Bahía Kino, named after a famous Jesuit missionary, Eusebio Francisco Kino, is a popular resort, particularly with sports fishermen, swimmers and campers

▶ Bahía Kino *78B3*

Virtually opposite Bahía de los Ángeles, but across the Gulf on the coast of Sonora, 107km west of Hermosillo, Kino is firmly divided into **Kino Viejo** and **Kino Nuevo**. The latter is geared to and mainly occupied by wintering Americans, its high-rise condominiums in marked contrast to the dilapidated fishing village of Kino Viejo. The original inhabitants of the area, the Seri people, are known for their traditional hardwood carvings of wildlife and intricate baskets, now hawked all over town.

▶▶ Bahía Magdalena *78B1*

Bahía Magdalena, a little-reached corner of Baja Sur, is accessible by a 57km surfaced road west from Villa Constitución which ends at the fishing village of **San Carlos.** The typically rocky Pacific coastline is protected by two elongated islands, **Isla Magdalena** and **Isla Santa Margarita**, which create a sheltered bay much favoured by grey whales for breeding (see page 93). The warm waters are rich in aquatic life, wrecks of galleons and mangrove inlets. Camping is, at present, the only option.

▶▶▶ Barranca del Cobre *78C2*

High in the Sierra Tarahumara, halfway between the Mar de Cortés and Chihuahua, stretches a landscape of spectacular canyons, known collectively as Barranca del Cobre (the Copper Canyon). These sculpted ravines, sliced out of the Sierra Madre Occidental, experience startling extremes in climate and have a wide variety of vegetation. In winter the pine forests at their rims (which reach 2,800m) are covered in snow, while their floors sprout tropical flora, a phenomenon that forces the area's primitive inhabitants, the Tarahumaras (see pages 100–1), to migrate twice-yearly.

The Barranca del Cobre is composed of five adjoining canyons that are collectively five times wider and one and a half times deeper than the Grand Canyon. It has become a firm favourite for hikers and riders and is being developed as an ecotourism destination with an increasing choice of accomodation available. Remote missions, ruined mining towns, wind-eroded rocks, waterfalls, lakes and uncharted caves combine with a cool climate to attract visitors, who arrive by the tortuous **Chihuahua–Pacífico** railway (see page 87) or by road to **Creel** (see page 88). More difficult to reach, but in a superb canyon riverside setting, is the former silver-mining town of **Batopilas▶▶**, 140km south of Creel and approached by the Camino Real, which snakes over 2,000m down to the canyon floor.

BARRANCA GOTHIC

In 1880 American politician Alexander Shepherd arrived from Washington with his family to preside over the prolific Batopilas silver mine. The only link with the outside world was by mule along five days of winding track, but Shepherd managed to bring pianos, pool tables and a railroad engine (in parts), as well as send back kilos of silver. Today his gothic adobe mansion is shrouded in wild bougainvillaea and open to the winds, but you can still see the remains of the family swimming-pool.

Cabo San Lucas, a still fledgling resort, backed by dramatic rugged sierra

CASCADE OF SAND
The presence of five underwater trenches, up to 3,000m deep, which nurture a high level of plankton, has blessed Los Cabos with a wealth of underwater life. An estimated 800 species of reef fish glide through the waters and include several unique to the region. You might also spot the world's largest fish, the whale shark, or the giant manta ray with its span of up to 7m. However, it is a submarine canyon located in the bay of Cabo San Lucas that provides a unique spectacle, that of a sandfall. Discovered in 1960 and filmed by Jacques Cousteau, it is a weird and wonderful sight to watch the sand cascading from the canyon edge to the shadowy depths below.

▶ Cabo San Lucas *78B1*

At the southernmost tip of the Baja peninsula, Cabo San Lucas is an expanding resort that, together with San José del Cabo, forms the much touted **Los Cabos.** This harmonious town, with low ochre-coloured buildings fronting a small marina and bay, is a destination for serious divers, golfers and sports fishermen, and is high on tourist facilities but low on authenticity. Its basic population fluctuates with the seasons; streets remain unfinished but nightclubs boom and hotels multiply while no fewer than six golf courses lie along the coast. **El Arco▶▶**, a massive natural rock arch terminating the headland, has become the local emblem and is viewed from boats leaving from the western end of the marina. At low tide boats stop off at the Playa de Amor, a fine, white sandy beach. Other trips go to **Cabo Falso**, where the Faro Viejo (old lighthouse) offers panoramic sea views that may include seals, sea-lions and whales on their way north.

▶▶ Casas Grandes *78C3*

Casas Grandes, about 300km by road south of the border town of Ciudad Juárez, is the most important archaeological site in northern Mexico. Presumed to date from ad 1000, it was abandoned in the mid-14th century following attacks by Apaches. Structures include pyramids, ball-courts, platforms, underground chambers and the remains of three-storey adobe houses. Excavations yielded Paquimé pottery (vessels decorated with natural pigments), necklaces of semiprecious stones and carvings of Quetzalcóatl. A superbly designed new museum, in circular form, gives background information besides choice exhibits (*Open* Tue–Sun 10–5).

The partially restored ruins of Casas Grandes indicate there was a high level of civilisation in the area

▶▶ Cascada de Basaseáchic *78C2*

Mexico's highest waterfall, whose torrents plunge over 300m to the foot of the Candameña Canyon, is in the Sierra Tarahumara, some 170km west of Cuauhtémoc and 140km north of Creel. Its scale and power are overwhelming, but access is notoriously difficult, requiring a bumpy car-ride followed by a short walk to the look-out point for the best view. A 1½-hour hike down to the bottom of the canyon brings you to the base of the waterfall.

One hundred and twenty species of cacti inhabit the Baja landscape, ranging from miniature cushions to the gigantic cardons. *Whether stretching in endless forests or standing as lone sentinels, they are not only visual symbols of the peninsula but also functional plants.*

Due to the semi-isolation of the Baja California peninsula, many of the area's plants are endemic and of the 120 species of cacti no fewer than 70 are unique to the region. From north to south the varieties change according to terrain, and their appearance alters with the seasons, seemingly lifeless in the high and dry summer but bursting with vigour and wreathed in flowers and vines in the rainy season and spring. Their ridges and grooves expand to absorb water which is retained by the waxy skin; they can hold water for up to five years.

Cardons and organ-pipes The tallest cacti on the horizon belong to the *cardon* family, a close relative of the *saguaro* of Arizona. These towering, fluted columns sometimes reach heights of over 20m. Thousands of them clothe the sierra as far north as San Felipe, and a dense forest grows inland from Bahía de Los Ángeles. In March and April the upper branches of *cardons* blossom with white flowers, followed by yellow fruits that split to reveal succulent red flesh. Pollination is carried out by bats, hawkmoths and humming-birds.

Branching towards the sky, the organ-pipe cactus of Baja, *pitahaya dulce*, is found in the southern half of the peninsula. Its nectar is much sought after by bats and was once favoured by local Indians who would gather to gorge themselves on it. The stimulating effect was such that tribal conflicts and marital ties were soon forgotten, much to the dismay of local padres. Another functional cactus is the *biznaga* or bulky barrel cactus which grows in the central part of the peninsula and served as an emergency source of water.

WHISPERED CONVERSATIONS

'The cacti stood in groups like people with feathered head-dresses leaning together and engaged in intimate whispered conversation... The cacti had no beauty – they were like some simple shorthand sign for such words as 'barrenness' and 'drought'; you felt they were less the product than the cause of this dryness, that they had absorbed all the water there was in the land and held it as camels do in their green, aged, tubular bellies.'

Graham Greene: *The Lawless Roads*, 1939.

BOOJUM TREES

Specific to the area between El Rosario and San Ignacio, as well as a small pocket of the state of Sonora, the hairy, undulating trunks of the boojum tree or *cirio* (related to the *ocotillo*) have also earned it the nickname of 'elephant tree'. In spring they burst forth with a mass of pink blossom creating a roseate haze in the middle of the desert.

One of Baja California's numerous species of cactus

DINOSAUR'S EGG
In 1993, the year 'Jurassic Park' ephemera invaded Mexican markets, the state of Chihuahua witnessed the discovery of a dinosaur's egg. Found by a local farmer who thought he had stumbled upon a 'curious stone', it was examined by palaeontologists and found to be the egg of a *critosaurus*, some 73 million years old. The exact location of the discovery in the southern part of the state was not revealed for fear of dinosaur-egg-plundering.

▶ Chihuahua *78C2*

The town of Chihuahua holds a few hidden secrets and makes an interesting stop-over. On its high plateau, against the impressive backdrop of the Sierra Madre Occidental, this prosperous city, with a population of one million, is the capital of Mexico's largest state. Today's riches come from cattle, timber, mining and industrial assembly plants whose chief customers lie across the border in the US. The little dog that bears the city's name did originate here but is nowhere to be seen.

The courtyard walls of the 19th-century Government Palace are lined with murals portraying memorable episodes in the history of Chihuahua

Hidalgo, Villa and Co Chihuahua was originally settled by silver-hungry miners in the early 18th century, but it suffered over the centuries from raids by Apaches from the north, as well as from uprisings by local tribes, goaded into action by the brutality of the Spanish overlords. During the War of Independence, Miguel Hidalgo fled here but was betrayed and subsequently executed. His head was exhibited in Guanajuato as a warning to similarly inspired individuals. Benito Juárez also installed himself in Chihuahua, but it was during the turbulent period of the Revolution that the city hosted its greatest hero, Pancho Villa, who set up his headquarters here.

Around the *zócalo* All Chihuahua's institutional monuments are within easy walking distance east of the *zócalo*, the **Plaza de Armas**. Dominating the square is the baroque **Catedral▶**, begun in 1726 but only completed in 1826 due to the expulsion of the Jesuit founders and Apache attacks. In this central area Porfiriato mansions jostle with modern buildings, while pedestrian streets are lined with cowboy-boot shops and ice-cream parlours. Two blocks east on **Plaza Hidalgo** (Avenida Carranza and Calle Libertád) stands the Correos (post office) and the **Palacio Federal▶**, an imposing building that saw Hidalgo's imprisonment in 1811. A small museum devoted to him opens on to the Calle Juárez side. Opposite stands the pale pink **Palacio del Gobierno▶▶**, originally a Jesuit college, faithfully rebuilt after a fire. Its courtyard walls incorporate a small altar on the site of Hidalgo's execution

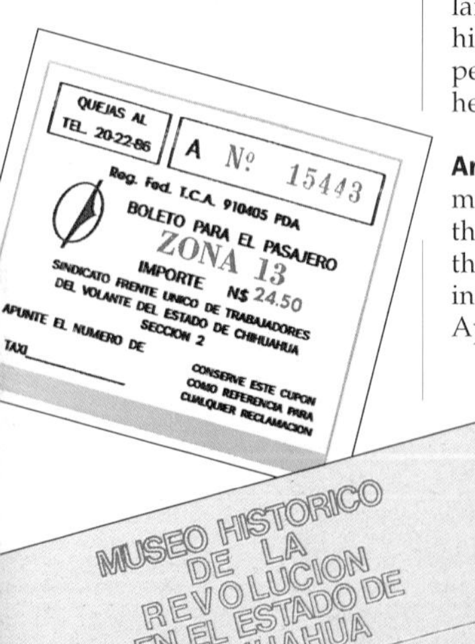

and have since been faced with murals by Aron Piña Mora depicting the history of Chihuahua.

South of the centre On the elegant Paseo Bolívar, a road which rings the historic centre, stands the extraordinary Quinta Gameros, a 1907 mansion that now houses the **Museo Regional▶▶**(*Open* Tue–Sun 9–1, 4–7). This displays art nouveau as a kitsch pastiche of the original. Angels, Little Red Riding Hood, gilded mirrors, stuccoed ceilings and stained glass exemplify the tasteless opulence of its pre-revolution days. The museum's only redeeming feature is a display of Paquimé pottery. Four blocks further south is the more tasteful Quinta Luz, now the **Museo de la Revolución▶▶▶** (*Open* Tue–Sun 10–1, 3–7), where Pancho Villa lived with one of his 25 *compañeras*, Señora Luz Corral de Villa, later recognised as his official wife. Its art nouveau murals, tiled walls and patio are evidence that despite his egalitarian principles Villa appreciated the good life, but the black 1922 Dodge peppered with bullet holes recalls his bloody fate in 1923. Exhibits are displayed throughout the elegant home and include photos, original documents, equipment, arms (including a 1900 Hotchkiss machine-gun), clothes and Villa's deathmask, making a fascinating record of this key period in Mexican history.

▶▶▶ Chihuahua–Pacífico Railway *78C2*

This celebrated railway, crawling through a deserted high altitude wilderness, winds through dramatic canyons, sierra and Alpine meadows before terminating on the Pacific coast at Los Mochis. The most spectacular section lies between Creel and Los Mochis, where it passes through 88 tunnels and 39 bridges, stops near the rim of the Copper Canyon at El Divisadero, then zigzags down past rock-faces and ravines to reach the tropical coastal plain. The first and second-class train leaves Los Mochis at 6am, and Chihuahua at 7am taking 12 hours in total, with Creel about halfway. Los Mochis is one hour behind Chihuahua (Central Standard Time). Accommodation is available in Creel, Divisadero, Posada, Bahuichivo and El Fuerte. For more information call 14-15 7756 or fax 14-109059 (Chihuahua).

CHIHUAHUA–PACIFICO DATA

This incredible feat of engineering was started at the beginning of the century, initiated by American mining companies under the name 'Kansas City, Mexico and Orient Railroad'. But it was not until 1961 that the Mexican government finally completed the most complex section of the 673km railway which involved blasting through solid rock (the longest tunnel measures 935m), building precipitous bridges (the highest stands at 110m marking the border between the states of Sinaloa and Chihuahua) and creating breathtaking loops around mountains. Official and unofficial contributors to its construction include President Adolfo López Mateos, the magnate Enrique Creel, Ulysses S. Grant, President Porfirio Diáz, Pancho Villa, Benjamin Johnson and the Tarahumara.

Bottom left: Tarahumara selling their crafts – one of the few ways they have to make a living

Below: the Copper Canyon is deeper than Colorado's Grand Canyon

THE MENNONITES
This austere, hard-working sect, founded by a Dutchman in the 16th century, adheres strictly to the words of the Bible. Refusal to bend to any other law led to persecution which drove them from Germany to Russia, Canada and finally, in the liberal, post-revolutionary days of the 1920s, to Mexico. Many travelled through the US and settled there. Mennonites only marry within their sect, thus they remain blonde-haired and blue-eyed, and speak an ancient German dialect. Men dress in checked shirts and denim bib-overalls, women in long skirts, shawls and headscarves. Their diligence has transformed the desert into fertile farmland.

Ciudad Juárez *78C3*

This sprawling, unattractive city of over a million inhabitants is a major border town linking El Paso in Texas with Northern Mexico's central route south. Dusty, mercilessly hot in summer, confusingly laid out and overtly geared to cashing in on cheap services of all kinds, it is best passed straight through. If you have time to spare, the **Museo de Arte Prehispanica▶** (*Open* Tue–Sun 10–6) in the Parque Chamizal, displays interesting examples of Paquime pottery alongside other pre-hispanic exhibits. The Plaza Principal holds the **Catedral** and **Palacio Municipal** and the Museo de Historia in the restored customs house.

▶▶ Creel *78C2*

Creel lies 2,338m up in the Sierra Tarahumara. This popular stop-over on the Chihuahua–Pacífico railway is well geared to visitors, without losing its frontier-town soul, though this will change with an additional 3,500 hotel rooms planned over the next decade. It consists of a main street and one main square against a backdrop of rock-faces and pine forests, and the atmosphere is heightened by its isolation, the echoing toots and shunting of trains and its colourful though impoverished Tarahumara inhabitants. Day-trips are organised from here on horseback or by van into the surrounding canyons, to Lago Arareco, Cascada de Cusárare, the hot-springs of Recohuata and Tarahumara cave dwellings, and there is a

Mission of San Ignacio de Arareco near the Arareco lake

bone-shaking six-hour ride to Batopilas (see page 83). Remember to make some purchases at the Jesuit mission shop, on the main square, which assists local Tarahumaras. A small ethnographic museum is located here, too.

▶ Cuauhtémoc *78C2*

This central market town for the Tarahumara people, and for Mexico's zealous Mennonite community, which established itself here back in the 1920s, lies in an undulating region of cattle farms and fruit orchards, 105km west of Chihuahua. The town's main monument is a statue of Cuauhtémoc, the last Aztec emperor, standing at the eastern end of the main street.

Durango's baroque Catedral, with its massive structure and domed bell-towers, dominates the principal square

►► Durango *78C1*

Durango lies in a rich mining area encircled by heavy industrial plants on a flat plateau, 310km north-east of Mazatlán. Much of its wealth comes from an iron ore deposit in one of the two hills looming over the town, the **Cerro del Mercado**. To the south the **Cerro de los Remedios** has been landscaped into a tranquil park with a chapel at the summit. Fourteen kilometres north of the town stand the reasons for Durango's more recent fame: a series of film sets constructed for Hollywood Westerns in the villages of **Villa del Oeste►** and **Chupaderos**. Tours are arranged by the tourist office (in the Palacio del Gobierno). The central Plaza de Armas is dominated by the domed bell-towers of the baroque **Catedral**, begun in 1695 but not completed for several decades. Fronting another beautiful square, the handsome 18th-century **Palacio de Gobierno** was originally built for a Spanish mining baron. Murals around the arcaded patio relate the history of the state of Durango. Even more elaborate in style is the **Casa del Condes de Súchil►►**, the stunning 17th-century colonial-style home of Spanish governors, part of which now functions as an up-market shopping centre.

► Ensenada *78A4*

The former gold-mining boomtown of Ensenada, on Baja's Pacific coast, now pays the price for its proximity to the border. Only 108km south of Tijuana, it is a favourite weekend destination for Californians. During the week it returns to its sedate fishing and shipping activities, but the scars remain. The local history museum, in former military barracks on the Avenida Gastelum, gives background information. Opposite the pier numerous stalls dish out fresh oysters, fish tacos or *ceviche* (raw fish marinated in lime or lemon), while the renowned *cantina* **Hussong's** attracts tequila and beer aficionados. Other interests include sports fishing, particularly from May to October; winery tours, the largest of which, **Bodegas Santo Tomás**, organises daily wine-tasting and has an impressive cultural centre in its recently converted original warehouse, and panoramic views of the coast from **El Mirador**. Good swimming beaches lie 10km south at **Estero**, while surfers slice through the waves at San Miguel, Tres Marías, California and La Joya.

LA BUFADORA (THE SNORTING ONE)

A strange marine phenomenon is visible, and audible, at Punta la Banda, 38km south-west of Ensenada and the southern headland of Bahía Todos Santos. Pounding surf periodically forces a jet of seawater up through a small blow-hole in the roof of an underwater cavern, producing a geyser effect as it explodes with a thunderous roar some 15m up into the air (best during high tide). Access to this sight is only possible by car or with a tour from Ensenada.

Street vendor, Ensenada

Spectacular scenery, talented actors and directors, dramatic plots and low wages made Mexico's film industry in the 1940s the world's most prolific after Hollywood. Great film-makers such as Sergei Eisenstein, Fred Zinneman, Luis Buñuel and John Huston also found their inspiration here, and Mexico's desert has frequently provided settings for foreign productions.

FILMING IN MEXICO
'*The Exterminating Angel* was made in Mexico, although I regret that I was unable to shoot it in Paris or London with European actors and adequate costumes. Despite the beauty of the house where it was shot and my effort to select actors who didn't look particularly Mexican, there was a certain tawdriness in many of its aspects. We couldn't get any really fine table napkins, for instance, and the only one I could show on camera was borrowed from the make-up artist.' Luis Buñuel: *My Last Breath*, 1983.

Although Eisenstein's *Que Viva Mexico!* (1932) was never publicly screened, the Russian's influence on the country's nascent film industry was powerful. The Revolution, arduous *campesino* lives, fiery characters and breathtaking scenery became fundamental themes that launched Mexico into a golden age of film by the end of the 1930s. Pioneers at that time included actor-director Emilio 'El Indio' Fernandez, Gabriel Figueroa (a master of camerawork) and actors such as Pedro Almedariz, Maria Felix and Dolores del Rio – already a Hollywood veteran.

A lighter touch The singing *charro* (cowboy), that quintessential Mexican figure, first featured in *Alla en el Rancho Grande* (1936), giving rise to the careers of Mexican pin-ups José Negrete and Pedro Infante, and the establishment of the *mariachi* figure beyond the borders of Jalisco. Making his first appearance at this time was Mario Moreno's popular comic character Cantinflas the unsophisticate who manages through a series of accidents to triumph and get the girl. Moreno was to make over 30 films. German Valdez's equally endearing Tin Tan character used the same formula in the 1950s.

Changing perspectives The end of World War II marked a change in direction. The subsequent lapsing of Mexico's 'equal partner' status with the United States, which had

The Exterminating Angel, *Luis Buñuel's 1962 film, received international acclaim*

Mario Moreno in the popular comic role of Cantinflas, playing alongside Janet Leigh

done much to advance the industry, together with rapid modernisation, led to films with more urban, socio-realist themes. After his epoch-making *Los Olvidados* (1950), Luis Buñuel was to make 18 more films in his adopted country. Many, such as *Viridiana* (1961) and *The Exterminating Angel* (1962), were to become internationally acclaimed. As Mexican film production flagged in the 1960s, American director John Huston's long love affair with the country that had begun with the classic *Treasure of the Sierra Madre* (1948) produced its greatest gem, the haunting *Night of the Iguana* (1964). However, his film version of *Under the Volcano* (1984) was unable to do justice to Malcolm Lowry's book, which depicted the horrors of the consul's *mezcal*-sodden descent into his private hell.

Modern Mexican cinema Several independent film-makers have made an impact, both in Mexico and abroad, in the modern cinema. Paul Léduc succeeded with *Reed: Insurgent Mexico* (1971), based on the American journalist's experience of the Revolution, and *Frida* (1985), about feminist cult-figure Frida Kahlo. Jaime Humberto Hermosillo pokes fun at bourgeois Catholic ideals in works such as *Doña Herlinda y Su Hijo* (1985). Later international hits have included Maria Novarro's *Danzon* (1992), a peep at life in the steamy port of Veracruz; Juan Mora's *Return to Aztlan* (1988); Nicolas Echeveria's *Cabeza de Vaca* (1989), based on a Catholic priest's journey through the northern deserts; Alfonso Arau's dreamy *Like Water for Chocolate* (1992), and Arturo Ripstein's gruesome *Deep Crimson* (1997), a true-life story of a Bonnie-and-Clyde-type duo.

Box-office targeting Film-makers now know that the only means of achieving fame outside Mexico is to win recognition on the art film circuit, to co-produce or to work directly in Hollywood. It is ironic that one of the most successful recent films about Mexico, *El Mariachi* (1993), was filmed by a 23-year-old Texan, Roberto Rodriguez.

LIKE WATER FOR CHOCOLATE

The greatest hit to have emerged from Mexico in recent years is undoubtedly *Como Agua para Chocolate*, a title which refers to Mexican hot chocolate made with boiling water; by extension someone who is (sexually) agitated is said to be 'like water for chocolate'. Directed by Alfonso Arau and released in 1992, it was based on the first novel of Mexican screenwriter Laura Esquivel, Arau's wife. With distinct surrealistic overtones, it recounts the frustrated love story of Tita and Pedro against a backdrop of revolution in the rugged northern state of Coahuila. As Pedro is forced to marry her elder sister, Tita transfers her sensuality into the realm of culinary seduction – what foodie can forget her lavishly and lovingly prepared quail in rose petal sauce?

THE 28TH PARALLEL
When crossing the 28th parallel from the north you are leaving the Pacific Time Zone and entering the Mountain Time Zone, one hour ahead. This was the meeting-point of the builders of the Trans-peninsular Highway in 1973, one team working northwards, another southwards. A plaque commemorates the spot where they met. Elaborate plans were developed for an underground museum and artefacts were actually installed. But then came Baja's heavy rains, the museum was flooded and the artefacts were removed, mostly to Mexico City.

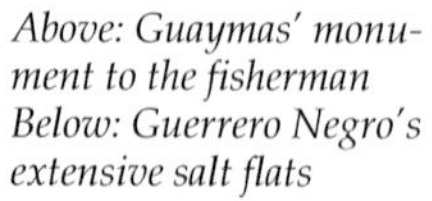

Above: Guaymas' monument to the fisherman
Below: Guerrero Negro's extensive salt flats

▶ Grutas de García 79D2

These caves, lying some 45km west of Monterrey in the Sierra del Fraile, were formed over 50 million years ago and are said to form Mexico's largest and most beautiful cave network. Discovered by a priest in 1843 they have become a popular local outing aided by direct buses from Monterrey on Sundays (from Saltillo at 9, 10, 11am). A 2.5km tour leads through 16 vast cave chambers thick with dramatically illuminated stalactite and stalagmite formations. Access is by cable-car from the car park.

▶ Guaymas 78B2

The main port of the state of Sonora on the Mar de Cortés has a spectacular mountain-backed harbour, but its revenue lies firmly in trade and commerce, not tourism. It was founded in 1701 by missionaries (the original **Mision de San José** lies 10km north of town), and over the years inspired the covetous ambitions of American, British and French invaders, most notably the French Comte Gaston Raousset de Bourbon, who twice attempted to establish a personal empire here but whose days were ended with a bullet in 1854. More interesting than the town itself are its surroundings. The nature reserve of **El Sahuaro▶▶** has a wonderful variety of cacti and other indigenous plants, the bays north of town towards San Carlos (see page 99) offer good fishing, swimming and snorkelling, and offshore islands attract sea-lions and aquatic birds. **Playa Miramar** has good facilities for visitors.

▶ Guerrero Negro 78A2

This dull town of salt-flats, vats and warehouses announces the end (or the beginning) of the monotonous Desierto de Vizcaíno, on Baja's 28th parallel. Salt from Guerrero Negro is transported in lighters to the Isla Cedros before being exported, mainly to the US and Japan. However, the big attraction here is nearby Laguna Ojo de Liebre, also known as **Scammon's Lagoon**, a protected national park where grey whales come to breed (December to March). Access to observe these giant mammals is by boat, or you can watch from look-out posts along the shore, about 24km from a turn-off on Highway 1. The colour grey continues in the extraordinary dunes of Don Miguelito.

Every autumn thousands of grey whales leave their summer grounds in the Bering Sea and migrate 8,000km southwards through the Pacific to the sheltered bays and coastal lagoons of Baja California to court, mate and give birth one of Mexico's greatest wildlife spectacles.

From the 1840s to the 1940s, when waves of whalers preyed upon the 'devilfish' so-called because of the mothers' ferocious protection of their threatened calves, the number of Californian grey whales fell from an estimated 24,000 to a mere few thousand. On the verge of extinction, the species finally received full protection from commercial whaling. In 1972 Mexico declared Laguna Ojo de Liebre (Scammon's Lagoon) and Laguna Guerrero Negro refuges for grey whales – the first such sanctuaries in the world. With the addition of Laguna San Ignacio in 1979 (now threatened by a massive salt-processing plant) in Bahía Magdalena, these gentle giants, weighing between 20 and 40 tons, have made a dramatic recovery and their numbers are now estimated at 20,000.

The next generation Courting and mating generally takes place at the entrance to the lagoon, where as many as 500 whales cruise in and out daily. The amorous giants lunge through the water, spouting vapour from their blowholes like geysers, in a promiscuous free-for-all copulation. With calving mothers outside the courting action in the shallower parts of the inner lagoon, the number of available females is greatly reduced, a factor which sometimes leads to indiscriminate mating of up to 20 whales at once. Meanwhile, the mothers-to-be (impregnated the previous season) produce their young after a nine-month period of gestation. The calves grow quickly on their mother's milk, which, at 53 per cent fat, is one of the richest in the world, and by winter's end have added over 1m to their length and doubled their weight. In March and April the whales begin the long haul north, followed by the mothers and calves, once the latter have accomplished a 'training session' in the mouth of the lagoon, consisting of an intensive work-out to build up their strength.

WHALE BEHAVIOUR
Heaving up and down, crashing through the waves, spouting water like a geyser, the grey whale displays still unfathomed behavioural traits that continue to intrigue whale-watchers. Swimming against the tide with its mouth wide open enables the whale to sieve huge amounts of water and trap rich plankton that blooms in the warm lagoon shallows. 'Bottom-grubbing' or stripping the lagoon floor with vacuum-cleaner suction techniques also provides food (mostly crustaceans).

Hermosillo's Plaza de los Tres Pueblos marks the site of the original Seri settlement

▶ Hermosillo *78B3*

The oven-like summer temperatures and industrialisation of Hermosillo, state capital of Sonora, mean that it is often bypassed by travellers. However, it is strategically placed on Highway 15, 277km south of the border town of Nogales and 136km from Guaymas. Although prosperous and modernised it still has charm and is scenically backed by the Cerro de la Campana. Hermosillo's colonial centre, founded in 1700, revolves around the shady **Plaza de Zaragoza▶▶**, flanked to the west by the **Catedral de la Ascensión** (1779) and to the east by the **Palacio del Gobierno**, where colourful murals depict Sonoran history. Local revolutionaries include General Alvaro Obregón. South of the centre lies the **Centro Ecológico de Sonora** (*Open* daily 8–6) a beautiful nature reserve full of indigenous and desert specimens, with a small zoo . The **Museo de Sonora** (*Open* Wed–Sat 10–5.30, Sun 10–3.30) housed in a converted penitentiary, presents an interesting display covering local history, archaeology and anthropology, including Seri carvings.

▶▶ Hidalgo del Parral *78C2*

The old mining centre of Hidalgo del Parral (or just Parral) lies 300km south of Chihuahua. The town is still dependent on the prolific mines in the surrounding hills which inspired its settlement in 1629. Its early history, however, is blackened by the slavery of local *indígenas*. Rebellions ensued and the **Templo de San Nicolás** was the site of a mass hanging of rebel leaders in 1676.

There are several elaborate 18th-century silver-miners' mansions, the most striking being the **Palacio Pedro Alvarado▶▶**. The **Templo de Nuestra Señora del Rayo**, completed in 1728, was reputed to have been financed by one of the Tarahumara who struck gold. Parral is famous, too, as the site of Pancho Villa's assassination in 1923 and the town commemorates this event with photos and memorabilia in the small **Museo de Pancho Villa** (*Open* daily 9–8).

▶▶ La Paz *78B1*

Great plans await La Paz, state capital of Baja California Sur, an expanding town with a life of its own outside tourism, unlike nearby Los Cabos. Set on a magnificent bay studded with outlying islands and backed by dramatic sierra, it has a pleasantly low-key atmosphere.

Its dark and difficult past was set in motion by Hernán Cortés in 1535 and involved vicious conflicts with local inhabitants, further exacerbated by droughts, famines, smallpox, pirates, American troops during the Texan War and, in 1853, the infamous William Walker, intent on installing a state of slavery.

Rumours of black pearls also spread and led to massive exploitation of the nearby oyster beds, finally wiped out by a mysterious disease in 1940. However, La Paz (meaning 'peace') was reborn when American sports fishermen discovered its waters and today its population of 250,000 has the highest per capita income in Mexico.

Although modernised, La Paz has preserved elements of its past, best reflected in the Mediterranean feel of the

THE END OF VILLA

At 8.30am on 20 July 1923 General Francisco 'Pancho' Villa, accompanied by six bodyguards, cruised unsuspectingly along Calle Gabino Barreda in Hidalgo del Parral. For the previous 103 days, nine conspirators had been lying in wait to ambush him ... the moment had come. Opening fire on Villa's black Dodge, they sprayed it with bullets and mortally wounded his bodyguards. Irrepressible until the bitter end, the dying hero of Mexico's revolution managed to fire a last, successful shot, killing one of the conspirators, before dying. The leader of the ambush, Jesus Salas Barraza, had no qualms about surrendering himself to the authorities, accusing Villa of dictatorial ambitions, and although sentenced to 20 years' imprisonment was mysteriously released a few months later.

La Paz's pleasant palm-shaded malecón *is perfect for strolling*

palm-fringed *malecón* (sea promenade). Stunning sunsets over the bay, superb beaches lining the Pichilingue peninsula to the north, island boat trips, good snorkelling and fishing, duty-free shopping, excellent seafood and reasonably priced hotels: these are its attractions. Buildings of note are limited to the 19th-century **Catedral de Nuestra Señora de la Paz**, built on the site of a 1720 mission in the central Plaza Constitución and faced by the **Palacio del Gobierno**.

For displays about the early Pericue, Cochimí and Guaicura indigenous communities, as well as Baja's numerous cave paintings, go to the **Museo Antropológico**▶▶ (*Open* Mon–Fri 9–6) three blocks inland from Plaza Constitución on Calle Altamirano.

Boat trips or kayaking trips take visitors to the islands of Espíritu Santo and Cerralvo, both blissfully unspoilt, or to Isla Partida, a seal sanctuary. All three are visited by scuba-divers for their rich marine life and transparent waters. Day-trips and longer expeditions are organised by Baja Expediciones, Sonora 585, El Manglito, La Paz (tel: 53828, fax: 53829).

BOATING FROM LA PAZ
La Paz has daily car-ferry services to Mazatlán and thrice-weekly boats to Topolobampo, the port of Los Mochis. The Mazatlán service normally leaves at 3pm, arriving at about 9am the next day. The Topolobampo service departs at 11am, arriving at 7pm. Timetables do, however, vary considerably with bad weather, the seasons and less definable factors. Tickets can be bought at the ferry terminal, about 22km north of town in Pichilingue, or more easily at any travel agency in the centre. For more information the tourist office at Paseo Alvaro Obregón 2130 will help.

Queuing up for a shoe-shine in La Paz

Loreto's Misión de Nuestra Señora has been restored after damage from earthquakes

▶▶ Loreto 78B2

Loreto, another southern Baja favourite with fishermen, as well as with hunters, lies on the Mar de Cortés 359km north of La Paz, beyond the magnificent purple contours of the **Sierra de la Giganta▶▶▶**. It was founded in 1697 by an Italian Jesuit, and is the region's oldest permanent settlement; it remained the capital of the peninsula until 1829 when it was virtually wiped out by a hurricane. From here Father Junipero Serra set out in 1769 to evangelise the Californias. The cloisters of the beautifully restored **Misión de Nuestra Señora de Loreto** incorporate the **Museo de los Misiónes▶▶** (*Open* Mon–Fri 9–4), an introduction to local Jesuit, Franciscan and Dominican activities. Around the church pedestrian streets lead down to the harbour and beach where Loreto's few hotels are situated. Loreto is slow-paced, with superb offshore islands such as **Isla Corondos** and beautiful beaches, snorkelling and dolphins on the way, as well as tennis and great sierra hiking. Although things may change with a 'mega-resort' planned 25km south at Puerto Loreto, though only a golf-course has appeared so far, 24,000 hectares are being conserved as a nature reserve.

Los Mochis 78B2

Los Mochis is unavoidable for anyone embarking on or disembarking from the Chihuahua–Pacífico train. This unexceptional town, with its over-priced hotels, rip-off taxis and giant mosquitoes (which spend the day at the airport and migrate to town in the evenings) is, along with nearby Culiacán, the centre of Mexican drug-trafficking, so gunfights are common. If you have to spend the night in the area try the little fishing port of **Topolobampo** or **El Fuerte▶▶**, two stops away on the Chihuahua railway.

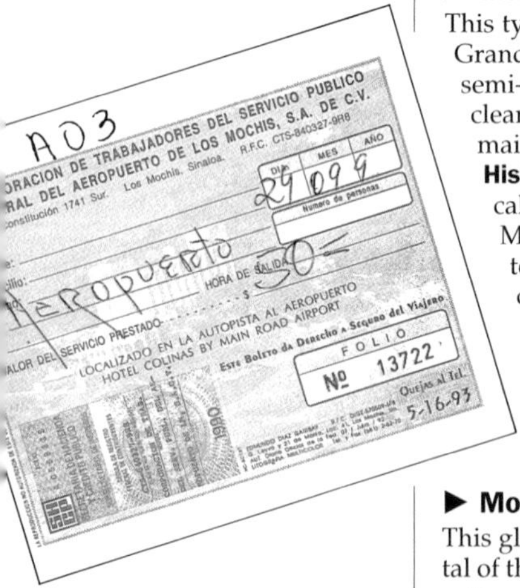

▶ Matamoros 79E2

This typical border town, lying on the estuary of the Río Grande across from Brownsville, Texas, offers the usual semi-planned vision of Mexico, although it is generally cleaner and less Tex-Mex than its counterparts. The main sight in Matamoros is the **Casa Mata Museo de Historia** (*Open* daily 9–6), an old fort in which historical exhibits cover confrontations during the Mexican–American war, other items of military history and local indigenous artefacts. Regional handicrafts, including leather goods, wooden furniture, ceramics and glassware, are sold at the Centro Artesanal on Calle 5a and Alvaro Obregon. The main beach of Playa General Lauro Villar, 37km east of town, has reasonable seafood restaurants along the seafront.

▶ Monterrey 79D2

This gleaming modern city (Mexico's third largest), capital of the state of Nuevo León and industrial capital of the nation, has a fast-paced life-style in keeping with its key location, 230km south of the Texas border on the Panamerican Highway. Its factories flourish and it is now concentrating on a cultural life to match its renowned business, commercial and educational facilities.

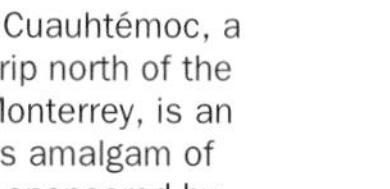

Monterrey's 1908 Government Palace

Monterrey nestles in the valley of the Sierra Madre Oriental, dominated by the mighty, saddle-shaped **Cerro de la Silla** (Saddle Hill). Spectacular contemporary architecture, a sleek new metro and imaginative city planning have made it an urban showcase. The main downtown area is concentrated around the **Gran Plaza** (popularly called the Macroplaza because of its size) and the adjoining **Plaza Zaragoza**. Beyond the new, elevated **Palacio Municipal** and a monumental sculpture by Rufino Tamayo, lies a blend of government buildings, fountains, the baroque **Catedral** and Monterrey's symbol of modernity, the orange tower of Luís Barragán's **Faro del Commercio** (Lighthouse of Business), whose green lasers are beamed across the city at night. A block further north stands the **Teatro de la Ciudad** and the **Esplanada de los Héroes** (with statues of Mexico's heroes). Immediately west of these plazas lies the busy **Zona Rosa**, full of upmarket hotels, shops and restaurants with a typical Monterrey buzz.

Monterrey's brightest jewel is the **Museo de Arte Contemporáneo▶▶▶** (*Open* Tue–Sun 10–5), an architectural masterpiece by Ricardo Legorreta which opened in 1991 next to the cathedral. Its 14 well-designed rooms display outstanding temporary shows. Equally impressive is the brand new **Museo de la Historia▶▶** (*Open* Tue–Sun 11–7), where interactive displays guide you through Mexican history.

ART, BASEBALL AND BEER

In the gardens of the Cervecería Cuauhtémoc, a short bus trip north of the centre of Monterrey, is an incongruous amalgam of attractions sponsored by Mexico's largest brewery, manufacturer of Tecate, Bohemia, Carta Blanca and Superior. Naturally enough, free beer is all part of the visit. The old 19th-century brewery houses the Museo de Monterrey, which holds good temporary exhibitions alongside its permanent collection of contemporary Mexican artists. Next door is the Salón de la Fama (Hall of Fame) with a collection of photos and memorabilia of Mexican baseball players and a Museo Deportivo (sports museum). Brewery tours take place three times a day (closed Mondays) but are not obligatory.

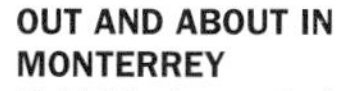

OUT AND ABOUT IN MONTERREY

Eight blocks west of Monterrey's Zona Rosa along Hidalgo is the 1946 Church of La Purísima. Designed by Enrique de la Mora, it was the first example of modern ecclesiastical design in Mexico. A kilometre further away, the more historical El Obispado stands on a small hill. Built in 1786, it served as a bishop's palace and military headquarters, but now houses the Museo Regional de Nuevo León as well as offering fine views over the city and mountains. For information on trips further afield go to the tourist office in the State Congress under the Gran Plaza.

Monterrey's Fountain of Life

NATURE'S LIVING LABORATORY

Thirteen kilometres northwest of the beaches of San Carlos and San Pedro lies the unusual island of San Pedro Nolasco. Despite its small size (3sq km) and proximity to the coast, it is one of the Gulf's most important islands for its rare but prolific flora and fauna. Seven types of native cacti and four species of reptiles are joined by frigate birds, pelicans, cormorants, penguins, kingfishers, herons, falcons and sea gulls. The rocky, craggy coastline, typical of the Gulf islands, also makes it a popular habitat for sea-lions, 25,000 of whom are estimated to inhabit this northern part of the Mar de Cortés. Boat trips are made from San Carlos.

▶▶ Mulegé *78B2*

This sleepy tropical town, backed by the Sierra de Santa Lucia, occupies a prime site on the magnificent **Bahía Concepción▶▶▶**, halfway down the Baja peninsula. It was founded beside Baja's only navigable river, which is lined with date palms and olive trees and dominated by the 1705 Jesuit **Misión de Santa Rosalía**. This stone structure overlooking the town, once an open prison, is now converted to the **Museo de Mulegé** (*Open* Mon–Sat 9–1). Eclectic exhibits range from the desk of Erle Stanley Gardner (creator of the *Perry Mason* sagas, who often withdrew to Mulegé, as did John Wayne) to old diving and mining gear. The beach below saw the disembarkation of American troops during the Mexican–American war, in which the invaders were victorious. Mulegé has since been rediscovered by American retirees and sports fishermen. It retains a lot of charm and offers numerous activities: scuba-diving, kayaking upriver or to outlying islands, trips inland on horseback or by jeep to see spectacular cave paintings in the **Cuevas de San Borjita** or exploring the ruggedly beautiful sierra. Hotels and restaurants remain, for the moment, low-key.

Mulegé is a delightful little oasis on the banks of the Mulegé River

Nogales 78B3

Nogales (the Spanish word for walnut tree) is the unavoidable border town for visitors heading south from Tucson, Arizona, and is the starting point for Mexico's Highway 15, which runs down the Pacific coast. Set in the vast Sonoran–Desert, a region of spectacular scenery and remarkable flora and fauna, it is also a major transit centre for travellers connecting with Greyhound buses or the Ferrocarril del Pacífico, so there is no shortage of accommodation.

►►► Real de Catorce 79D1

The extraordinary town of Real de Catorce lies high in the Sierra Madre Oriental, roughly halfway between Saltillo and San Luis Potosí, with access through a 3km mining tunnel. This once-thriving silver-mine town, with a population of 40,000, now echoes with the footsteps of a thousand odd survivors, though tourism is boosting their numbers. It was founded in the mid-18th century and reached its zenith in the late 19th century when its silver veins were considered second only to Guanajuato (see pages 134–7), but from the 1920s it sank into a rapid decline. Today many mansions are shuttered up, although once a year life is re-injected into the town when thousands of pilgrims flood in for the festival of San Francisco (4 October). The baroque **Parroquía de San Francisco**, with its image of St Francis of Assisi and hundreds of naïve *ex-votos* and offerings, is proof of an undying faith. Three other relics of the town's heyday remain: a recently restored **Plaza de Toros** (bullring), the **Palenque de Gallos** (cockfighting arena), designed in Roman amphitheatre style and today a cultural centre, and the **Casa de Moneda** (mint).

►► Saltillo 79D2

Saltillo, capital of the state of Coahuila, is well known for its walnut trees, vineyards, pleasant high-altitude climate and old colonial buildings, and makes a relaxed and interesting stop-over. This former cattle-farming centre is a much smaller and less frenetic place than Monterrey, 85km northeast, although it is now attracting new industry and modernising fast. Downtown activity and sights are concentrated around the **Plaza de Armas** and, two blocks north-west, the **Plaza Acuña**. Flanking the former is the impressive Churrigueresque **Catedral de Santiago►►**, built between 1746 and 1801, its ornate façade crowned with two towers (which can be climbed). Facing it is the elegant **Palacio del Gobierno** (1808). Saltillo is famous for its colourful handwoven *serapes* (shawls), much in evidence at the lively **Mercado Juárez** on Plaza Acuña.

► San Carlos 78B2

San Carlos, 16km north of Guaymas on the Sonoran coast of the Mar de Cortés, is rapidly being over-developed. Two of Mexico's largest marinas, a string of trailer parks and motor homes, a golf course and over-priced services conspire against the attraction of its magnificent bay setting. However, good beaches win out, and fishermen and divers revel in the prolific waters around the outlying islands.

BATHING IN THE BAHIA

Pelicans, gulls, sea-lions and dolphins are all part of the marine paradise of Bahía Concepción, a deeply indented bay which starts from Punto Chivato and curls past Mulegé and El Coyote to end in a peninsula. Studded with islands and lined with beaches renowned for their wealth of sea shells and marine life, it has become a favourite destination for campers. To the south of Mulegé, Playa Punta Arena, Playa Santispác and El Requesón are all stunning beaches, while to the north Punto Chivato offers a luxury hotel as well as more stretches of blissful white sand strewn with shells.

Weaving demonstrations of Saltillo's sought-after serapes *(shawls) are held at a workshop next to the Casa de la Cultura*

The Tarahumara, scattered over the magnificent but harsh gorges of the Sierra Madre Occidental, manage to live outside the confines of civilisation, preferring a life close to the earth in the bleak, rocky ravines. Northern Mexico's largest indigenous group, they have preserved a unique, albeit impoverished life-style.

The Sierra Tarahumara is incomparable, with its wild, rugged mountains, canyons and gorges covered by cacti, forests and lush vegetation

NATURE'S STRANGE SIGNATURES

'Tarahumara country is full of signs, of shapes, of natural effigies which do not seem to exist by chance, as if the gods, who are omnipresent here, had wanted to prove their powers in these strange signatures ... Of course this is not the only place on earth where Nature, moved by a sort of capricious intelligence, sculpted human forms. But this is a different case, because it is over the entire geographic expanse that Nature decided to speak.' Antonin Artaud: *Un Voyage au Pays des Tarahumaras*, 1945.

Some 50,000 Tarahumara live in the region surrounding the Barranca del Cobre and the Barranca de Urique in the south-western corner of the state of Chihuahua. Their rugged homeland covers about 35,000sq km of mountains, gouged by the rushing torrents of the Río Fuerte and the Río Conchos. It is on the arable land along the tributaries of these rivers that most Tarahumara choose to live, often in caves, farming the canyon tops (at over 3,000m) for most of the year, descending with their sheep and goats to the semi-tropical floors during winter.

The running people Related to the Apaches, the Tarahumara call themselves the Rarámuri, the 'running people', a result of their legendary ability to sprint barefoot up rocky mountainsides or even outrun deer – often spurred on by copious consumption of *tesquino*, a potent corn-beer. Respect for the individual is their greatest ideal

to which is linked a unique certainty in their control over time, an intense spirituality and belief in life after death. Long isolated, reserved, disdainful of 'civilisation', and in close touch with the land, they claim telepathic powers. Their innate mystical bent incorporates *peyote* (see page 149) into rituals which have fascinated many a Westerner, not least the French writer and actor, Antonin Artaud, who spent several weeks observing the Tarahumara in 1936.

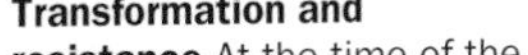

Transformation and resistance At the time of the Spanish Conquest the Tarahumara occupied over 45,000sq km. Change soon came in the wake of the Jesuits who, despite strong local resistance, established numerous missions by the mid-17th century. Christianity was absorbed into the Tarahumara calendar, providing the social focus of Sunday worship, but for everyday problems they still clung to their traditional belief in the spiritual world as the exact reverse of the physical one: while the body sleeps, the soul is at work. More transformation came with the opening of silver mines, which brought in foreign blood, from *mestizos* to Africans and Indians from Central Mexico. By the early 19th century mixed-race individuals outnumbered the indigenous people (in 1980 the proportion had risen to 6 to 1). By the late 19th century this state of affairs triggered violent revolts and forced many Tarahumaras to retreat to less accessible and less fertile areas. The same period saw large-scale exploitation of Chihuahua's pine forests by American lumber interests, leading to the construction of logging roads and the Chihuahua railway. Only the disruption of the Mexican Revolution stopped the wholesale destruction of the Sierra Tarahumara forests, but it also saw widespread losses of Tarahumara cattle and crops to Pancho Villa's indiscriminate forces.

Today's status Although the 1950s saw the return of parts of the sierra to the Indians under the *ejido* (communal holding) system, many supplement their income by working in sawmills in a rotational system aimed at ensuring work for everyone. Subsistence farming remains their main activity but this meagre existence has led to the death of thousands through malnutrition, parasites and general hygiene-related diseases. Although their population remains stable, in the 1960s 80 per cent of Tarahumara children died before the age of five. Today this has been reduced by half largely thanks to the humanitarian intervention of Jesuits who also attempt to improve illiteracy rates. Yet, however integrated the Catholic missionaries may be in the Sierra, they still have not managed to eradicate the Tarahumara gods Raiénari (the sun and protector of men) and Mechá (the moon and protector of women).

EASTER *FIESTA*

The Easter procession most dramatically displays the Tarahumara synthesis of Christianity and ancient rites. Men with painted bodies and mud-caked hair, dressed in headbands and loincloths, divide into two groups: the Pharisees (with turkey-feather headdresses) and the soldiers (with wooden swords). Processions and dances to drums and flutes lead up to Good Friday, when effigies of Judas appear and dances reach their climax around the church altars. By the next day Judas has been ritually stabbed during an orgy of *tesquino* consumption and the Tarahumara go home.

Misión de San Ignacio, one of Baja California's most beautiful mission churches

▶ San Felipe 78A3

Nearly 200km south of the Baja border town of Mexicali lies San Felipe, at the end of Highway 5. Sports fishermen discovered San Felipe in the 1950s, and since then this fishing village has mushroomed into a modestly scaled fishing and boating resort, now with two golf-courses. Big tides make the main beach south of town a popular target for dune-buggying, and it is lined with an increasing number of up-market hotels, trailer parks, beach camps, bars and restaurants. The road south is only partly paved but acceptable for most vehicles.

▶ San Ignacio 78A2

San Ignacio is the second of central Baja's oasis towns after Mulegé, and marks the point where the Transpeninsular Highway veers from the west to the east coast. Its shady central plaza lined with small stores and old colonial buildings focuses on the **Museo de las Pinturas Rupestros▶** (*Open* Mon–Fri 8–3) and the **mission church**. Originally built in adobe by the Jesuits in 1728, it was replaced with the present stone Dominican structure in 1786. In the nearby Sierra de San Francisco, excellent for hiking, are **native cave-paintings▶▶**, but they can only be reached by mule or four-wheel drive with a local guide. **Laguna San Ignacio**, 70km west, is good for whale-watching (Dec–Mar).

▶▶ San José del Cabo 78B1

San José, the more traditionally picturesque town of the Los Cabos partnership, dates back to 1730 when its Jesuit **mission** was founded. A ceramic frieze over the church entrance shows Brother Tamaral being 'martyred' by Pericué in 1734. However, the stone and stucco 19th-century houses that line Paseo Mijares, San José's broad, main street, prove that perseverance paid off. Today the town presents a clean, prosperous face to its mainly American visitors. From the small, shady plaza by the church the avenue passes the stately **Palacio Municipal**, real-estate agencies, smart boutiques, restaurants and a few lively bars before descending to the hotel-lined coast.

Although condominium and hotel development is happening fast, San José's 40,000 inhabitants are also employed with cattle and agriculture: mango, avocado

CATAVIÑA DESERT

This spectacular region of sculptural rocks lies in Baja's Parque Natural del Desierto Central, roughly halfway between San Quintín and Bahía de los Ángeles. In among the other-worldly boulders scattered across the desert is a unique display of desert vegetation. Cardons, cirios, ocotillos and hairy boojum trees create a weird and wonderful landscape, although many of the boulders beside the highway have become defaced by graffiti. Camping is the only way to truly savour these unique surroundings.

Shaded avenue in the developing resort town of San José del Cabo

and orange trees are abundant. There are horseback excursions to **La Playa** (a popular surfing beach 2km east of town), which lies beyond the ecological reserve and lagoon, home to 200 bird species. At the river estuary the **Centro Cultural** (*Open* Tue–Sun 9–5, Wed 9–1) illustrates local history and enthography. To the west lies the 'corridor' of luxury hotels and golf-courses, ending at Los Cabos.

▶ San Quintín *78A3*

The bay and town of San Quintín lie 192km south of Ensenada, reputedly the windiest spot in Baja where, at certain times of the year, chilly sea mists roll inland towards the dry, brown desert. The beautiful beaches are popular for fishing, diving, surfing and their fertile clam-beds. This service-town is seeing a growing number of hotels being built, in addition to the existing trailer parks.

▶ Santa Rosalía *78B2*

Santa Rosalía owes its existence to a 19th-century French mining company, El Boleo Copper. Built in the 1880s, it remained a company-owned town for nearly 70 years and, although El Boleo closed in 1953, a Mexican company kept operations going until 1985 when it shut down for good. Copper and manganese were shipped from a man-made harbour, now expanded to include floating docks with ocean-cruiser capacity, regularly used by the Guaymas ferry. The town's main monument is the prefabricated iron-plated **Iglesia de Santa Barbara▶▶**, designed by a contemporary of Gustave Eiffel and exhibited in Paris in 1889 before being shipped here in 1895. Adjacent streets are lined with elegant weatherboard houses, some with wrought-iron verandas, the most impressive being the graceful **Palacio Municipal**.

CAVE PAINTINGS
In the sierras of San Francisco and Santa Lucía, near San Ignacio lies a fantastic concentration of prehistoric cave paintings, unfortunately all difficult to reach. Executed by Paleo Indians, probably to invoke the favours of the gods for successful hunting, they mostly depict hunters standing with their prey of horned animals. Panels are larger and more numerous than the celebrated paintings of France's Lascaux Caves – those at Cueva Pintada reach 2m. Trips can be arranged from hotels in San Ignacio such as Posada San Ignacio, tel/fax: 115-40313.

THE 'CORRIDOR' BEACHES
Linking Cabo San Lucas and San José del Cabo is a 30km highway known as 'the corridor'. Foothills covered with scrub and cacti front a blissful stretch of cobalt blue ocean and the best beaches of Los Cabos. Developments leap out of this otherwise harmonious landscape and include five golf courses. In 30 years Los Cabos may have changed radically, but the waves haven't – they can still be dangerous. Areas that are safe to swim from are, working west to east, the city beach of El Medano, Playa Cementerio (4km); Playa de las Viudas (11km); Bahía Chileno (14km) and Playa Palmilla (27.5km).

Clapboard frame houses built by El Boleo still line Santa Rosalía's streets

DAMIANA
Todos Santos is the place to sample a drink of the real *Damiana*, a regional speciality which is brewed from the twigs and leaves of the *damiana* plant. Reputed to have great curative powers against flu, chills and general lethargy, it also claims aphrodisiac qualities. In its most kitsch Los Cabos form, *Damiana* is marketed as a yellow liqueur in a bottle shaped like a woman's body, but in Todos Santos you are more likely to find it brewed as tea.

Tijuana *78A4*

Before heading for Tijuana, remember that this is the world's busiest border, with 30 million crossings a year. Catering solely for those from across the border and above all from San Diego, just a few kilometres north, Tijuana offers a range of services and attractions from cheap marriages, souvenirs, divorce, prostitution, auto-repairs, drugs, liquor and dentists to betting on horses, greyhounds and *jai alai* ... the list is endless. These very services lend the town a fascination of its own and two million inhabitants live off the proceeds. The result is a modern city bristling with skyscrapers, where many Americans choose to live, crossing the border to work.

Historical sights are non-existent but Tijuana's city authorities have invented alternatives. **Mexitlán**, a cultural theme park, provides an instant overview of Mexico's centuries of civilisation, covering an entire city block with 150 scale-models of pre-Hispanic and colonial sites, folk-dance performances, restaurants and 'craft' shops. The **Centro Cultural**▶▶ (*Open* Tue–Fri 11–7, Sat–Sun 11–8), a spectacular building designed by Pedro Ramírez Vázquez, houses a history museum, theatre, handicraft shops, restaurants and the Omnimax Theatre where spectators are propelled into the landscapes and sites of Mexico, projected on to a 180-degree screen.

Town beaches are crowded and not particularly clean so head for **Rosarito**, half-an-hour south by road. This once-small seaside village mushroomed during the 1980s and is now a modern resort with condos in all directions. Its seafood restaurants claim the world's best lobsters, particularly good at the **Rosarito Beach Hotel**, or 1950s Hollywood Fantasy.

▶ Todos Santos *78B1*

This tropical town, founded in 1724, lies 65km north of the Cabo San Lucas and now boasts an expanding American community. Its Pericu inhabitants were decimated by diverse epidemics and the town was resettled by *mestizos* who set up a sugar industry. Mango groves compete with date palms for supremacy but it is the long deserted beaches that are the chief attraction here, in particular **Punta Lobos** which lies at the foot of a dramatic rocky bluff.

Tijuana's unusual Centro Cultural is an ambitious example of contemporary architecture

Drive

Baja California

This circuit takes you away from the developments of Los Cabos along rough, unsurfaced roads to a stretch of coast that few visitors reach. Allow a full day for negotiating the terrain and for swimming stops.

From **San José del Cabo** drive 8km north on Highway 1 (in the direction of La Paz) and at **San José Viejo** turn right towards **Palo Escopeta**. Depending on the time of year this normally dry, scrub landscape can look lush, with thousands of cacti draped in wild flowers or vines, and the odd palm tree in the valleys. Watch out for cattle that stray into the road – penalties are high for injuring them. The bumpy track leads through the occasional village where ambiguous-looking turnings can be identified by the friendly inhabitants. Stark, cacti-studded hills predominate while roadrunners, hares and zebu cattle are the most conspicuous fauna. Certain stretches of the road have been much improved and you can pick up speed. When glimpses of cobalt blue appear on the horizon (1½ to 2 hours later), the hardest stretch of the drive is nearly over.

Along the coast take your pick of the endless beaches and warm waters of the **Mar de Cortés**. For a good lunch and proximity to the coral reef of Los Pulpos, drive through Punta Lobera to a high rocky outcrop at **Los Frailes**, Baja's most easterly point. Here a discreet, though pricey hotel overlooks a sheltered beach, making an excellent swimming stop. The reef surrounds most of Cabo Pulmo, immediately to the north, where the road regains a viable tarmac surface. Pass Punta Arena's small **lighthouse** and at La Rivera turn left to cut across to the village of **La Cueva** on Highway 1.

On the drive south back to **Los Cabos** the magnificent **Sierra de la Laguna** looms to the west all the way.

Westin Regina Resort, Los Cabos

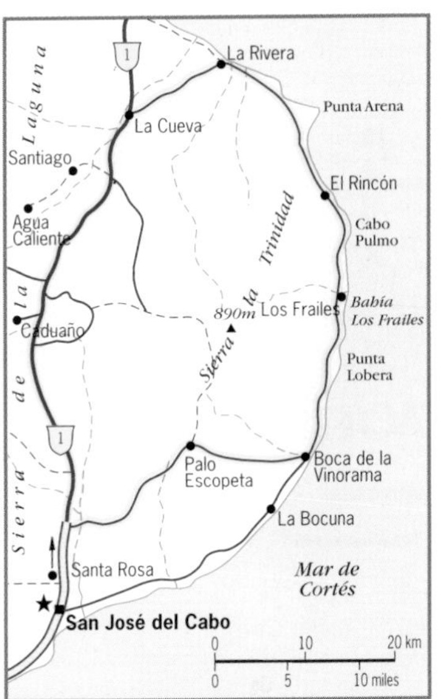

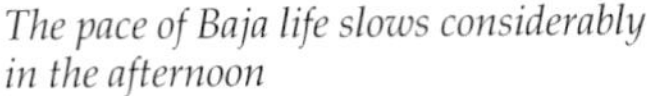
The pace of Baja life slows considerably in the afternoon

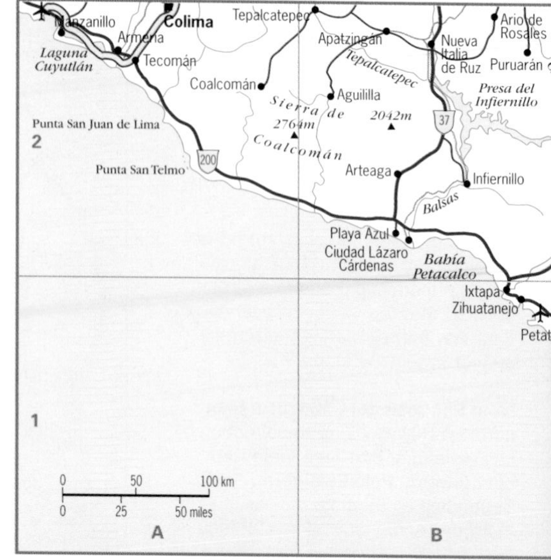

Right: the Pacific Coast (south)

The Pacific Coast

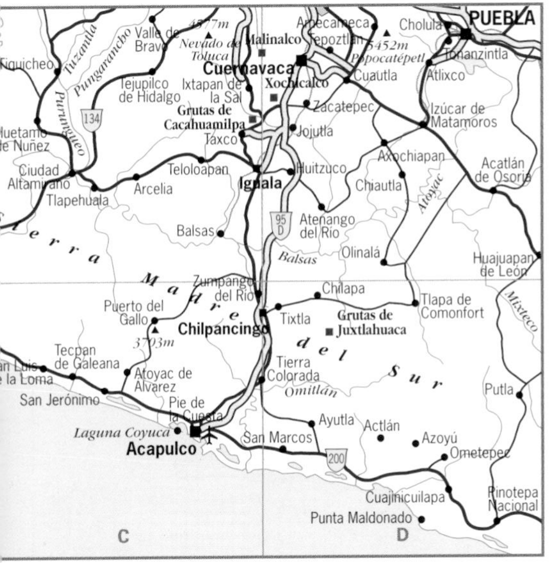

THE PACIFIC COAST From Mazatlán to Acapulco, the Pacific coast cuts south-east down the states of Sinaloa, Nayarit, Jalisco, Colima, Michoacán and Guerrero before moving into Oaxaca (see **The South**, page 188). This is Mexico's most spectacularly beautiful coastline, backed by the craggy mountain ranges of the Sierra Madre Occidental and the Sierra Madre del Sur. Not surprisingly it has been a long-standing target for sun-worshippers, jet-setters, sports fishermen and surfers, who are drawn to its thundering waves, elevated temperatures, tropical blooms and technicolour sunsets. Mega-resorts continue to expand but there are still long tracts of coast that remain undeveloped and industrial pollution is limited. Short forays can be made inland to mountain villages where history has not been completely erased, while out in the deep blue of the Pacific every possible water-sport can be enjoyed. Bus routes connect most inhabited destinations but to reach more remote areas a car is essential. Not everything about the area is idyllic. Socio-economic problems in the state of Guerrero have produced sporadic armed attacks, and this, too, was where Hurricane Pauline struck in October 1997. Although the tourist infrastructure escaped damage, poorer homes were ripped apart and 135 people died.

BACKGROUND Before the Spanish descended to the Pacific coast the area was inhabited by local tribes now loosely described as 'Culturas del Occidente'. Nayarit, Jalisco and Colima together formed the epicentre of this civilisation, thought to date from between 300 BC and AD 150. As their artefacts were all probably looted from underground tombs the term 'tomb culture' is often used. Only one important site remains from this era, at Ixtlán del Río. Although maritime trade already existed before the arrival of Cortés, it was in the 1560s that a direct link with the riches of the Orient was created from the ports of Acapulco, Barra de Navidad and Manzanillo. San Blas

▶▶▶REGION HIGHLIGHTS

Previous page: visitors to the state of Guerrero can enjoy vast expanses of beautiful deserted Pacific beach, if the glitz and glamour of places like Acapulco palls

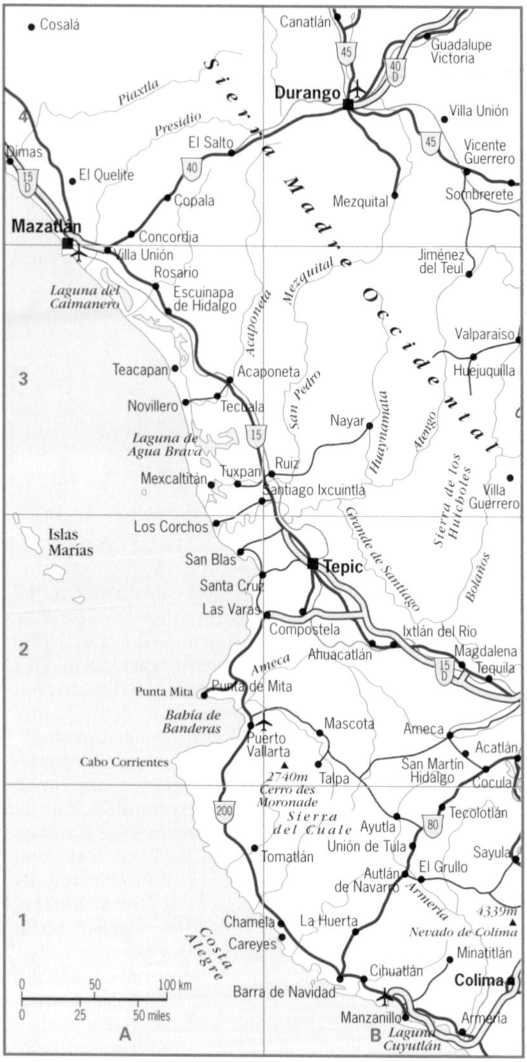

Right: the Pacific Coast (north)

Coconuts drying in the sun to make copra

saw the first missionaries set sail for Baja California in 1768, while Mazatlán thrived as an important fishing port. Along with this external input came a new ingredient to the population, African slaves, brought in to do the work the native Mexicans were not considered capable of. Their influence is particularly visible in the villages of Guerrero and in Acapulco itself. After Independence the area lost its colonial trading importance and lapsed into a long period of decline. Then came the 1950s, the first commerical airlines and Acapulco's phoenix-like rise from the ashes, soon followed by Puerto Vallarta and, more recently, Mazatlán, Manzanillo and Ixtapa-Zihuatanejo, one of the latest of Mexico's artificial mega-resorts.

TODAY'S HIGH PROFILE... The Huichols and Coras, some of Mexico's least acculturated indigenous groups, still

inhabit the sierras of Nayarit and Jalisco, but because of their remoteness they make little imprint on the coastal towns. Above all, the Pacific is geared towards the great outdoors: fishing, diving, surfing, parasailing, and sun worshipping. Celebrities such as Elizabeth Taylor and Richard Burton drew the wealthy here in the 1950s. As a result, the area today is one of Jacuzzi-infested hotels, happy-hour bars and time-share condos, and the luxury villas advance over the horizon. Little can stop the tidal wave of visitors who flood into the international airports for a two- week binge of sea and sun, and their needs are well catered for.

Colourful hammocks for sale – the coolest way to spend a night on the beach or have a siesta

...AND LOW PROFILE Commercialism plagues the large resorts, but explore the coastline between them and you enter an ecological paradise of lagoons, secluded coves and steep slopes thick with tropical vegetation. Careyes may cater for an exclusive clientele, but a few kilometres away lie the still low-key resorts of Barra de Navidad and Chamela. Between San Blas and Mazatlán is a long stretch of undeveloped, scenic land, part tropical jungle, part open lagoon, perfect for those wishing to escape the crowds. Other last frontiers are dotted along Michoacán's coast, east and west of Playa Azul. The only problem is the ferocity of the Pacific waves, a challenge for surfers, attractive for sports fishermen, but often dangerous for swimmers and divers.

Local women wash clothes in the time-honoured way

ENTICING PLUNDER
Plying the Acapulco–Manila route were sturdy new trading galleons, *naos de China*, constructed of Filipino teak by Malays and Chinese and laden with the riches of Nueva España and the Orient. Cargoes of silver, spices, ivory, porcelain and silks soon became prime targets for covetous Dutch and English buccaneers who included Sir Francis Drake and Thomas Cavendish. Pichilingues (Dutch pirates), buccaneers, corsairs, filibusters and pirates added new colour to the high seas and to local vocabulary, but the amount they plundered was a mere drop in the ocean compared to the immense wealth the Spanish Crown was amassing. From Acapulco their colonial plunder was loaded on to mules and trekked across country to Veracruz, from where it was shipped home to the courts of Spain.

High diver, La Quebrada, Acapulco

▶ Acapulco *107C1*

However much the myth has been shattered, nothing can alter Acapulco's breathtaking site commanding two bays and backed by the dramatic Sierra Madre del Sur. About 380km south of Mexico City by a fast toll-road, it attracts plane-loads of package tourists geared up for its resort offerings. A tacky concrete nightmare for some, a steamy playground for others, Acapulco specialises in extremes. Beachlife or nightlife, these are the alternatives, yet this fun-loving settlement of nearly 1 million inhabitants lies on the coast of one of Mexico's poorest states, an oasis in the wilderness.

Before the crowds Acapulco's early development was due, quite simply, to its status as the nearest Pacific port to Mexico City. The 'place where the big reeds grow' was reached by Cortés and others around 1530 and port facilities were soon established in the generous natural harbour. In 1565 the first Spanish galleon set sail from Manila to Acapulco, marking the beginning of a trade route that saw the wealth of the Orient exchanged with that of Nueva España. With Independence the Spanish ships sailed away for ever, Acapulco went into decline and by the early 20th century had all but ceased to exist. However, in 1927 a paved road from Mexico City and, finally, an international airport in the 1950s brought it back to life.

Layout The 11km curve of horseshoe-shaped Acapulco Bay starts in the east at the headland of Punta Bruja, crowned with a giant illuminated crucifix, with the water-sports bay of **Puerto Marqués** at its feet. Sweeping past the main tourist developments and beaches along La Costera to the old town, it ends at Punta Grifo on the **Peninsula de las Playas**. Here **Caleta** and **Caletilla**, two adjacent beaches, attract visitors with their calm waters and are the embarkation point for **Isla de la Roqueta▶▶**, an island popular for more gentle waves, lush vegetation and the submerged bronze statue of the **Virgin of Guadalupe**. To the west of the promontory is the celebrated **La Quebrada**, where daredevil divers plunge 40m into the waters below, and **Playa la Angosta**, another sheltered cove. From here the road follows the coast to **Pie de la Cuesta▶▶**, a landspit edged by sea and lagoon, now a favourite with budget travellers.

Central sights and beaches Fronting the main harbour is the old town, a surprising encounter with Mexico in what is otherwise an anonymous international resort. Narrow, lively streets lead off the shady central plaza and uphill to the **Fuerte de San Diego▶▶** (*Open* Tue–Sun 10–5), built between 1615 and 1617 to protect the port from pirate attacks and now converted into an interesting history and anthropology museum, with panoramic views over the bay and mountains. A few streets north is the sprawling **Mercado de Artesanías** with good deals on handicrafts and clothes. Further east is the **Parque Papagayo**, an amusement park that lies right behind **Playa Hornos**, where fishermen unload their catch. In the middle of the bay is **Playa Condesa**, the hottest

The curving sweep of Pie de la Cuesta, famous for its sunsets
Inset: Paradise restaurant

beach in town, where sun-posing wins over swimming. Another hive of entertainment clusters around the Centro Internacional Acapulco, further along La Costera, and includes the aquariums, dolphins and water-rides of the **CICI** children's park.

PIE DE LA CUESTA
Ten kilometres north-west of Acapulco, a long narrow spit of land separates the thundering Pacific Ocean from the mangrove- and palm-fringed Laguna Coyuca. Once a birdwatchers' paradise, and now a favourite with water-skiers, the lagoon extends 10km west and is dotted with tropical islands. Horseback riders and sunset fanatics home in on the beach of Pie de la Cuesta, almost impossible to swim off due to its pounding surf and strong undertow, although locals show off their fearlessness in the towering waves. The modest hotels and seafood restaurants that line the shore suffered severe hurricane damage in 1997.

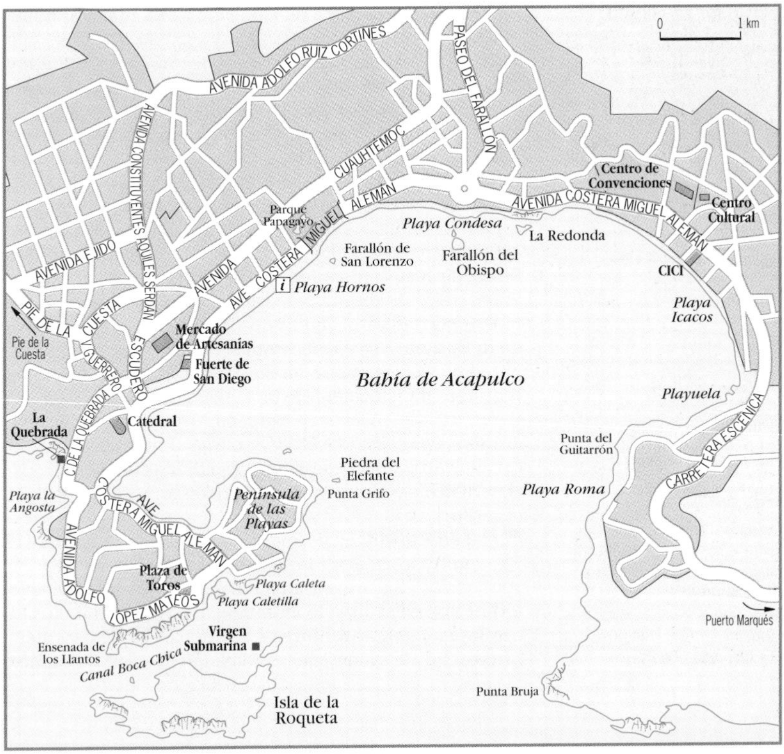

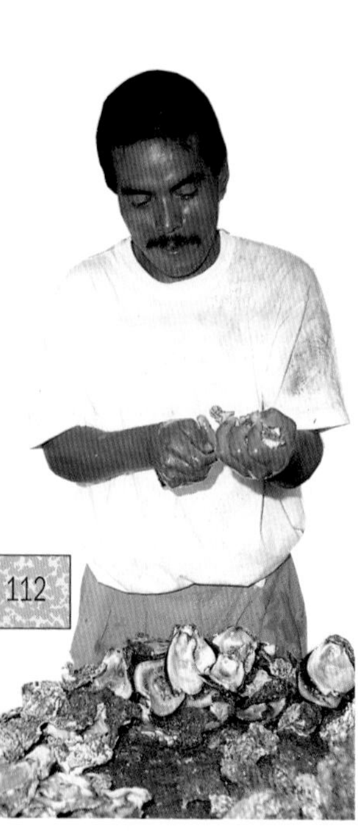

Preparing oysters at a beachside restaurant

VOLCANOES
Still occasionally emitting blasts of sulphurous smoke, El Fuego (Volcán de Fuego) rises 3,900m into the skies of Colima just north of the state capital. A national park has been created around it and dirt roads run high enough up the slopes to enable the summit to be reached on foot. Further north looms El Nevado (Nevado de Colima), which peaks at over 4,200m. Also known by its Náhautl name of Zapotépetl, it is Mexico's sixth highest volcano, now extinct. This whole region is a dramatic spectacle of hills, valleys and deep gulleys crossed by bridges – well worth exploring on the highway to Guadalajara.

►► Barra de Navidad *108B1*

This tiny, picturesque fishing village and relaxed resort marks the southern point of Jalisco's majestically mountainous and indented coastline and lies at the eastern end of the wide sweep of Bahía de Navidad. The main street is named after Miguel López de Legazpi, the Spanish captain who set sail from here for the Philippines in 1564. Well supplied with modest hotels and seafood restaurants, the village culminates in a sandbar recently extended with a seawall promenade. To the west is a sandy beach, good for surfing in the winter months, and to the east lies a vast lagoon, sheltered by the peninsula of **La Culevra**. A public boat serves its pretty waterfront village of **Colimilla►**, lined with low-priced seafood restaurants nestling in tropical vegetation. A huge luxury resort with a 27-hole golf-course profits from all this, and although Barra suffered from an earthquake in 1994 it remains an enticing destination.

►► Careyes *108B1*

Careyes occupies a prime stretch of Jalisco's tropical coast, where palm-strewn hills roll into the Pacific, small sandy coves offer sheltered waters and turtles are a common underwater sight. Largely reserved for the very well-heeled, the area has been targeted by several exclusive resort-hotels, including a 1,500-hectare resort owned by an Italian millionaire, Gianfranco Brignone. It also has an incongruous polo club in the jungle and a wildlife reserve and exclusive hotel run by Isabel Goldsmith. For less fortunate mortals, there is a well-maintained campground on Bahia Careyes.

►► Colima *108B1*

Barely 60km inland from the Pacific coast, in the foothills of the Sierra Madre del Sur, is the placid capital of the tiny state of Colima (which covers exactly 0.27 per cent of the Mexican Republic). With a warm, year-round climate, numerous tropical parks and gardens, stately buildings and a good archaeological museum it makes a refreshing climatic and cultural change from the Pacific trail. It was the third city established by the Spaniards in Mexico, in 1523, but most of its monuments date from the 19th century. Exceptions are the **Convento de Almoloyan**, a former 16th-century convent, and the Plateresque **Iglesia de San Felipe de Jesús**, inhabited in 1772 by the priest and subsequent instigator of Independence, Miguel Hidalgo. A few blocks north-east of the Plaza Principal stands the **Casa de la Cultura**, a modern complex that combines galleries, libraries, workshops and a theatre with the **Museo de las Culturas de Occidente►►** (Museum of the Western Cultures). Its many pre-Hispanic artefacts include the famous stylised pot-bellied Colima dogs, modelled in every conceivable pose as well as other, often humorous, clay figurines (*Open* Tue–Sun 9–1, 4–8).

►► Concordia *108A4*

This pretty town is set in lush tropical vegetation, on the spectacular Highway 40 which winds north and distinctly uphill from Mazatlán to Durango. It is well known for its fine hand-carved furniture and pottery. On the tiny main square the imposing 18th-century **Iglesia San Sebastián**

Concordia's Iglesia San Sebastián is the focal point of the main square

THREE RIVERS PROJECT
Two broad rivers, the Humaya and the Tamazula, cross the state of Sinaloa and on reaching the state capital of Culiacán join to create a third, the Río Culiacán, which eventually flows into the Pacific. Trees and vegetation line these watercourses and the surrounding fertile valleys are considered to be Mexico's breadbasket (and unofficial drugbasket). A massive development project already under construction will create 10 bridges, 46km of riverside promenades and 32km of new highway, as well as harness the waters of an unruly *arroyo* (stream) into El Bledal reservoir.

has a fine baroque façade, its pink stone contrasting with the modestly scaled, whitewashed houses. The surrounding hills are much visited by locals for their abundant mineral and hot-water springs and this lush, fresh region, only 48km from Mazatlán, makes a welcome change from the heat of the coast.

▶▶ Copala *108A4*

About 24km further north of Concordia, the picture-postcard village of Copala, founded in 1565 and once noted for its silver mining, clings to the Sinaloan mountainside. Two-storey houses with decorative ironwork balconies line cobblestone streets which wind precariously around the verdant slopes. The late-18th-century **Iglesia de San Joseph** incorporates a 16th-century belltower and atrium.

▶▶ Cosalá *108A4*

Another of Sinaloa's treasures, this former mining town lies lost in the inland sierra between Culiacán and Mazatlán, about two hours' drive from the latter. Red-tiled roofs of whitewashed houses retreat into the shade of cedar trees and the main square offers an interesting **Museo de Minería e Historia** (*Open* Tue–Sun 9–1, 3–5) housed in a colonial mansion. The main church, the 18th-century **Templo de Santa Ursula**, has an unusual sundial, but more curious is the Palacio Municipal clock, which functions by means of a 24-hour pulley weighted by a rock.

The charming town of Copala is surrounded by gently rolling slopes that form the foothills of the Sierra Madre Occidental

LAS HADAS
This completely self-contained, Moorish-style fantasy of domes, towers and arches offers every imaginable luxury in a high-class Disneyworld setting. The product of the imagination of Bolivian tin magnate and multi-millionaire, Antenor Patiño, it was initially conceived as an ultra-deluxe resort where he and his friends could gather at any time of the year for the temperate weather and suitably exclusive atmosphere. Bo Derek and Dudley Moore tested the pool here while shooting the film *10* and since then the 220 rooms, 18-hole golf course, private marina and beach have been ranked among the world's top 10 hotels.

Ixtapa's wide, sandy beaches, set against a tropical background, have become a firm favourite with Mexican families

▶▶▶ Costa Alegre *108A1*

This newly coined name refers to Jalisco's spectacular and still relatively undeveloped coastline which curves north-west from the Bahía de Navidad and ends at the Bahía de Chamela, a distance of about 100km. It is truly tropical, with superb beaches fronted by rocky islands, and amenities range from the luxury developments of Careyes to more affordable options in Melaque, Chamela or Tenacatita.

Melaque▶, also known as San Patricio, lies at the western end of the lovely Bahía de Navidad facing Barra (see page 112) and is popular with Mexican families. To the north, the growing coastal settlement of **Chamela▶▶** sits on an 11km stretch of beach facing numerous outlying islands, 150km south-east of Puerto Vallarta. An international airport is planned.

▶ Ixtapa *106B1*

Now twinned with nearby Zihuatanejo (see page 122) as a major goverment-sponsored resort, Ixtapa, 240km west of Acapulco, was nothing more than a coconut plantation until the mid-1970s. Development has brought the coastal highway and an international airport, but the lush tropical valley remains, ending on the white sands of the lovely **Playa del Palmar**. The town lacks the majestic scale and history of Acapulco, but high-rise hotels, restaurants, bars, discos, shopping centres, golf-course, marina and endless watersports keep visitors happy. The soul of Mexico retreats behind the Sierra Madre del Sur, but can be found on **Isla Ixtapa▶▶**, an island wildlife sanctuary where armadillos, deer and raccoons vie with *palapa*-style seafood restaurants for attention. Beaches here are more sheltered for swimming than Playa del Palmar and snorkelling and diving are more rewarding. Horses can be hired at **Playa Larga**, to the north.

▶ Ixtlán del Río *108B2*

Nayarit's only archaeological site, **Los Toriles** (*Open* daily 8–5), which flourished during the 2nd century AD, lies 81km east of Tepic on the highway to Guadalajara. Several low structures surround the circular **Temple of Quetzalcóatl**, mounted via four staircases and with walls perforated by cruciform openings. These could have referred to a pre-Hispanic concept of the universe. Other ruins date from around AD 400; the site is thought to have remained occupied until the Spanish conquest. On the outskirts of the small town of Ixtlan del Rio, it is worth seeing for those whose route takes them this way.

▶ Manzanillo *108B1*

Manzanillo was founded in the early 16th century as a major shipyard and port for the trade route to Asia and is said to have hosted junks from the Orient long before the Spaniards arrived. Today it is a sprawling, unattractive town curving around an immense, mountain-backed bay. Ocean liners, cargo boats, fishing boats and yachts dot the harbour. The main town is situated on an isthmus separating the Pacific from the Laguna Cuyutlán. Resort hotels, condominiums and the better beaches lie across the bay on the road west to Playa de Oro airport. Most famous of all the hotels is **Las Hadas** (The Fairies), (see panel opposite).

This tropical port was named after the camomile tree (*manzanilla*) and is known as the 'Sailfish Capital of the World'. It is renowned as a base for deep-sea fishing expeditions. From October to May, sports fishermen track down abundant red snapper, marlin, sea bass and giant tuna. Manzanillo sprouts an abundance of vegetation, but the general atmosphere is run-down and harbour installations are less than picturesque. It is home to the Mexican navy and ranks as Mexico's most important west coast shipping centre, with a railway link inland to transport local produce (coconuts, limes, bananas, mangoes, avocados and sugar-cane) to Guadalajara. For visitors the main interest lies in the white or black volcanic beaches lining the Bahía de Santiago at the chic western end of the main bay: **La Audiencia**, **Santiago**, **Olas Altas** and **Miramar**. The last two have good surfing and the cove of La Audencia is ideal for swimming and water-skiing. This area is slated for residential and tourist developement surrounding the new marina, **Puerto Juluapan**.

OLAS VERDES

The Pacific waves round Manzanillo are known for a spectacular nocturnal phenomenon, that of an emerald-green phosphorescent microscopic organism which sporadically invades the water. This naturally illuminated plankton creates a most remarkable effect and if you plunge into the green waves (*olas verdes*) at the right time you will emerge covered in sparkling pinpoints of light.

Manzanillo is a popular base for fishing expeditions

Valentino's Disco Club, a Moorish-style palace by the sea at Punta Camaron, is a long-time favourite in Mazatlán

►► Mazatlán *108A4*

This booming resort town, with over half a million inhabitants, is rapidly expanding along the coast of Sinaloa. As a major commercial fishing port it boasts Mexico's largest shrimp fleet and superlative sports-fishing, with eight fleets of charter-boats that originally set tourism in motion here. Less sophisticated than its chief resort rivals, Mazatlán still has a life of its own, with an atmospheric old town sitting on a headland which firmly separates harbour and tourist activities. Three hills and the distant Sierra Madre create scenic interest, but Mazatlán is celebrated above all for its 21km *malecón* (sea boulevard), lining the bay. Its position due east of the southern tip of Baja California, at the confluence of the Mar de Cortés and the Pacific, endows it with warm water, a constantly balmy climate and abundant year-round shoals of marlin and sailfish.

Mazatlán was founded in 1531, but did not really develop until the mid-19th century. Relics from this era can be found in the relaxed old town which revolves around the Plaza Principal with its Moorish-style **cathedral** and, two blocks south, the 1860s **Teatro Ángela Peralta►►**. Other sights are the **Mercado Central**, brimming with crafts and foodstalls, and the small **Museo de Arqueología** at Sixto Osuna 76 (*Open* Tue–Sun 10–6), displaying pre-Hispanic artefacts and contemporary art. Towering over this downtown area is the **Cerro de la Nevería** (Icebox Hill), with panoramic sea views. A short hike to the end of the peninsula ends at **El Faro►►**, a lighthouse open to the public, which claims to be the world's second highest – after Gibraltar's. A tourist office is located in this area at Paseo Olas Altas 13000, in the Banco de México building.

From the surfing beach of **Playa Olas Altas** at the base of Cerro de la Nevería (where high-divers plunge from a tall rock), the celebrated *malecón* runs north-west past the

Laying bricks out to dry in the sun

Playa del Norte and into the **Zona Dorada** (Golden Zone). Here condominiums, large hotels, discos and restaurants look out across Mazatlán's best beaches and surf to outlying islands. **Isla del Venado** offers great swimming, snorkelling and diving. Boat trips leave daily at 10am from the beach next to El Cid hotel. Trips to **Isla de la Piedra** and **Isla del Chivo** leave from near the freighter docks. Mazatlán also has the **Acaurio Mazatlán** (*Open* daily 9.30–6.30) with 50 aquariums, a marine museum and a botanical garden, as well as 60 tennis-courts and two golf-courses.

Time-share sharks abound but with tracts of plum real estate still empty, Mazatlán keeps an attractively imperfect air. Despite the visitors who pour into its international airport and a giant tourist complex taking shape at its eastern end, Mazatlán strikes a good balance between old and new.

▶▶ Mexcaltitán *108A3*

Once thought to be the legendary island of Aztlán, the original home of the Aztecs, Mexcaltitán lies 70km northwest of San Blas along Nayarit's lagoon-indented coast, and is reached by ferry from the town of **Santiago Ixcuintla**. Local transport is by canoe through a network of narrow canals criss-crossed by causeways – which have given rise to the nickname the 'Venice of Mexico'. No tourist facilities exist but Mexcaltitán has not been not forgotten: Mexican presidents periodically visit the island village in a symbolic gesture to its quintessential Mexican character.

▶▶ Playa Azul *106B2*

Squeezed between the states of Guerrero and Jalisco is the remote, undeveloped coastline of Michoacán, with an immense, polluted black-spot at the industrial port of Lázaro Cárdenas, but otherwise offering several low-key destinations. Playa Azul is popular with Mexican tourists who flood down from inland Michoacán, but it remains a pleasant resort with a beautiful beach and good surfing – its waves compare with those in Hawaii. Stingrays and strong currents present some dangers, but these are outweighed by the dramatic setting of mountains descending sharply into the sea, the cheap accommodation and the string of open-air seafood restaurants that line the waterfront.

CARNAVAL

Every year since 1898, during the week before Ash Wednesday, Mazatlán has burst into life with its Mardi Gras, one of Mexico's liveliest fiestas. Activities take place all over town but the main festivities concentrate along Playa Olas Altas. Wandering *mariachis* keep the background sounds going till late, fireworks shoot over the bay, mock sea-battles take place and fancy-dress balls propel inhabitants and visitors into a fantasy world. This is considered the world's third best carnival after Río de Janeiro and New Orleans, which means that Mazatlán's many hotels are fully booked. If you want to take part in the fun, make reservations several months ahead.

MAZATLAN'S ISLANDS

Of the outlying islands, the Isla de la Piedra (Stone Island) is the most ecologically appealing, for its salt-water canals, thick, lush mangrove swamps, numerous seabirds and superb uncrowded beaches. Boats leave from Mazatlán's *embarcadero* (landing place) in the docks behind the old town, right beside a huge tuna, sardine and shrimp packing plant. Three islands lie a short distance out from the Zona Dorada: Lobos, Isla del Venado and Pájaros. Isla del Venado (Deer Island) is particularly good for snorkelling and diving and also boasts some interesting old cave paintings. Boats leave from the Muelle Pier, just east of the lighthouse, and from larger hotels.

No other nation can claim such a profound 20th-century architectural imprint as that of Luís Barragán on Mexico. Inspired by Juan O'Gorman, Barragán's vivid, geometric lines have spawned hundreds of copies all over the country and created a typically Mexican school of contemporary architecture.

OMNIPRESENT ARCHITECTURE
'Mexico has always been a country of architects, from pre-Columbian times to the present. Nearly all our towns and the majority of our villages possess remarkable edifices and monuments, and some of them are really grandiose. The number of these buildings and urban complexes that have miraculously survived the ravages of time is surprising.'
Octavio Paz: *Labyrinth of Solitude*, 1950.

In every city of Mexico, from Monterrey to Acapulco, Mexico City to Puerto Vallarta, modern architecture is a high-profile element in the urban picture. Sleek office buildings, innovative museums, sophisticated villas, luxury hotels and even bus stations all bear the signatures of Mexico's new generation of architects. Their work follows an architectural tradition that started with the great Maya and Aztec temples, was nurtured by the Spanish, and peaked in grandiose excess under Porfirio Díaz. Post-revolutionary Mexico saw a new democratic accent on integrating art, architecture and the applied arts, stimulated by the flourishing muralist movement and much influenced by the theories and designs of Juan O'Gorman.

Precursors Behind the post-revolutionary thrust of new forms was the figure of José Villagram García who propounded the theory of 'contemporary Mexican architecture as the result of the historical development of our art... and of a form of expression suited to our culture.' His rejection of the copying of European forms, which had monopolised the Porfiriato style, was adopted by his students, who included Juan O'Gorman, Enrique de la Mora and Enrique Yañez. O'Gorman, the son of Irish immigrants, advocated the Bauhaus principles of functionalism, but combined this with the burgeoning new spirit of Mexican identity. His private houses, built in the early 1930s in San Ángel, are among the country's first modern buildings. One major landmark is the indigo and red studio he designed for Diego Rivera and Frida Kahlo, which regenerated the brilliant colour that once coated pre-Hispanic façades. The ultimate symbol of this cultural renaissance was Mexico City's Ciudad Universitaria (1951–5), an astonishing collaboration between nearly 100 architects and engineers that remains a show-case for decorative passion and generous use of space.

Modern architecture at the New Stock Exchange, Mexico City

Barragán O'Gorman's emphasis on utilitarian rationalist forms and colour was taken one step further by Luís Barragán, who,

The Westin Regina Resort, Los Cabos

MAGIC
'Architectural publications no longer contain the words: beauty, inspiration, bewitchment, magic, spell and also serenity, silence, intimacy, astonishment. All these words have been warmly received in my heart.'
Luís Barragán.

FEEL A BARRAGÁN
To really experience Barragán's architectural innovations and fully understand the subsequent cloning, make a visit to his studio-house in Mexico City, now run by a foundation which provides guided tours (in Spanish and English). Appointments can be made by calling 5-515 4908 on weekdays 11am–2pm.

inspired by a visit to Spain's Moorish palace, the Alhambra, sought to inject beauty, emotion and spirituality into modernist forms. Together with Enrique de la Mora and Mathías Goeritz, Barragán embarked upon a style of architecture where bold wall colour, scale and angle defined a space in which, when possible, nature was fully integrated.

Their own private homes, built in the 1940s on Calle Francisco Ramírez in Tacubaya, Mexico City, became the controversial models for a style which left its signature on countless commissions over the following decades. Light, volume, thick walls and small openings laid out in geometric purity juxtapose planes of pink, ochre, violet and peach. Water may be channelled along pathways, gush from overhead aqueducts or lie tranquilly in a pool. An exhibition of Barragán's work at New York's Museum of Modern Art (MoMA) in 1976 confirmed his satellite status, acknowledged in 1980 with the Pritzker Prize (architecture's equivalent of the Nobel). In 1988 Barragán died at the ripe old age of 86 leaving a legacy of 20th-century monuments and an enduring Mexican style, much copied since.

Zealous disciples Following close behind the trail-blazing Barragán is Ricardo Legorreta, now considered the doyen of contemporary architecture. Using Barragánesque colour juxtapositions and openings, he has applied himself to luxury hotels in Cancún and Ixtapa. One of his best known designs is Monterrey's spectacular art museum, MARCO, which Legorreta describes as 'a traditional Mexican building (where) movement is achieved through a central patio'. However, Legorreta's more recent work lacks the purity of his early days and leaves the way open for the next generation. The 1990s have seen no abatement in Mexico's talent for architectural innovation, most recently displayed in Mexico City's new Centro Nacional de las Artes at Tialpan. This huge arts complex was rushed to completion before the end of Salinas' presidential term in 1994. Again, vividly coloured façades combine with dramatic scale to represent the Mexican identity.

Mexico City's Satellite Towers, by Barragán and Goeritz, 1957

A BREATH OF HISTORY
Originally called Las Peñas, Vallarta's history goes back to 1851 when a certain Guadalupe Sánchez built the first house on the banks of the Río Cuale. He developed a successful mule operation, hauling minerals from inland mines to the small port for shipment and bringing salt from the outlying Islas Marías. As word of the area's great beauty spread, other settlers arrived and in 1886 the small town was officially recognised. When Las Peñas changed its name to Puerto Vallarta in 1918 to honour Jalisco's governor, its population stood at 200. In 1954 an airport was built and Puerto Vallarta began to be touted as a Pacific paradise. Then 10 years later along came John Huston...

The guardian angel of fishermen, one of many diverse sculptures dotting Puerto Vallarta's malecón

▶▶▶ Puerto Vallarta *108A2*

Rip-off taxis, Chevrolets, fuming buses, taco stands, '2 for 1' happy-hour bars – Puerto Vallarta is blatantly aimed at the tastes and wallets of *gringos* (foreigners) who flood through the international airport to the high-rise hotels lining this spectacular, mountain-backed bay, the world's second largest. The early development of this now legendary resort was jumpstarted in 1964 by the filming of John Huston's *Night of the Iguana* starring Ava Gardner and Richard Burton. Elizabeth Taylor came too, and the famous couple set up home in the winding cobblestone streets of what is now termed Old Vallarta. The rest, as they say, is history.

South of Río Cuale The main downtown area is divided by the Río Cuale with an elongated island at its mouth, which has become home to a modest museum (*Open* Tue–Sat 10–3, 4–7, Sun 10–2), shops and various bars and restaurants. To the south lies the once down-market side of Vallarta, where chic restaurants are invading streets such as Badillo. Modest hotels and restaurants make it the best place for budget travellers and those looking for some flavour of Mexico. The waterfront here claims the town's 'in' beach, **Playa de los Muertos** (now renamed Playa del Sol) and a string of hotels and condos clusters around the lively Plaza Lazaro Cardénas. At the back, the main road leads south out of the centre to wind round the spectacular cliff, past more luxury hotels, villas and beaches before reaching the end of the bay at **La Mismaloya**, the cove of *Iguana* fame, now graced with a monstrous hotel block.

Town centre This is the focus of the town's main action, sandwiched between a steep hill and the sea. Red-tiled houses along the central streets are now smart galleries, clothes or craft shops and the palm-lined *malecón* (seafront) is lined with the liveliest bars and discos. The much modernised main square, **Plaza de Armas**, is flanked by the curiously crowned **Nuestra Señora de Guadalupe** (1902) and the modern **Palacio Municipal**, which also houses a helpful tourist office. Climb the steep and picturesque streets inland from here and you touch the pulse of Vallarta's fishing-village origins.

Beyond the old town centre the highway crosses a completely soulless hotel zone, passes the port (packed with cruise ships, battleships and trawlers) and ends at **Marina Vallarta**. This self-contained commercial and residential area, which includes a golf course and an American school, lies just before the bold pink forms of the airport. Yet Vallarta and the Bahía de Banderas do not end here. More coastal developments are mushrooming in an area to the north named Nuevo Vallarta. Finally, at **Punta Mita**, the northern headland of this mighty bay, are the bay's best surfing beaches.

Out and about in Vallarta There is no shortage of excursion opportunities in Vallarta, and you hardly need to search them out as tour agents promote their services liberally. Snorkellers and divers should head for **Mismaloya**, where an underwater park lies around the outlying rocks of **Los Arcos▶▶**, or take a speedboat to the **Islas**

Marietas▶▶, about an hour away, where reefs and underwater caverns teem with marine life. **Punta Mita▶▶**, the bay's northern headland is also a worthwhile destination. Deep-sea fishing is particularly profitable from November to May, as is whale-watching between December and April. Vallarta's best swimming beaches can only be reached by boat and lie at the southern end of the bay. The most visited is **Yelapa**, but **Quimixto▶** and Playa de las Animas remain relatively uncrowded. Jungle trekking, kayaking, diving, horseback riding and a wide range of watersports are also available, and nobody leaves this resort without an extra suitcase full of Huichol crafts and cheap, but stylish clothes.

DANGERS
Vallarta is knowingly on the make, so there are some factors to bear in mind for a more peaceful and less costly holiday. Visitors are the easy victims of well-practised tricks. A taxi-driver may insist that your desired restaurant is closed or that he knows a better one. This is where his commission lies. Avoid it. Worse still are the oily tones of the touts who offer 'tourist information' or unbeatably cheap jeep-rental. They are in fact attached to timeshare developments and use all the tricks of the commission trade. Beware!

Tourist policewoman

Some of Vallarta's former charm lies hidden in its steep, cobblestoned streets

MORE ECOLOGICAL DELIGHTS
Around the border of Nayarit and Sinaloa, roughly halfway between San Blas and Rosario, stretches a region of cattle ranches, undulating hills clothed in tropical vegetation, *palapa*-roofed villages and wetlands punctuated by the occasional rocky outcrop. Lagoons and islands fringed by vast coconut plantations are havens for diverse birdlife as well as abundant marine species. At Escuinapa, 22km south-east of Rosario, follow the road to Teacapán, past lagoons, to reach the pristine and still undeveloped beaches of La Tambora, Las Cabras and Los Angeles, where great seafood can be savoured while watching the sun set over the Pacific.

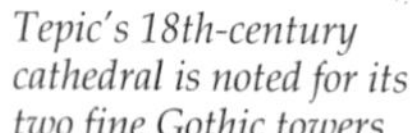

Tepic's 18th-century cathedral is noted for its two fine Gothic towers

▶▶ Rosario 108A3

Seventy-five kilometres south-east of Mazatlán, Rosario is a relic of the region's former mineral riches, now a centre for the less illustrious cultivation of mangoes. Founded in 1655, it had become the richest town in the north-east by the late 18th century. Over 70km of underground tunnels were dug in a frenetic search for its prolific gold and silver, and mining continued until 1945. The **Misión de Nuestra Señora del Rosario**, finished in 1759, contains the ultimate symbol of this former glory, a massive and elaborate gold altarpiece. The church, now located on the main square, had to be moved stone by stone from its former site, where the tunnels below had led to its collapse.

▶▶ San Blas 108A2

Gnats, birds and surf are the outstanding features of San Blas, a sleepy fishing town and resort that lies 130km north-west of Puerto Vallarta. Surrounded by lush mangrove-fringed lagoons and estuaries, palm groves and 30km of beaches, it would be a tropical paradise were it not for the clouds of voracious insects which descend at dusk. However, with a correctly screened hotel and plenty of insect repellent, San Blas becomes an atmospheric destination offering good facilities, historic sites, ecological interest and, reputedly, the longest (as opposed to highest) waves along the Pacific coast, perfect for surfers. The **Bahía de Matanchén** was an important 16th- to 18th-century departure point for Spanish expeditions including that of Father Junípero Serra, who set off in 1768 with 14 other Franciscans to 'conquer' the Californias. Ruins from this period include the old **Aduana** (Customs House) by the port and, on a hill overlooking the town and estuaries, the **Fuerte de Basilio▶▶** and a 1769 church, the subject of Longfellow's poem *The Bells of San Blas*.

Jungle boat trips go to the lagoons of **La Tovara▶▶** and **Camalota**, inhabited by turtles, iguanas, alligators, herons, egrets and cormorants, and from November to March ornithologists come to see 200 or so species of migrating birds join 150 native species. The entire area is considered one of the most important natural bird refuges in the Western hemisphere.

▶ Tepic 108B2

The modest capital of Nayarit is a crossroad town for rail, bus and car travellers. This is the departure point for the coastal destinations of San Blas and Mexcaltitán, the inland road to Guadalajara and the coast route to Puerto Vallarta. It also serves as a weekend market town for the Cora and Huichol peoples who live in remote villages of the sierra to the north-east, beyond the rolling fields of sugar-canes. The **Museo Regional de Antropología e Historia▶** (*Open* Tue–Sun 10–2, 5–8) gives a good background to their unique *peyote*-inspired crafts (see page 149) and displays 'tomb culture' artefacts.

▶▶ Zihuatanejo 106B1

Zihuatanejo is the 'fishing-village' partner in the much promoted Ixtapa-Zihuatanejo resort project (see page 114), a distinctly tarted-up version of the real thing. However, its fabulous bay setting and fine swimming beaches more than compensate. Dirt streets are replaced with cobble-

stones, pedestrian malls invade the old town and hotels front the beaches, but Zihuatanejo still has only 35,000 inhabitants, a far cry from the Pacific's mega-resorts. The **Playa Principal** bordering the old town is the least attractive beach, but south-west across a canal and around the bay there are far better propositions. **Playa Madera**, lying beyond a headland, offers cheap accommodation and restaurants and is a popular family beach. Better still is **Playa la Ropa**, backed by cliffs (with good views) and fringed with palm trees, not surprisingly the target for the town's better hotels. At the end of the bay lies **Playa las Gatas▶▶**, a lovely sheltered beach flanked by palms, naturally protected by an underwater reef and easily reached by boat from the town pier or by a rocky path from Playa la Ropa. Open-air *palapa*-roofed restaurants dish up fresh lobster, and scuba and snorkelling gear can be hired here – the only drawback is the fly invasion, so take insect repellent.

The fishing village of Zihuatanejo offers a relaxed contrast to its high-rise neighbour, Ixtapa

THE BELLS OF SAN BLAS

What say the bells of San Blas
To the ships that southward pass
From the harbor of Mazatlán?
To them it is nothing more
Than the sound of surf on the shore,
Nothing more to master or man.

But to me, a dreamer of dreams,
To whom what is and what seems
Are often one and the same, –
The Bells of San Blas to me
Have a strange, wild melody
And are something more than a name.

Henry Wadsworth Longfellow's last poem, 1882.

La Sirena Gorda restaurant, Zihuatanejo

3er. CAMPEONATO
Superior
CHARRO
GUADALAJARA
1 9 9 4
Conmemorando el 452 aniversario
de la ciudad de Guadalajara
LIENZO CHARRO JALISCO

Cerveza
especial
"Noche Buena"
CERVECERIA MOCTEZUMA, S.A.
Orizaba, Ver., Guadalajara, Jal.
MARCA REGISTRADA HECHO EN MEXICO

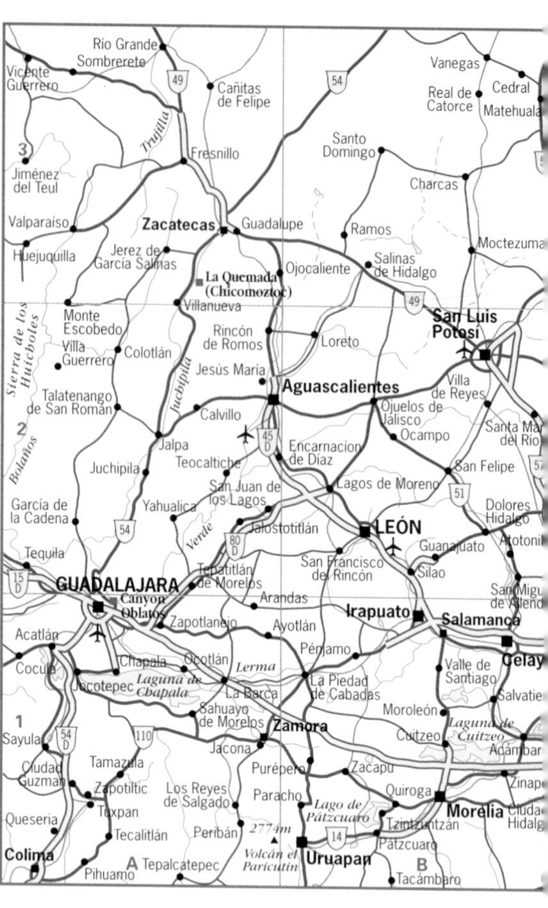
Río Grande
Sombrerete
Vicente Guerrero
49
Cañitas de Felipe
54
Vanegas
Real de Catorce
Cedral
Matehuala
Trujillo
Fresnillo
3
Jiménez del Teul
Santo Domingo
Charcas
Valparaíso
Zacatecas
Guadalupe
Ramos
Moctezuma
Huejuquilla
Jerez de García Salinas
La Quemada (Chicomoztoc)
Ojocaliente
Salinas de Hidalgo
Villanueva
Sierra de los Huicholes
Monte Escobedo
Villa Guerrero
Colotlán
Rincón de Romos
Loreto
San Luis Potosí
Jesús María
Juchipila
Aguascalientes
Talatenango de San Román
Calvillo
Villa de Reyes
Ojuelos de Jalisco
Ocampo
2
Bolaños
Jalpa
Teocaltiche
Encarnación de Díaz
Santa María del Río
Juchipila
San Juan de los Lagos
Lagos de Moreno
San Felipe
García de la Cadena
Yahualica
51
Dolores Hidalgo
54
Verde
Jalostotitlán
LEÓN
80 D
Guanajuato
Tequila
San Francisco del Rincón
Silao
15 D
GUADALAJARA
Tepatitlán de Morelos
Arandas
San Miguel de Allende
Canyon Oblatos
Zapotlanejo
Irapuato
Salamanca
Acatlán
Ayotlán
Pénjamo
Celaya
Cocula
Chapala
Ocotlán
Lerma
Valle de Santiago
Jocotepec
Laguna de Chapala
La Barca
La Piedad de Cabadas
Salvatierra
1
Sahuayo de Morelos
Moroleón
Sayula
54 D
110
Zamora
Cuitzeo
Laguna de Cuitzeo
Jacona
Acámbaro
Ciudad Guzmán
Tamazula
Purépero
Zacapu
Zapotiltic
Los Reyes de Salgado
Paracho
Quiroga
Queseria
Tuxpan
Lago de Pátzcuaro
Morelia
Ciudad Hidalgo
Tecalitlán
Peribán
2774m
Tzintzuntzán
14
Colima
Volcán el Paricutín
Uruapan
Pátzcuaro
A
Tepalcatepec
Pihuamo
B
Tacámbaro
45 D

The Central Highlands

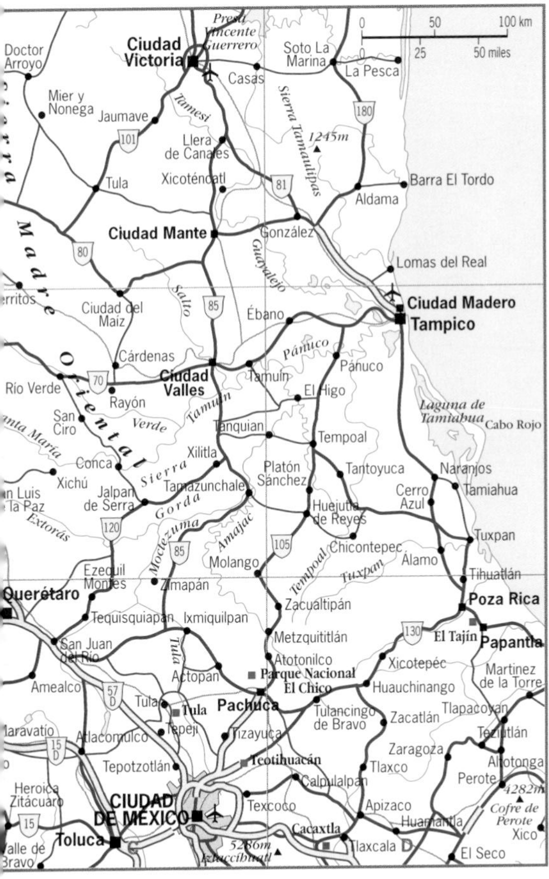

THE CENTRAL HIGHLANDS North-west of Mexico City extends a network of colonial cities, spectacular embodiments of the nation's former wealth. From the high plateau of Zacatecas, the northern plains break up into a series of low ranges sandwiched between the two mountainous spines of Mexico: the Sierra Madre Occidental and the Sierra Madre Oriental, which run down the west and east of the region respectively. In the triangle formed by the historic old towns of San Luis Potosí, Querétaro and Aguascalientes lies the area known as the Bajío, where fertile valleys alternate with arid sierra, source of much of the nation's mineral wealth. To the west the Bajío culminates at Guadalajara, Mexico's second largest city and gateway to the Pacific, while to the south unfold the lush hills of the state of Michoacán. Here, abundant water has created a welcoming habitat that year after year attracts 35 million monarch butterflies. These apparently fragile creatures wing their way over 3,500km to escape Canada's severe winter. Between December and March a walk through the forest sanctuary of Angangueo (off Highway 15 north of Zitacuaro) reveals clouds of brilliant orange butterflies hibernating on fir branches.

Above: once almost a ghost town, Real de Catorce is now being revived by tourism
Previous pages: the Mil Cumbres in the Sierra Madre Occidental National Park

►►► REGION HIGHLIGHTS

HISTORY The Central Highlands were originally inhabited by diverse indigenous peoples who were allied through agricultural needs and trade. No major sites remain which can compare with those found further south, although the Purépechas (later called the Tarascans by the Spanish) are known to have rivalled the Aztecs in power and culture. From their base around Michoacán's Lago de Pátzcuaro they withstood Chichimec attacks from the north and Aztec attempts at domination from the east. Their advanced craft techniques were subsequently nurtured by the enlightened first Spanish bishop of Michoacán, Don Vasco de Quiroga. Most of the other sites in this central region were left by the bellicose Toltecs who, between the 10th and 13th centuries, forged north beyond the state of Zacatecas from their base at Tula. The site of La Quemada reflects their influence and the importance of the turquoise trade. Otomís and Huastecs, the latter a mysterious Maya-linked culture based around the Gulf coast, occupied much of the area when the Spanish arrived in the 16th century.

PRECIOUS METALS Lusting after the gold, silver and gemstones buried in the dry hills, the Spanish wasted little time in establishing a silver route from Zacatecas through Aguascalientes, Guanajuato, San Miguel de Allende, Querétaro and San Juan del Río south to Mexico City. Another branch of the route came from San Luis Potosí, further east. Every one of these towns flourished with the riches pouring out of the deposits and by the late 18th century reached a peak of production, exploitation of indigenous labour and world renown. However, posterity has inherited the benefits in the form of magnificent structures erected as proof of the cities' prosperity. Hand in hand with Spanish colonialism went Catholicism, inspiring ambitious cathedrals, convents, monasteries and gilded chapels.

The area was also the source of the early 19th-century Independence movement. The ball was set rolling in Dolores by the recalcitrant priest Hidalgo, aided by Ignacio Allende, and soon the towns of San Miguel, Guanajuato, San Luis Potosí, Zacatecas and Morelia were drawn into their net. After the leaders' capture, the banner was taken over by José María Morelos, a native of Morelia (then called Valladolid).

NEW FACES Today these colonial cities are rimmed with 20th-century industrial concerns. Textile and shoe factories, plus other light industries have left their urban mark and visitors must fervently believe in the attractions of each city to want to penetrate beyond the barrier of ugly, anarchistic constructions. An exception is Guadalajara, the region's most Americanised city and Mexico's capital of high-tech, whose voracious tentacles spread from a much modernised centre.

Agriculture remains an important economic factor, particularly in the more fertile states of Michoacán, Querétaro and Aguascalientes, while Zacatecas and Guanajuato continue to occupy the top of the nation's table of mineral production. Yet at the heart of these towns lies an awesome choice of monuments, always conveniently laid out around an animated central square, typically called the Plaza de Armas. Some towns are now remarkably preserved with strict conservation regulations, notably Morelia, Guanajuato, San Miguel and Pátzcuaro, and many museums are housed in beautifully restored convents or 18th-century mansions.

PURCHASES
Tarascan traditions have left a wealth of crafts (woodwork, ceramics, embroidery, weaving, papier mâché). These are still practised in the villages near Pátzcuaro, at Uruapan, famed for its lacquerware, and at Santa Clara del Cobre, where gleaming copper pots and vases fill the village. High-quality glass, furniture, pottery and Huichol beadwork and yarn paintings are made in and around Guadalajara, and there is the superbly crafted 'cowboy' leatherwork of Zacatecas. Silver, too, is a favourite purchase although Taxco, south of Mexico City, is the acknowledged capital. The state of Querétaro continues its craft traditions, embodied in wickerwork, but more ostentatiously in jewellery studded with precious and semi-precious stones.

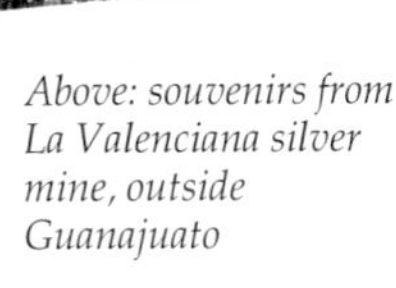

Above: souvenirs from La Valenciana silver mine, outside Guanajuato

Left: rancheros *driving cattle near Paricutín, Michoacán*

Relief of Venustiano Carranza, in Aguascalientes

LOCAL SPECIALITIES
Aguascalientes means 'hot springs' and here visitors can sweat it out in the local mineral pools. The best known and most convenient is the Balneario Ojo Caliente. Further afield is the Balneario Valladolid, about 20km north of town. Both are set in recreational parks. The town is also known for its clothing and textile industry: numerous outlets offer factory-priced goods while *aguítas*, open-work embroidery, can be purchased at the Centro Comercial Plaza Vestir.

GETTING AROUND
Buses between cities in Mexico are frequent and many luxury lines ply the routes, making colonial city-hopping an easy and relatively inexpensive occupation. Bus stations are increasingly being moved to the outskirts of larger cities – in the extreme case of Guadalajara its modern terminals are located over 5km from the city centre.

▶ Aguascalientes *124A2*

'Clear waters, blue skies, good land and good people' is the motto of the city of Aguascalientes, capital of one of Mexico's smallest states and generally considered the geographical centre of Mexico. Constant attacks by hostile Chichimecs delayed Spanish settlement until 1565, when Aguascalientes became a strategic garrison on the silver route from Zacatecas to Mexico City. Discovery of local silver-veins in the 18th century generated new wealth and independent statehood was granted in 1857. It is a booming industrial city, although its prosperity also derives from agriculture, vineyards and cattle ranches in the fertile surrounding plain. The old colonial centre livens up considerably in late April when Mexico's oldest and longest fair, the Fería de San Marcos, draws thousands of visitors – to avoid disappointment, book your hotel well in advance at this time.

Monumental splendour lies in the **Palacio del Gobierno▶▶**, located on the south side of the Plaza Principal, which was begun in 1665 but has been much remodelled since. Built of volcanic rock and pink quarry stone, its elegant courtyard made a fitting residence for the wealthy Rincon Gallardo family. Today its walls are faced with murals by Oswaldo Barra, relating local history. Opposite stands the 18th-century **Catedral de Nuestra Señora de la Asunción▶**, whose religious paintings include major works by Miguel Cabrera. Alongside is the ornate Porfiriato **Teatro Morelos** where the Convention of Aguascalientes failed to reconcile Revolutionary leaders in 1914; and half a block down Carranza is the **Casa de Cultura**. This 17th-century former mansion and convent now hosts numerous cultural activities. More culture is on show at the **Museo Regional de Aguascalientes▶▶** (*Open* Tue–Sun 10.30–5) mainly devoted to the works of native artist Saturnino Herrán, and the **Museo José Guadalupe Posada** (*Open* Tue–Sun 10–2, 5–9) displaying this 19th-century artist's satirical and political prints.

▶▶ Cuitzeo *124B1*

The pretty, rural town of Cuitzeo lies on the shores of a large lake, 34km north of Morelia. Access from the south is across the lake causeway to a promontory where colonial Cuitzeo was founded in 1550 by Augustinian monks. Their beautiful **Monastery of Santa María Magdalena**, profusely decorated by Tarascan artists, is the town's main monument. Apart from this and the 18th-century Franciscan hospital, Cuitzeo presents a harmony of 19th-century architecture. Unfortunately the lake has become severely polluted by waste from Morelia and, like Chapala, is also being choked by water-hyacinths.

▶ Dolores Hidalgo *124B2*

Fifty-four kilometres north-east of Guanajuato lies the town which witnessed the start of the Independence movement. On the Plaza Principal, the **Parroquía▶▶**, an 18th-century building with an impressive Churrigueresque façade, was where the priest Miguel Hidalgo uttered his famous *grito* (cry), inciting the population to rise up against their Spanish rulers. Two museums illustrate the movement: the **Museo de la Independencia Nacional** (*Open* Tue–Sun 10–5) gives statistical and

Dolores Hidalgo, where the church bells rang out for revolution in 1810

The parish church of Our Lady of Sorrows in Dolores Hidalgo is a magnificent example of 18th-century Mexican baroque architecture

documentary information about the conditions, decline and sporadic rebellions of the *indígena* population; the **Museo Casa de Hidalgo** (*Open* Tue–Sat 10–6, Sun 10–5), former home of the national hero, displays personal items and documents. Dolores now thrives on its cheap, colourful ceramics, sold at countless roadside shops.

►► Guadalajara *124A1*

Guadalajara is often unjustly dismissed as a large, overbearingly industrialised city (Mexico's second largest), but in fact it has a compact centre laid out on an easy grid pattern, a refreshing climate, relaxed pace and helpful, though conservative inhabitants. Now promoted as Mexico's Silicon Valley, it is one of the world's leading producers of high-tech electronic goods. With nearly five million inhabitants (and a high proportion of resident Americans), this overtly prosperous, much modernised city is also the source of numerous Mexican traditions – from *mariachis* and tequila to the Mexican Hat Dance.

History The city was founded in 1542 on the site of today's historic centre. For centuries it vegetated, although its position halfway between the central colonial cities and

HIDALGO'S *GRITO*

Miguel Hidalgo's *grito* ('call to arms') was uttered on the evening of 15 September 1810 and inspired the momentous national struggle to throw off the Spanish cloak. Ten months later Father Hidalgo was captured and executed in Chihuahua, thus ending a life of unorthodoxy which included questioning the authority of the Pope and having a mistress. Much influenced by the legacy of Don Vasco de Quiroga, Michoacán's 16th-century bishop, Hidalgo's sympathies lay firmly with the *mestizo* and indigenous population and his leadership of the angry mob of insurgents again set him aside from conformity within the Church.

JOSÉ CLEMENTE OROZCO
Orozco, Guadalajara's most famous 20th-century artist (1883–1949), along with Rivera and Siqueiros, was one of Mexico's *Tres Grandes*, the three pioneers of muralism. Orozco was the most tragic and dramatic, revealing in his monumental works a humane spirit and fierce sense of identification with his times. In the early 1930s he left for the US to escape public criticism of his work and there his great talent was recognised. On his return to Guadalajara he was given major public commissions. His masterpieces are less overtly political, but more emotive than his fellow muralists' work, and are among the city's greatest sights. His former home at Avenida Aceves 27 has been converted into a museum.

Below: Independence Day parade
Far right: Guadalajara's urban facelift camouflages some deeply entrenched traditions

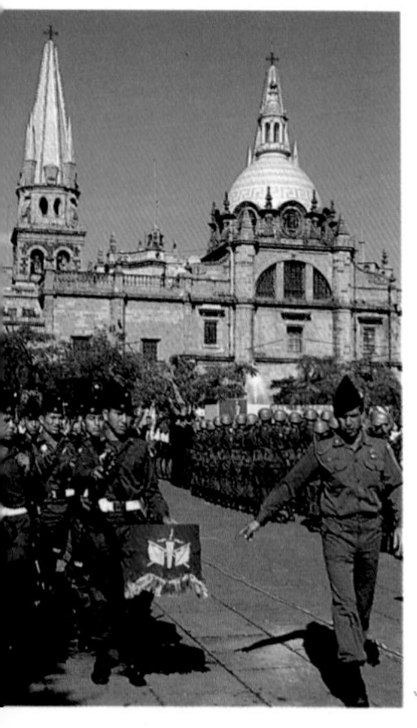

the Pacific port of Manzanillo brought commerce and the whole fertile region became an agricultural hub. It was only in 1920, with the extension of the Southern Pacific Railroad from California to Jalisco, that Guadalajara's fate was sealed. When the railway was sold off to the Mexican government 30 years later, the city was still a quiet provincial town of cobbled streets, but since then it has boomed, integrating its forward-looking industries into a new urban façade. Much of today's wealth stems from its traditionally close links with the US.

Central monuments Guadalajara's historic sites all stand conveniently around the central plazas, four of which surround the cathedral, while the fifth, the Plaza Tapatía, stretches nine blocks east from the Teatro Degollado along a revamped pedestrian esplanade. Immediately visible are the yellow-tiled spires of the **Catedral▶▶**, a massive edifice begun in 1561 but not completed for over 50 years. Toppled by an earthquake in 1818, the spires were rebuilt in Byzantine style, and other architectural influences create a curious amalgam of Gothic, Moorish, Tuscan and Corinthian styles in a baroque wrapping. On the south side is the animated Plaza de Armas, surrounding a Parisian kiosk and flanked by the **Palacio de Gobierno▶▶**, dating from 1643, but considerably altered in the 18th century. Here, in 1810, Hidalgo declared an end to slavery, an event captured by Orozco's powerful staircase murals, which continue in the Sala Jalisco, the legislative chamber on the second floor devoted to portraits of Mexican statesmen and revolutionaries.

To the north of the cathedral, overlooking a rotunda memorial, is the excellent **Museo Regional▶▶▶** (*Open* Tue–Sat 9–7, Sun 9–1.45), housed in a magnificent seminary dating from 1701. The collection covers prehistory and pre-Hispanic eras, while upstairs 17th- and 18th-century paintings include works by Miguel Cabrera and José de Ibarra. Caricatures by Rafael Ponce de León and numerous elements of Jalisco's history and ethnography (Huichol and Cora) complete this wide-ranging museum. Behind the cathedral, the Plaza de la Liberación ends at the neo-classical **Teatro Degollado▶▶**, Guadalajara's cultural pride and joy. The theatre is home to the state symphonic orchestra and also the Grupo Folklórico of the University on Sundays and Thursdays. The gilded, five-tiered interior was inaugurated in 1866 by the celebrated soprano Angela Peralta, watched over by a ceiling mural of Dante's *Inferno*.

From here the Plaza Tapatía stretches east past fountains, sculptures, trees and benches to the impressive **Instituto Cultural Cabañas▶▶▶** (*Open* Tue–Sat 10–6, Sun 10–3), designed by Manuel Tolsa in 1805 as an orphanage. It is now the focal point of the city's cultural activities. The 26 linked, arcaded patios planted with grapefruit trees create a harmonious backdrop to Orozco's masterpiece, the 1930s mural *Man of Fire*, painted on the chapel's central dome. Symbolic representations of air, water and earth surround a central figure of fire and damnation, while other panels depict the sufferings brought by the Spanish Conquest. The museum here exhibits over 100 works by Orozco, a native of the city, as well as temporary exhibitions of contemporary art.

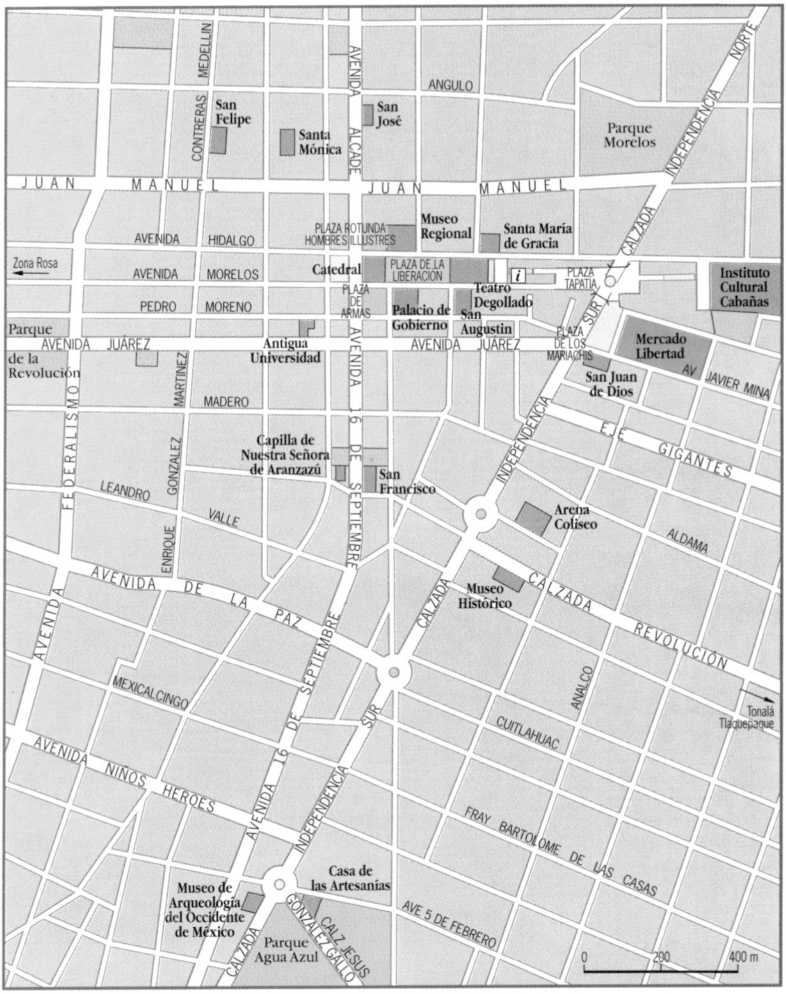

Medellin
Avenida Alcade
Angulo
Independencia Norte
Contreras
San Felipe
Santa Mónica
San José
Parque Morelos
Juan Manuel
Juan Manuel
Calzada
Plaza Rotunda Hombres Illustres
Museo Regional
Santa María de Gracia
Avenida Hidalgo
Zona Rosa
Avenida Morelos
Catedral
Plaza de la Liberacion
i
Plaza Tapatia
Instituto Cultural Cabañas
Plaza de Armas
Teatro Degollado
Pedro Moreno
Palacio de Gobierno
San Augustin
Sur
Parque de la Revolución
Avenida Juárez
Antigua Universidad
Avenida Juárez
Plaza de los Mariachis
Mercado Libertad
Av Javier Mina
San Juan de Dios
Martinez
Madero
Federalismo
Avenida 16 de Septiembre
Independencia
Eje Gigantes
Capilla de Nuestra Señora de Aranzazú
San Francisco
Gonzalez
Leandro Valle
Enrique
Arena Coliseo
Aldama
Avenida de la Paz
Museo Histórico
Calzada Revolución
Avenida
Calzada
Mexicalcingo
Analco
Tonalá Tlaquepaque
Avenida 16 de Septiembre
Sur
Cuitlahuac
Avenida Niños Heroes
Independencia
Fray Bartolome de las Casas
Casa de las Artesanías
Museo de Arqueología del Occidente de México
Ave 5 de Febrero
Gonzalez Gallo
Calz Jesus
Parque Agua Azul
Calzada
0 200 400 m

Restaurant at Tlaquepaque's El Parián

South of the centre Immediately south of the Instituto Cultural Cabañas lie two monuments to Guadalajara's deeply-rooted traditions: the **Mercado Libertad▶▶** and the **Plaza de los Mariachis▶▶**. The former, a gigantic market, occupies four city blocks and claims to be the largest in the Western hemisphere. Shoes, belts, guitars, chairs, hats, pottery and onyx as well as fruit, fish, meat and vegetables are hawked in this multi-storeyed edifice by aggressive vendors. One street south, beside a small church, is the pedestrian alleyway of the *mariachis* (see page 138), where sidewalk cafés and restaurants spill outside and the city's musicians gather late into the evening.

Several blocks south of the cathedral, down Avenida 16 de Septiembre, stand two churches, relics of a Franciscan monastery destroyed during the Reform period. To the east the **Templo de San Francisco▶** has a wonderful

Shoes for sale at the huge Mercado Libertad

Plateresque façade. Across the street, the more severe mid-18th-century **Capilla de Nuestra Señora de Aranzazú▶▶▶** surprises with its two magnificent Churrigueresque altars and impressive ceiling and wall paintings.

Further south on the same street, at the junction with Calzada Independencia, is the city park, **Parque Agua Azul▶**, fronted by a stark modern entrance and offering plenty of recreational escape for children. The **Museo de Arqueología del Occidente de México▶** (*Open* Mon–Fri 10–2, 4–6, Sat–Sun 11–2.30) opposite the entrance, contains a display of pre-Hispanic artefacts from the western states, while on the northern side the up-market **Casa de las Artesanías▶** sells a wide selection of high-quality local craftwork. Children especially enjoy the **Parque Huentitan** and its zoo (*Open* Tue–Sun 10–6), near the spectacular **Barranca de Oblatos**, about 11km north of the centre.

Tlaquepaque and Tonalá Guadalajara's urban sprawl now engulfs the villages of Tlaquepaque and Tonalá, both

TEQUILA
Fifty kilometres west of Guadalajara, on Highway 15, lies the small town of Tequila, Mexico's main tequila-producing area (see page 217). This industry has functioned since the 18th century. Fields of *agave tequilana*, a spiky-leafed succulent of the maguey family, surround the town where many familiar brands are distilled. The two largest distilleries, Sauza and Cuervo, offer tours and sampling: the Sauza plant contains a striking mural by Gabriel Flores illustrating early production methods.

easily reached by bus from the centre. Although it is definitely geared to foreign purses, **Tlaquepaque▶▶** makes a picturesque outing. Its elegant 19th-century mansions, which were once summer retreats for wealthy *tapatíos* (Guadalajarans), have been converted into craft boutiques or restaurants. The village atmosphere centres around the **Jardín Hidalgo** and adjoining **El Parián▶▶▶**, an arcaded structure dating from 1878 but remodelled in 1978. Its shady courtyard is where Guadalajarans and visitors gather for protracted weekend lunches to the tunes of the ubiquitous *mariachis*. Meanwhile, the surrounding pedestrian streets have an endless and eclectic display of jewellery, glass, leatherwork, ceramics and antique furniture – the best that you will see in Mexico. The **Museo Regional de Cerámica y los Artes Populares▶▶** (at Independencia 237) displays fine Huichol embroidery, ceramics by contemporary potters and Jaliscan folk art in a pretty, old building.

A few kilometres south-east lies **Tonalá▶**, a less pretentious village where many of the craft workshops and factories are to be found, particularly for stoneware pottery and glass. The **Museo Nacional de la Cerámica▶** is here at Constitución 110. Tonalá is best visited on Thursday or Sunday, when a huge market invades the streets. There are superb views over the city and plains of Jalisco from the 2,500m **Cerro de la Reina**, site of a historic battle between Tonaltecan rebels and the pernicious *conquistador* Nuño de Guzmán.

▶▶ Guadalupe *124A3*

In a little village 7km east of Zacatecas stands one of Mexico's most remarkable religious museums, the **Convento de Guadalupe▶▶▶** (*Open* Tue–Sun 10–5), founded in 1707 as a Franciscan seminary. The ornately gilded pink interior of the church is best viewed from the elevated choir, reached through the labyrinthine museum. Paintings and furniture collected from churches throughout the state of Zacatecas form a treasure-trove of 17th- to 19th-century religious images and artefacts, superbly displayed within the monasterial stone structure. In an adjoining building, the **Museo Regional** displays an extraordinary collection of early modes of transport, from old stage-coaches and carts to a 1930 Cadillac convertible.

ZONA ROSA

Modern and prosperous Guadalajara is best experienced in the area west of the centre, which starts at Avenida Chapultepec, often known as the Zona Rosa. Wide, leafy streets are lined with chic shops and restaurants and the overall feel is more American than Mexican. The Plaza del Sol is the largest of the city's many shopping centres and is crowned by a giant hotel, its latest addition being a glass pyramid for special events.

CANYON

Escape the 20th century by going 10km north of the city, up Calzada Independencia, to the Cañon Oblatos, a 600m gorge cut by the Santiago and Verde rivers. Panoramic views from the rim stretch endlessly over the surrounding landscape. Nearby is Parque Natural Huentitán, where an open zoo houses monkeys, elephants and giraffes alongside the colourful animal sculptures of local artist Sergio Bustamante. Other offerings include a planetarium, a science and technology centre, an aviary and a snake-house.

Government Palace

Guanajuato, once the richest city in the land

HIDDEN PLAZAS
The town's first public garden, the Jardín de la Unión, was laid out in 1861 and is the focus of evening action, but there are countless other pretty plazas tucked away in the maze. The Plazuela de San Fernando, just north of Juárez, has a spirit typical of the town and is lined with bookshops, small restaurants and some craft shops. A winding alley to the west leads to the Plaza de San Roque, dominated by a 17th-century church. Both plazas are used during the October Festival Cervantino for outdoor performances. More formal is the nearby Jardín de la Reforma, with its neo-classical columns and arched stairs opening on to Juárez.

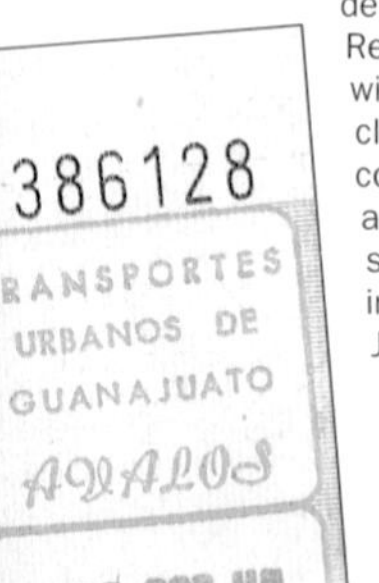

▶▶▶ Guanajuato *124B2*

The charm and beauty of Guanajuato lie as much in individual monuments as in the overall harmony and liveliness of the city. This mosaic of brightly coloured houses sprawls over a narrow valley rimmed by mountains – its Tarascan name means 'mountainous place of frogs'. Frogs are now thin on the ground, but Guanajuato is firmly placed on the national calendar for its October arts festival, the **Festival Cervantino**. This lively university town, riddled with underground tunnels, overground *callejónes* (alleys), pretty plazas and charming hotels, is central Mexico's most seductive and stimulating destination.

Background Though Guanajuato was sparsely settled by Chichimecs in the early 16th century, by 1554 the area's rich silver veins had been discovered and Real Minas de Guanajuato was founded. Barons flourished and the indigenous people suffered. However, in 1810 Miguel Hidalgo's call for Independence at nearby Dolores led to the famous battle in Guanajuato when the Alhóndiga (granary) was captured by Hidalgo's forces, greatly aided by local citizens. Retaliation by the Spanish was ferocious: after reconquering the town they held a lottery, randomly choosing citizens to be tortured and hanged. Redistribution of wealth after Independence led to the erection of many of Guanajuato's elegant mansions, but violence reappeared during the Revolution and in religious conflicts between 1927 and 1946. Since 1945, when the University was founded, the town has regained peace and prosperity, further stimulated by the Festival Cervantino, which began in 1972. In 1988, Guanajuato was declared part of Unesco's world cultural heritage.

Layout The tunnels that carry heavy traffic beneath the centre are confusing to some, but an essential element in Guanajuato's uniqueness. Although their stone arches, vaulted ceilings and winding steps appear straight out of the Middle Ages, they actually date from 1883–1908, when these former rivers were flooded, and have been sporadically extended up until 1970. Above ground two main arteries, Pocitos and Juárez, preserve visitors from

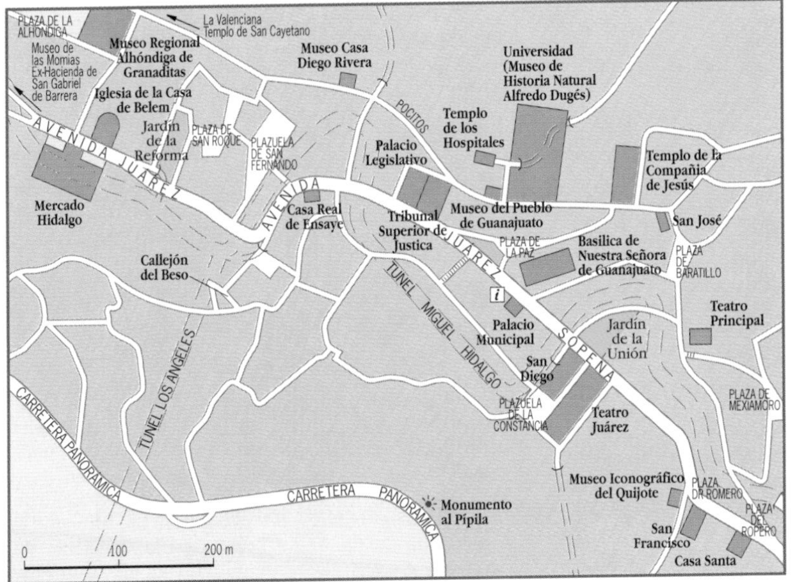

this subterranean purgatory, and their slopes, twists, plazas and branches add to the urban quaintness. Most of the main sights lie along these roads, while to the north and south is a maze of steep, picturesque *callejónes*: the narrowest was romantically named the **Callejón del Beso** (Alley of the Kiss) as courting couples could actually kiss from their opposing balconies.

Sights Between Juárez and Pocitos stands the forbidding **Museo Regional Alhóndiga de Granaditas▶▶** (*Open* Tue–Sat 10–2, 4–6, Sun 10–3.30), built as a grain warehouse in the late 18th century, used as a fortress in 1810 and subsequently the macabre showcase for the heads of

The striking baroque Basilica of Our Lady of Guanajuato

AL PIPILA
Standing high on a hilltop south of town on the Carretera Panoramica is a monument dedicated to José de los Reyes Martínez, 'Al Pípila', the miner who burnt the doors of the Alhóndiga for Hidalgo's forces but died in the process. The pink-stone statue can be climbed and offers fabulous views over the city. The easiest means of access is by bus (marked 'Pípila') running west along Juárez, but don't miss the twisting downhill walk back.

the captured rebels. The hooks from which they were suspended can still be seen, but the fortress has since been converted from a prison into a museum of Guanajuato's archaeology, ethnography, mines and history, and displays Chávez Morado's mural of the struggle for Independence.

High up on the Carretera Panoramica stands another of Guanajuato's highlights, the **Museo de las Momias▶▶** (*Open* daily 9–6). This decidedly gruesome museum exhibits 117 mummified bodies excavated from the local cemetry whose mineral-rich soil preserved them so well. Propped up in glass cases which line the tunnels beneath the cemetery, some mummies still wear their boots, others their ragged suits, while child mummies are dressed up like dolls and a mummified foetus is proudly displayed as 'the world's smallest'.

South of the Alhóndiga, along Juárez, stands the enormous cast-iron 1910 **Mercado Hidalgo**, selling crafts upstairs and produce downstairs. The main road continues east past the 17th-century **basilica▶**, a sober construction whose main interest lies in a jewel-encrusted Spanish statue of the Virgin Mary, said to date from the 7th century. Far more impressive is the **Templo de la Compañia de Jesus▶▶▶**, which lies behind and uphill from the basilica, next to the University. Built in 1746, its pink-stone façade is one of Mexico's outstanding examples of Churrigueresque exuberance and is surmounted by a

Below: statue of Peace, Plaza de la Paz
Right: the pink-stone Templo de la Compañía (Jesuit church) is a jewel of Churrigueresque architecture

19th-century neo-classical cupola. The restored interior displays paintings by Miguel Cabrera, the prodigious 18th-century artist.

To the west looms the grandiose, crenellated façade of the **University**, completely remodelled in 1955 from a 16th-century Jesuit college. On the top floor is the **Museo de Historia Natural Alfredo Dugés▶** (*Open* weekdays only). To the left of the main entrance is Guanajuato's first parish church, the **Templo de los Hospitales** (1560–5). Opposite the University, at Pocitos 7, the **Museo del Pueblo de Guanajuato▶▶** (*Open* Tue–Sat 10–2, 4–7, Sun 10–2) is housed in a lovely 17th-century mansion where mainly colonial paintings are displayed. Further west along Pocitos, at No 46, is the **Museo Casa Diego Rivera▶** (*Open* Tue–Sat 10–2, 4–7, Sun 10–3), where the painter was born in 1886, and which now displays his family's belongings alongside a few paintings and sketches.

Guanajuato's soul lies in the **Jardín de la Unión▶▶▶**, a small, shady plaza lined with hotels, bars and restaurants and fronted by a magnificent church and the Teatro Juárez. The original **Templo de San Diego▶▶** was damaged by a flood in the late 18th century and rebuilt in ornate baroque style, in contrast to the adjacent **Teatro Juárez▶▶▶** (*Open* Tue–Sun 9–1.45, 5–7.45), begun in 1873 and inaugurated by President Porfirio Díaz in 1903. Its superbly crafted, Moorish-inspired interior, incorporating elaborate art-nouveau touches, makes a fitting memorial to the excesses of that epoch. Further along Sopena is the **Museo Iconografico de Quijote** (*Open* Tue–Sat 10–6.30), displaying images of Cervantes' legendary hero, Don Quixote.

Out of town An integral part of Guanajuato's history and beauty lies 5km north along the winding panoramic highway at **La Valenciana**. By the time this mine was registered in 1770, it was producing 25 per cent of the Americas' silver. After several closures it reopened in 1968 as a co-operative. Visitors can walk around the site but the mine-shaft is strictly off-limits. On the main road stands the exquisite **Templo de San Cayetano▶▶** (*Open* Tue–Sun 9.30–6.30), erected in 1775 by the Count of Valenciana and another outstanding showcase of Churrigueresque design and detail. The high-relief gold altars are masterpieces of this style, while the sacristy, completed in 1788, contains some fine original furnishings.

The immense private wealth generated by Guanajuato's mines is exemplified in the **Ex-Hacienda de San Gabriel de Barrera▶▶** (*Open* daily 9–6), a museum and park that lies a few kilometres west of the town on the main road to Irapuato. This late 17th-century *hacienda* belonged to Captain Gabriel de Barrera, who used the extensive grounds for processing the precious ores. It is now completely re-landscaped into a delightful patchwork of garden styles (Roman, English, Oriental, Arab, Italian and French). The beautifully restored mansion displays 17th- to 19th-century furniture and *objets d'art* from France, Spain and England and has a small crafts shop.

LAS CALLEJONEADAS

Take a seat in the Jardín de la Unión at nightfall for a free show of Guanajuato's typically provincial vibrancy.
By 8pm flower-sellers, *mariachis* and children are replaced by high-spirited students perpetuating a tradition which dates from 1963. Following the rediscovery of student songs of Spanish origin, a vociferous procession (*callejóneada*) now takes place daily, led by the younger generation. The route winds through narrow *callejónes* (passageways) south of the Jardín, pausing in the Callejón del Beso, and finally culminates in the Plazuela de los Angeles two hours later; songs and wine accompany students and visitors all the way.

Sit in any self-respecting Mexican restaurant and you will be assailed by the brass and string sounds of a sombrero-hatted mariachi *band. Hard to ignore, these musicians are part of a well-entrenched and much-loved tradition that expresses the Mexican soul in melodramatic odes to love and death for the sake of honour.*

MARIACHI HAUNTS
Apart from Mexico City's Plaza Garibaldi, Guadalajara is the best place to experience top-quality interpretations by these traditional musicians. From the classic rendezvous of the Plaza de los Mariachis to the chic restaurants west of the city centre, you may encounter local figures such as Machete, Bigotes (moustache) or Pato (duck) plucking, blowing and vocalising Jaliscan emotions. However, this once male bastion is now being encroached upon by women: watch out for Las Perlitas Tapatías (Guadalajara's Little Pearls) or, in Mexico City, track down the pastiche cabaret act of Astrid Hadad, Mexico's answer to Madonna.

The state of Jalisco is the birthplace of the *mariachi* tradition. Accepted legend has it that these troubadour bands first became popular in the mid-19th century during the brief reign of Emperor Maximilian. He had them play at marriage feasts in Mexico City's Chapultepec Castle. The name *mariachi* is thus said to derive from the French word *mariage*. However, another, more convincing theory contends that the tradition existed well before then and that the word derives from a Cocula word for 'tree', which described the platform the musicians played on.

Whatever its origins, the roving minstrel practice has successfuly taken root all over the country: double-basses disappear over the brow of a sierra, guitars are packed into buses and trumpets flash at a lakeside jetty as the *mariachi* groups travel from one gig to the next. As the sun sets, town *zócalos* (main squares) are monopolised by figures in uniformed finery inspired by *charros* (Mexican cowboys): felt hat, high-waisted jacket, white shirt, embroidered belt, gilt or silver chains and trims – a distant cousin of Spain's flamenco costume. When café or restaurant customers finally rise to the occasion and demand their favourite lament, these slick musicians embark on a rousing repertoire of *ranchera* music in which love, death and destruction, suffering, alcohol and defeat assume uniquely Mexican proportions.

The basic instruments are the *guitarrón* (a domed bass guitar), the *vihuela* (small treble guitar), violins, trumpets and regional instruments, which in Veracruz include the *marimba* (wooden xylophone). The sign of a truly inspiring *mariachi* band is when the participating customers end the evening in empathetic tears ...

Mariachi *music originated in the state of Jalisco and now resounds all over Mexico*

► Lagos de Moreno *124B2*

This rarely visited, peaceful riverside colonial town lies 82km south-east of Aguascalientes on a major highway crossroads. Its pretty streets climb up the hillside, culminating at the summit with a monastery and superb views over the green hills of Jalisco. A few small hotels and restaurants are inevitably clustered around the *zócalo*, as are the historical sights. These include the baroque **Iglesia de Santa María de los Lagos**, the turn-of-the-century **Teatro Rosas Moreno** and the **Convento de Capuchinas**, now converted into a museum.

►► Laguna de Chapala *124A1*

At certain points over 30km wide and almost 100km long, Laguna de Chapala is Mexico's largest lake, situated 48km south-east of Guadalajara. The temperate climate (it lies at an altitude of 1,524m) and beautiful, mountain-circled setting lured many a wealthy Mexican earlier this century, including Porfirio Díaz, who built his summer residence there, and it has since been discovered by North American artists, writers and retirees, now numbering over 6,000. Another invasion is that of water hyacinths: along with consequent silt build-up and toxic waste, they bode ill for the lake's aquatic life. Three main towns lie along its northern shore: **Chapala**, an expatriate focal point which still boasts some grandiose turn-of-the century mansions and an old railway station, now being converted into a museum. **Ajijic** with an emphasis on arts and crafts, and **Jocotepec** is home to the 1529 Church of Señor del Monte. Boat trips visit the two islands of **Los Alacranes** and **Mexcala**, the former thick with willows, *tabachines* (orange-flowered trees) and the lake's most scenic fish restaurant.

LITERARY CHAPALA
Two celebrated authors inspire today's Chapalan pen-pushers: D H Lawrence and Sybille Bedford. It was in Chapala in the early 1920s that Lawrence wrote the first draft of his novel *The Plumed Serpent*, while comfortably housed in a villa on Calle Zaragoza. This has now been converted into a pricey hotel, the Quetzlcóatl Inn. Much of Sybille Bedford's inspired travelogue, *A Visit to Don Octavio*, is set on the shores of Lake Chapala, where she stayed in the early 1950s. Her descriptions of the area, and its expatriate and local personalities, make a colourful, penetrating and amusing read.

Boats for hire (above) and fine copperware for sale, Lake Chapala

► La Quemada *124A3*

The ruins of La Quemada, also called Chicomoztoc (Place of the Seven Caves), lie 40km south of Zacatecas. This impressive hilltop fortification rising out of the cacti-strewn sierra was probably erected to guard against Chichimec invasions, and was one of the most northern outposts of civilisation during Toltec times (roughly 10th to 13th century). Platform pyramids and walled courts occupy the summit, and outside the walls, on the lower slopes, the ceremonial centre contains a small pyramid and remains of a colonnaded hall.

▶▶▶ Morelia 124B1

Aristocratic Morelia, capital of the undulating and fertile state of Michoacán, lies 311km west of Mexico City. It was founded in 1541 under the name of Valladolid, and attracted many families of the Spanish nobility. At Independence its name was changed to Morelia in honour of Morelos, a native son and key figure in the movement. This dynamic, yet compact university town of half a million inhabitants was declared a historical monument by Unesco and it takes this dual role very seriously, restoring and maintaining the homogenous centre while keeping cultural activities alive and visitors happy.

In and around the *zócalo* Pride of the central Plaza de Armas is the massive pink-stone **Catedral▶▶▶**, said to be the third largest in Latin America. It was begun in 1640 but not completed till 1744. The baroque twin towers and tiled dome surmount a neo-classical interior whose main features are a monumental German organ consisting of 4,600 pipes, an ornate silver altarpiece and a much revered cornpaste Christ (see panel, page 143). Eighteenth-century arcades and imposing colonial buildings surround the buzzing plaza, the north side being a favourite for outdoor cafés. The **Palacio de Gobierno▶▶** is worth entering for its grandiose courtyard and gallery murals. Further east along Avenida Madero stands the baroque masterpiece, the **Templo de las Monjas▶▶** (1729–37). In the south-western corner of the plaza is the **Museo Regional Michoacano▶▶▶** (*Open* Tue–Sat 9–7, Sun 9–2), founded in 1886 and housed in a magnificent mansion. The extensive collection covers geology, archaeology, Tarascan ethnography and colonial history and contains some rarities: look out for the Mayan *chacmool* (a reclining statue on which sacrifical offerings were laid) found at Ihuatzio on Lake Pátzcuaro. Flanking the western end of the *zócalo* is another baroque mansion, the **Hotel Virrey de Mendoza▶**.

North-west of the Plaza de Armas lie more rich historical finds. First along Madero is Mexico's oldest college, the **Colegio de San Nicolás▶**, founded in 1540 in Pátzcuaro but later transferred to Morelia. Former students include Morelos and Hidalgo, whose statue dominates the patio, while the heart of another Mexican hero, Melchor Ocampo, is preserved in a memorial room upstairs. On the corner of Nigromante, the **Palacio Clavijero▶▶▶** is a superbly proportioned construction with a large, elegant patio. It was built in 1660, and originally functioned as a Jesuit school; it has since been converted into municipal offices which include the tourist office and a library.

Converted convents One block down Nigromante lies Morelia's oldest building, the **Templo de las Rosas▶▶** (1590), which adjoins a former convent, now a music academy. North-west of here stands another ecclesiastical conversion, the **Ex-Convento del Carmen▶▶**, built in 1596 but extended in the 17th and 18th centuries. It now functions as the **Casa de la Cultura**, a lively centre for arts workshops and performances, and also houses the **Museo de la Máscara** (*Open* daily), with

THE AQUEDUCT AND TARASCAN SPECIALITIES

Almost 2km of arched stone aqueduct runs from the eastern end of Avenida Morelos, beyond the Bosque Cuauhtémoc, the city park. Built between 1785 and 1789 to supply water to the expanding city, its 253 arches are now superbly illuminated at night. Marking the beginning of the aqueduct is the Fuente Tarasca, a not-so-splendid 1960s fountain with sculptures of bare-breasted Tarascan maidens holding a platter of Michoacán fruits. Crystallized versions of these fruits (*cubitos de ate*) can be sampled at the Mercado de Dulces (Candy Market), an elevated market area which flanks the western side of the Palacio Clavijero. Made from guava, coconut or quince and cooked with milk, these *dulces* (sweets) are an integral part of Morelia's fame.

Morelia's pink-stone cathedral overlooks the main square

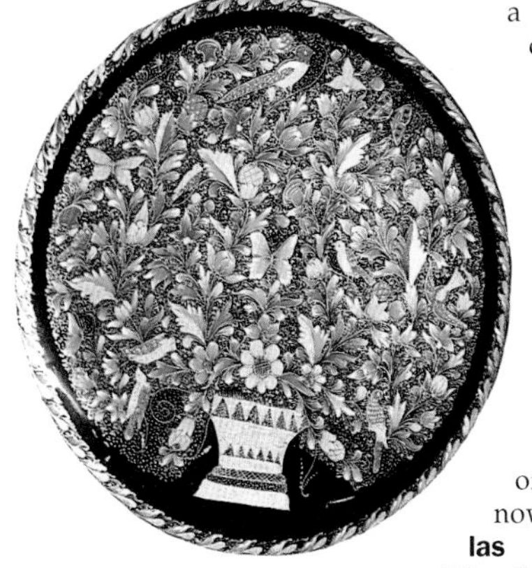

Left: a fine example of Michoacán craftsmanship

a small but choice display of regional masks. Even Morelia's bus station once echoed with the footsteps of Carmelite nuns, but a more inspiring conversion is the former convent of San Francisco, now the **Casa de las Artesanías**►►. The cloisters, cells and arcades are now invaded by traders of Michoacán's richly diverse handicrafts. Demonstrations of craft techniques can be seen in the upstairs rooms. It lies due east of the *zócalo* on Plaza Valladolid. A few blocks east is the **aquaduct** (see panel).

JOSÉ MARIA MORELOS
Like Hidalgo, Morelos was an enlightened, active priest and rapidly assumed leadership of the Independence movement after Hidalgo's execution in 1811. Born in a house on the street of Corregidora in 1765, Morelos later bought a residence one block east, where he lived from 1801. He too succumbed to government forces and in 1815 was executed. Both houses have been converted into museums of memorabilia devoted to this priestly freedom fighter.

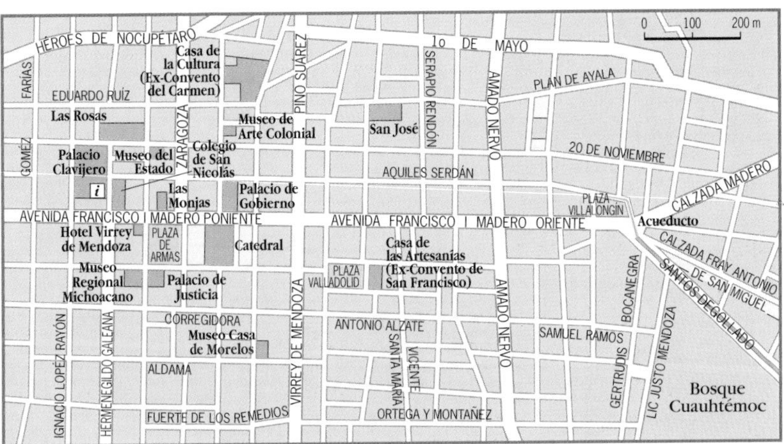

The island of Janitzío rises up sharply from the middle of Lake Pátzcuaro

QUIROGA AND UTOPIA
Quiroga, the most visionary of all the first Spanish settlers, was sent by the colonial government to straighten out the havoc wrought in the area by the merciless *conquistador*, Nuño de Guzmán, whose massacres and slavery had shattered the Purépechan kingdom. From his first base in Tzintzuntzán, Quiroga moved to Pátzcuaro in 1540. From here he worked incessantly to establish models of egalitarian communities, directly based upon the philosophy of his English contemporary, Thomas More, outlined in his book *Utopia* (1516). He built hospitals and schools and travelled from village to village inspiring trades and crafts, converting rapidly as he went. Today, the devout descendants of the Tarascans are amongst Mexico's most talented crafts people.

▶▶▶ Pátzcuaro *124B1*

The town of Pátzcuaro lies at an altitude of 2,130m, just over 60km west of Morelia in the heart of Michoacán. It is set in a pastoral region of lakes and pine forests where wood-smoke fills the air and quaint cobbled streets wind uphill from the scenic lake lying at its feet. The Purépechas (later called Tarascans) appeared in the area in the early 14th century and still flourish, partly thanks to the enlightened policies of Michoacán's first bishop, Don Vasco de Quiroga, who established the state capital in Pátzcuaro in 1540. They remain faithful to traditional costumes and crafts, and their presence in and around the town gives it a unique atmosphere which, combined with its architectural harmony, makes Pátzcuaro a fascinating living crossroads of the two cultures.

Around Plaza Vasco de Quiroga Two plazas constitute the core of the town. The grander of the two, the arcaded **Plaza Vasco de Quiroga**, is flanked by stately 18th-century mansions, many of which have been converted into hotels, restaurants and craft shops. The streets east of here wind uphill to the heart of Pátzcuaro, located along Calle Enseñanza. On the corner of Alcantarilla is the delightful **Museo de Artes Populares▶▶▶** (Museum of Folk Art, *Open* Tue–Sun 9–6), housed in the former Colegio de San Nicolás, founded by Don Vasco in 1540. Local pottery, masks, textiles, straw figures, lacquerware, copper and *ex-votos* (votive offerings) are beautifully displayed in this ecclesiastical setting, surrounding a verdant patio. Towering across the street is the once-Jesuit **Templo de la Compañia▶** (1540), Pátzcuaro's first basilica which, although modified with baroque elements, has kept its simple, barrel-vaulted ceiling. The massive adjoining hospital has been converted into a cultural centre. Buried under the church foundations is a Tarascan pyramid similar to that of Tzintzuntzán. Immediately opposite stands the walled church of **El Sagrario**. A livelier destination

Weaving in the House of Eleven Patios

The pace of life is slow in Pátzcuaro

tucked away down a nameless side street is the **Casa de los Once Patios▶** (House of the Eleven Patios), a former Dominican convent (1745) which is now home to a plethora of small craft shops. One block north on Enseñanza stands the **Basilica de Nuestra Señora de la Salud▶▶**, started in 1554 but rebuilt in 1883 after countless catastrophes. It contains Don Vasco's mausoleum and the more celebrated cornpaste image of the **Virgen de la Salud** (Virgin of Health), made for their bishop by local Tarascans and a miraculous survivor of the basilica's fires. The church plaza comes alive on the eighth day of every month when pilgrims flock to the church to make healing requests, although any service here is striking for the fervour of the Tarascan worshippers.

Around Plaza Gertrudis Bocanegra The smaller but livelier **Plaza Gertrudis Bocanegra** (named for a heroine and martyr of the Independence movement) lies one block north of the main square and is where the town's shoeshiners, *colectivo* buses, street vendors and cheaper hotels are clustered. Dominating the northern end is the **Biblioteca Bocanegra▶**, which occupies the former church of San Agustín. Next door stands the **Teatro Emperador Caltzontzín**, a former convent, while immediately to the west a lively market area full of stalls selling *serapes* (blankets), hats and food extends towards the **Santuario de Guadalupe** (1833). In the evening the plaza end of the market is transformed by gas-lit stands where local specialities are dished up to a colourful crowd of diners.

Down to the lake From Plaza Gertrudis Bocanegra streets of whitewashed houses with red-tiled roofs run downhill to the main highway, railway and Lago de Pátzcuaro beyond. Boats leave the main *embarcadero* (landing place) for **Janitzío▶▶**, a picturesque, though commercialised, pilgrimage island crowned by a giant statue of Morelos, which commands fabulous views over the lake. Fishermen with their famous butterfly nets trawl the tranquil waters and their freshwater catch can be sampled at countless restaurants along the jetty or on Janitzío itself. Boats to smaller, less visited islands leave from the Embarcadero San Pedro, to the west of the main jetty down a side road.

CORNPASTE SCULPTURES

Even before the Spanish arrived, the Tarascans were making figures of their idols out of a special paste, *pasta de caña*. This modelling paste was made from the ground kernels of sweetcorn mixed with gum derived from a type of orchid. With Franciscan approval of the substance and technique, it was used to create images of Christ and the Virgin, which are found in several Michoacán churches. Most famous and revered is that of the Virgin of Health in Pátzcuaro's Basilica: her miraculous powers have even been credited with the figure's expansion, though this is due, more prosaically, to temperature changes.

Of the many religious festivals that punctuate the Mexican calendar, the Día de los Muertos *(Day of the Dead) is the most spectacular and closest to the indigenous spirit. Celebrated throughout the country on 1 and 2 November, it is the focus for extremes of artisan imagination as well as nocturnal spectacles of moving ritual.*

AZTEC POEM
We only come to dream,
We only come to sleep;
It is not true, it is not true
That we come to live on Earth.

Where are we to go from here?
We came here only to be born,
As our home is beyond,
Where the fleshless abide.

Does anyone really live on Earth?
The Earth is not forever,
But just to remain for a short while.

Symbols of the Day of the Dead adorning a street lamp

All Saints' Day is the moment when the whole of Mexico plunges into a unique celebration of death, the culmination of weeks of preparation in order to communicate with departed family members. Not only does it reinforce the family bonds, it also strengthens community relationships, while the placing of offerings on family altars continues a tradition that dates from pre-Hispanic times. Whether at Mixquic or Milpa Alta (Valley of Mexico), Iguala (Guerrero), Lago de Pátzcuaro or the mountains of Oaxaca, the Day of the Dead is a highly charged occasion which reveals the depths of the Mexicans' spirituality and their ambivalent relationship with death.

Death During their rule, the Aztecs were known as the 'people of death', believing that after a fleeting encounter with life, man entered the realm of nine underworlds in the infinite cycle of the cosmic process. Two months of the year were dedicated to worshipping the dead – one for departed children and the other for adults; the latter included massive human sacrifices associated with the god Huitzilopóchtli. Five centuries later the fusion of this tradition with Catholic teachings can be seen in symbolic sugar skulls (relics of pre-Hispanic *tzompantli* or skull-racks), bread-rolls shaped like human bones (*pan de los muertos*) and grotesque papier-mâché skeletons.

Preparations In the preceding weeks craftsmen achieve heights of fantasy making elaborate altars for private homes, while bakers and confectioners create miniature candy coffins and animals. Market places spill over with inventive goods and food (particularly in the Valley of Mexico and adjoining states), from decorative candles of all sizes and shapes and wreaths of fresh and plastic flowers to candlesticks, incense-burners, pots and sugar *calaveras* (skulls). Households are cleaned from top to bottom and women prepare traditional dishes to be placed on the altar: *mole* (Puebla's celebrated sauce), desserts, *tamales* and, of course, *calaveras*. Personalised offerings can include cigarettes, a glass of tequila, clothes, hats or anything related to the occupation of the departed – from an ear of corn to a plough or machete. All depends on regional customs as much as the tastes of the dead person.

Celebrations To ensure that the departed find their way from the cemetery, flower petals are strewn along the path leading to the family altar, where the souls of the dead will feed on the aromas from the offerings and enjoy their

favourite music. Church bells start tolling on the evening of 31 October to announce the visit of child spirits and continue throughout the next day to herald the arrival of the adult souls, for whom the altar is rearranged. In some areas *calaverear* (door-to-door chanting and praying for the souls that nobody remembers) is carried out in the evening. The family's offerings are then collected up and consumed in the church itself. However, American Hallowe'en traditions are fast replacing this old custom.

On 1 and 2 November there are nocturnal family pilgrimages to cemeteries where candles are lit, food offerings made, pictures of saints installed and wreaths laid. This is also an occasion for picnicking, heightened by the ritual consumption of *pulque* (maguey beer). The Day of the Dead culminates with visits to relatives to distribute offerings, interspersed with welcome glasses of *mezcal* or tequila.

DEAD SPECIALS
The famous Day of the Dead celebrations around Lago de Pátzcuaro now draw hundreds of visitors. From sunset on 1 November, Tarascan celebrants from lakeside villages canoe across the dark waters to the island of Janitzío, where candle-lit processions, accompanied by chanting and dancing, lead to the cemetery. The all-night cemetery vigil is now out of bounds to tourists to preserve a necessary intimacy, but other ceremonies can be observed at the nearby pyramid site of Tzintzuntzán. At the village of Mixquic (some 50km from Mexico City), rituals involve masked dances and processions to the cemetery: the skeleton assumes a high profile here.

Some of Mexico's greatest art celebrates death. Papier-mâché skeletons like this one are produced by the thousand for the Day of the Dead

LA CORREGIDORA
Querétaro's indisputable heroine, Doña Josefa Ortíz de Domínguez (*La Corregidora*), wife of the royal governor (*el corregidor*), is widely commemorated in the city. Her statue crowns a semi-circular square bearing her name at the northern corner of the pedestrian zone and the Palacio de Gobierno is often referred to as the Casa de la Corregidora. She saved the lives of the insurgent plotters who often met secretly at her home. When her husband learned of her involvement, he locked her in a room of their house but she managed to get a message out through a keyhole, saving the revolutionaries from imminent discovery. Immediately after, Miguel Hidalgo's *grito* sparked off the independence movement.

►► Querétaro *125C1*

The sprawling, dusty city of Querétaro, whose hard-edged atmosphere and commercialism reflect its proximity to Mexico City, 220km away, is considered the crossroads of the nation. Yet within the untidy outskirts, a renovated historic centre evokes memories of key events in Mexican history and has enough monuments to occupy a full day's visit. Querétaro was originally an Otomí settlement, later conquered by the Aztecs, and was taken over by the Spanish in 1531. By the late 17th century it had become the third city of Nueva España, but it was the following century that saw the building of most of Querétaro's surviving monuments. The Independence movement began here in 1810, and in 1848 the notorious Treaty of Guadalupe was signed, which handed over half of Mexico to the US. Twenty years later Querétaro witnessed Emperor Maximilian's last stand, his execution and finally, in 1917, it saw the birth of the new Mexican constitution.

Querétaro's hub is the Jardín Zenea (formerly Jardín Obregon). Rising on its eastern side is the striking church of **San Francisco**►► (*Open* daily 6.30–2, 5–9), built 1540–50, with a tiered sandstone tower and a cupola faced in *talavera* tiles. The adjoining monastery is now the excellent **Museo Regional**►►► (*Open* Tue–Sun 10.30–5). Aspects of local history and archaeology are displayed beside a collection of religious iconography. Particularly remarkable is a corridor of paintings by Miguel Cabrera. Military history also figures prominently, as does the 1917 Constitution. Behind these landmarks radiates an extensive pedestrian area, where flowery, cobbled streets packed with street-vendors lead uphill to the Plaza de Armas. Here, superb 18th-century mansions now function as government buildings: at the northern end is the **Palacio de Gobierno**, from where the governor's wife sent her secret warning (see panel). On the eastern flank is the **Méson de Santa** Rosa, now an elegant hotel.

Directly east and uphill from this square stands the impressive Franciscan monastery, the 17th-century

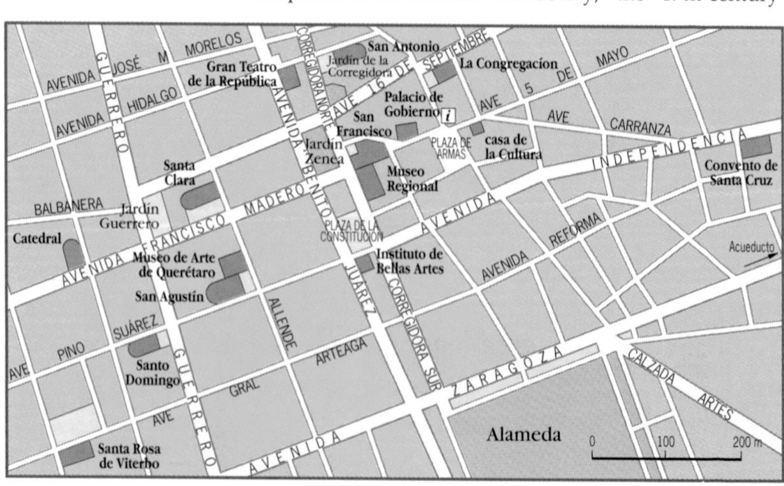

The Church of Santa Rosa

Convento de Santa Cruz▶▶ (*Open* Mon–Fri 9–2, 5–8.30, Sat–Sun 11–6) built on the site of the Otomí defeat in 1531, and once Emperor Maximilian's prison. Its religious function continues today and visits are by guided tour only, although it is well worth stopping off for a number of curious features, including a tree sprouting cross-shaped thorns. Beyond the monastery is the start of Querétaro's **aqueduct** (1726–38), its 74 stone arches rising 23m over the town.

West of the centre On the Jardín Guerrero, a square which is thick with laurel trees and graced by a 1797 fountain of Neptune, stands one of Querétaro's baroque masterpieces, the **Templo de Santa Clara▶▶▶** (1633) (*Open* daily 6–1, 5–8.30). The austere exterior of this former convent belies its interior, a gilded riot of high-relief altarpieces which cover practically every wall. Two blocks south is the equally magnificent **Templo de Santa Rosa de Viterbo▶▶▶** (1752) (*Open* daily 6.30am–8.30pm), its flying buttresses carved with masks and its interior boasting a Churrigueresque altar-piece, an ornately carved choir and a unique inlaid marble pulpit. Between these stands another former convent, San Agustín, now revitalised by the **Museo de Arte de Querétaro▶▶** (*Open* Tue–Sun 11–7), whose collection of 16th- to 20th-century paintings is overpowered by the scale and mastery of the stone carving in its 18th-century cloister.

THEATRICALITY

The Gran Teatro de la República, one block north of the Jardín Zenea, was the setting for several momentous historic events. It was inaugurated in 1852 with the name Gran Teatro Iturbide, and in 1867 was the meeting place for the Council of War which condemned the luckless Emperor Maximilian to death. In 1917 it witnessed the formal signing of the Mexican Constitution: the stage backdrop still lists the names of the delegates. Finally, in 1929, it saw the beginning of 70 years of one-party rule when the PRI (Partido Revolucionario Institucional) was founded there.

Querétaro, renowned for its opals and other gems, is an elegant city despite undergoing rapid industrialisation

MASKS
One of Mexico's most compelling displays of ceremonial masks is found at the Museo de la Máscara, opposite the Teatro de la Paz on the Plaza del Carmen in San Luis Potosí. Over 700 examples reveal the fertile imagination of pre- and post-Hispanic Mexican communities and are displayed to reflect the nation's social, political and religious history. Traditional costumes and descriptions of dances contribute further to understanding the incredible rituals which still play a fundamental role in Mexican life.

San Luis Potosí's attractive zócalo

► San Juan del Río 125C1

The market town of San Juan del Río is set in vineyards 52km south-west of Querétaro. It is famous for its lapidary business, which originated with the mining of local opals, but now extends to the polishing of gemstones from all over Mexico. The old colonial centre is notable for the **Templo de Santo Domingo**, a 17th-century baroque church and former convent, the multi-domed **Templo de Sagrado Corazón** and adjoining **Parroquía**, both dating from the 18th century and overlooking the Plaza de la Independencia, and the hilltop ex-convent of **Santa Veracruz**►► which houses a small history museum. The main crossroads of Juárez and Hidalgo is where most craft shops are next to some bars and restaurants.

► San Luis Potosí 124B2

San Luis Potosí, capital of the vast state of the same name, was founded in 1592 when silver and gold were discovered in the area. With a particularly bad record for mistreatment of the indigenous population, it redeemed itself somewhat when it became the site for Juárez's government-in-exile and later nurtured revolutionaries, particularly Francisco Madero. Since then industry has left its mark, although the majestic centre still offers a wonderful array of colonial architecture. On the Plaza de Armas the twin-towered **catedral**►►, completed at the turn of the 18th century, faces the **Palacio de Gobierno**. One block north-east on the Plaza de Fundadores stands the main university building, once a Jesuit college (1653), flanked by its exquisite baroque chapel, the **Capilla de Loreto**►► (1700). To the south, the quieter Plaza de San Francisco is dominated by a former Franciscan convent and church with a lovely baroque sacristy. The convent now houses the rather dusty **Museo Regional** (*Open* Tue–Sat 10–1.45, 4–5.45, Sun 10–2), whose outstanding feature is the Churrigueresque **Capilla de Aranzazú**►►. However, the jewel in Potosí's crown is the 1764 **Templo del Carmen**►►►, two blocks east of the cathedral, with its richly carved exterior and Chapel of the Virgin, entirely faced in gilded cherubim and decorative carvings. Not to be missed either is the **Museo de la Máscara**►►(*Open* Tue–Fri 10–2, 4–6, Sat–Sun 10–2). (See panel).

Year in, year out, the Huichol people of Nayarit and Jalisco struggle hundreds of kilometres across the central highlands to the northern region of San Luis Potosí, in search of the precious peyote *plant; at once their drug, god and raison d'être.*

The Huichols are thought to have been based originally in the sierra of San Luis Potosí before they fled from the Spaniards. Today they have become one of Mexico's purest and most isolated indigenous groups. Scattered on farms throughout the inaccessible mountains and canyons of Nayarit and Jalisco, they have systematically rejected outside influences and maintained their own mythology, which sees everything as divine, or possessing a soul. As a result the rugged landscape is dotted with natural shrines where they leave offerings and make requests. Their celebrations blend complex healing traditions passed down through generations of shamans with Huichol legends and gods, namely the sun, fire, water, corn, deer and *peyote*. Considered the fount of life, the sacred *peyote* 'button' is chewed in mystical rituals to stimulate predictions of the future, and diagnosis and healing of sickness. To gather the year's provisions of this hallucinogenic cactus, the Huichols trek 43 days across the Sierra Madre to Wirikuta, following a highly ritualised route.

***Peyote* creations** The role of the Huichol shaman (*maarakame*) is primordial. Only he can communicate directly with the gods, interpret the divine will and translate the hallucinations brought about by *peyote*. As a result, other Huichols channel their visions into art and offerings, above all *nierika* (yarn paintings), psychedelic expressions of their mythology. Vividly coloured and contrasting yarns are pressed into a wax base (derived from a form of *peyote* juice) to create an effect similar to their beaded gourds and wooden objects. Both yarn paintings and gourds are coated with beeswax before glass beads are placed, using a cactus thorn, in symbolic designs. The glass beads represent another change in tradition: brought by the Spaniards, they gradually replaced the traditional decoration of seeds, nuts, pebbles and corn kernels.

***PEYOTE* EFFECTS**
The unassuming appearance of the small tufted cactus known as *peyote* belies the radical effect created by its alkaloid ingredient, mescalin. It is by no means a monopoly of the Huichols: its use by the Aztecs (their relatives) was described with disgust by Spanish chroniclers and under colonial rule it was soon banned. In addition to giving frightening hallucinations, which can last three days, *peyote* is reputed to build up physical strength, give a sense of invulnerability and reduce appetite and thirst, all of which help the Huichols accomplish their annual jaunt. The drug is banned in Mexico for everyone except indigenous people.

Huichol

The pink Parroquía was apparently inspired by a postcard of a Gothic cathedral in Europe

►► San Miguel de Allende *124B2*

San Miguel was founded in 1542 by a Franciscan monk. During the colonial period it was a busy crossroads for the great mining towns of the Bajío region, Guanajuato and Zacatecas. Climbing up a steep hillside, in a region of arid sierra dotted with ranches and goatherds, San Miguel is now home to a community of artists, writers and retirees from the US. Up-market restaurants, hotels, galleries and craft shops have followed in their wake, reactivating the elegant old mansions of the centre and lending the town a unique, albeit *gringo*, flavour.

CRAFTS AND MARKETS

Behind San Felipe Neri is a market area with a very traditional Mexican feel. Indian women chop cactus leaves and men sit in front of mountains of eggs, backed by rows of *huachipiles* (leather sandals). Descend some steps and you come to the 'crafts market' where vendors aim some remarkably kitsch wares at tour groups. Far more attractive goods can be found in the town's numerous craft shops, which line the streets leading off the Plaza Allende.

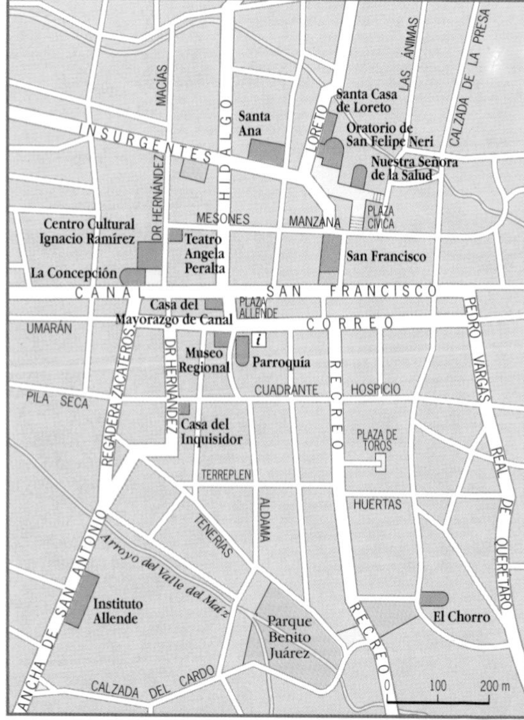

In and around the Plaza Allende One of the few towns in Mexico to be designated a national monument, San Miguel has an attractive harmony of narrow cobblestone streets, low-lying red-roofed houses, tree-lined patios and elegant mansions on the Plaza Allende. There are no major monuments, although the lofty, fluted spires of the extraordinary neo-Gothic **Parroquía▶▶** are a wonder in themselves. The church was designed in 1880 by local mason Zeferino Gutiérrez. Across the side-street stands the 18th-century **Casa Allende**, birthplace of Ignacio Allende, who engineered Mexico's independence movement along with Miguel Hidalgo. Now the **Museo Regional▶▶** (*Open* Tue–Sun 10–4), it displays the city's archaeology and history, with strong emphasis on Independence. On the north-west corner stands the **Casa del Mayorazgo de Canal** (*Open* Tue–Sun 10–4), once home to the Count of Canal and now used for temporary art exhibitions. The **Casa de los Conspiradores** is where Allende and fellow conspirators plotted in the basement as the bourgeoisie danced on the first floor.

Churches Along Calle Canal's uphill route stands the Churrigueresque-style **Iglesia de San Francisco**, begun in 1779. Two blocks north, flanking a terraced plaza, stand three 18th-century churches. To the east, the **Iglesia de Nuestra Señora de la Salud** has a pretty, scalloped stone entrance, but it is the **Oratorio de San Felipe Neri▶▶** (1712) that is of more interest, with its indigenous-style vegetal motifs on the façade and paintings of the life of St Philip Neri. To the west is the beautiful gilded chapel of **Santa Casa de Loreto▶▶** (often closed).

Cultural centres San Miguel's finest building is the **Bellas Artes▶▶▶**, housed in the 18th-century **Convento de la Concepción**, whose church boasts one of Mexico's largest domes. The spacious cloister now serves as San Miguel's lively **Centro Cultural Ignacio Ramírez**. Art exhibitions and murals line the arcades and one room is devoted to an unfinished work by Siqueiros. Several blocks south of here, at San Antonio 20, is the celebrated **Instituto Allende▶**, an arts and language school founded in 1951 that drew the first Americans to San Miguel. Housed in the imposing 1735 *hacienda* of the Conde de Canal and set in a lovely park, it is still a magnet for North American students.

ATOTONILCO

Fifteen kilometres north of San Miguel, on the road to Dolores Hidalgo, is the tiny Indian hamlet of Atotonilco, an important pilgrimage site closely linked to the struggle for independence. It is dominated by a 1740 church, scene of Miguel Allende's wedding in 1802 and, eight years later, the first destination for the insurgent forces on their march from Dolores to San Miguel. The object of their visit was a banner depicting the Virgin of Guadalupe, which was seized and held aloft by Hidalgo and Allende's followers as they triumphantly entered San Miguel. The banner now hangs in San Miguel's Museo Regional.

Detail on church façade

A rare empty street in San Miguel: most are packed with craft and furnishing shops

VOLCAN PARICUTIN
Uruapan's lush, rolling hills may be famous for their avocados but it is the volcano of Paricutín which draws the visitors. It looms 2,774m over the horizon, 15km west of town, and is accessible from the village of Angahuán, where horseback tours can be organised. A vast, furrowed, black field of lava covers the slopes and it is here that you can see the church spire of the village of San Juan Parangaricútiro, buried for eternity when the volcano erupted in 1943 in a cornfield, much to the horror of the local farmer. It spewed fire and lava more or less continuously for nine years, engulfing two villages and petrifying the region in the process, but now stands inactive.

FRANCISCAN MISSIONS
The Franciscans were an official and integral part of the Spanish Conquest, particularly active in the state of Querétaro, from where they sent missionary expeditions to the north and into the US. It was not until 1750, however, that the celebrated Franciscan Junípero Serra managed to set up churches in five mission towns of the inaccessible Sierra Gorda. Each one is a work of art, its fine, descriptive baroque carvings reflecting a synthesis of Spanish and indigenous art. Jalpan, Tancoyol, Concá, Tilaco and Landa are all dominated by these magnificent structures, the most ornate being that of Landa where the façade is alive with figures of saints.

►► Sierra Gorda *125C2*

This mountainous region lies in the north-east of the state of Querétaro and crosses into Hidalgo and San Luis Potosí. Roads climb dizzily through pine forests to 2,500m before descending to warmer valleys. In 1600, indigenous resistance to the activities of Franciscan missionaries led to war, but by 1750 five unique missions had been built by Father Junípero Serra, together with native artisans. Their highly ornate style is described and explained at the small **Museo Historico de la Sierra Gorda** (*Open* Tue–Sat 10–3, Sun 10–1) at **Jalpan de Sierra**, the regional crossroads, which has its own striking mission church and good visitors' facilities. Other missions can be seen further afield at Conca, Tancoyol, Tilaco and Landa, the last easily accessible on Highway 120 (see panel).

► Tampico *125D2*

This sprawling industrial city, the southernmost and largest in the state of Tamaulipas, is completely monopolised by the oil industry. It was first inhabited by the Huastecs and later came under Aztec rule, before being settled by the Spanish in 1534. The port was sacked by pirates in the 17th century and rebuilt in the 19th century, but it was the discovery of oil in 1901 that led to its heyday. Transformation came along with British and American oil men and its waters soon became an environmental disaster. Things are cleaner now and the **Playa de Miramar** and **Playa Altamira**, just north of town, are suitable for swimming. The **Museo de la Cultura Huasteca** (*Open* Tue–Sun 10–3), in the satellite town of Ciudad Madero, is well worth a visit for its fine collection of ceramics and sculptures. Fishing fanatics should head for the freshwater lagoons of **Chairel** and **Carpintero**, both with popular fishing camps.

► Tequisquiapan *125C1*

Tequisquiapan is the last major town before Highway 120 climbs into the Sierra Gorda, and is popular for its temperate climate, thermal springs, wines, cheese and crafts. The town is 180km from Mexico City, and the area's many spas have spawned numerous hotels and restaurants catering for weekend crowds from the capital. It depends economically on its basketware, wickerwork, jewellery and ceramics all sold at the central market. About 17km to the north is the archaeological zone of **Ranas**, inhabited between the 7th and 11th centuries and, 15km east of this, the ruins of the ceremonial centre of **Toluquilla**.

►► Tzintzuntzán *124B1*

On the eastern shores of the Lago de Pátzcuaro (see pages 142–3 and 156–7) is the village of Tzintzuntzán (Place of the Hummingbirds), one of the three cities which once formed the 14th-century Tarascan League and the first base for the enlightened bishop of Michoacán, Vasco de Quiroga, in 1538. Today the village has become a crafts centre for handpainted ceramics, straw figures and woodcarvings, and also attracts a growing number of affluent lakeside residents. The Purépecha site of **Las Yácatas** (*Open* daily 9–5.30), is located up a slip-road to the south of the village. A row of five stepped, circular pyramids

The former city of Tzintzuntzán was dedicated to Curicaveri, the god of fire

(*yácatas*) offers lake views and a small museum gives the background to this once flourishing kingdom. The 16th-century **Templo de San Francisco** is now partly in ruins, but its peeling interior and atmospheric, rambling garden of pine and olive trees (reputedly planted by Quiroga himself in defiance of an edict forbidding their cultivation) are well worth the visit.

▶ Uruapan *124B1*

Uruapan, famous for its fine lacquerware, makes a delightful stop-over on Michoacán's main road south to the Pacific. It lies in a beautiful, lush, subtropical region, one of Mexico's chief fruit-growing areas, with avocados figuring prominently. Urupuan's main attraction is the **Parque Nacional Eduardo Ruíz▶▶**, in which rises the source of the Río Cupatitzio at the northern end of town and is thick with mossy trees, tropical vegetation and man-made waterfalls. On the Plaza Principal stands the **Museo Regional Huatapera▶** (*Open* Tue–Sun 10–6) housed in one of Bishop Quiroga's first hospitals (1533), which exhibits Michoacán crafts with a special emphasis on lacquerware. Between the *zócalo* (main square) and the park, craft shops and workshops line Calle Independencia, finishing at the Mercado de Artesanías opposite the park entrance.

Fine church detail, Uruapan

Uruapan's attractive cathedral

A short trip by cable-car takes you up the Cerro de la Bufa to the Patrocinio Chapel

CERRO DE LA BUFA
The easiest way to the top of this hill is via cable-car from the slopes of the Cerro del Bosque, also accessible from the northern exit of the El Edén mine. Views across the city are spectacular, particularly at sunset, and the hill can be descended by a path which leads directly back to the centre. At the summit an 18th-century chapel contains a much-revered portrait of the Virgin Mary: pilgrims sometimes spend the night in the courtyard. Behind stands the Museo de la Toma de Zacateca with memorabilia concentrating on Villa's victory over the Federales.

Beside the craggy summit stand three monumental statues of the Revolutionary leaders and at the top is an observatory.

▶▶ Xilitla *125C2*

In the remote mountains of southern San Luis Potosí, the village holds a curious attraction: the fantasy home of English eccentric Edward James (1907–84) – see panel, opposite. On his arrival in 1954 he invested in a tract of hillside where he built a whimsical, Daliesque complex. His mentor, a Yacqui, meanwhile constructed a village home in a parallel anarchistic spirit (see panel, page 155). Now called El Castillo, it has been converted into a comfortable *posada* (inn). The 36 surrealist structures of **Las Pozas** are now being rescued from encroaching vegetation. River-rafting is another attraction here from May to November.

▶▶▶ Zacatecas *124A3*

The mining city of Zacatecas, gateway to the north, blankets a magnificent plateau at an altitude of 2,500m, rimmed with arid hills. With few visitors and even fewer indigenous residents, it epitomises the prosperity of colonial Spain. Baroque monuments pepper the pink-stone centre at the foot of the Cerro de la Bufa (2,667m), but it also has a lively market area that contributes to the friendly atmosphere. A panoramic cable-car, silver crafts, semi-precious stones, leatherwork and a robust local wine add to the attractions.

Silver town The founding of Zacatecas in 1546 was directly linked to its silver deposits, already exploited by the Zacateco people, and within a few years industrialists were sending wagon-loads of the precious ore south to Mexico City. Fortunes were rapidly made, but the political upheavals of the 19th and early 20th centuries, including Pancho Villa's capture of the city in 1914, announced the end of the boom. However, silver is once again the city's main resource and it now mines a large percentage of the nation's production. One of the major sights is **La Mina del Edén▶**, north-west of the centre at the foot of Cerro del Bosque. Guided tours start with a ride on a small train. This drives straight into the heart of the 16th-century mine where you continue on foot past garishly illuminated shafts, multi-levelled galleries, chasms, pools and even a shrine. Guides reveal horrifying statistics which describe mining conditions of the past and their Zacateco victims.

Central sights Two parallel streets cut through the centre: Avenida Hidalgo (becoming Avenida González Ortega) and Calle Tacuba. Dominating their junction is the **catedral▶▶▶**, completed in 1752 and one of Mexico's outstanding expressions of baroque. Its northern side is flanked by the Plaza Hidalgo and the **Palacio de Gobierno**, a former silver baron's mansion, as is the imposing **Palacio de Mala Noche** opposite. South of the cathedral the city's up-market shopping centre, **El Mercado**, is housed in a cast-iron market building. Across Avenida Hidalgo stands the elegant 19th-century **Teatro Calderón.**

Uphill to the west lies the pretty **Templo de Santo Domingo▶▶▶** (1746), the richest in Zacatecas, filled with baroque gold-leaf altar-pieces. Its former monastery now houses the remarkable **Museo Pedro Coronel▶▶▶** (*Open* Fri–Wed 10–2, 4–7), where a remarkable collection of

Celebrating Independence Day in Zacatecas' zócalo

SILVER CENTRE
Zacatecas' silver tradition continues at the Centro Platero, located in the former *hacienda* of Bernandez on the outskirts of the city. Visitors can watch silversmith techniques in the workshops or make purchases at the shop to encourage this recently revived tradition.

A DESTINY OF ECCENTRICITY
Edward James spent much of his time and fortune patronising artists of the Surrealist movement. During World War II he fled from Europe to the safer delights of Beverly Hills, where he wined and dined the likes of Humphrey Bogart and Orson Welles. But the fascination of this existence soon palled and he began his Mexican episode in the village of Xilitla. With the help of his Yaqui mentor he started putting his marijuana and *peyote*-inspired dreams into practice, directing a team of local builders to create his personal delirium of Oriental temples, Greek columns, arches and bridges, which was never finished.

exhibits cover every civilisation from Ancient Greece to Asia and Africa. Another private collection of the Coronel family is the **Museo Rafael Coronel**▶▶ (*Open* Thu–Tue 10–2, 4–7), housed in the baroque monastery of San Francisco, still revealing damage from Villa's bombardment. This striking complex at the northern end of town (bus 5 or 8) includes a vast collection of Mexican masks, puppets and sketches by Diego Rivera.

South of the centre Avenida Hidalgo runs south past 19th-century buildings to Avenida Juárez, which marks the end of the old centre. To the west it is the **Alameda**, for centuries the fashionable Zacatecan promenade. Southwest of here lies the **Parque Enrique Estrada**, flanked to the west by the **Museo Francisco Goitia** (*Open* Tue–Sun 10–1.30, 5–8), a memorial to this famous Zacatecan painter. Here, too, are the remains of an 18th-century aqueduct. Just behind this is the luxury **Quinta Real**▶▶ hotel, constructed around a 17th-century bullring. A few streets northwest the **Jardín Independencia** becomes the shoeshiners' domain and beyond this the rambling market streets of Zacatecas begin.

Pancho Villa looks out over Zacatecas, the city he liberated from General Huerta during the revolution

Drive

Lagos de Pátzcuaro and Zirahuén

This pastoral circuit of Lago de Pátzcuaro and Lago de Zirahuén takes you through the small lakeside villages of Michoacán. Pyramids, early Franciscan churches, a Utopian-style village and, above all, thriving local crafts are the reasons for visiting this area. Allow a full day.

From **Pátzcuaro** (see pages 142–3) follow the road down to the lake and turn right on to the road to Tzintzuntzán, which leaves the main highway at Tzurumutaro. Skirting the lake through lush green farmlands you can make a short detour left to **Ihuatzío** (signposted) to see the unexcavated lakeside ruins of an old Tarascan town. The main road continues away from the lake through gentle hills of eucalyptus trees and after 6km descends to **Tzintzuntzán** (see pages 152–3). On your right before entering the village is a turn-off winding uphill to an important Tarascan archaeological site where five circular pyramids (*yácatas*) overlook the lake. The village itself is known for its elaborate wood-carving, displayed along the main street, woven straw figures and for a particular style of hand-painted pottery. Visit the 16th-century **Franciscan church** and its gardens behind the main square.

From here the road continues past old and new lakeside houses, flat pastures and roadside crafts vendors to the main junction at **Quiroga**, the busiest and largest commercial town on the lake. Turn left at the arcaded main square and drive a few kilometres on to **Santa Fé de la Laguna**, the first of more than a dozen Indian villages hugging the lake. It was here in Santa Fé that Don Vasco de Quiroga, Michoacán's first bishop in the 1540s, tried to set up a model of Thomas More's *Utopia*. The 16th-century hospital and chapel still stand and the village square has recently been completely renovated.

Continuing on MEX 14 you pass pine woods and several local restaurants serving freshwater fish straight from the lake. Just beyond Chupícuaro the road branches: turn left to **San Jerónimo**, a sprawling village

Boarding the ferry for Janitzío Island

Young Tarascans enjoying a bag of popcorn

of dirt roads, red roofs and spires on a lakeside promontory. The main activities here are wood-carving and boat-building.

A few kilometres further through verdant countryside the road goes south through San Andrés to the villages of **Puácuaro** and **Napízaro**, a mere 2km apart. The inhabitants of these villages are pure Purépechas and they specialise in basket-making. A short distance on is the large fishing village of **Erongaricuaro**, whose Purépecha name means 'lookout tower on the lake'. Visit the 16th-century **Franciscan church** and **seminary** for good lake views and admire the old Spanish-style architecture. Crafts include fine inlaid furniture, weaving and embroidery.

Two kilometres south lies **San Francisco Uricho**, a tiny village whose 16th-century church boasts a superb altar. **Arocutin**, the next stop, is known for its fine embroidery. From here you can reach the island of **Jarácuaro**, which specialises in hat-making. Another 2km further is **Tocuaro**, the main village on Lago de Pátzcuaro for making masks, and as you round the southern shores of the lake you come to the *pulque* distilling village of **San Pedro**. The lake road finally rejoins MEX 14 back at Pátzcuaro. From here follow signs to Uruapan until the road branches off to the left to the small Lago de Zirahuén, a peaceful and scenic spot to relax.

Lake Zirahuén is noted for its clear blue waters

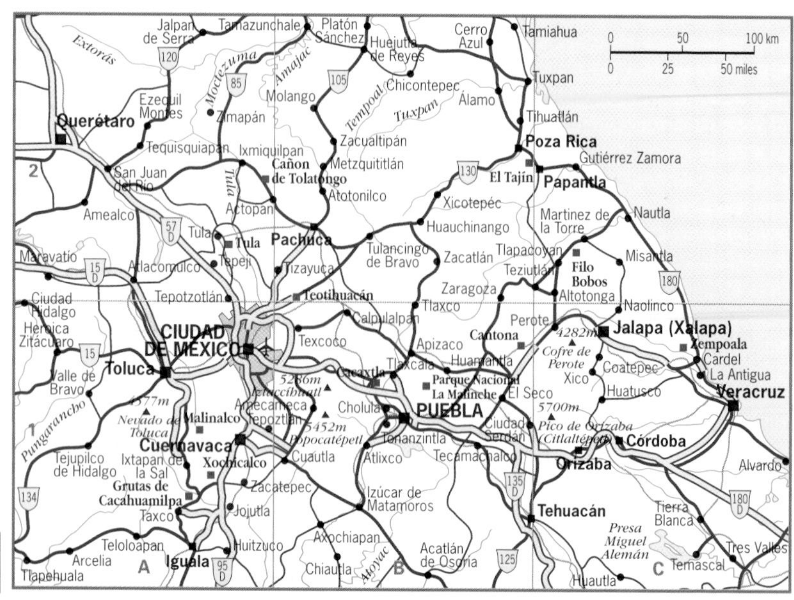

Jalpan de Serra
Tamazunchale
Platón Sánchez
Huejutla de Reyes
Cerro Azul
Tamiahua
0 50 100 km
0 25 50 miles
Extorás
120
Moctezuma
Amajac
85
105
Chicontepec
Álamo
Tuxpan
Tempoal
Ezequil Montes
Zimapán
Molango
Tihuatlán
Querétaro
Zacualtipán
Poza Rica
Tequisquiapan
Ixmiquilpan
Cañon de Tolatongo
Metzquititlán
Gutiérrez Zamora
2
San Juan del Rio
Tula
130
El Tajín
Papantla
Atotonilco
Xicotepéc
Amealco
Actopan
Martinez de la Torre
Nautla
57 D
Tula
Pachuca
Huauchinango
Tulancingo de Bravo
Zacatlán
Tlapacoyan
Maravatío
15 D
Atlacomulco
Tepeji
Tizayuca
Teziutlán
Filo Bobos
Misantla
Zaragoza
180
Ciudad Hidalgo
Tepotzotlán
Teotihuacán
Tlaxco
Altotonga
Naolinco
Heroica Zitácuaro
Calpulalpan
Perote
CIUDAD DE MÉXICO
Cantona
4282m
Jalapa (Xalapa)
Texcoco
Apizaco
Cofre de Perote
Zempoala
15
Toluca
Tlaxcala
Huamantla
Cardel
Valle de Bravo
Cacaxtla
Xico
Coatepec
La Antigua
5286m
Parque Nacional La Malinche
El Seco
Iztaccíhuatl
Huatusco
Veracruz
Pungarancho
Nevado de Toluca
Amecameca
Cholula
5700m
Malinalco
Tepoztlán
5452m
PUEBLA
Pico de Orizaba (Citlaltépetl)
1
Popocatépetl
Tonanzintla
Ciudad Serdán
Córdoba
Cuernavaca
Tejupilco de Hidalgo
Ixtapan de la Sal
Xochicalco
Cuautla
Atlixco
Tecamachalco
Orizaba
Alvarado
Grutas de Cacahuamilpa
Zacatepec
135 D
134
Izúcar de Matamoros
Tierra Blanca
Taxco
Jojutla
Tehuacán
180 D
Presa Miguel Alemán
Axochiapan
Teloloapan
Huitzuco
Acatlán de Osoria
Tres Valles
Arcelia
A
Iguala
95 D
Atoyac
B
125
C
Temascal
Tlapehuala
Chiautla
Huautla

The Central Valleys & the Gulf

THE CENTRAL VALLEYS AND THE GULF From Toluca in the west to Veracruz in the east, the central valleys of Mexico dance across high plateaux and even higher, snowcapped peaks, sweeping across fields of corn or maguey and up into pine forests before sloping down to the coastal plain of the Gulf. Some of the country's richest and poorest inhabitants live in this region: wealthy refugees from the big city who reside in the hills of Morelos, and farmers scraping a living on the arid slopes of Hidalgo. Between these two extremes are the industrialised cities of Puebla and Cuernavaca, the artisan villages of the vast state of Puebla and the idyllic tropical garden of the state of Veracruz. It was not for nothing that so many of Mesoamerica's dynasties graduated to these fertile valleys, and the relics of their civilisations add greatly to the region's attraction. Sites continue to be excavated and restored. These include Filo Bobos, north of Jalapa, in lush, forested hills full of parrots and toucans. West of Cofre de Perote lies Cantona, a vast site with Olmec characteristics that reveals strong defensive structures.

FROM THE BEGINNING TO BAROQUE One of Mesoamerica's most astounding sites is Teotihuacán, its sheer scale and symmetry being ample evidence of this

Previous pages: the magnificent Nevado de Toluca, Mexico's fourth highest summit at 4,680m. The two lakes in the volcano's crater are named after the sun and the moon

civilisation's sophistication. It can be visited on a day-trip from the capital or incorporated into a wider exploration of the state of Hidalgo. Less spectacular is what remains of Tula, home to the militaristic Toltecs. To the south of Mexico City lies scenic Xochicalco and, to the east, the exquisite murals of Cacaxtla, the massive pyramid of Cholula and spectacular El Tajín. You can follow the trail the *conquistadores* took over mountain passes from Veracruz to Tlaxcala and Cholula before besieging the Aztec capital. Some of their earliest buildings can be seen, as well as sublime heights of baroque design, from the extraordinary church at Tepotzotlán and the encapsulation of Indian imagination at Tonanzintla to Puebla's Santo Domingo and Taxco's Santa Prisca. The whole region is rich in a minefield of historical connections. The state of Morelos is named after the radical priest José María Morelos, who was instrumental in bringing about Mexico's independence, basing himself for a time at Cuautla. French intervention in 1862 and 1863 centred upon Puebla, while Cuernavaca echoes with the doomed footsteps of Emperor Maximilian and Carlota. Revolutionary machinations reverberate in Veracruz, scene of Venustiano Carranza's US-backed government in 1915 and, closer to the soil, in Morelos, where guerilla forces were mobilised by Emiliano Zapata's cry of *tierra y libertad* ('land and liberty').

UNADULTERATED NATURE No fewer than nine national parks cover the slopes of the mountain ranges ringing Mexico City. Closest to the capital and most symbolic is

Below: the Atlantes of Tula

Colourful bark painting

the Parque Nacional Popocatépetl–Iztaccíhuatl, but the Pico de Orizaba (Mexico's highest peak), La Malinche (near Puebla), the Nevado de Toluca (south-west of Toluca), the Cofre de Perote (west of Jalapa) and El Chico (near Pachuca) all offer stunning landscapes.

The central Gulf Coast, although not equalling the splendour of Pacific beaches or the turquoise waters of the Yucatán, makes a pleasant low-key destination. Costa Esmeralda, the narrow coastal strip below Jalapa, is lined with lagoons, fishing villages and lush vegetation, as well as a few hotels, but also plays host to Mexico's only nuclear energy plant, Laguna Verde, at the southern end. You can test the water in one of the many spa towns of Morelos, although in some cases a theme-park atmosphere has been overemphasised. Man has left his agricultural mark too, with coffee, vanilla, tobacco, sugarcane, grain, fruit, vegetables and flowers widely cultivated throughout the valleys.

URBAN VISITS The most popular destinations in the region are Puebla, Cuernavaca and Taxco, along with Veracruz. The first two, although both of unique cultural interest, have become quite polluted, a situation aggravated by fast highway connections to Mexico City. Taxco, the 'world silver capital', offers a slower pace of life.

On a smaller scale, and therefore often more atmospheric, are towns such as Tlaxcala and Jalapa. Jalapa's landmark Museum of Anthropology should be a priority for anyone interested in the cultures of the Gulf, and it can be combined with a visit to the nearby sites of El Tajín and Zempoala.

THE TREE OF LIFE

The region surrounding Mexico City is rich in craft traditions – embroidery, weaving and onyx work from the villages of Puebla, Talavera tiles from Puebla itself. The handicraft which is perhaps most associated with Mexico, however, is the *arbol de la vieda*, or 'tree of life.' The centre of manufacture is the village of Metepec, just south of Toluca. These elaborate, colourful clay constructions develop a theme which originated in the Middle East and was brought, via a tortuous route, first to Spain and then to Mexico. Commemorating the story of Adam and Eve in the Garden of Eden, they depict flowers, foliage, the couple and their imminent fall, symbolised by a snake or a skeleton.

SPAS
The state of Morelos is renowned for its thermal springs, many of which have been transformed into large recreational centres aimed at pollution-fleeing inhabitants from the capital and Cuernavaca. The region's largest spa is found 10km north of Cuautla at the Centro Vacacional Oaxtepec: 25 pools, an artifical lake, sports facilities, cable-car, hotels and cabins make this a favourite weekend playground, sponsored by the Mexican Social Security. El Recreo and El Bosque offer similar amenities, though on a smaller scale. Another cluster of spas is found due south of Cuernavaca around the towns of Zacatepec, Jojutla and Tehuixtla, the latter boasting five sulphurous baths.

►► Actopan *158A2*

The town of Actopan, 37km north-west of Pachuca in the lush foothills of the Sierra Madre Oriental, is known, above all, for the superbly preserved **Convento de San Nicolás►►►**(*Open* daily 9–5), now housing a museum of colonial art. Constructed in 1548 by Augustinian monks, it was one of a series of imposing, fortified monasteries founded throughout the state of Hidalgo. Behind the Plateresque façade its cloisters and stairwell contain beautiful black and white frescoes painted by the monks. On the walls of the vaulted *capilla abierta* (outdoor chapel) are more colourful visions of hell and damnation painted by indigenous artisans. A similar structure is found at **Ixmiquilpan**, 40km further north.

►► Cacaxtla *158B1*

Open: daily 9–5.30

On a hilltop 25km south-west of Tlaxcala are the ruins of an Olmeca-Xicallanca site, unearthed in 1975, now joined by the pyramid of **Xochitécatl►** excavated in 1993–6, the fourth largest in Mexico and at least 1,000 years older. A winding rural path connects the two sites, or you can drive by road. Xochitécatl has three structures, including a circular pyramid, and views towards Popocatépetl and Iztaccíhnatl. Cacaxtla itself flourished in the 8th to 10th centuries and bequeathed Mesoamerica's most descriptive frescoes. Technically very advanced, these paintings depict

Discovered as recently as 1975 by tomb robbers, Cacaxtla's spectacular murals are fading, in the sun and wind, despite efforts to preserve them

elaborately costumed warriors and priests, ceremonies and battles. The main battle-scene mural is on the northern wall of the **Plaza Norte** and others cover the walls of Edificio A. The complex is roofed for protection against destructive sunlight but this is sadly not preventing these exceptional paintings from fading. The design of the roof also channels dusty winds, so go there before it is too late.

►► Cantona *158A2*

Open: daily 9–5

Although it was discovered in the mid-19th century, the site of Cantona opened to the public only in 1996. Barely one per cent of this 12sq km fortified city has been excavated, but archaeologists recognise that at its zenith, between AD 600 and 1000, it rivalled Teotihuacán. It lies in dry, volcanic hills, that gave the 80,000 Olmec-Chicalanca

The Templo de Nuestra Señora de los Remedios crowns the Gran Pirámide

inhabitants their main trade, obsidian. The main restored area is the ceremonial centre, where long avenues and 10 ball-courts surround the acropolis. Access is along a rough road from the village of Tepeyahualco, about 65km west of Jalapa and 98km from Puebla.

▶ Cholula *158B1*

Cholula was famed as a ceremonial town dedicated to Quetzalcóatl. It was the victim of plundering and a massacre by Cortés' army and his Tlaxcalan allies on their march to Mexico City. The invaders replaced the temples with shrines and churches, including the **Convento Franciscano▶▶** (1549) and the later 49 domes of the **Capilla Real**. However, it is the **Gran Pirámide▶▶** (*Open* daily 9–6), the largest in the Americas, which dominates the otherwise uninspiring town. Built on a massive scale, it reflects Cholula's importance as a spiritual centre, although the partly overgrown slopes now diminish the impact. The colonial **Templo de Nuestra Señora de los Remedios** (1594) crowns the summit, while beneath the pyramid 8km of passages have been dug to reveal the remains of murals. A small museum near the tunnel entrance fills in the background and displays a reproduction of a mural depicting a *pulque*-drinking session.

▶ Cuautla *158B1*

Cuautla's temperate climate makes it a popular retreat for the capital's jet set. Just over 40km east of Cuernavaca, and little more than an hour's drive from Mexico City, it is famous for its spas. In 1812 the town played a major role in the Independence struggle when Morelos set up base here in an attempt to attack Mexico City. Although a three-month siege resulted in his defeat, Morelos is honoured by a small museum in the **Ex-Convento de San Diego▶▶**. **Agua Hedionda** on the east side of the river, is famous for its sulphurous waters which fill two large pools.

IN THE EYES OF A *CONQUISTADOR*

'Cholula is situated on a plain with many other towns around it ... It is a land rich in maize and other vegetables, and in peppers, and in the maguey from which they brew their wine. They make very good pottery of red and black and white clay painted in various designs, and they supply Mexico and all the neighbouring provinces with it At that time the city had many lofty towers, which were the temples and shrines in which they kept their idols, in particular the great *cue* [temple pyramid] which was higher than that of Mexico, although the *cue* at Mexico was very grand and tall. '
Bernal Díaz: *The Conquest of Mexico*, 1568.

BEYOND CUERNAVACA

'How continually, how startlingly, the landscape changed! ... a strange planet where, if you looked a little further, beyond the Tres Marías, you would find every sort of landscape at once, the Cotswolds, Windermere, New Hampshire, the meadows of the Eure-et-Loire, even the grey dunes of Cheshire, even the Sahara, a planet upon which, in the twinkling of an eye, you could change climates and, if you cared to think so, in the crossing of a highway, three civilisations; but beautiful, there was no denying its beauty, fatal or cleansing as it happened to be, the beauty of the Earthly Paradise itself.'
Malcolm Lowry: *Under the Volcano*, 1947.

Cuernavaca's Palace of Cortés, built by the conquistador in 1529

EXPATRIATE LEGACIES
Cuernavaca's expatriate residents have firmly left their mark. The town first achieved world fame through Malcolm Lowry's novel of human despair, *Under the Volcano* (1947), later made into a film. The former Japanese-style residence of Barbara Hutton, the Woolworths heiress, which includes contemplation pools with stones placed by a priest flown in from Kyoto, now functions as a Japanese restaurant (Restaurant Sumiya). Behind the cathedral in the former Franciscan convent, is the Museo Casa de la Torre, which displays valuable paintings and antiques from all over the world, collected by Robert Brady, who lived in the building until his death in 1986.

▶▶ Cuernavaca *158A1*

Cuernavaca is said to have the greatest number of swimming pools per capita of any city in the world. This overtly prosperous, increasingly polluted town with a population of over one million is only 76km south of Mexico City and has long been a popular weekend and retirement spot – the Aztec nobility, Hernán Cortés and Emperor Maximilian all vacationed here. Many Mexicans from the capital live here in splendid isolation behind high-walled properties, and expatriate renown has drawn droves of visitors, imparting a lively cosmopolitan air and generating countless bars and chic restaurants.

Unable to pronounce its Náhautl name, the Spaniards substituted their word for 'cow horn', hardly a promising start. In 1522 Cortés set about building a massive fortress-palace, followed by an equally bulky cathedral, placing these two edifices among Mexico's oldest colonial monuments. The **Palacio de Cortés** now houses the **Museo Cuauhnáhuac▶▶▶** (*Open* Tue–Sun 10–5), an extensive collection covering regional archaeology, colonial history and the Revolution, with strong emphasis on the role of Zapata, who was born and assassinated in this state. A first-floor loggia displays a masterful mural by Diego Rivera depicting the Conquest of Mexico and cruel subjugation of the indigenous people, factors which are further symbolised by the ruins of a pyramid visible beneath the fortress. Fronting its towering façade are Cuernavaca's lively main squares, focal point for nightly promenades, hawkers and people-watching.

Two blocks west up Calle Hidalgo is the **catedral▶▶▶**, built by Franciscan monks in 1530. It stands at the back of a walled garden, flanked by the 16th-century Capilla Abierta and the **Capilla de la Tercer Orden▶▶**. The uniquely renovated interior is the main interest. Contemporary design elements, including stained-glass windows bt Mathias Goeritz, create a purist style which highlights another curiosity, delicate 17th-century murals painted by a Japanese convert, depicting the martyrdom of 25 Franciscan missionaries in Japan. *Mariachi* masses are celebrated on Sundays at 11am.

Opposite the cathedral precinct, on the other side of Avenida Morelos, is the **Jardín Borda**►► (*Open* Tue–Sun 10–5.30). This beautiful landscaped garden surrounds a mansion financed by the French silver magnate José de la Borda in 1783, and was once a favourite retreat for Emperor Maximilian and Carlota. The house displays historical documents, folk art and temporary art shows. The man-made lake is the site of an open-air theatre. Maximilian's country residence, the **Casa de Maximiliano**► (*Open* daily 9–5) includes the cottage of his native Mexican mistress and now houses a museum of herbal medicine and a botanic garden. It lies south of the centre at Calle Matamoros 200 in Acapatzingo.

►►► El Tajín *158B2*

Open: daily 9–5

Twenty-four kilometres south-east of the industrial town of Poza Rica, in the state of Veracruz, lie the magnificent ruins of the Totonac civilisation (4th- to 12th-century). This vast, undulating site, most of which is still engulfed by rampant vegetation, is the most impressive north of Teotihuacán. In the central excavated area stands the **Pirámide de los Nichos**, a modestly scaled, tiered edifice perforated with 365 niches (representing the solar year), which looms over numerous other buildings and at least 10 ball-courts. The walls of the main ball-court are carved with fine bas-reliefs depicting warriors, ballplayers, human sacrifices and a *pulque*-drinking bout. Uphill, behind the main pyramid, lies another centre, **El Tajín Chico**, a network of buildings dominated by the **Edificio de las Columnas**. Many of the massive columns have mosaics similar in motif and technique to those at Mitlá, Oaxaca (see page 195). At the entrance to the site an immaculately designed modern museum displays artefacts from the site, with explanatory panels. The 20m pole in the forecourt outside is used by the celebrated *voladores* (flying dancers): their dangerous ritual is enacted daily around midday (see page 170). The nearest hotels are at Papantla.

MEXICAN LEGACIES
David Alfaro Siqueiros, one of Mexico's three great muralists along with Rivera and Orozco, had his workshop and home in Cuernavaca, where he worked from 1964 until his death in 1974. Located at Calle Venus 7, the Taller y Museo Alfaro Siqueiros displays four unfinished murals, photos and assorted memorabilia. About 5km from town, at Atlacomulco, is the Hacienda de Cortés, a 17th-century construction which belonged to Martin Cortés, who succeeded his father, Hernán, as Marquis of the Valley of Oaxaca. During the revolution it served as Zapata's military base before being abandoned. Now completely restored, it functions as a luxury hotel and restaurant.

Totonac voladores *preparing to 'fly' in El Tajín. This ritual dates back to pre-Hispanic times*

Cacahuamilpa's spectacularly lit cave system contains graffiti by historic figures such as the Empress Carlota

MORE CAVES

Further south in the mountainous wilds of the state of Guerrero are the caves of Juxtlahuaca and Oxtotitlán, the former situated 52km east of Chilpancingo and the latter further north, 12km from Chilapa. The Grutas de Juxtlahuaca contain a spectacular underground pool overhung by stalactites. There is also one cave chamber where rock paintings dating back 3,000 years show a human couple, a snake and a jaguar. At the Grutas de Oxtotitlán strong Olmec influences have been found in cave paintings, one of which depicts a richly costumed figure on the back of a jaguar. It is thought to be a personification of the god of fertility and rain.

Ixtapan de la Sal is a relaxing weekend destination appreciated by capital-dwellers

▶▶▶ Grutas de Cacahuamilpa 158A1

Open: daily 10–5

Between Cuernavaca and Taxco, about 30km from the latter, lies the national park of Cacahuamilpa, which shelters a network of extraordinary underground caves riddled with 16km of man-made tunnels. Although no cave paintings have been found here, these caverns are impressive for their outstanding rock formations, stalagmites and stalactites, many named according to the shapes they create. Hourly guided tours lead visitors through cleverly illuminated passages and into 16 vast chambers, where there is a spectacular sound and light show.

▶ Ixtapan de la Sal 158A1

The spa resort of Ixtapan de la Sal, in a lush mountainous region 80km south of Toluca on Highway 55, has rich mineral waters whose curative properties have long been associated with relief from muscular and circulatory problems. The largest and smartest establishment is the Balneario Nuevo Ixtapan, which has been developed into a recreational area of artificial lakes and waterfalls.

▶▶▶ Jalapa *158C1*

High in the *tierras templadas*, 135km inland from Veracruz, Jalapa is a lively university town of around 250,000 inhabitants which has preserved its colonial heart of steep winding streets. Jalapa's altitude and subtropical surroundings, overlooked by the Cofre de Perote volcano, endow it with a micro-climate of clear sunny mornings and cooler, misty afternoons. Gardens and parks proliferate, the most celebrated being the **Parque Juárez▶**, a small, formal terraced garden created during Porfirio Diaz's regime, that serves as the town *zócalo*. It is flanked to the north by the arcaded **Palacio Municipal** and to the west by the **Palacio de Gobierno**, seat of the Veracruz state government and home to a 1962 mural by Mario Orozco Rivera. Opposite stands the 18th-century **Catedral**, whose main features are a steeply sloping floor and an antique English clock in the bell-tower. From here the main street, Enriquez, continues east into a lively zone of shops and cafés. One block downhill, Calle Zaragoza is the focus for colonial hotels and budget restaurants. At the foot of the hill lies the **Paseo de los Lagos▶**, a pretty lakeside park with its **Casa de Artesanías** and, at its southern end, the university campus. East of the centre on the main road to the bus station is the **Galería del Estado▶▶**, a beautifully renovated colonial building which houses temporary art exhibitions.

Jalapa's main interest, the superlative **Museo de Antropología▶▶▶** (*Open* Mon–Fri 9–6, Sat–Sun 9–5), lies at the northern end of town on Avenida Xalapa. This remarkably designed museum (1986), second only to Mexico City's in scale and quality, slopes gently down a landscaped hillside, its terraced marble halls opening onto sunlit patios. The vast collection concentrates on the three great Gulf Coast cultures; Olmec, Totonac and Huastec. The Olmecs' extraordinary giant carved basalt heads from San Lorenzo reflect the sophistication of Mexico's oldest civilisation (1200 BC to 400 BC), equally apparent in their tiny clay sculptures of baby heads and jade masks. The later Totonac culture, is exemplified by their wonderful 'smiling' sculptures, expressive clay figures, votive *hachas*, and the astounding life-size Cihuateco sculptures. The Huastecs, believed to be distantly related to the Maya, are represented by volcanic rock sculptures of gods, shell carvings and superb pottery.

FROM COFFEE TO WATERFALLS
Jalapa is the centre of an extensive region of coffee and tobacco plantations, both of which have contributed to the fame of the state of Veracruz. Just south of Jalapa is the lushly situated town of Coatepec, an orchid-growing centre and major coffee producer: cafés in Jalapa serve the real, freshly ground brew. A few kilometres further south lies Xico, a picturesque town of brightly coloured houses surrounded by exuberant tropical vegetation and plantations. Just outside the centre is the spectacular waterfall of Texolo, equalled by the 80m Naolinco waterfall which lies 32km north of Jalapa amongst hills, valleys and ravines.

Exhibit in Jalapa's Museum of Anthropology

▶ Malinalco *158A1*

Open: daily 9–5

The hilltop ceremonial centre of Malinalco, reached from a turn-off on Highway 55, 50km south of Toluca, displays some rare, well preserved examples of Aztec stone sculptures. Built after its annexation to the Aztec kingdom in 1476, the principal structure, the **Templo de los Guerreros Aguila y los Tigres** (Temple of the Eagles and Jaguars), is a circular pyramid carved out of the mountain. The summit temple displays two seated jaguars flanking the central stairway while through the entrance, in the form of an open-mouthed snake, stand eagles and a recumbent jaguar. **Building IV** was once the Templo del Sol, focus for major Aztec festivities every 260 days.

No other ancient civilisation in the world had such a profound taste for blood as the Aztecs. Possessed, obsessed, they sent thousands of young men up the temple steps to the sacrificial altar in regular attempts to pander to their gods. Even the favourite pre-Hispanic sport, the ball-game, had more sinister undertones.

PEPPERS AND TOMATOES
'... we saw our comrades who had been captured in Cortés' defeat being dragged up the steps to be sacrificed ... they made them dance in front of Huichilobos. Then after they had danced the *papas* laid them down on their backs on some narrow stones of sacrifice and, cutting open their chests, drew out their palpitating hearts which they offered to the idols. Then they kicked the bodies down the steps and the Indian butchers who were waiting below cut off their arms and legs and flayed their faces which they afterwards prepared like glove leather and kept for drunken festivals. Then they ate their flesh with a sauce of peppers and tomatoes.'
Bernal Díaz: *The Conquest of New Spain*, 1568.

The ball-game is thought to have originated with the Olmecs (see pages 30–1) but it took many centuries for it to assume the strictly defined shape of the courts at El Tajín, Monte Albán, Tula, Xochicalco and Chichén Itzá. Using a rubber ball that was propelled by the players from their hips and knees, the game had deep religious significance and its outcome was literally one of life or death. Players would wear protective belts and knee-pads but this did not prevent their fate: the losers (or winners – this remains uncertain) were sacrificed. The court also became the macabre stage for the sacrifice of captives, whose blood was smeared over the ground afterwards. The most graphic depictions of these ceremonies are in the bas-reliefs surrounding the south ball-court of El Tajín, in which the skeletal and ever-ravenous Death God features prominently.

Divine appetite With the Aztec concept of death as a means of approaching the gods, sacrifice was considered an honour. The souls of victims of war or sacrifice went directly to the paradise of the Sun God, where they were incarnated as humming-birds, while their blood assured the equilibrium of the cosmos and the daily return of the sun. Priests, painted or dressed in black and with hair matted in blood, were the purveyors of this food of the gods in an emotive ceremony that would last all night, conch shells blasting, drums beating and copal burning. Victims would be led to the sacrificial altar crowning the pyramid, where their hearts were removed and burnt for the gods' consumption. They were finally decapitated and flayed and their skin donned by the priest in recognition of their passage into the realm of the divine.

Monte Albán's famous ball-court

▶ Pachuca *158B2*

Pachuca, capital of Hidalgo, one of Mexico's poorest states, has a history of silver mining which dates from 1534, although it never attained the same importance as the great mining centres to the north-west. The mines on the edge of town and at Real del Monte still function and also bring with them a Pachucan speciality, the local *paste* (meat pie), introduced by miners from Cornwall in England in 1825. Try one at **La Blanca** on the *zócalo*. These immigrant workers also inspired Mexico's present-day national passion – football.

Sandwiched between two mountain ranges at an altitude of over 2,400m, Pachuca is a smaller version of Guanajuato, though winding streets, plazas and colonial buildings alternate with modernised parts. At its centre is the **Plaza de la Independencia**, crowned by an ornate clock-tower erected in 1910 with sculptures representing Independence, Liberty, the Constitution and the Reform (a tourist office is located inside the tower). A few blocks south-east of here is Pachuca's oldest building, the **Iglesia de la Asunción▶▶** (1533) and the adjoining **Convento de San Francisco** (1596). The church contains the mummified body of St Columba, brought from Sens in France, where she was martyred in the 3rd century; and the monastery has now become the **Centro Cultural de Hidalgo▶▶** (*Open* Tue–Sun 10–6). Permanent structures here include the **Museo Nacional de la Fotografía** and the **Museo Regional**. The photography collection exhibits early photographic apparatus with selected prints from its archives of over 1½ million photos, dating back to 1873. The small Museo Regional covers Hidalgo's history, archaeology (the Toltecs) and ethnography.

Other sights include the **University**, housed in a former hospital (1758) and, on the north side of the market square (Plaza de la Constitución), the **Cajas Reales** (1675), which was used for storing the infamous Quinta Real, the King's Fifth (a fifth of all precious metals was sent directly to the Spanish Crown).

MINERAL REAL DEL MONTE

Vast fields filled with rows of maguey plants, from which *pulque* is produced, cover the high slopes surrounding Pachuca, but 10km east lies the source of much of the state's former prosperity, Real del Monte. Silver, gold, lead and precious stones were mined here during its peak in the 18th century, but notoriously evil conditions led to a historic strike in 1766. No longer able to tolerate their exploitation, miners rose up and killed the mayor. The mine later passed into the hands of an English company.

The clock-tower that symbolises Independence rises above Pachuca's main square. Its carillon imitates London's Big Ben

Totanac descendants of the ancient Veracruz culture still live in Papantla today

▶ Papantla 158C2

The small town of Papantla, 210km north-west of Veracruz and 40km inland from the coast, lies in a veritable garden of Eden. Citrus orchards, vanilla plantations and cattle ranches cover the lush slopes of a region still strongly steeped in Totonac traditions. It is visited mainly for its proximity to the site of El Tajín, but it has a sleepy, picturesque charm of its own. Sprawling up a hillside, it culminates in the central plaza, the Parque Téllez, dominated by a rather ordinary church. In its turn this is towered over by an immense hilltop statue of a pipe-playing *volador* (flying dancer), symbol of Totonac tradition. The lofty pole in front of the church was once used by *voladores* every Sunday but is now reserved for major festivals. At one corner of the square is a busy daily market which sells vanilla 'sculptures' (made from vanilla bean pods), embroidery, jewellery and the costumes worn by many of the local men: loose baggy white trousers and tunics.

VOLADORES

For centuries man has attempted to fly, not least the *voladores* of Papantla. Re-enacting an ancient pre-Hispanic ritual, five men dressed in traditional costume climb a 30m pole crowned by a tiny platform where a short ceremony takes place. The chief starts a giddy dance to the tune of his pipe and drum, turning to each of the four cardinal points in honour of the Sun god. Meanwhile the four *voladores* wrap themselves in rope, fastened to a suspended frame. Launching themselves headfirst into space they plunge to the ground, spinning exactly 13 times each, their arms outstretched to greet the sun, while the rope slowly unwinds.

▶ Parque Nacional El Chico 125C1

Nature reserves are a recent development in Mexico, with over five per cent of land now protected by government regulations. El Chico National Park is high in the Sierra Madre Oriental, just over 30 twisting kilometres north of Pachuca. It offers great hiking terrain through pine forests, past lakes, rock formations and into caves. The mining town of **Real El Chico** lies on its western side and to the north, on Highway 105, is the 16th-century Augustinian monastery of *Atotonilco*.

▶▶ Parque Nacional La Malinche 158B1

From Tlaxcala or Puebla, it is a short drive or bus-ride to the base of this volcano, which stands at number five in Mexico's volcanic peak roll-call, at 4,461m. The road goes as far as La Malintzi, already over 2,900m, and from here a footpath leads up the ridge to the summit (about four hours).

▶▶ Parque Nacional Pico de Orizaba 158C1

Pico de Orizaba, also called Citlaltépetl ('Mountain of the Star'), stands 148km east of Puebla on Highway 150. Although its slopes are gentler than either Popocatépetl or Iztaccíhuatl, its superior height (over 5,700m) makes it

Popocatépetl as seen from the national park that surrounds it. You can climb 'Popo' in six to eight hours

LEGEND
The towering forms of Mexico's twin peaks inspired a Náhautl legend. A warrior (Popocatépetl) fell desperately in love with a beautiful princess (Iztaccíhuatl), but her father would allow their marriage only if Popocatépetl conquered a neighbouring tribe. This he did, but on his return found that the princess, fearing him dead, had died of a broken heart. He carried her body to the site of two hills, laid it on one and watched over her in eternal sorrow from the other. The shape of Iztaccíhuatl is said to resemble the profile of the recumbent princess, and that of Popocatépetl, the kneeling warrior.

a serious climbing challenge, and the lack of infrastructure imposes more preparation. Departure points are from the villages of **Ciudad Serdán** or **Tlachichuca**, reached by a turn-off running west from Highway 140. Transportation can be arranged here to reach a base camp where limited lodging and camping are available. An exhausting 10-hour hike is necessary to reach the peak but easier trails criss-cross the lower pine-clad slopes. This spectacular mountainous region marks the point where the tropical airstreams from Veracruz and the Gulf meet the cooler air of the central plateau: the result is often a permanent misty drizzle (particularly in October and November), which considerably reduces visibility.

►► Parque Nacional Popocatépetl-Iztaccíhuatl *158B1*

Along Mexico's central plateau rises a series of volcanoes that forms the transvolcanic region (see page 28). Towering over a region between Mexico City and Puebla are the second and third highest peaks, Popocatépetl (5,452m) and Iztaccíhuatl (5,286m). Climbing the snowcapped peak of Popocatépetl ('smoking mountain') was once a popular pastime for the capital's more energetic inhabitants, but volcanic activity has now put it strictly out of bounds. From a turn-off at Amecameca on Highway 115 the road winds up between the two peaks, to the **Paso de Cortés**, where there is a rare monument to Cortés (who supposedly first saw the lake city of Tenochtitlán from here). Another road winds north to the parking area for Iztaccíhuatl. This is where serious climbers set off for the base-camp of **La Joya** to start the long haul to the peak of 'Itza'. Serious rock-climbing is involved and it is advisable to hire a guide at Amecameca.

The baroque, born in early 17th-century Italy, soon spread to Spain and by the 18th century dominated Mexican architecture. Exuberant decoration and expansive, curvaceous forms blossomed above all in the nouveau riche colonial cities of central Mexico, where they characterised heights of ecclesiastical extravagance.

END OF AN ERA
Mexico's increasingly baroque style of architectural adornment, which gripped the national imagination for many prolific decades, would doubtless have brought about its own demise through an aesthetic reaction against its excesses. However, the style came to a uniquely abrupt end in 1783, when by order of the Spanish Crown it was replaced by neoclassism.

EIGHTH WONDER OF THE WORLD
The inauguration of Puebla's Capilla del Rosario inspired a book entitled *The Eighth Wonder of the World at the Great Chapel of the Rosary*. This details the decoration and transcribes every sermon pronounced during the nine days of opening ceremonies.

Eighteenth-century Mexican baroque – a style that defines the country for many people – was the embodiment of Mexico's social and economic confidence. Early examples were limited to surface decoration in a development of the Plateresque, a Renaissance style characterised by finely carved ornamental motifs and named after the *platero* (silversmith), that had held sway since the Spanish Conquest. However, by the 1730s Mexican baroque had become an elaborate, highly charged ornamentation named after the Spanish architect Churriguera (1665–1725), who specialised in lavishly carved retables (decorative frames situated at the back of the altar). Churrigueresque masterpieces of decoration and architecture pepper the mineral-rich cities of central Mexico, as well as Oaxaca and San Cristóbal, and are as visible a part of the national heritage as pre-Hispanic pyramids.

Relative restraint The birth of early baroque can be seen in Oaxaca's San Felipe Neri and the later Basilica de la

The interior of Puebla's Chapel of the Rosary is richly decorated with gold leaf, tiles, sculptures and carvings

Soledad (1682), both of which display intricately carved green-stone façades. In Querétaro the restrained stone entrance of the Ex-Convento de San Agustín (started in 1731) develops into a harmoniously proportioned cloister dominated by superbly carved stone pillars. Moorish influence, brought by the Spaniards from Andalucia, is particularly evident in the tiled *mudejar* domes which crowned many churches of central Mexico from the 17th century on. The most astonishing precursor, Cholula's Capilla Real (1540), boasts 49 domes. However, one exception in the early baroque period pointed the way to the Churrigueresque: the Capilla del Rosario in Puebla's Santo Domingo. Completed in 1690, the profusely carved chapel was described by contemporaries as the eighth wonder of the world.

TWENTY-FIVE YEARS OF HARD LABOUR
The astonishing Sanctuario de Octotlán, which overlooks Tlaxcala, is a typical example of Churrigueresque top heaviness. Above the delicately carved white stucco façade rise twin towers which widen towards the top. Inside, in the Camarin del Virgen, and in front of the main altar, the riotous gilded and painted decoration is the result of a quarter of a century of concentrated work by Francisco Miguel. The octagonal shrine to the Virgin is taken for a yearly outing to other Tlaxcalan churches on the third Monday of May.

Churrigueresque By the mid-18th century the ultra-baroque style had swept the country, producing delirious peaks of craftsmanship in carved, gilded altars, polychrome stucco-work and lace-like stone façades. Ignoring the classical rules of design, Churrigueresque architects often worked without plans, concentrating on drama as opposed to harmonious proportions. Paintings and sculptures were integrated into massive, high-relief altar-pieces and classical order was inverted by placing more delicate elements at the base. Extensive use of the *estípite*, a type of pilaster tapering towards the base and often elaborately carved at the top, helped give Churrigueresque its characteristic top-heavy impact. Floral motifs, sashes, scallops, bows and scrolls were entwined with countless cherubs and organically shaped abstract motifs in a distinctive style which swept through the country's ecclesiastical buildings.

The ultimate expressions of this labour-intensive and costly offering to the glories of Christianity can be seen at Taxco's Santa Prisca (created in the 1750s by Spanish students of Churriguera and financed by the mining baron José de la Borda), Mexico City's El Sagrario, and Guanajuato's Templo de la Compañia (1746) and La Valenciana (1775). Other prominent examples are Tepotzotlán's Camarín de la Virgen in San Francisco, Zacatecas' Santo Domingo (1746) and Catedral (1752), San Luis Potosí's San Francisco and Querétaro's Santa Clara and Santa Rosa (1752). The pulpit of Santa Rosa is entirely encrusted with an intricate marquetry of marble, tortoise-shell, ivory and mother-of-pearl.

Indigenous input However Spanish the origins of the baroque were, it was also an expression of indigenous creativity by local artists in their own interpretations of the Bible. Outstanding in this field is the church of Santa María, near Tonanzintla, which is entirely faced in sculpted *indigenas* figures paying homage to the Virgin Mary, surrounded by an abundance of naïve angels, fruits and flowers. In Oaxaca the magnificent church of Santo Domingo was decorated by Zapotec artisans, as were several churches in the valley, notably San Jerónimo at Tlacochahuaya.

Carved with consummate skill, countless figures of saints and angels adorn the façade of Tepotzotlán's church

MOLE* AND *CHILES EN NOGADA

Whether or not mole originated in the nuns' kitchen at Santa Rosa is questionable, but it is dished up in restaurants all over town, traditionally accompanying turkey or chicken. The list of ingredients in this spicy brown sauce includes fresh and dried chilli, pepper, peanuts, cloves, almonds, cinnamon, aniseed, tomato, onion, garlic and chocolate as well as virtually any other available herb or spice. Another visually more inspiring speciality is *chiles en nogada*, a delicious combination of stuffed chillies in a creamy walnut sauce topped with pomegranate seeds, traditionally available only in August and September but now served all year round.

 Puebla

158B1

Puebla sits in the foothills of the Sierra Madre, rimmed by four volcanoes. Mexico's fourth largest city is famed for its Spanish character and hand-made Talavera ceramics, and was already an important manufacturer of pottery when Spanish settlers founded the strategic stronghold in 1531. Its historical highpoint came on 5 May 1862 when the superior forces of French invaders suffered a rare defeat at the hands of General Ignacio de Zaragoza's troops: the event commemorated in streets named Cinco de Mayo all over Mexico, is celebrated annually. No celebration is made, however, of the French army's subsequent victorious siege, which left Puebla an occupied town for four years.

Ecclesiastical monuments At the heart of this sprawling, industrialised city lies the enormous Plaza Principal. The much-vaunted **catedral►►** is a vast, stylistic hotch-potch crowned by a tiled dome, whose construction dragged on from 1575 until 1649. Inside are a beautifully carved choir, no fewer than 14 chapels and some notable baroque paintings in the sacristy. Immediately behind is the **Palacio Episcopal**, which houses the tourist office, a prestigious library and the Casa de la Cultura. The city's crowning glory, however, is two blocks north of the square up Avenida 5 de Mayo at the **Templo de Santo Domingo►►►** (*Open* daily 7–12.15, 4–7), where the

Buildings in Puebla make lavish use of Talavera tiles

PROBLEMS
Despite its high cultural profile, Puebla is under serious attack from environmental lobbies. The daily dumping of 1,800 tons of solid waste allows toxic sludge to seep into underground aquifers and outmoded industrial plants lack basic anti-pollutant safeguards. In 1993 Governor Díaz unveiled the controversial Angelopolis programme, offering a radical solution mainly aimed at multiplying profits. It includes the creation of an industrial corridor, a low-cost housing area and a downtown riverwalk. The latter will become the Río San Francisco commercial and tourist zone, bulldozing what are deemed to be 'unprofitable' colonial buildings and evicting Puebla's traditional potters who have worked there with open-air kilns since 1653.

Capilla del Rosario (1690) constitutes the most sumptuous Dominican construction in the world. A profusion of gilded and carved stucco covers the dome and walls, framing polychrome statues, huge paintings, tiles and the bejewelled Virgin, resplendent in her freestanding altar.

More religious history comes to the fore at the 17th-century **Ex-Convento de Santa Rosa▶**, five blocks further north. This is now the **Museo de las Artesanías** (*Open* Tue–Sun 10–4.30), and every nook and cranny is filled with craftwork from the state of Puebla, making the obligatory guided tour a lengthy process. The last stop is the nuns' kitchen, faced in superlative Talavera tiles, where it is said that Puebla's famous *mole* sauce was invented. Two blocks north is the **Ex-Convento de Santa Mónica▶** (*Open* Tue–Sun 10–6) another 17th-century convent, where 80 years of clandestine activities followed the closure of monasteries and convents in 1857 by President Juarez. It now functions as a museum of religious art, and is a masterpiece of disguised doorways and secret passageways.

Domestic architecture and museums Puebla's originality lies in its feast of decorative mansions around the central streets, usually incorporating Talavera tiles and often dripping with ornate stuccowork. The **Casa del Alfeñique▶▶** houses the Museo Regional, opposite a crafts market, **El Parián**, and on the edge of an 'artists' quarter. Here, too, stands the **Teatro Principal** (1759), said to be Mexico's oldest theatre. On the main boulevard of 3 Poniente, two blocks west of the *zócalo*, the **Museo Bello▶▶** (*Open* Tue–Sat 10–4.30) displays an eclectic private collection of European, Asian and Mexican antiques. Two blocks south-east of the *zócalo* the **Museo Amparo▶▶▶** (*Open* Wed–Mon 10–5.30) exhibits Puebla's archaeological and vice-regal collections in a state-of-the-art setting that was originally a 16th-century hospital. For a guided tour of Talavera workshops, go to **Uriarte**, Avenida 4 Poniente, 911 (*Open* Mon–Sat 9–6.30, Sun 11–6).

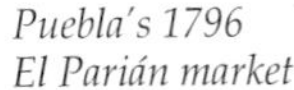

Puebla's 1796 El Parián market

MR SPRATLING
William Spratling was a professor of architecture in New Orleans before he came to Taxco in 1929. His passion for pre-Hispanic art extended to silver design and in 1931 he set up a workshop with a silversmith from nearby Iguana. He soon had 400 workers under him and, as the years went by, his apprentices set up their own workshops. By the time he was made a 'Son of Taxco', in 1953, the town had achieved international recognition as the silver capital of Mexico. He survived financial ruin brought on by a disastrous business partner, but his life ended tragically with a car accident in 1967.

Taxco's parish church is a fine example of Churrigueresque architecture, a florid extension of baroque

 ▶▶▶ Taxco 158A1

Taxco has long been established as a destination for silver-hungry tourists, but its spectacular natural site manages to compensate for the commercialism, notably the *pase pase* ('come in') refrain of the shopkeepers. Spilling down the slopes of Monte Atache, high in the forested mountains of Guerrero, it has grown considerably from its early days as a staging post on the royal road south to Acapulco, yet still maintains the quality of an Andalucian village. Silver was already flowing in the 1530s but it took two more centuries for Taxco to blossom, hand in hand with the fortunes of José de la Borda, an enterprising Frenchman who left his mining-magnate's mark here and in Cuernavaca. Another protagonist was William Spratling, who was responsible for regenerating the dormant silver industry in 1932 (see panel).

Exploring the maze Red-roofed, whitewashed houses pile on top of each other in the jumble of Taxco's crooked cobblestone streets, which zigzag uphill from the main road. At the centre of the web lies the small Plaza Borda, a social focal point and site of the **Iglesia de Santa Prisca y San Sebastián▶▶▶** (1758), built in seven years, and entirely financed by Borda. The church is one of Mexico's most harmonious and complete expressions of the Churrigueresque style, its interior crafted by students of the Spanish architect Churriguera. No expense was spared, as can be seen from the exquisitely carved façade, the luminous high-relief of the 12 gilded altarpieces, the many paintings by Cabrera and the German organ, brought in pieces by mule from Veracruz.

On a tiny plaza behind the church the **Museo Guillermo Spratling▶▶** (*Open* Tue–Sun 10–5) exhibits pre-Hispanic artefacts mostly from Spratling's private collection. (His collection was assembled according to personal aesthetic

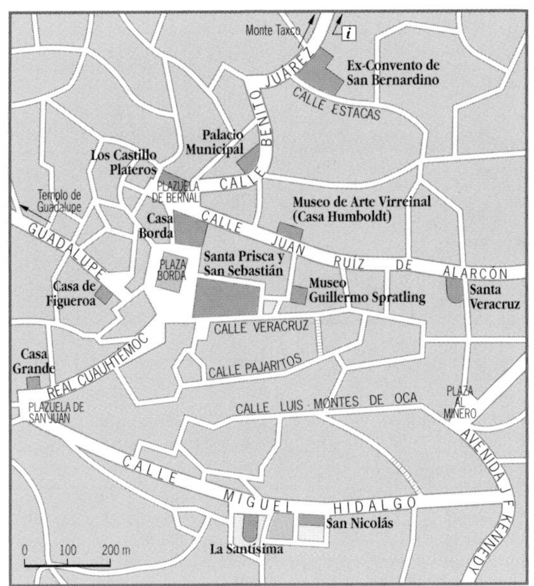

MR BORDA
'God gives to Borda, so Borda gives to God' were the words attributed to José de la Borda when he decided to finance the extravagant construction of Santa Prisca and import artisans from France and Spain. Legend goes that he had been lured to Taxco by stories of untold riches lying below its surface. His search proved fruitless until one day his horse slipped on a steep slope, dislodged a stone and in doing so revealed a mother lode of silver!

The town is known principally for its exquisitely crafted silverware

criteria only, thus authenticity is not assured). A few twisting steps down from here, on Calle Juan Ruíz de Alarcón, stands a museum honouring another of Taxco's illustrious foreign residents, the German explorer Baron von Humboldt, who lived here in 1803. The **Casa Humboldt** now houses the **Museo de Arte Virreinal▶▶** (*Open* Tue–Sat 10–5, Sun 9–3), a collection of colonial art assembled from Taxco's many mansions and churches. Curiosities include a rare 18th-century *catafalque*, a tiered funerary altar found in Santa Prisca during restoration in 1988. Other fine mansions and churches (notably the **Casa de Figueroa**, the **Casa Grande**, the **Ex-Convento de San Bernardino** and the hilltop **Templo de Guadalupe**) nestle in Taxco's maze, while a lively market area sprinkled with silver shops occupies the narrow streets below Santa Prisca.

Above the labyrinth The winding main road from Mexico City passes under **Los Arcos**, the last remaining arches of a 16th-century aqueduct which once continued past the Hacienda del Chorrillo, up a sliproad. The main tourist office is beside the arches and the gardens of the *hacienda*, now an applied arts school, harbour the *teleférico* terminus, the fastest and most scenic means of getting to the summit of **Monte Taxco▶▶** (7.30am–7pm). Views from the cable-car and the hotel at the top take in pine forests, waterfalls, the town's ramshackle hillside houses and, on a clear day, the distant peaks of Popocatépetl and Iztaccíhuatl.

Museo de Arte Virreinal
Casa Humboldt — J. Ruiz de Alarcón 6 — Tel. 2 55 01
Tasco, Gro. — C. P. 40200 — México
Cooperación N $ 5.00 — Nº 977

▶ **Tehuacán** see page 182

The Avenue of the Dead runs the length of Teotihuacán. At a time when most European cities were little more than villages, Teotihuacán was probably the biggest city in the world

NEW THEORIES, NEW QUESTIONS

Until recently it was thought that Teotihuacán was governed by pacifist priests dedicated to advancing the arts and sciences. However, recent discoveries made in the citadel and the Temple of Quetzalcóatl point to the practice of human sacrifice and have modified Teotihuacán's purist image. A sacred city that attracted pilgrims from afar, it was also a thriving and aggressive centre of trade with specialised quarters for potters, jewellers and other artisans. The end came between 650 and 700 when the city was abandoned, but several question marks remain. Archaeological finds indicate that it was set on fire, but by whom and why is not known. The growing strength of rival dynasties was certainly instrumental in its downfall.

▶▶▶ Teotihuacán *158B2*

Open: daily 8–5

Monumental Teotihuacán, site of the most urbanised civilisation in Mesoamerica, was designed to be seen from the heavens. It once covered an area of 20sq km and by AD 450 had a population of 85,000. Today, over 1,200 years after the fall of its sophisticated and influential civilisation, the ruins remain awesome, particularly as 80 per cent has been restored – not always well. Distances here are vast so visitors should be well prepared for the adversities of the Valley of Mexico climate: intense sun and/or afternoon storms in the summer months. Numerous paths branching off the main, well-trodden avenue lead to smaller and less-visited ruins which still impart a sense of the greatness of the sacred city.

Layout Some 50km north of Mexico City, Teotihuacán can be entered from the south, location of a restaurant, or from the pyramids farther north. Despite its incredible symmetry Teotihuacán is aligned slightly off the north–south axis, a factor believed to be inspired by astronomical calculations. Crossing the city east–west is the modified course of the Río San Juan and bisecting it south–north is the 4km-long Calle de los Muertos (Avenue of the Dead), which culminates in the shadow of the volcano, Cerro Gordo. Lining this broad avenue are Teotihuacán's major monuments: opposite the southern entrance lie the fortified walls of the vast Ciudadela (citadel), which enclose the magnificent tiered pyramid of the Templo de Quetzalcóatl; further north, past ruins of palaces, looms the Pirámide del Sol. In its southern shadow stands a superb modern museum – essential viewing. The next major monument along the Avenue of the Dead is the Palacio de Quetzalpapálotl (Palace of the Quetzal Butterfly), on the left before the Pirámide de la Luna (Pyramid of the Moon).

Main monuments Like the main pyramids, the **Temple of Quetzalcóatl**, in the citadel belongs to Teotihuacán's earliest period (CAD 200), although it was later built over. Stone carvings (366) depict the plumed serpent (Quetzalcóatl), the rain god (Tláloc) and the fire serpent; these were once brightly coloured, as were all Teotihuacán's structures. The **Pyramid of the Sun**, 70m high and with base walls measuring 222m, follows Egypt's Cheops pyramid and that of Cholula in scale.

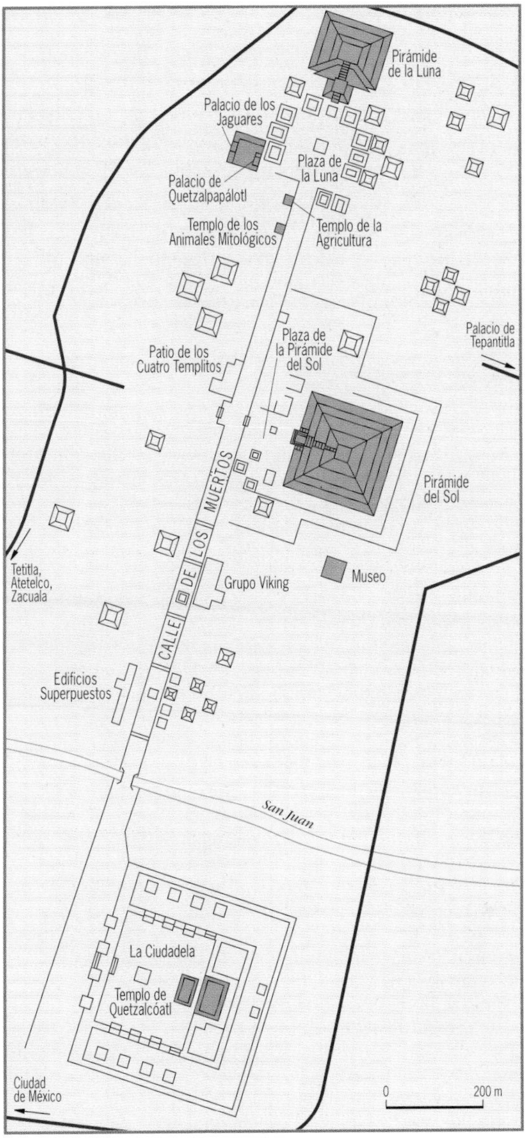

Although it was substantially altered by misguided excavations and reconstruction between 1905 and 1910, its ceremonial significance was confirmed in 1971 by the discovery of an underground tunnel filled with religious artefacts. The **Palace of Quetzalpapálotl** lies in a restored, elevated patio of square columns carved with bird and butterfly designs, its walls partially faced with a mural. At the back of this palace lie more patios with murals and carvings depicting the jaguar god, decorated conch shells (a recurring Teotihuacán motif) and birds. Dominating a large plaza lined with 12 temple platforms, the **Pyramid of the Moon** offers the final sweeping view of Teotihuacán from its summit.

MURALS
Practically every wall of Teotihuacán was once painted with gods, mythical creatures, plants, shells, animals (real and imaginary) and priests in allegorical and eloquent expressions of the population's complex culture. The most visited murals are those in the Palace of Quetzalpapálotl and its sub-structures, but 500m east of the Pyramid of the Sun stands a priest's residence (Tepantitla) filled with murals dedicated to Tláloc. A more legible full-scale copy of this is displayed at the Museo de Antropología in Mexico City. In the far west lie the palaces of Atetelco, Tetitla and Zacuala, where jaguars, coyotes, snakes and eagles are easily discernible.

Mural fragment in the site museum

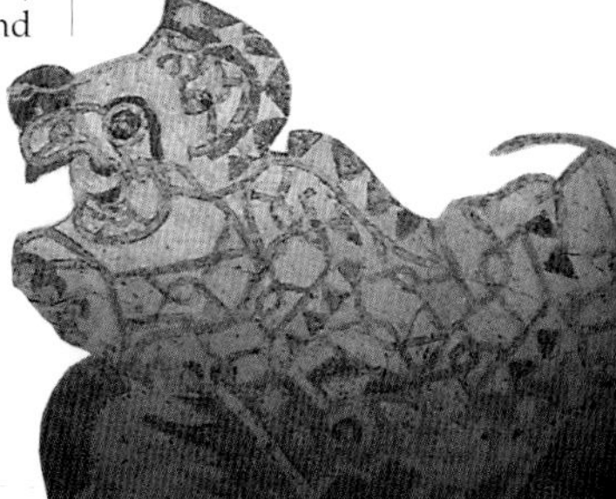

For the Mesoamericans the gods were omnipresent. Their identities and their importance differed from one culture to the next, but a recurring deity was that of Quetzalcóatl, the plumed serpent, worshipped from Teotihuacán to Chichén Itzá. In some places, even today religious practices combine aspects of traditional gods with Christian traditions.

AZTEC LEGEND
During the final flood of ancient times, the sky fell to earth. Quetzalcóatl and Tezcatlipoca changed themselves into two trees that grew and grew, pushing the sky back to its original position. Finally leaving the trees in place, one at each end of the earth, the two deities climbed over the rim of the sky and met at the centre of the Milky Way. Thus they became the 'lords of heaven and of the stars'.

MAYAN GENESIS
'In the beginning there were no people, no animals, no trees, no stones, there was nothing, all was desolation and emptiness ... In the silence of the mists lived the gods called Tepeu, Gucumatz and Hurakan, names that guard the secrets of creation, of life, death, of the earth and of the beings that inhabit it ... The gods conferred and agreed on what was to be done ... and light was created in the void.'

From the *Popoh Vul*, the sacred book of the Quiché Maya, discovered at the beginning of the 18th century.

Passion, fervour and an obsession with the supernatural dominated Mexico's civilisation when the Spaniards arrived. Every gesture, thought and act was governed by divine personalities to the extent that faith was even stronger than the basic instinct to survive. Intricately linked with, and visible in the sun and stars, Mesoamerican gods also entered nature as animals, plants or the land itself, and nearly every native civilisation had – and, in some cases, still has – its god of corn.

Primal pairs For the Aztecs, violence was a way of life. Their belief that the world had passed through four cataclysmic cosmic ages before entering the final Fifth Sun featured titanic fights between Quetzalcóatl and Tezcatlipoca to dominate each cycle. God of sorcery, creator of sky and earth and considered the supreme Aztec power, the invisible Tezcatlipoca ('Smoking Mirror') was only manifest as a shadow or as the wind, but his antics constantly opposed Quetzalcóatl, the benign creator of mankind from his own blood. Duality was thus firmly established, echoed in the origins of the terrible Huitzilopochtli, the Aztec god of war who started life in conflict. According to legend, his widowed mother Coatlicue (an earth goddess) was made pregnant by a ball of feathers, much to the horror of her 400 sons (the stars) and daughter (the moon). To prevent her disgrace they decided to kill her, managing her decapitation but not preventing the birth of the fully armed Huitzilopochtli. Thus born in anger, he proceeded to slay his sister, defeat his brothers and develop an insatiable thirst for warrior blood.

This 'pairing' of gods is also found amongst the Lacandon (Hachakyom and Kisin) and the

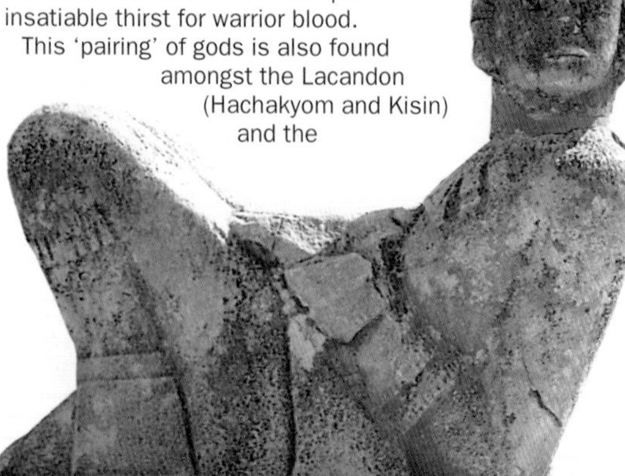

To appease the gods the hearts of sacrificed victims were removed and placed on a chacmool *altar such as this one at Chichén Itzá*

Tarahumara (Elder Brother and Younger Brother). In its contemporary expression, the primal father and mother have been absorbed into the Christian God and the Virgin is identified with the sun and moon.

Gods of nature For such an agriculturally dependent race, rain assumed primordial importance. At Teotihuacán an entire mural in the palace of Tepantitla depicted the paradise of Tláloc, the rain god who was central to Aztec agricultural rites. At the end of the dry season mass sacrifices of young children took place on mountains to appease him. His paradise also offered idyllic retirement for anyone who died a water-related death such as drowning. More terrifying was Xipe Totec, the god of spring and rebirth of vegetation, represented by priests wearing the flayed skin of sacrificial victims. Nature also reincarnated the dead: the Aztecs believed that the souls of warriors could return as birds or butterflies.

In the Yucatán, the Maya corn god Yam Kax governed all agricultural rites and Chac, the rain god, would not suffer any delay in sowing (the date was announced by the first seasonal appearance of the winged ant), a factor that actually halted the Indian attack on Mérida during the bloody 1840s War of the Castes. Maya fidelity to their ancient beliefs is still reflected in their view of heaven: seven levels are pierced by the sacred *ceiba* (cohune palm) and it is by climbing this tree that dead souls progress to the divine summit, home of the God of Christianity.

ANIMAL MAGIC
Belief in the magic function of animals was widespread. The main deity depicted by the Olmecs, Mexico's mother race, combined a snarling jaguar with a fat baby, often squalling and gesticulating, a concept that spread as far as the cave paintings of Guerrero. For the Maya the jaguar's spotted coat represented the night sky (he was a god of the underworld), while the macaw with its brilliant plumage was an agent of the sun god. The dog, although not a deity, had a major role in leading souls across the river to the Aztec underworld, a belief that recurs amongst Tarascans, Mixtecs and Tzotzils.

Images of Chac, the god of rain, adorn the temples at Chichén Itzá

Natural spring at Tehuacán

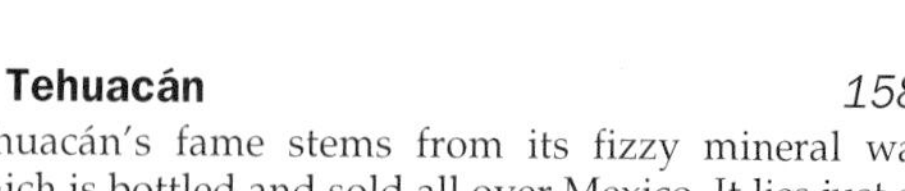

► Tehuacán *158B1*

Tehuacán's fame stems from its fizzy mineral water, which is bottled and sold all over Mexico. It lies just over 110km south-east of Puebla on the mountainous main road south to Oaxaca. A former monastery now houses the **Museo del Valle de Tehuacán**, which exhibits significant archaeological finds from the region and over 6,000 mineralogical specimens. Mineral baths which date from pre-Hispanic times still function on the outskirts of town.

►►► Tepotzotlán *158A2*

Barely 30km north-west of Mexico City on the way to Tula, this small colonial town is known for its fabulously ornate **Templo de San Francisco Javier►►►** and the adjoining monastery, now home to the **Museo Nacional del Virreinato►►►** (Viceroyal Museum). This Jesuit church was built in the 1670s but most of its rich ornamentation, both inside and out, dates from the mid-18th century. It displays superlative religious paintings, statues, reliquaries and chalices, as well as furniture, *objets d'art*, arms and costumes from the 16th to 19th centuries (*Open* Tue–Fri 10–5, Sat–Sun 10–6). Off the pretty cloister is the **Capilla Doméstica**, another baroque flight of fantasy.

Tepotzotlán's church

►► Tepoztlán *158A1*

Tepoztlán's isolated setting in a beautiful valley edged by towering cliffs made it a favourite retreat for mystics of the 1960s and '70s. Just 25km north-east of Cuernavaca, it has become a popular weekend outing. Dominating the town centre is a 16th-century Dominican monastery and church, the **Ex-Convento Domínico de la Natividad.** In a street just behind is the **Museo Arqueológico►** (*Open* Tue–Sun 10–6), which displays a small but fine selection of pre-Hispanic figures collected by the poet Carlos Pellicer. A colourful food market in the main square expands to crafts at the weekend, and up-market restaurants cater for wealthier visitors. Tepoztlán's setting can best be appreciated from the **Pirámide de Tepoztec►►**, high on a hilltop north of town. A good hour's climb up a steep path leads to this ruined Tlahuican temple dedicated to the Aztec god, Tepoztécatl.

HIGH BAROQUE WHIMS

The zenith of Tepotzotlán's Church of San Francisco, considered the ultimate expression of Churrigueresque detail, is reached in the Camarín de la Virgen, an eight-sided chapel with mirrors, cherubs, flowers, fruit and geometric motifs in a delirium of gold-leaf and colour. The spectacle of the main church nave and chapels is equally dazzling: floor-to-ceiling gilded altarpieces incorporate paintings and statues of saints, all glowing in the soft light of alabaster windows.

►► Tlaxcala *158B1*

The town of Tlaxcala was instrumental in Cortés' victory over the Aztecs, and was immediately granted special privileges by the Spanish emperor, but its population was decimated by a plague between 1544 and 1546. Today it remains a small, quiet town, capital of Mexico's tiniest state (of the same name). The lovely main square, the **Plaza de la Constitución**, is rimmed by fine 16th-century government buildings incorporating Moorish architectural elements and the magnificent baroque **Basilica**. Here too is the **Palacio del Gobierno▶** (*Open* daily 8–8), with extensive murals illustrating local history. Off the southeast corner, up a slope, stands **San Francisco▶▶**, Mexico's oldest church (1521). Its monastery contains the **Museo Regional▶▶** (*Open* Tue–Sun 10–5) with historical and archaeological exhibits arranged around its cloisters. In the neighbouring church a beautifully decorated wood ceiling and tiled *azulejo* floor lead to a side chapel, the **Capilla del Tercer Orden**, whose font is said to have been used to baptise the four chiefs of Tlaxcala. Three blocks north-west of the zócalo, set in the riverside gardens, is the **Museo de Artes Populares▶** (*Open* Tue–Sun 10–6), with craft demonstrations. On the outskirts overlooking the valley stands the dazzling white church of **Ocotlan▶▶▶** (1541). High relief sculptures continue inside in breathtaking gilded form.

▶ Toluca *158A1*

This growing town, 60km west of Mexico City, is the highest in the country. The **Cosmo Vitral▶▶** (*Open* Tue–Sun 10–6) on Plaza Garibay was once a market but has been converted into a large botanic garden illuminated by stained-glass windows. The **Mercado Juárez** now sprawls along the south-west periphery of the city on and off Paseo Tollocán, next to the bus station. Museums include the **Bellas Artes▶** (*Open* Tue–Sun 10–6), concentrating on colonial and modern paintings, and the **Museo de Antropologia▶** (*Open* Tue–Sun 10–6). To the southwest (40km) looms the **Nevado de Toluca▶▶**, the world's only drive-in volcano. You can park at 4,500m and gaze at the crater lakes of the Sun and the Moon.

PEACE WITH THE TLAXCALANS

'And when we came within a mile of Tlascala these same Calciques (chiefs) who had gone ahead came out to meet us, bringing with them their sons and nephews and many of the leading inhabitants ... There were four parties in Tlascala and their subjects came from all parts of the country, wearing their different costumes which, although made of sisal, there being no cotton to be had, were very lordly, and beautifully embroidered and decorated.'
Bernal Díaz: *The Conquest of New Spain*, 1568.

Stained glass window at the Cosmo Vitral in Toluca

The interior of Tonanzintla's church is encrusted with every conceivable decorative medium

TOLTEC CARVINGS
Militarism, human sacrifice, mortality and supernatural creatures all have a high profile in Toltec carvings. The 4.6m-high Atlantes at Tula, supposedly representing Quetzalcóatl as the morning star, are armed with spears and arrows, and sport feathered helmets and butterfly-shaped breastplates. More warriors and gods, prowling jaguars, human heart-devouring eagles, coyotes and incarnations of Quetzalcóatl once faced every wall or column. Legend and fact merge, even leaving in question the fate of the Toltec Quetzalcóatl, alias their king, Topiltzin. This great king fled a *coup d'état* around 987 and arrived on the Gulf of Mexico. Did he then perform an act of self-sacrifice? Or did he set sail on a raft built of serpents – to return one day from the east?

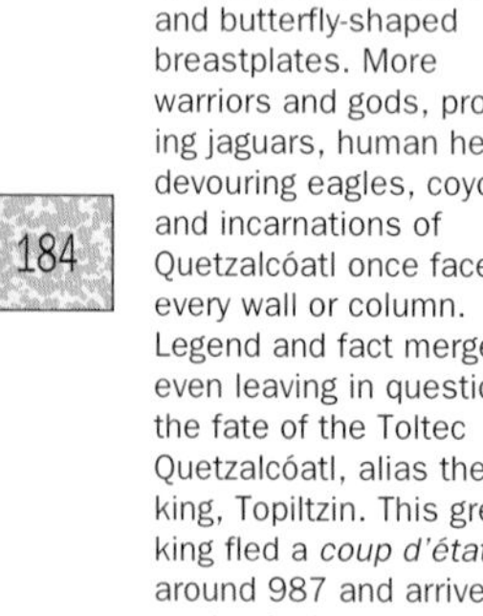

►► Tonanzintla *158B1*

A few kilometres west of Puebla and south of Cholula, off Highway 190, the village of Tonanzintla boasts the remarkable **Iglesia de Santa María** (*Open* daily 10–6). Carrying 18th-century baroque decoration to the extreme, every surface is embellished with gilded and polychrome stucco, wood and painting. What makes it unique is the fact that this is a perception of heaven created by indigenous people. Barbarous and sublime, it combines pagan atavism (winged angels, vegetable offerings, naïve perspectives) with Christian symbols in a rare hybrid expression of spirituality. Further south, at Acatepec, another baroque marvel, the **Templo de San Francisco**►►► (1788), recalls the proximity of Puebla in its riotously tiled façade and contains a richly decorated interior. Five kilometres on, the village of **Tlaxcalancingo** is home to yet another extraordinary church, ornamented with fine Talavera tiles.

►► Tula *158A2*

Open: Tue–Sun 9.30–4.30
The ruins of the mighty Toltec kingdom of Tula lie 84km north-west of Mexico City. From 950 to 1150 it filled the central Mexican power vacuum between the Teotihuacán civilisation and the Aztecs. The site has more academic than real interest as excavations are limited and the most important sculptures have been replaced with copies (the originals are exhibited in Mexico City's Anthropology Museum). The Aztecs told stories of the magnificence of Tula, and were probably also responsible for early looting. Overlooking an arid, undulating landscape, the focal point is the **Pirámide de Quetzalcóatl** (known as the Templo de Tlahuizcalpantecuhtli). Its summit is dominated

by four heavily armed Atlantes, giant stone warriors that once supported the roof of the temple. Square columns aligned behind them are carved with relief images of crocodiles, warriors and the head of Quetzalcóatl. Along the northern wall of the pyramid base is the 40m **Coatepantli** (Serpent Wall), a bas-relief depicting a series of snakes devouring human skeletons. Flanking the west side is the **Palacio Quemada** (Burnt Palace) with more columns, low benches and bas-reliefs. In front a roofless colonnaded hall contains two reclining *chacmools* (stone figures with bowls probably used for receiving the hearts of sacrificial victims) and opens on to a large plaza. Beyond this lies another, larger pyramid, only partially excavated. Two ball-courts complete the site, all of which is explained at the entrance museum, which has some important artefacts.

Like grim-faced sentinels guarding the past, the Atlantes of Tula form a dramatic silhouette on top of their platform

▶ Valle de Bravo *158A1*

The little town of Valle de Bravo nestles in a wooded valley 76km west of Toluca. Narrow cobbled streets lined with pristine white houses with red roofs create a pattern along the shore of an artificial lake, Laguna de Avándaro. It is popular for its watersports, from water-skiing to sailing; the surrounding hills are good for hiking and riding. Crafts also have a high profile and the Sunday market around the main square caters for the weekend hordes. Hotels are expensive, reflecting the resort's appeal for wealthy escapists from the capital.

▶▶▶ Veracruz *158C1*

Veracruz was the first landing-point for Cortés and his army in 1519 and for centuries was Mexico's major seaport. Perhaps more Caribbean than Mexican, this colourful, tropical port resounds to the marimba as its residents and seafaring visitors play hard and long into the night. Countless hawkers, musicians and bars cater well for their needs while adequate beaches stretch south of the centre. Veracruz had the monopoly on trade between Spain and her colony despite devastating epidemics of yellow fever and pirate attacks (notably Sir Francis Drake and John Hawkins). The French military also disembarked here in 1838 and again in 1861. Bombarded by the Americans in 1847, it was later occupied by them in 1914. Apart from the fort of San Juan de Ulúa, built in 1562, most public buildings date from the Porfiriato period.

CARNIVAL

The festive atmosphere of Veracruz reaches an annual peak during the week preceding Ash Wednesday. Mexico's number one carnival pulls in visitors from every corner of the nation so, if you are intent on joining the fun, book a hotel well in advance. Every day has a special theme embodied in brilliantly coloured floats and processions which wind their way through the streets, accompanied by the inevitable and very Caribbean sounds of steel drums and marimbas (large wooden xylophones). Fireworks, dances (Veracruz is particularly strong on lively traditional dances with a marked heel-tapping Spanish influence), endless food stalls and, of course, plenty of alcohol to keep spirits on a permanent nine-day high.

VERACRUZAN BEACHES
Boats from the main quay leave in the mornings for the Isla de Sacrificios, the island site of an important pre-Hispanic shrine where the Spaniards first discovered traces of human sacrifice. Today's visitors should be careful not to find themselves sacrificed to the waves, as currents are strong, but the beaches are attractive. On the mainland south of town the best destinations are Mocambo (9km) and Boca del Río (13km). Both are easily reached by bus from Zaragoza. Hotels, seafood restaurants and reasonably clean water make Mocambo a desirable weekend getaway, while at Boca del Río the estuary is dotted with purveyors of the freshest Veracruz catch.

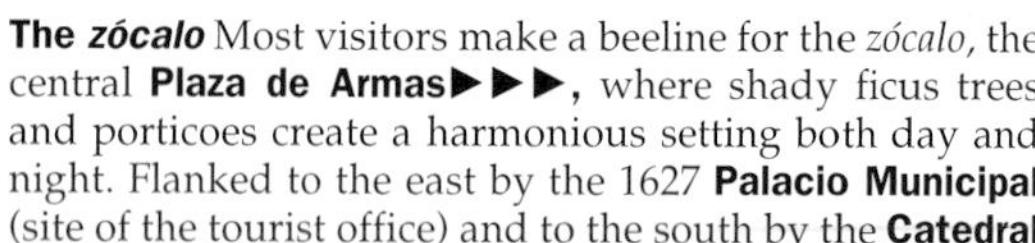

The *zócalo* Most visitors make a beeline for the *zócalo*, the central **Plaza de Armas▶▶▶**, where shady ficus trees and porticoes create a harmonious setting both day and night. Flanked to the east by the 1627 **Palacio Municipal** (site of the tourist office) and to the south by the **Catedral**

Veracruz's cathedral stands on the Plaza de Armas – said to be the oldest zócalo *in Mexico*

(1734), the square is surrounded by hotels, bars and restaurants, whose tables spill outside. As *mariachis* tune up, vendors of every age hawk hammocks or sunhats, while others stagger beneath giant model galleons, and entire families anchor themselves for the evening entertainment.

Towards the harbour A few blocks south, on Zaragoza, is the **Museo de la Ciudad▶▶** (*Open* Mon–Sat 9–4), which offers some unusual perspectives on Mexican history, notably the role of the Arab world in maritime history and the socio-economic effects of three centuries of slave-trafficking. On an opposite corner stands a violet-coloured 18th-century hospital, now the **Centro Cultural▶**, whose pretty patios are the venue for cultural events and a crafts shop. Two blocks east stands the **Baluarte Santiago▶** (Santiago Bastion), last survivor of nine 16th-century forts which lined a defensive wall, although cannons now point curiously inland. The interior hosts a small museum of pre-Hispanic jewellery (*Open* Tue–Sun 9–4).

Down by the harbour at the lighthouse is a modest **museum▶** dedicated to Venustiano Carranza, who based his government here while formulating the Constitution between 1914 and 1915 (*Open* Tue–Sun 9–5). The elegant 19th-century building is also home to the Mexican Navy High Command: naval officers gladly point the way. The quay, towered over by a hideous 1960s Pemex building, is the departure point for

A copy of the Marigallante *in Veracruz harbour*

Café de los Portales, the former Café de la Parroquía, Veracruz

harbour boat tours. At the town end is a covered **Mercado de Artesanías** (crafts market), which fronts a string of small shops, all selling shellwork, crochet, embroidery and souvenirs.

Towards San Juan de Ulúa On the seafront side of the *zócalo*, the traffic-laden **Plaza de la República** is lined with grandiose Porfiriato buildings: the civil registry building, customs house, post office and station. From the Aduana (customs house) buses leave for **San Juan de Ulúa▶▶▶** (*Open* Tue–Sun 9.30–5) and the main port area north of town. Formerly an island fortress, San Juan de Ulúa is now linked to wharves by a causeway. It was established in 1528, and extended in the 17th and 18th centuries, and its ramparts, towers and bridges create an intriguing structure. Some areas are still used by the National Arsenal and a small museum hides under the central arches. Across the moat are the dungeons which were used for Porfirio Díaz's political prisoners.

▶▶ Xochicalco *158A1*

Open: daily 10–5

Built on an elevated defensive site in rolling hills, Xochicalco ('house of flowers') flourished between 650 and 900. This coincided with profound transformations in the Mesoamerican balance of power, sparked off by the fall of Teotihuacán. It is thought to have been the commercial meeting place for Maya, Olmecs and Zapotecs, where they also shared their astronomical knowledge. Its main structure is the **Pirámide de Quetzalcóatl** (also known as the Pirámide de las Serpientes Emplumadas), a platform carved with superb bas-reliefs of the feathered serpent god, cross-legged figures resembling Mayan priests and calendric references. The large, reconstructed ball-court was possibly the first in the central plateau.

▶▶ Zempoala (Cempoala) *158C1*

Open: daily 9–5

Halfway between Jalapa and Veracruz on the Gulf Coast lies the Totonac site of Zempoala, whose gleaming white buildings, reflected in the sun, seemed to Cortés and his men to have been built of silver. From 1521 Zempoala was to play a key role in facilitating Cortés' victory. The excavated area stands against a mountainous background with many structures scattered in nearby villages and fields. A wall encircles the **Templo Mayor**, **Templo de las Chimeneas** (named after the 'chimney' form of its semicircular columns), the **Gran Pirámide** and the adjoining **Templo del Díos del Viento**. Beyond the wall stands the **Templo de las Caritas**, once decorated with rows of little carved heads.

NUMBER ONE

On the coast road between Veracruz and Zempoala, the picturesque village of La Antigua was the site of the first Spanish settlement on Mexican soil in 1519, named Villa Rica de la Vera Cruz. A ruined Ayuntamiento (town hall), a restored church (Eremita del Rosario) and the ruins of the Casa de Cortés, said to have been built for the *conquistador* himself, are all that remains of those early years.

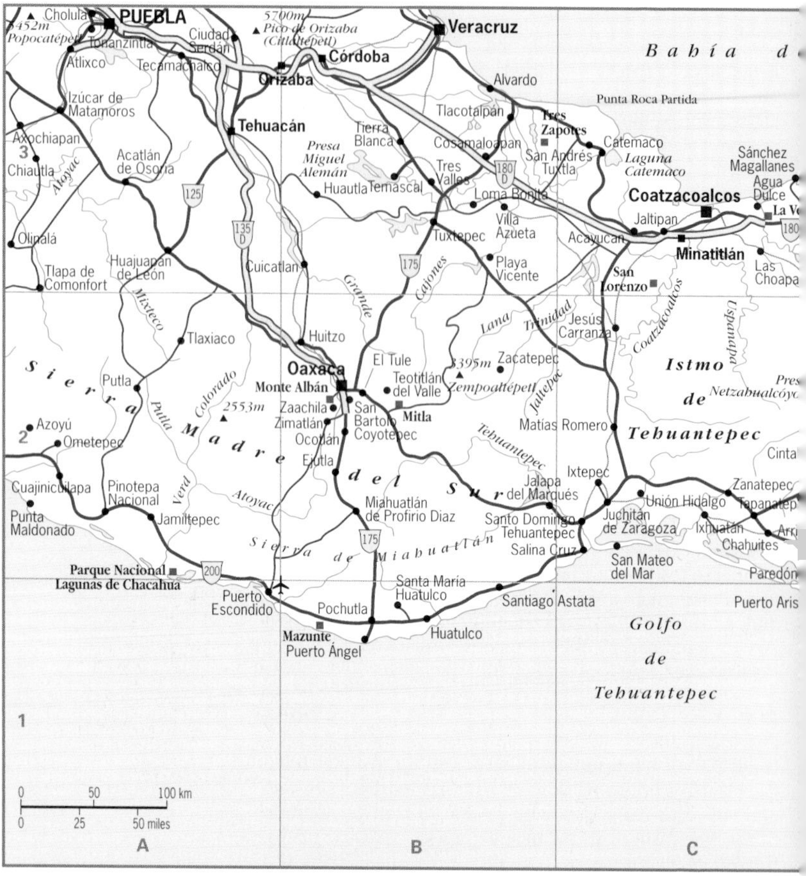
Cholula
PUEBLA
5452m
Popocatépetl
Tonanzintla
Atlixco
Ciudad Serdán
5700m
Pico de Orizaba (Citlaltépetl)
Tecamachalco
Orizaba
Córdoba
Veracruz
Bahía d
Alvardo
Punta Roca Partida
Izúcar de Matamoros
Tehuacán
Tlacotalpán
Tres Zapotes
Axochiapan
3
Chiautla
Atoyac
Acatlán de Osoria
125
Presa Miguel Alemán
Tierra Blanca
Cosamaloapan
180 D
San Andrés Tuxtla
Catemaco
Laguna Catemaco
Sánchez Magallanes
Agua Dulce
Huautla
Temascal
Tres Valles
Loma Bonita
Coatzacoalcos
La V
135 D
Olinalá
Villa Azueta
Tuxtepec
Jaltipan
Acayucan
180
Minatitlán
Huajuapan de León
Cuicatlán
175
Cajones
Playa Vicente
San Lorenzo
Las Choapa
Tlapa de Comonfort
Mixteco
Grande
Lana
Trinidad
Jesús Carranza
Coatzacoalcos
Uspanapa
Tlaxiaco
Huitzo
Sierra
El Tule
3395m
Zacatepec
Istmo
Oaxaca
Monte Albán
Teotitlán del Valle
Zempoaltépetl
Jaltepec
Pres
Netzahualcóyo
de
Putla
Colorado
2553m
Zaachila
Zimatlán
San Bartolo Coyotepec
Mitla
Azoyú
Putla
Madre
Matías Romero
Tehuantepec
2
Ometepec
Ocotlán
Tehuantepec
Cinta
Ejutla
del
Sur
Ixtepec
Jalapa del Marqués
Zanatepec
Cuajinicuilapa
Pinotepa Nacional
Verd
Unión Hidalgo
Tapanatep
Atoyac
Miahuatlán de Profirio Diaz
Santo Domingo Tehuantepec
Juchitán de Zaragoza
Ixhuatán
Arri
Punta Maldonado
Jamiltepec
Chahuites
Sierra de Miahuatlán
175
Salina Cruz
San Mateo del Mar
Parque Nacional Lagunas de Chacahua
200
Paredón
Santa María Huatulco
Puerto Escondido
Santiago Astata
Puerto Aris
Pochutla
Mazunte
Huatulco
Golfo de Tehuantepec
Puerto Ángel
1
0
50
100 km
0
25
50 miles
A
B
C

The South

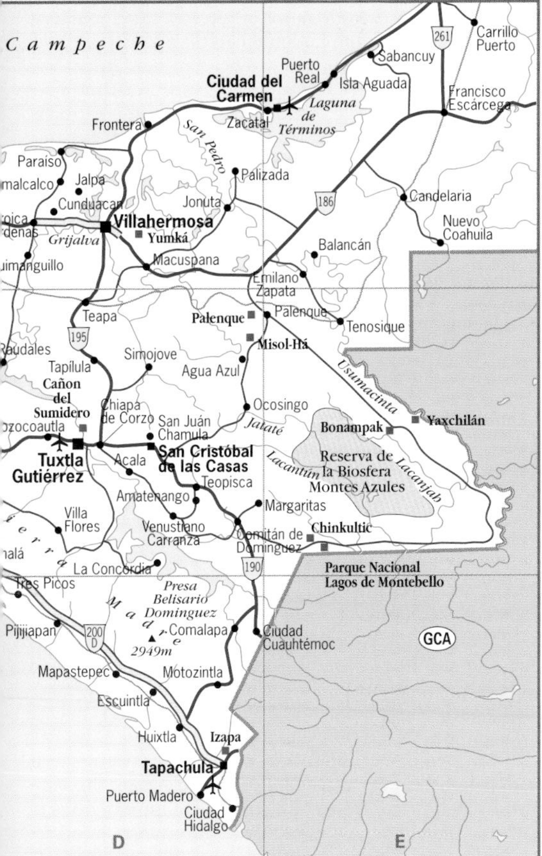

THE SOUTH The difference between central Mexico and the south is very marked. Socially, economically, geographically and historically the south (which would be more accurately described as the east) brandishes its own banner. From southern Veracruz to Oaxaca, Chiapas and Tabasco, steamy coastlines, dry sierra, forested mountains and tropical rain forest announce the beginning of Central America. Home to the densest concentration of Mexico's indigenous population (for example, 70 per cent of the state of Oaxaca's inhabitants are of native descent), the area is redolent of Olmecs, Zapotecs, Mixtecs and Maya, and it is their craft traditions, way of life and spiritual beliefs that define the region's character. Decades behind the development of central and northern Mexico, the cities shrink noticeably in scale and in number and, following the same equation, poverty gains the upper hand. The exception is the more sophisticated state of Tabasco, the heart of Mexico's oldest civilisation, the Olmecs, which has made a quantum leap into the late 20th century with the discovery there of rich oil deposits. Surprisingly, the states of Oaxaca and Chiapas are both exceptionally well organised for visitors, and eco-tourism is developing fast. This is often arranged in conjunction with local people, and can include guided walks, horse-trekking or simple accommodation in villages.

EXCEPTIONS TO THE RULE
The south has a few geographic anomalies among its contours. In southern Veracruz the flat, hot plain suddenly breaks into volcanic sierra around San Andrés Tuxtla and Catemaco. Refreshing temperatures, lakes and pastoral slopes have led to this region being dubbed the 'Switzerland of Mexico'. In Tabasco, the region bordering the Yucatán evolves into an idyllic, unspoiled land of banana groves, palm trees and estuaries. Similarly, there is a life after the rainforest, found in the moody beauty and changing hues of the Lagos de Montebello on the Guatemalan border.

Previous page: countless varieties of cacti flourish in the arid mountains of the Sierra Madre del Sur, which dominate the states of Guerrero and Oaxaca
Below: the Sierra Madre del Sur

RESISTANCE Although most of the southern cultures were under Aztec domination when the Spanish arrived, it took several years for them to bend to new rule. Even then, there were sporadic indigenous rebellions and land disputes, which have continued up till the present. Chiapas was brought under control in 1524 by the *conquistador* Diego de Mazariegos, not without provoking thousands of suicides by *indígenas* who heroically leapt into the gaping depths of the Cañon de Sumidero. One group was never conquered: by retreating into the rainforest of Chiapas the Lacandons preserved their Mayan traditions for centuries. Ruled by the Spanish colonial administration of Guatemala, Chiapas only joined Mexico in 1824, another factor which contributed to its slow development. Oaxaca, too, held out valiantly against the Spanish but the *encomienda* (land grant) system soon wrought its havoc, depriving *indígenas* of their land and enslaving hundreds of thousands on tobacco and sugarcane estates. Disease and deplorable conditions took their toll, despite one bright light in the long dark tunnel of oppression: the Dominican bishop Bartholomé de las Casas who, in 1550, managed to have slavery banned in Chiapas.

OAXACAN TERRAIN The steamy and tropical coastal plains of southern Veracruz rise rapidly into the central mountainous spine, convergence of the Sierra Madre del Sur and the Sierra Madre Oriental. From Puebla and Veracruz, roads lead south through vast, empty landscapes then climb to the hot, dry region of Oaxaca where Zapotecs and Mixtecs live scattered throughout the valley. Archaeological interest is particularly strong here, whether at the sublime capital of Monte Albán, the masterfully decorated site of Mitla, the more remote ruins of Yagul or in the city museums. Nor is baroque architecture unrepresented: Oaxaca's churches more than compensate for the relative absence elsewhere. To the south the state of Oaxaca descends to the relaxed Pacific resorts of Puerto Ángel and Puerto Escondido and the newly developing Huatulco, destined for mega-resort status with an international airport.

▶▶▶ REGION HIGHLIGHTS

Near San Cristóbal de las Casas

INTO CHIAPAS Moving east, Mexico narrows into the plains of the Isthmus of Tehuantepec where the Pacific is 'only' 225km from the Gulf, a distance which once inspired thoughts of an alternative Panama Canal. From here the furrowed, pine-forested hills of Chiapas rise to San Cristóbal de las Casas and its troubled and mysterious mountain villages before descending again to humid jungle around the major Mayan site of Palenque and the shrouded ruins of Bonampak and Yaxchilán. Water is abundant throughout Chiapas: reservoirs produce almost 30 per cent of the nation's requirements and waterfalls such as Agua Azul offer much-needed relief from the humid heat. The Río Grijalva, the main waterway artery to the Gulf, courses through Tuxtla Gutiérrez, the Cañon de Sumidero and Villahermosa to end in the flat, marshy delta of Tabasco – the last of the Mexican 'south' before the country twists northwards into the Yucatán peninsula.

ZAPATISTAS

In the early hours of New Year's Day 1994, some 2,000 armed indigenous Mexicans, men and women, took over five towns in Chiapas, including San Cristóbal de las Casas and Ocosingo, in a highly organised uprising aimed at drawing attention to agrarian and human rights' issues (see page 17). Led by the charismatic but incognito 'Marcos', Zapatista negotiations produced some immediate results. Chiapas was awarded $250 million for road and infrastructure projects, while in the state of Oaxaca, where 4,000 native Mexicans had followed Chiapas' example by taking over public buildings, social aid was increased to $153 million. Despite these gains, the Chiapas situation has not been resolved, so travellers should be careful outside the main towns.

Brahmin cattle, Chiapas

Agua Azul's jungle waterfalls present a dazzling display of cascades tumbling over limestone rocks

CAST A SPELL
Catemaco's fame as Mexico's number one centre for witchcraft has led to a proliferation of local *brujas* (witches) and *curanderos* (healers), who offer services ranging from home-made cures for illnesses to love potions or occult predictions.

AGUA AZUL
N$ 5.00
CONTROL
Fecha
19___
Nº 1118

PARQUE NATURAL TURISTICO
Cascadas de Agua Azul
ADMINISTRADO POR CAMPESINOS
del Pob. Agua Azul Mpio. de Tumbalá, Chis.
La presente cuota se destinara para la protección, preservación, conservación y administración del parque Turistico, para conservar la Belleza Natural la Flora y la Fauna nuestra, ayúdenos a conservar la Ecología para nuestra futura generación, demuéstrelo.
ADMINISTRACION ENTRADA AUTOMOVIL
Fecha de Entrada ___ de 199 ___
N$ 5.00
Reg. No. 13519 S.T.
Conserve limpio el Parque
Nº 1118

LIKE A LIZARD
'Before us lies the gleaming, pinkish-ochre of the valley flat, wild and exalted with sunshine. On the left, quite near, bank the stiffly pleated mountains, all the foot-hills, that press savannah-coloured into the savannah of the valley. The mountains are clothed smokily with pine, *ocote*, and, like a woman in a gauze *rebozo*, they rear in a rich blue fume that is almost cornflower-blue in the clefts. It is their characteristic that they are darkest blue at the top. Like some splendid lizard with a wavering, royal-blue crest down the ridge of his back, and pale belly, and soft pinky-fawn claws.'
D H Lawrence: *Mornings in Mexico*, 1927.

▶▶ Agua Azul *189D2*

Deep in the jungle of Chiapas, the spectacular waterfalls of Agua Azul ('blue water') cascade down natural limestone rock terraces to create a series of turquoise pools strung out through a national park. They are just over 60km south of Palenque on the road to San Cristóbal, and their beauty has inevitably made them a prime target for tourist buses from Palenque. However, if you walk some way upstream to smaller falls and pools, not only will you escape the masses but you will also be able to swim in safer waters.

▶▶ Bonampak *189E2*

Bonampak ('City of Painted Walls') lies in remote, tropical forest 140km south-east of Palenque. Boat, bus and camping trips are organised from Palenque and San Cristobal, usually combining Bonampak with Yaxchilan over two days. A pricier alternative is to join a tour by small plane. When it was discovered in 1946, Bonampak made headlines for its 150sq m of 8th-century murals, the only such paintings in the Mayan world. However, high humidity and rainfall had taken their toll, and the murals had faded dramatically. Restoration began in 1984, and today their colours have been restored as closely as possible to the originals. There are three structures but it is the **Templo de las Pinturas** (Temple of Paintings) that is remarkable. It depicts images of battles, palace life and festivities of the Late Classic period (AD 600–900).

▶▶▶ Cañon del Sumidero *189D2*

From Chiapa de Corzo the Río Grijalva winds its way 15km north between the sheer walls of the Sumidero Canyon to end at the Chicoasén dam. The canyon plunges to depths of over 1,000m and possesses an amazing diversity of flora and fauna on its upper slopes. Boat trips leave (when full) from the *embarcadero* (landing place) at Chiapa de Corzo and take two to three hours to cover the round trip; otherwise the precipitous canyon can be viewed from look-out points on its western face in a national park area (*Open* daily 6–5), easily accessible by road from Tuxtla Gutiérrez.

Viewed from the top or from a sightseeing boat below, the Sumidero Canyon is awe-inspiring

► Catemaco *188C3*

In the southern tobacco-growing part of the state of Veracruz, 175km south-east of Veracruz itself, is the sleepy lakeside town of Catemaco. Famed as a centre for witchcraft, Catemaco is a relaxed little town. The lake is rimmed by verdant volcanic hills, with waterfalls (Salto de Teoteapan), water-skiing, beaches and islands reached by boat from the town quay. Most popular is the **Isla de los Changos** (Monkey Island), where a troop of lively macaques has been brought from Thailand. Waterfront restaurants dish up the lake speciality, *mojarra* (a type of perch), eels and *tegogolo*, a freshwater snail. The town itself has a run-down appeal and only one sight, the charming **Iglesia de Nuestra Señora del Carmen**, which nevertheless pulls in hordes of pilgrims every mid-July. Not to be outdone, the witches convene annually on the 1,650m summit of the Volcán San Martín.

►► Chiapa de Corzo *189D2*

Chiapa de Corzo lies 20km east of Tuxtla Gutiérrez, just before the road climbs to San Cristóbal, at the head of the Cañon de Sumidero. Although it is one of the most ancient sites of southern Mexico (going back to 1500 BC), its pre-Hispanic ruins consist of only one small pyramid. However, the town possesses a certain elegance, with good riverside restaurants and an arcaded *zócalo* dating from 1528. At its centre stands **La Pila**, a unique octagonal fountain structure (1562), said to have been inspired by the shape of the Spanish crown. The **Museo de la Laca**►► (*Open* Tue–Sun 8–5) exhibits diverse lacquer techniques, from China to Uruapan, with strong emphasis on local lacquered gourds and masks. This is housed in the beautiful monastery adjoining the **Templo de Santo Domingo** (1554), that flanks the square. It claims one of Latin America's oldest and most sonorous bells, made of silver, copper and gold.

LACQUERWARE

Centuries ago, the simple gourd provided Mesoamerican hunters with essential food and water vessels. It is not known when lacquering was first developed but it already existed when the Spanish arrived. Mexico's main centres of lacquerware are at Uruapan, Olinalá and Chiapa de Corzo. During the colonial period the latter produced a stunning range of lacquered furniture, lecterns, frames and crosses but today, apart from a few wooden boxes and crosses, lacquering is only applied to gourds. The craftswomen of Chiapa de Corzo fix layer upon layer of coloured powder, alternating with the waxy fat of the *aje* insect, which is finally polished and painted with a floral design.

Huatulco's nine interlocking bays with white-sand beaches are set against a backdrop of dense jungle

OUT AND ABOUT IN HUATULCO

Even if your trip does not coincide with Huatulco's whale season (Aug–Oct), you are quite likely to see dolphins. Underwater life is richer still, although coral reefs are mostly dead. Scuba-diving outfits can be found at Tangolunda and Santa Cruz, but if you just want to don a snorkel and mask, stalls at Bahia Maguey rent them out.

PETRIFIED WATER

Water may seem scarce in the arid hills surrounding Mitla, but drive a further 45km south-east along a rough dirt road and you will be proved wrong. Here, frozen in time, is Hierve el Agua, a uniquely petrified irrigation system used over 2,000 years ago. Sulphur springs have led to recent structuring with basic *cabinas*.

► Comitán *188D2*

This small town, founded in 1527, is a major staging post between Tuxtla, the capital of Chiapas, and Guatemala. The altitude creates a pleasant climate and there are several relics from colonial days, as well as two good museums, the **Museo Arqueológico** (*Open* Tue–Sun 10–6) and the **Casa Museo Dr Belisario Dominguez**, home of the local Republican martyr killed in 1912 (*Guided tours* Tue–Sat 10–6.45, Sun 9–12.45). Comitán is also the gateway to the Lagos de Montebello (see page 206).

► El Tule *188B2*

This tree is claimed to be the widest in the Americas. It stands in the village of Santa Maria del Tule, 13km east of Oaxaca. Over 41m tall and with an ever expanding girth, the *ahuehuete* cypress is thought to be over 2,000 years old. It has certainly been around longer than the vividly painted 17th-century **Templo de Santa Maria**, beside it.

►► Huatulco *188B1*

The most recent of Mexico's government-planned mega-resorts lies 285km south-east of Oaxaca in a stunning mountain- and jungle-backed setting. Until the early 1980s this group of nine interlocking bays had only an isolated fishing village, with no water or electricity and was accessible by a dirt path. The terrain, similar to Acapulco's, is formed by the rugged Sierra Madre del Sur, abutting the Pacific to create sandy coves. In 1983 the first luxury hotels and a six-lane road network were built, soon followed by an airport, golf-course and a marina. However, the 1994–5 financial crisis slowed progress so for the moment Huatulco remains pleasantly undeveloped.

So far, there are three structured bays: **Tangolunda** (the most exclusive), **Chahue** (still embryonic), and **Santa Cruz**, where amenites are clustered around the marina. The lively services village of **La Crucecita** is good for budget hotels, bars and restaurants. Activities include diving, river-kayaking, jungle-trekking, horse-riding or boat trips to deserted beaches. The best way to profit from it is to take a package deal from Oaxaca or Mexico City.

▶▶ Misol-Há *189D2*

Like Agua Azul, Misol-Há makes welcome relief from the often stifling heat of lowland Chiapas and is even nearer to Palenque – 22km south of town. In a beautiful jungle setting 35m of water thunders down a cliff into a large pool which is safer for swimming than Agua Azul's rushing and rocky currents. Local buses stop just over 1km from the falls, next to camping facilities, cabins and a small restaurant.

▶▶ Mitla *188B2*

Open: daily 8–5

The fascinating archaeological site of Mitla is easily reached from Oaxaca on Highway 190, 44km to the south-east. The village is also home to the **Frissell Museum▶▶** (*Open* daily 9–5), an extensive private collection of Zapotec and Mixtec artefacts that is well worth visiting before the uphill climb to the red-domed church and site. Mitla (Place of the Dead) was occupied by the Zapotecs between AD 400 and 700 and, following the decline of Monte Albán, blossomed into a major ceremonial centre. Much of the rich decoration was added by the Mixtecs, who alternated with the Zapotecs in the regional balance of power until the arrival of the Spanish in 1521. Their geometric stonework is remarkable for its complex inlay technique, well preserved in the priestly **Grupo de las Columnas**: up the main stairs and behind a rectangular colonnaded hall is the **Patio de las Grecas**, faced in intricate stonework friezes. Downhill another large patio structure incorporates two underground cruciform tombs and, in the 16th-century church grounds to the north, the **Grupo de la Iglesia** displays the remains of Mixtec murals. The **Columna de la Vida** (Column of Life) is a large stone which, when embraced, is said to reveal how long you have to live by the distance left between your fingertips. Beside the site car-park is a very commercial crafts market and in the main village street numerous small shops sell local embroidery, crochet and weaving. There are also numerous *mezcal* bars, whose products come from local distilleries.

MR FRISSELL

To the left of the main square at the entrance to Mitla stands the legacy of Erwin Robert Frissell, a retired real-estate broker from Minneapolis who was bitten by the Zapotec antiquities bug in the 1940s. By 1950 Frissell had bought the Posada La Sorpresa (The Surprise). He soon filled the rooms with his vast collection of Zapotec and Mixtec artefacts from the valley. On his death administration of the museum was transferred to the University of the Americas, which encourages donations to maintain the free entrance for the benefit of local Zapotecs.

Mitla's local market sells Teotitlán rugs as well as Guatemalan handicrafts

Mitla's colonial church

Only about one-fifth of Mexico's original rainforest remains, mostly concentrated in Chiapas and the Yucatán, near the Guatemalan border. High rainfall and constant humidity create steamy jungles where howler monkeys scream from the branches, but jaguars and quetzals hover on the brink of extinction.

IGUANA STEW
Mexico boasts over 1,000 species of reptiles, more than any other country. Some of these are tried-and-tested gastronomic delicacies, not least the iguana. As a result, green and black iguanas, both of which are impressively large lizards with serrated dorsal crests, are becoming a rarity. However, if you see a *basilik*, you won't forget it. This prehistoric-looking creature, nicknamed the Jesus Christ lizard, possesses the extraordinary ability to walk on water – rising on to its hind legs, it makes record-breaking sprints across rivers, in total contrast to the average iguana basking on the shore.

Mexico blooms in the most impossible places

Since the 1960s, deforestation has left its mark on the tropical forests that once stretched from the state of Veracruz through Tabasco to Chiapas, Campeche and Quintana Roo. Other environmental threats – such as the reclaiming of coastal wetlands for development, hunting and the illegal traffic in rare species – are enough to put the future of this complex ecosystem in real jeopardy. However, regional governments have responded by creating a network of biosphere reserves that now protect some 1,700,000 hectares, while allowing local inhabitants to continue a controlled rural existence within their boundaries. Montes Azules in Chiapas (part of the Selva Lacandon bordering the Río Usumacinta and the last bastion of true rainforest in Mexico), Calakmul in Campeche (see page 230), Sian Ka'an in Quintana Roo (see page 245) and the cloudforest of El Triunfo near Tapachula (see page 212) all offer the chance to enter a tangled realm of interdependent flora and fauna where flashes of vivid butterflies and the deafening racket of cicadas regularly assault the senses.

Jungle symbiosis Trees laden with bromeliads soar over 50m, creating a dense leaf canopy and an ideal environment for 50 species of brilliantly coloured orchids. Mahogany is one of the many precious hardwoods and, like any vigorous jungle growth, a potential victim of the powerful strangler fig. In between the ant-trees, the sapodillas (provider of chicle – chewing gum), the towering guanacastes and the poisonwood trees thrives a dense mass of climbing plants and ferns whose existence depends on the shade provided by the canopy. Gracefully draped lianas such as the wild grapevine offer pure drinking water when cut open, while the gnarled bullhoof vine, if boiled and consumed, will halt internal bleeding. In this complex ecosystem, one of the richest in the world, each plant has a role and every aggressor an antedote.

From spiny anteaters to howlers The jungle is hospitable territory for tropical fauna, but also fertile ground for

poachers. Jaguars, pumas, ocelots and margays are favourite targets and as a result are fast disappearing. More easily spotted, and more numerous, is the spiny anteater, a toothless mammal which feeds on ants by means of a tapered nose and long, sticky tongue. Equally common are tapirs, armadillos and coatimundis (racoon-like creatures), which root around on the forest floor, but watch out for the tree-climbing porcupine, whose spines – erected at the slightest provocation – can penetrate skin and muscle. Monkeys are ever present, crashing around in the tree-tops but not easily visible. Spider monkeys are the most common in the Maya rainforest and spend much of their time performing acrobatics high in the tree canopy, only descending to drink. Often audible, but rarely sighted, are howler monkeys, whose screams and grunts can be heard up to 10km away, especially in the early morning.

Hyacinth macaw, a typical rainforest inhabitant

Winged creatures From the cloudforests of Chiapas down to the tropical rainforest there are an estimated 750 species of bird, which are joined by millions of migrating northern comrades every winter. Aracaris and toucans (vividly coloured, fruit-eating birds with voluminous, multi-coloured bills), are still relatively common, but the magnificent turquoise-coated quetzal, despite its long-standing role in Mexican mythology, is fast approaching extinction. Still abundant are the numerous types of tiny, iridescent humming-birds which hover and dart about in search of nectar. Shrill green parakeets, amazon parrots, macaws and king vultures (which combine a naked technicolour head with black and white body plumage) are all present, but spotting these elusive creatures is no easy task.

JUNGLE HIDEOUTS

Eco-tourism in southern Chiapas is still in its infancy, although biological and tourist stations are slowly appearing on the outskirts of Montes Azules. The most direct access is from Palenque to Bonampak, about two hours' drive, where camping and trails are in place. Escudo Jaguar offers 'eco' accommodation in thatched huts, and from here a 45-minute boat-ride reaches Yaxchilan. Alternatively, boat trips can be organised from Tenosique, through the heart of the rainforest along the Guatemalan border. Ecogrupos de México (Mexico City, tel: 661 9121, fax: 662 6354) offers camping and boat tours to the area. Tourist offices in Tuxtla, Palenque, San Cristóbal and Tapachula have further information on 'eco' retreats.

NUMBERS

Together with the Petén rainforest in Guatemala, the Lacandona forms part of the largest tract of tropical rainforest north of the Brazilian Amazon. The 330,000-hectare Montes Azules Biosphere Reserve forms at least half of Mexico's remaining tropical rainforest. In just one hectare there are an estimated 15 species of tree, 25 of orchid, 20 of bird, 10 of mammal, 150 of –butterfly and more than 2,500 of insect.

TREASURE OF TOMB 7
The treasure of Tomb 7, discovered in the 1930s, is now displayed in Oaxaca's Museo Regional (see page 201). Jewellery of gold, silver, turquoise, jade, seed-pearls, rock crystal, obsidian, coral and amber, cups of alabaster, beads of finely incised jaguar molars – the diversity, richness and craftmanship is astounding. Dating from the Mixtec post-Classic period (1350–1521), the treasure also includes exquisite examples of gold jewellery made with the lost-wax technique (using moulds of clay and beeswax) – bird-head ear-rings, mask brooches, skull necklaces. The owner of the treasure was a Mixtec dignitary who was buried along with two other bodies, probably sacrificed servants.

Example of Monte Albán's intriguing 'dancers'

▶▶▶ Monte Albán *188B2*

Open: daily 8.30–5

The Zapotecs chose the perfect site for their capital. After levelling a hilltop, they constructed a city commanding spectacular 360-degree views, heightened by the clear, dry air of Oaxaca. Monte Albán ('White Mountain') was founded around 500 BC, and peaked between AD 500 and 600 with an estimated population of 24,000, before being abandoned in the 8th century. During the final stages of the post-Classic period (1350–1521) the Mixtecs used the palaces and tombs for offerings and burials. Only 10km west of Oaxaca, this magnificent site should be a top priority for any visitor to the south.

Layout From the entrance and sleek new museum, a path winds up the hill to the corner of the Plataforma Norte, where the breathtaking **Gran Plaza** opens up at your feet. Flanked to the east by a ball-court, a palace and small temple platforms and to the west by three large temple complexes, the plaza sweeps 300m south to finish at the majestic pyramid of the Plataforma Sur. Other structures are aligned down the centre, yet the sense of space remains absolute from any vantage point. Most buildings date from Monte Albán's third phase, roughly the last two centuries of its power, the final structures overlapping with the period when the Zapotecs were building their shrines in the valley below.

Structures The huge **Plataforma Norte** (North Platform) is mounted via a steep flight of steps to a spot where immense columns once supported a roof. Beyond this lies a sunken patio (a characteristic of Teotihuacán) containing an altar, and to the west it is flanked by a structure considered to be a Mixtec addition. A fork from the main access path leads behind this platform to a group of five tombs (there are nearly 190 dotted around Monte Albán), the most elaborate being **Tomb 104**. Over the entrance a clay urn represents Tláloc (the rain god), and inside there are superb frescoes of deities, and hieroglyphs. At the opposite end of the plaza towers the **Plataforma Sur**, with sweeping panoramas from the summit (its second level is temporarily closed awaiting renovation). Beside it in the corner stands Edificio M, an echo of the tunnelled structure of Edificio IV at the other end. Between these two is perhaps the most outstanding sight, the **Palacio de los Danzantes** (Building of the Dancers), named after the bas-reliefs of 'dancers' carved on slabs around its base. The building consists of several tomb chambers opening on to a central courtyard.

The interconnected structures aligned down the centre of the plaza terminate at **Edificio J**, a triangular building that is crossed by a tunnel and thought to have been an observatory due to its alignment with the star Capella. Debate continues over the function of the other central buildings, approached from staircases on all four sides.

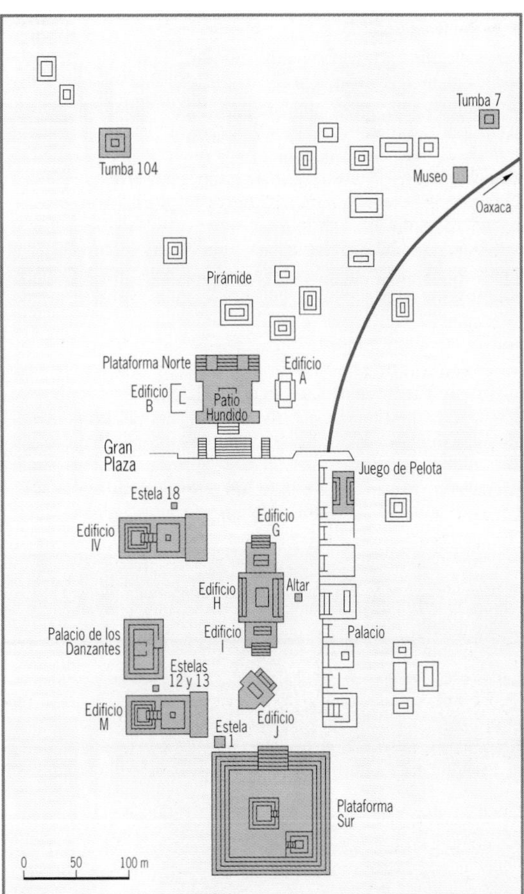

DANZANTES

Still controversial are the strange subjects of the carved tablets which lined the Danzantes edifice and the tunnel beneath the observatory. Deformed beings, hunchbacks and figures exhibiting odd gestures and movements, some with severely mutilated genitals, appear to dance or swim. Royal victims or sick people? For the moment debate favours the royal captives theory. Strong Olmec influence can be seen in certain Negroid features, while many figures are accompanied by name glyphs, bar-and-dot numerals and calendric glyphs, further evidence of Zapotec sophistication in astronomy and mathematics. The best preserved examples are displayed in the site museum.

View north over the Zapotec ruins of Monte Albán, from the South Platform
Inset: detail of another 'dancer'

BENITO JUAREZ
Oaxaca's far-sighted political son, Benito Juárez, is commemorated in a small museum at García Vigil 609. This Zapotec Indian, who considered the priesthood before becoming a lawyer, dedicated himself to improving the lot of impoverished villagers. His political career took off in 1855 when he became Minister of Justice in the new liberal government. His radical Reform Laws at last broke the stranglehold of the reactionary Church, but resulted in civil war. Elected President in 1861, Juárez closed monasteries and confiscated Church property, but he was soon ousted by the French invasion. On his return to power in 1866 he implemented a series of laws making free primary education mandatory and stimulating industry. He died in office in 1872.

Oaxaca *188B2*

For travellers coming from the north, Oaxaca's main attraction is its tranquillity – no fuming buses, no traffic snarling up the centre. Ringed by beautiful forested hills to the north and west, with dry unpolluted air, the city has low buildings and a colourful pedestrian area, making it a pleasure to visit. These positive factors have also created a negative side: an overwhelming flow of visitors concentrated in a small town. The state of Oaxaca is not a prosperous one, and this has produced the inevitable disparity between poor Zapotecs and Mixtecs and relatively wealthy tourists.

History and monuments Oaxaca was founded in 1486 by the Aztecs, but was renamed Villa de Antequera by the Spanish in 1526. It soon made its living from cochineal production and textiles. Although recurring earthquakes caused considerable damage over the centuries, Oaxaca still claims some major baroque monuments, most impressive being the **Templo de Santo Domingo►►►** (*Open* daily 10–1, 4–8). Set on a large plaza lined

The Church of Santo Domingo, jewel of Oaxaca

with crafts shops, the church and adjoining monastery were built by Dominicans in the late 16th century. The interior stucco relief was elaborately gilded and painted by top Mexican craftsmen in the mid-17th century and the vaulted ceiling is completely inset with 36 paintings. Other highlights include the richly gilded altar, the magnificent **Capilla del Rosario** and the famous genealogical tree, with its crowned figures and cherubs, which winds across the ceiling inside the main entrance. This represents the family of Santo Domingo de Guzmán, 13th-century founder of the Dominican order. The

FESTIVALS
Oaxaca's lively religious festivals are legendary. Holy Week is widely celebrated but specific to Oaxaca is Lunes del Cerro (Monday of the Hill), celebrated on the last two Mondays of July. This brings together 16 different ethnic groups in a fantastic display of music and dance, the *Guelaguetza*. Most curious of all is the Night of the Radishes (23 December), when the animated *zócalo* is invaded by booths displaying figures and biblical scenes carved out of giant radishes. Follow tradition – eat a *buñuelos* (crisp pancake), make a wish and smash your plate to make it come true!

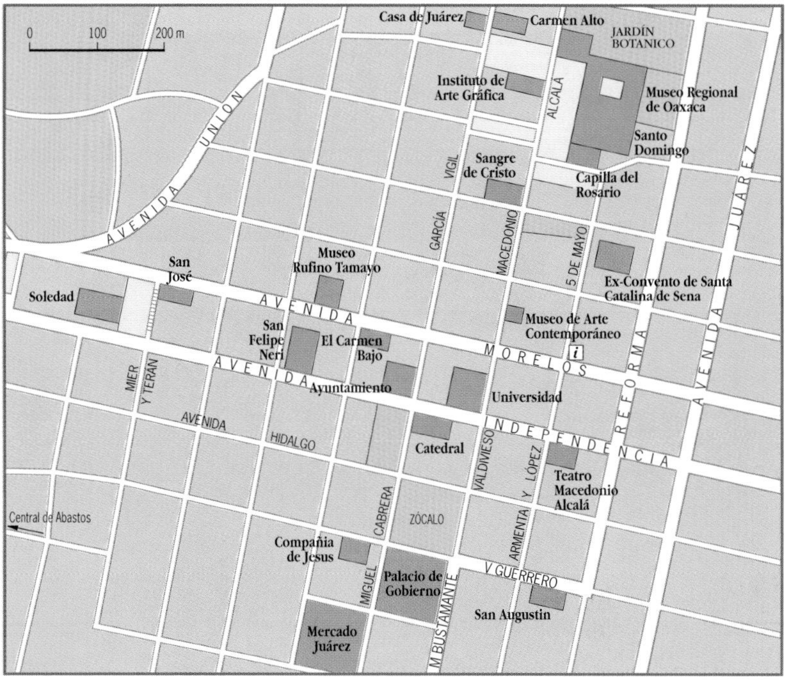

monastery now houses the **Museo Regional▶▶▶** (*Open* Tue–Sat 10–6, Sun 10–5), which displays the Mixtec treasure from Monte Albán's Tomb 7 (see page 199) and Zapotec and Mixtec artefacts. The cultural pluralism of Oaxaca state (16 linguistic groups developed over a period of 12,000 years) is demonstrated in the ethnographic collection.

On the west side of town stands the imposing **Basilica de la Soledad▶▶** (1682), a carved green and sandstone edifice containing the much-revered statue of the Virgin Mary, resplendent in jewel-encrusted robes. Don't miss the eccentric small church museum at the back (*Open* daily 10–2). Back towards the *zócalo,* the 1633 **Templo de San Felipe Neri▶** presents another green stone baroque façade. One block north stands the **Museo Rufino Tamayo▶▶▶** (*Open* Mon, Wed–Sat 10–2, 4–7, Sun 10–3). Tamayo spent over 20 years collecting pre-Hispanic antiquities and this small, select museum is the result. The rooms devoted to Olmec, Occidente, Totonac and Maya artefacts are exceptional.

Pre-Columbian artefact in the Rufino Tamaya Museum

A few minutes' peace away from the Saturday market

VILLAGE MARKETS
Hire a car or take a bus to experience the colour, bustle and aromas of a Oaxacan village market. There are markets on Monday at Miahuatlán (breads, *mezcal*, leatherwork), Tuesday at Zimatlán (pottery, vegetables), Wednesday at San Pedro y San Pablo Etla (breads, cheese, flowers), Thursday at Zaachila (meat, nuts) and at Ejutla (*mezcal*, embroidered blouses), Friday at Ocotlán (flowers, vegetables, meat), Saturday at Oaxaca (everything) and Sunday at Tlacolula (ceramics, *mezcal*) and Tlaxiaco (leather, blankets and *agua ardiente*, the local liquor).

Chapulines – edible grasshoppers

Round the *zócalo* Oaxaca's *zócalo* pulsates with *mariachis*, shoe-shiners, beggars, vendors and tourists. At sundown the State Band dutifully tunes up and the evening entertainment moves into gear. Towering over the square is the **Catedral►►**, started in 1533 but not finished till two centuries later (it suffered earthquake damage in 1727). It contains an extensive collection of 16th- and 17th-century paintings. Two blocks east is the **Teatro Macedonio Alcalá►**, a 1909 Porfiriato extravaganza, and, occupying the entire southern flank of the square, the elegant **Palacio de Gobierno►** (1882), another victim of Oaxaca's recurring earthquakes. To the north of the Catedral, on Avenida Independencia 607, is the **Ayuntamiento**, home to the helpful state tourist office and craft shop.

Arts and crafts Two blocks south of the *zócalo* lies the daily **Mercado Juárez**, full of tasty Oaxacan specialities and crafts. Two blocks further south is the **Mercado de Artesanias**, packed with enticing craftwork. The vast market at the **Central de Abastos►►**, south-west of the centre, opens daily. However, Saturday is when the sprawling alleys become a hub for vendors of cheese, breads of all shapes, fresh or dried giant prawns, herbs, incense, ropes, chillies and tortillas. One section of this bewildering cornucopia is allocated to craft stands, where bargaining is essential. For more up-market buys, the shops in and off the pedestrian-only street of **Alcalá**, which joins the *zócalo* to Santo Domingo, sell beautiful gold and jade reproductions of Mixtec jewellery, Taxco silver, black San Bartolo pottery, painted mythical animals (*alebrijes*), handwoven rugs and plenty of beautiful embroidery and weavings. Calle Alcalá is also home to the **Museo de Arte Contemporáneo** at No 202 (*Open* Wed–Mon 10.30–8), and, at the northern end the **Instituto de Arte Gráfica** (*Open* Wed–Mon 9.30–8). This institute, founded by artist Francisco Toledo, exhibits contemporary graphic art shows in a superb colonial mansion. In the parallel street of 5 de Mayo more quality shops are clustered around the Camino Real, a luxury hotel housed in the beautiful 16th-century **Ex-Convento de Santa Catalina de Sena►►**.

Political frontiers cut through a region that shares a common Maya heritage as well as geographical and physical characteristics. From Chiapas the Maya route continues into the rainforest and mountains of Guatemala, a nation whose troubles of a recent past have spilled over the Mexican border. Winding through the Selva Lacandon, the mighty Río Usumacinta is the only stretch of the Guatemalan border that is not a straight line drawn on the colonial map. During Spanish rule, Chiapas was administered from Guatemala and after independence, in 1823, the state actually joined an independent federation of Central American states.

Chiapas' participation in an independent federation of Central American states was short lived – 62 per cent of Chiapanecos voted to join Mexico in 1824. Since 1954 Guatemala has been ruled by military dictatorships with CIA backing, a situation finally ended when the Clinton administration cut funding. After decades of military coups and oppression, Guatemala attained a relatively democratic régime when Alvaro Arzu was elected in January 1996.

Massacres In the early 1980s violence erupted between opposing groups of extreme-right army and guerrillas, with indigenous Guatemalans (55 per cent of the population) caught in the firing line. Women, old people and children were massacred in a government attempt to erase dissent. The worst trouble-spots were in the inhospitable sierra of Huehuetenango and Quiché near the Mexican border and refugees were soon streaming down the slopes to escape the butchery. The initial reception was unhelpful, but the sheer mass of people finally forced the hand of the Mexican government. Refugee camps were set up around Comalapa and the Lagos de Montebello, while half the refugees were moved to camps in Campeche and Quintana Roo, out of range of Guatemelan soldiers who came across the border to attack them.

Hope By 1986 glimmers of democracy appeared in Guatemala when Venicio Cerezo was elected at the head of a 'constitutional' government and started the long, slow return to democracy. His *apertura* (opening) signalled a renewed popular involvement in politics. In 1991 the UN finally made moves to bring about the return of some 30,000 refugees, but it was in 1993 that the world became aware of what was happening. Led by Rigoberta Menchú (winner of the Noble Peace Prize), a group of 2,200 Guatemalans made a symbolic and ceremonial return to their homeland. It has been estimated that in the period 1960–96, about 100,000 Guatemalans were killed. Today the situation has been reversed, as the relatively peaceful Guatemala watches disturbing events in Chiapas.

CROSSING THE BORDER
The main entry points into Guatemala are at Tapachula and Comitán. From Tapachula there is a choice of crossing at Talismán bridge to El Carmen or, 38km to the south, from Ciudad Hidalgo to Ciudad Tecunumán. The other main crossing is from Ciudad Cuauhtémoc (80km south-east of Comitán) to La Mesilla and on to Huehuetenango along a spectacular, mountainous route which was, until a few years ago, a battle-ground between guerillas and the Guatemalan army. Visas should be obtained at Guatemalan Consulates in Mexico City, Comitán, Ciudad Hidalgo or Tapachula, although border-posts do theoretically issue them.

Palenque's Palace complex is over-looked by its square tower

PALENQUE TOWN
Seven kilometres east of the archaeological zone, the long, straggling village of Palenque caters almost solely for the needs of visitors. Although most hotels and restaurants are close to the *zócalo* (or *jardín*), a few more select places are set in superb tropical grounds on the road to the ruins. Travel agencies organise trips to Misol-Há, Agua Azul and further afield to Bonampak and Yaxchilán. Two more accessible waterfalls (Motiepa and Otulum) lie off the access road to the ruins.

▶▶▶ Palenque *189D2*

Open: daily 8–5

The fabulous site of Palenque, shrouded in humid tropical growth, would be a moving experience were it not for the armies of tourist groups. The airstrip receives flights from Mexico City, Cancún, Villahermosa and Tuxtla all year round – lunchtime seems to offer the only lull in the flow. Palenque is the most important archaeological site in the northern Maya region, 120km east of Villahermosa in the foothills of the Chiapas Highlands. Giant liana-draped trees and dense undergrowth encircle the ruins, which spread over an area of 6sq km. At its peak between AD 600 and 800, this great ceremonial city was eventually abandoned in the 10th century for reasons still unknown.

Site monuments Once brightly painted, the grey stone monuments of Palenque have been extensively restored, although only a fraction have been excavated. The first and most impressive is the **Templo de las Inscripciones** (Temple of the Inscriptions), a stepped pyramid rising to a summit temple and descending 25m inside to the extraordinary tomb of King Pakal (*Open* daily 10–4). Hieroglyphic inscriptions (including the date AD 692) are carved into three panels lining the temple, and the crypt contains a carved sarcophagus and walls decorated with fine figurative stucco reliefs. The fantastic jewellery and jade-encrusted mask found here are now exhibited in Mexico City's Museum of Anthropology. Next to it, **Templo XIII** contains the remains of the Reina Roja, excavated in 1994; her ornaments are at the site museum. Virtually opposite this pyramid is **El Palacio**, a complex of courtyards, corridors and tunnels crowned by a tower which probably functioned as an observatory. Bas-reliefs and modelled stucco friezes stud the walls and pillars inside and out, and remarkably carved slabs were discovered in this maze. Across the stream on the hillside is a group of four temples (notably the restored Templo de la Cruz), some with reconstructed roofcombs and all displaying carved slabs related to their religious functions.

From this group a path follows the stream north past the **Juego de Pelota** (Ball Court) to another complex, the **Grupo Norte** (Northern Group) and the **Templo del Conde** (Temple of the Count), where three tombs were found. The Grupo Norte is composed of five temples built at different periods but presenting a beautiful architectural unity. From here a path leads east, past maintenance buildings and downhill through thick jungle. A small group of ruins stands evocatively in a forest clearing and, beyond a pyramid, the path veers left to a bridge across a rushing waterfall. The exit to the main road leads to the excellent museum. The main entrance and car park is a hot 1.5km uphill walk from here, so make sure you have organised return transport.

Museum This airy, well-designed museum opened in 1993 with exhibits of some of the most important artefacts found on the site, so should not be missed. Hieroglyphic panels (notably the Tablet of the Palace covered with 262 glyphs), pots, intricately sculpted plaster and clay heads and figures (some with deformed foreheads) are exhibited beside the celebrated Tablet of Slaves (7th- to 8th-century), which depicts priests and priestesses making offerings to a central deity. Restoration workshops, a gift shop and open-air cafeteria complete complex.

DEFORMATIONS AND MUTILATIONS

One of the Maya's cultural peculiarities, though also found to a lesser extent amongst the Totonacs, was their practice of mutilating the body for aesthetic ends. Foreheads were deformed from birth by binding a baby's head between concave wooden tablets: this produced their much admired sloping forehead. The Maya also filed their teeth and encrusted them with obsidian and jade, perforated their lobes for earrings, and painted and tattooed their bodies, although the latter practice was probably reserved for priests and nobles. Many of Palenque's superb sculptures depict the results of these practices.

Mayan stone carving in the courtyard of the Palace

Set in mountainous jungle scenery, the Lagos de Montebello are popular for fishing and trekking

DANGER!
Visitors arriving on Oaxaca's idyllic Pacific coast are often so bewitched by its relaxed veneer and superb setting that they forget basic survival tactics. Remember that despite a booming tourist industry, certain regions of Mexico remain severely impoverished and crime thus becomes a very real problem. Both Puerto Ángel and Puerto Escondido are notorious for theft, particularly the latter, where visitors tend to be more affluent. Other threats lie in fierce undertow, prowling tarantulas and relentless mosquitoes.

►► Parque Nacional Lagos de Montebello *189E2*

The Lagos de Montebello lie 56km east of Comitán, on the border of Guatemala, on the edge of the Lacandon rainforest. Strewn across a hilly, forested region are dozens of lakes of all sizes and colours, ranging from a delicate pale blue to emerald and shades of violet, each hue determined by the different mineral deposits present and the physical surroundings. Some basic accommodation and a camp site are available and public transport serves the park regularly from Comitán. The beautiful park is crossed by tracks which offer lovely walks as they wind past the various lakes, rocky outcrops, pine and oak forests, the Mayan site of Chinkultic and a few remote villages.

► Parque Nacional Lagos de Chacahua *188A2*

Stretching 32km along Oaxaca's south coast, 86km west of Escondido, the coastal lagoons of Chacahua make a great birdwatching destination. Reached from the village of Zapotalito (off Highway 200), the extensive lagoons and their mangrove-edged islands can only be toured by boat: aim for early morning or late afternoon for good sightings of ibis, egrets and cormorants, as well as deer and alligators. Bring your insect repellent as mosquitoes thrive in this swampy land.

►► Puerto Ángel *188F1*

The delightful secluded beaches and tropical setting of the low-key fishing-port of Puerto Ángel have kept budget sunbathers, swimmers, surfers and snorkellers happy for years. However, in 1997 Hurricane Paulina struck, causing extensive damage to homes, beach-huts and vegetation. Rebuilding is underway, but it will take time for the swaying coconut-palms to regrow. Visitors can still enjoy the balmy evenings, vivid sunsets, transparent waters, simple hotels and seafood restaurants.

Puerto Ángel itself lies at the eastern end of the mountain-backed bay. Its amenities are basic (bank, tourist office, decent hotels, restaurants). The main beach, **Playa del Pantéon**, offers easy swimming in calm, shallow water dotted with fishing boats. A kilometre or so east of

Puerto Ángel has long been a favourite hideaway for those seeking a quiet existence

here lies the pretty creek and peaceful beach of **Estacahuite**, and a few kilometres west by road is **Zipolite▶**, once a paradise for surfers, backpackers and nudists, though renowned for its treacherous undertow. More than anywhere else, this generous, white-sand beach, ending in a dramatic headland, suffered from the hurricane, as beach-bars and cabins were mostly lightweight affairs. Twenty minutes further by road lies **San Agustinillo▶▶**, a beautiful beach where the sea is protected by craggy rocks. Its hammocks and palapa restaurants are popular with local families. Further west still is **Mazunte▶**, home to a turtle-research centre and museum (*Open* Tue–Sat 10–4.30, Sun 10–2.30) where live residents represent nine of the world's 11 types. The wild, long beach sees armadas of up to 200,000 Olive Ridley turtles from July to December.

▶▶ Puerto Escondido *188A1*

Seventy kilometres west of Puerto Ángel, by a twisting, mountainous road, is the coastal resort of Puerto Escondido. This has much to offer the comfort-seeking tourist, without losing its fishing-village character. Originally visited for its world-class surfing, its attraction lies in the string of beaches stretching from the main bay (Playa Principal), frequented by fishermen, pelicans and local bathers. This is edged by a pedestrian promenade, the heart of a relaxed tourist zone. Uphill behind this area lies a more authentic quarter, where cheap lodging and restaurants can be found. To the east of the central fishermen's haunt is palm-fringed **Playa Marinero**, but beyond the rocky headland stretches the long, sandy beach of **Zicatela**, a surfers' paradise, although its strong undertow can make it dangerous for swimming. To the west lies the beautiful cove of **Puerto Ángelito**, accessible by boat or taxi from downtown, and a popular weekend destination. Beyond the headland is **Playa Carrizalillo**. From Playa Principal a concrete walkway winds west around the rocks, offering sweeping seaviews.

Puerto Escondido – 'hidden port' in Spanish

CHAMULAN BELIEF
Independent-minded San Juán Chamula, site of strong anti-Spanish resistance and a major rebellion in 1869, now functions with its own political, civic and religious structure, represented by the crosses facing the church. Draped in pine branches, they are the earthly symbols of Mayan cosmic forces as well as the starting point for Christ's embodiment as the sun. Inside the gloomy church row upon row of flickering candles, clouds of incense and chanting worshippers reinforce this intense spiritual belief. However, all is not rosy. San Juán's strange atmosphere derives partly from the dichotomy of tourism versus local poverty but more so from religious persecution and expropriation of land by local drug syndicates. This is a region where visitors should be wary of solitary wandering: attacks are on the increase.

▶ San Andrés Tuxtla *188C3*

About 150km south-east of Veracruz the flat coastal swamps rise into the fertile rolling green hills of Los Tuxtla, a volcanic region which was once Olmec territory. This is now the last bastion of agriculture and fishing before the Gulf Coast plunges into industrialisation and oil at Minatitlán. San Andrés is known, above all, for its puros, cigars made from local tobacco, and makes a good, economic base for visiting the Olmec site of **Tres Zapotes▶**, the **Laguna Encantada▶▶** (Enchanted Lagoon) in the crater of an extinct volcano and, further afield, Lake Catemaco (see page 193). There is good hiking in the biosphere reserve of San Martin, to the north.

▶ San Bartolo Coyotepec *188B2*

This small village 12km south-east of Oaxaca is renowned for its black pottery, which is made using an ancient Zapotec technique. Water-jars and *mezcal* containers, among other things, are baked in sealed-off, underground kilns. The black sheen is created by the soot and smoke that impregnates and colours the clay. A final lustre is achieved by staining and polishing. The pieces sold at the artisans' market here are generally cheaper than in Oaxaca.

▶▶▶ San Cristóbal de las Casas see pages 210–11

▶▶ San Juán Chamula *189D2*

Set high in the Chiapas Highlands, the village of San Juán Chamula offers an extraordinary vision of an ethnic group (one of 22 Tzotzil villages in the area) clinging fiercely to its unique traditions in the face of overwhelming odds. On Sundays, this religious and commercial hub for over 65,000 Chamulans scattered around the mountains is invaded by tour groups from San Cristóbal as a huge market occupies the central square. Apart from the colourful costumes of the Chamulans, the main interest is the church, where worship combines Christian and Mayan spiritual practices. A ticket to enter the church must be obtained from a small office across the square and photography is strictly forbidden. Next door is the **Museo de Chamula** (*Open* daily 9–6), a small informal museum with ethnographic exhibits.

San Juán Chamula's parish church, cannot be entered by visitors during festivals

The Lacandons, the last pure survivors of the Maya, live in the heart of the Mexican rainforest, where they are thought to have fled from colonial invaders. This tiny ethnic group offers a unique window on the beliefs of the ancient Maya. Only 'discovered' about a century ago, today's Lacandons number about 400. Despite attempts to protect the community from the march of the 20th century, the younger generation is now only too aware of what modern life has to offer.

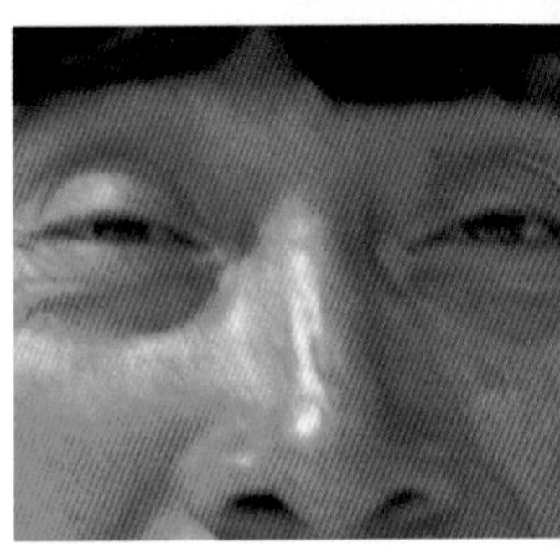

Mostly untouched by Christianity, apart from a few converts by American missionaries, many Lacandons continue to worship at the temple site of Yaxchilán, where their gods include Metsaboc, god of rain and of the heavens and his opposite, Kisin, god of the underworld and bringer of sickness. Ceremonial dates are calculated using the 260-day cycle, harking back to the Maya lunar calendar (see pages 228–9). However, their forecast of the world's destruction may soon apply to their own ethnic group: massive enforced relocation will doubtlessly announce the end of their traditions. Military check-points also abound in this area, as a result of Chiapas' political turbulence.

Life-style Based around the lakes of the Selva Lacandon, between the rivers Usumacinta and Jacate, the Lacandons make their living from hunting, fishing, gathering wild jungle fruits and cultivating crops. These highly distinctive, diminutive Maya wear their hair long with a fringe, and dress in unbleached cotton *huipils* (tunics). Men may sport nose-rings and women necklaces of berries or beads but precious metals are non-existent: they are a primitive people who still use digging-sticks for sowing seeds and clear land with slash-and-burn techniques.

Lacandon houses are simple structures consisting of four posts supporting a palm-leaf roof which is tied down with lianas. These units were created for single families and have completely supplanted former clan villages. They raise the problem of inbreeding, something which is difficult to measure. A good source of information on the Lacandons is the institution of Na-Bolom in San Cristóbal de las Casas (see page 211), which also makes accommodation permanently available to them.

LACANDON ORIGINS
Linguistically the Lacandons have no connection with any other Chiapan group, something which has given rise to long speculation on how and when they arrived in the rainforest. Their own name for themselves is *masswal* (meaning 'low class'), probably an Aztec word related to their primitive life style. What is certain is that they are a Mayan group, probably from the Yucatán peninsula, as their language bears strong similarities to an archaic Yucatecan dialect.

The Church of Santo Domingo is an excellent example of the Mexican high baroque style

OUT AND ABOUT IN CHIAPAS
San Cristóbal makes the ideal base for exploring nearby villages known for their fine, varied textiles and fiercely guarded ethnic traditions (particularly San Juán Chamula, Zinacantán and Amatenango). There is no shortage of organised tours by bus, horseback or on foot, some going as far as Yaxchilán. Volunteer work is also possible. Notice boards pop up all over town: those outside the tourist office, at Casa Margarita and at El Puente are particularly good sources of information about what is on offer.

▶▶▶ San Cristóbal de las Casas *189D2*

No longer the remote, picturesque mountain town that it was 20 years ago, San Cristóbal attracts an increasing number of visitors and much of its centre is dedicated to their needs. Restaurants, bars and charming hotels, together with very visible ethnic traditions, give San Cristóbal a unique and upbeat character. Colourful buildings, cool mountain air, a wealth of local handicrafts, fascinating institutions and the interest of nearby Tzotzil and Tzeltal villages all combine to make San Cristóbal a stimulating place to stay. The Acteal massacre in late 1997, and the ensuing conflicts in the surrounding area have had surprisingly little effect on the town itself. Life goes on in the hip coffee bars while tragic social conditions are the rule just a few kilometres away.

San Cristóbal de las Casas lies high in pine forested mountains

Resistance and persecution San Cristóbal's inhabitants put up fierce resistance to the *conquistadores* but were subsequently forced into the Spanish *encomienda* system which used indigenous slave labour on 'Spanish-owned' land. De las Casas' valiant championship of their rights in the 1540s freed Tzotzil slaves, but as recently as the 1960s there was still a curfew on indigenous Mexicans in town after dark. San Cristóbal's progress has been slow, with agriculture as the main money-earner: so it was not surprising when it hit the headlines in 1994 with the *zapatista* uprising (see page 17). Army presence is still very noticeable and care should be taken in the area. Other problems stem from religious persecution and the power of drug syndicates, all of which has resulted in an estimated 20,000 Chamulans swelling San Cristóbal's population over the last decade.

Layout and sights A grid of streets surrounds San Cristóbal's *zócalo*, dominated by the remodelled 16th-century **catedral▶** and the **Palacio Municipal**, home to the tourist office. Two parallel streets running east, Real de Guadalupe and Madero, form a concentrated area of hotels and restaurants. Insurgentes, the main street south, leads past churches, more hotels and restaurants to the bus station on the Panamerican Highway. Uphill to the north stands the **Templo de la Caridad▶** (1712), but far more striking is San Cristóbal's oldest church, **Santo Domingo▶▶▶**, which rises beside it. Started in 1547, the church was substantially transformed in the 18th century, leaving a fine, lacy façade of vine-draped columns and vegetal motifs. The interior walls integrate paintings and statues with gilded, baroque altars, equalled in ornamentation by the carved pulpit. On the terraces surrounding the two churches a colourful **crafts market** springs to life daily. Santo Domingo's monastery now houses the **Museo Regional▶** (*Open* Tue–Sun 9–4), which concentrates on San Cristóbal's history and ethnography. Here, too, is the weavers' co-operative, **San Jolobil▶▶** (meaning 'the Weavers' House' in Tzotzil), founded to revive and perpetuate the ancestral weaving traditions of Chiapan villages and now claiming 800 members (*Open* Mon–Sat 9–2, 4–6.30). More handicrafts can be seen in the labyrinthine **Mercado** (*Open* daily 6–3), a couple of blocks further north. On Sundays this is the best place to admire brilliantly attired families on shopping sprees: they should be photographed only with discretion.

Na-Bolom A living institution, **Na-Bolom▶▶▶** ('House of the Jaguar') is fascinating for anyone interested in the Lacandon. The sprawling colonial mansion, 10 blocks east of Santo Domingo along Calle Comitán, was, from the 1950s, a social and professional hub for countless anthropologists, writers and artists (including Diego Rivera), thanks to its late owners, the Danish explorer Frans Blom and his Swiss photo-journalist wife Trudy. It now functions as an artefact-packed cultural guest-house, library (with 14,000 books on Chiapas), botanic garden and introduction to local environmental and ethnic issues (*Open* Tue–Sun; guided tours at 11.30 in Spanish and 4.30 in English and Spanish).

VILLAGE UNIFORMS
Chiapan costumes are renowned for their intricate embroidery and weaving, skills which have always had a ritualistic significance. Tzotzil and Tzeltal villages differentiate themselves by colours, motifs and even the cut of their clothing. *Huipiles* (tunics), *quechquemitls* (shoulder-capes) and *rebozos* (shawls) are often predominantly red and white – looking pink from a distance – or blue, but many other fine distinctions come into play. Tassels, pompons and ribbons appear on men's flat palm hats or swinging from their tunic, while women's looped plaits are tied up with vivid bows. More sober, certain Chamulans dress in belted cream wool tunics over white trousers – a style imposed by the Spaniards who were shocked by the Indians' tasselled loincloths.

The courtyard of Na-Bolom

NATURAL DYES
The fast disappearing natural dyes used by Mexican weavers produced an astonishing palette of subtle tones. Roots, bark, berries and leaves created soft reds and browns, while blue came from mixing acacia leaves with black clay or, more often, with the indigo plant. Yellow came from dahlia flowers or the mora tree. Animal dyes were chiefly obtained from the cochineal, a tiny parasite found on cacti which, when crushed, yields a dense crimson colour. Sea-snails were another important dye source: their secretion turns a brilliant lilac on contact with the air and families would camp out on Oaxacan beaches dipping their yarn into the precious liquid.

▶ Tapachula 189D1

Tucked away in the south-east corner of Mexico is the major border-town of Tapachula only 17km from Guatemala. Visas can be obtained from the Guatemalan Consulate and the town buzzes with Guatemalans, formerly refugees and now shoppers. Worth seeing is the archaeological site of **Izapa▶▶**, 10km east of town. The incredibly hot but fertile surrounding plain was home to a flourishing civilisation in the last two centuries BC and shows a distinctive art style. Numerous temple platforms have revealed carved stelae (stone slabs), which form the vital link in time and space between the Olmecs and the Maya. Artefacts from the site are at the **Museo Regional** (*Open* Tue–Sun 10–5), on Tapachula's *zócalo*. The cloud forest reserve of **El Triunfo▶▶**, home to 300 bird species, including the elusive quetzal, lies nearly 130km north-west (for information on tours contact the Instituto de Historia Natural in Tuxtla Gutiérrez, tel: 961 23663).

▶▶ Tehuantepec 188B2

Tehuantepec is the most historically significant of three towns clustered around the Isthmus, the narrowest point of Mexico. Salina Cruz is its industrialised neighbouring port, while Juchitán has a more modernised façade, concealing even deeper traditions. The women of the Isthmus are known for their strength, beauty and elaborate dress (long flowing skirts and embroidered tunics), but it is their commercial astuteness that reigns. The market on Tehuantepec's arcaded main square is mainly run by women. One block away is the 1544 Dominican church and monastery, the latter now converted into the Casa de Cultura, with informative exhibits. The dramatic ruined hilltop fortress of Guingola, built by the last Zapotec ruler, Cosijoesa, is 15km north of town.

Tehuantepec's main rival, **Juchitán▶**, is 27km east. Little love has been lost between their respective inhabitants since 1866, when defeated Tehuantepec led the French army to Juchitán. Thanks to a spirited female defence, the latter held out. Today, the main interest is the market

Women play a dominant role in many aspects of daily life in Tehuantepec

Standing-room only for young and old in one of Tehuantepec's motocarros

(sample an iguana stew or invest in local craftwork on the upper floor) and its female vendors. The **Casa de Cultura** holds temporary exhibitions. Nature-lovers should head 20km north to natural springs and refreshing bathing-pools at **Tlacotepec▶**, once used by Zapotec royalty.

▶ Tenosique *188B3*

This small agricultural town is set in a hot, humid region of exuberant tropical vegetation, about 200km south-east of Villahermosar and only one hour by train from Palenque. It makes a useful crossroads for intrepid travellers intent on adding the Guatemalan site of Flores to their Maya checklist. Boats from La Palma (one hour away) follow the Rio San Pedro to the border. An alternative is to follow the Usamacinta River north into the delta wetlands of **Centla▶▶**, a protected habitat for jaguar, crocodile and ocelot. Immediately to the south of Tenosique is the magnificent canyon of **Boca del Cerro▶**. Rafting trips can be arranged in town. Tenosique's own archaeological museum displays artefacts from Yaxchilan and local sites, including **Pomoná**. Small hotels and restaurants make it eminently visitor-friendly.

▶ Tuxtla Gutiérrez *189D2*

The state capital of Chiapas, 293km south of Villahermosa, is the centre of a thriving coffee-growing region and source of Mexico's famed marimba music now revived at the **Parque de la Marimba**. Its steamy heat is all-enveloping, but less than two hours away and 1,500m higher lie the cool mountain villages around San Cristóbal. Tuxtla's *zócalo* is a revamped square awash with marble fountains and dominated by the modern **catedral**. The **Museo Regional▶▶** (*Open* Tue–Sun 9–5), in the Parque Madero, displays Olmec and Mayan artefacts together with colonial and ethnographic exhibits. A theatre, children's recreation area, botanic garden and *Orquideario* (orchid garden) complete the park offerings. An alternative claim to fame is the **zoo▶▶▶** (*Open* Tue–Sun 8.30–5.30), south of town and best reached by taxi. An enlightened approach to animal captivity has created large enclosures housing 239 species native to Chiapas. You will see ocelots, jaguars, pumas, howler monkeys and the Vivario's unappealing community of spiders and insects. All this is set in a 100-hectare tropical park of hardwoods and cedars.

Transportación Fray Matías de Córdoba S.A. de C.V.
☆☆☆☆☆
Transportes Terrestre Aeropuerto Terán - Tuxtla
R.F.C. TFM-920122-JDO
Rel. Ext. No. 09002372
N$ 10.00
Nº 04438
ZONA ORIENTE
TUXTLA GUTIERREZ, CHIAPAS TEL. 5-31-95
USUARIO

FRUIT-THROWING

Each *barrio* (quarter) of Tehuantepec celebrates its patron saint over several days to the tunes of the marimba. Most telling of all is the local custom called *tirada de frutas*, which takes place at numerous fiestas throughout the year. The first sign of this is a Tehuana woman staggering under lacquered gourds piled high with sweets, toys and mangoes which she distributes to the crowd. If only to show who wears the pants (or *huipil* in this case), women dressed in dazzling finery then climb on to the rooftops and throw fruit at the inferior males in the streets below.

Doll wearing local costume in Tuxtla Gutiérrez

Brilliantly coloured, woven and embroidered clothes are an enduring tradition all over Mexico. Oaxaca and Chiapas, home to the highest proportion of indigenous people, continue weaving techniques bestowed on them by none other than Quetzalcóatl.

THE RHOMBUS
The rhombus, a recurring motif in Chiapan embroidery, represents the Maya universe. Its four sides denote the limits of time and space, while smaller rhombuses in each corner symbolise the four cardinal points. Mitla-style 'Greek' hooks (a motif which was used in ancient Greece), which fill the margins of the rhombus, are stylised butterflies.

Separation of the secular and the sacred is impossible in Mexico. Craftwork expresses a highly personal view of the world, of life and death, and of the forces of nature. Never static, indigenous costume has developed over the centuries by assimilating outside influences. The arrival of the Spaniards brought new techniques and symbols imbued with Arab skills imparted by the Moors, an input that greatly stimulated creative potential. With the opening of Mexico's gate to the Orient through direct trade with the Philippines, a subtle synthesis of world cultures came about. Far less positive is the impact of 20th-century synthetic dyes and machines which, in extreme cases, have reduced what was once a spiritual exercise into a mechanical industry aimed at tourist purses. However, the geographical isolation and low standard of living in parts of Oaxaca and Chiapas have perversely ensured the survival of certain weaving and embroidery traditions.

Mixtec woman weaving, Oaxaca

Cloth For the Aztecs, weaving was an art invented by Xochiquetzal, goddess of flowers and patron of weavers, and every self-respecting girl was expected to lend a hand at the spindle and the loom. In their hierarchical society, costume variations distinguished the privileged from the poor as well as symbolising the wearer's tribe and origin, something that still holds despite the passage of over 400 years. Although clothes made of rabbit fur or twisted feathers disappeared long ago, certain Chiapan villages (Zinacantán, for example) still interweave downy feathers into ceremonial *huipils* (tunics), and Tzotzil and Tzetzil costumes are heavily decorated with swinging pompons, tassels and flowing satin ribbons.

Cotton remains the predominant cloth although wool, introduced at the time of the Conquest and mainly used for striped *serapes* (shawls), is rapidly being replaced by acrylic. In Chiapas they beat rough wool to give it a felt-like texture and are careful not to remove the natural oils during the cleaning stage: garments for the cold and damp highlands must be waterproof. Back-strap looms (attached to the back by a belt) are commonly used by women who make their own and their family's clothes; they often weave complex designs without diagrams or models and relying entirely on intuition, memory and imagination.

Dress styles Indigenous women still favour the *enredo*, a wrap-around skirt held in place by a separate waist sash, a highly decorative and essential element. Over this, or tucked inside, is the tunic-like *huipil*, which displays most of the intricate weaving patterns and/or

embroidery and thus becomes the most personalised garment in a woman's wardrobe. Finally, the versatile *rebozo* (a rectangular shawl introduced during the colonial period) serves as a wrap or baby-carrier. Male dress has evolved even more radically with the loin-cloth (banned from settlements by the Spaniards) replaced by trousers, while bare, once-painted torsos are now covered in shirts, topped with a *serape*. Belongings are carried in shoulder-bags woven from cotton, wool or vegetable fibres. In the Chiapan villages near San Cristóbal many Tzotzils and Tzeltals wear richly embroidered and trimmed tunics, yet another sign of their proud sense of identity; these are among the richest, most varied and elaborately worked textiles in Mexico. A variation is the typical Chamulan male outfit of wide hat, shirt, belted natural-wool tunic and trousers – a dashing Spanish legacy.

Design motifs Abstract, symbolic snakes, deer, butterflies, birds, flowers and foliage are combined with pre-Hispanic geometric forms – chevrons, triangles, zigzags, rhombuses and squares. Astutely aware of the tourist market, many local embroiderers have copied designs from archaeological sites such as Mitla or Yaxchilán, although in some cases these may have genuinely survived. Entire zoos invade the colourful Mixtec embroidery of Oaxaca, even depicting exotic, non-indigenous animals such as lions, but more likely to be crocodiles, iguanas or scorpions.

CHINA POBLANA

A well-entrenched legend regarding Mexican costume highlights the Oriental influence as Spanish galleons sailed between Manila, in the Philippines, and Acapulco. The story goes that in the 17th century a Chinese princess was captured by pirates, then rescued by gallant Spanish mariners who brought her to Acapulco. Abandoned to her fate, she made her way to Puebla, where she spent her life helping the poor. Scorning the elegant Spanish fashions of the day, she wore simple, full skirts and a loose, frilly blouse covered with a shawl, thus innovating a colourful, peasant-chic style. *China Poblana* (Chinese-Pueblan) is now Mexican national costume.

Dazzling embroidered weavings, San Cristóbal de las Casas

At La Venta schoolchildren investigate an Olmec head dating from the 4th century BC

COLOSSAL HEADS
The American archaeologist Matthew Stirling first uncovered the Olmec mystery, the massive carved basalt heads which reach heights of nearly 3m and weigh over 40 tons. Throughout the 1930s and '40s Stirling and his wife excavated three major Olmec sites: Tres Zapotes, La Venta and San Lorenzo. They became convinced that these civilisations predated the Maya. Vehemently opposed by Mayan specialists, Stirling was subsequently vindicated by carbon-dating. However, many questions remain: how were they created? How were they moved? Where did their Negroid features originate? Are they warriors or kings?

► Villahermosa *189D3*

The steamy capital of Tabasco is a booming metropolis at the heart of the state's oil industry. The layout follows the course of the Río Grijalva, which carries much of the trade to the interior of Chiapas and out to the port of Frontera. Not the most appealing of cities, Villahermosa's main interest lies in **Parque la Venta►►** (*Open* Tue–Sun 9–8), north-west of town. This is an outdoor museum of the original Olmec site of La Venta, some 120km west devoted to the city, which was unearthed by oil engineers in the 1940s. Roughly dating from 1000–600 BC, La Venta is represented here by 31 stone artefacts, including three colossal sculpted heads which have been transferred to this lush jungle setting. A zoo, a children's playground and a lagoon complete the attractions. More Olmec masterpieces can be seen at the excellent **Museo Regional de Antropología►►** (*Open* Tue–Sun 9–8), part of the CICOM (Centro de Investigaciones de las Culturas Olmeca y Maya) complex situated south of the centre. Naturalists and families should escape 10km south-east to **Yumka**, a vast nature reserve of jungle, savanna and wetlands with an excellent visitor's structure.

►►► Yaxchilán *189E2*

Nestling in thick rainforest on the Guatemalan border, in a loop of the Río Usumacinta, the extensive Mayan site of Yaxchilán is a major highlight of southern Mexico. Most people visit Yaxchilán by bus to **Frontera Corozal**, then take a 45-minute boat-ride. Alternatively there are plane tours from Palenque or San Cristóbal. The main buildings display intricately carved lintels, statues and walls inscribed with glyphs that have been deciphered to reveal Yaxchilán's secrets. Its heyday was in the mid-8th century, when it was ruled by the Bird Jaguar (*Pájaro Jaguar*) but, like all Mayan cities, it declined and by 900 was abandoned. The most important building is the richly decorated **Edificio 33**, a monumental temple on a levelled-off hilltop behind the riverside structures of the main plaza. Its main feature is a towering roofcomb framing a 7m niche which once contained an enthroned statue of a god. This is now kept inside the temple and still forms part of an annual ritual performed by the Lacandons.

Ritual pulque-drinking bouts were an important part of pre-Hispanic culture, depicted in friezes and on murals in many archaeological sites such as El Tajín (see page 165), but it was the Spanish who brought the distilling techniques which produced tequila and mescal.

Three alcoholic drinks dominate the *cantinas* and *pulquerías* (male-only bars) of Mexico: tequila, mescal and pulque. All are distilled from species of the agave or maguey (century plant) but there is a vast difference in strength – pulque is like a mild beer while tequila and mescal are hard liquor (over 40 per cent alcohol). Only one type of maguey produces true tequila, several produce mescal (thriving in warm, lowland climes, particularly Oaxaca) and over six will yield the basic juice for pulque (suited to cool, dry central highlands). Tequila is named after the Jaliscan town of Tequila (see page 132), centre of agave *tequilana* plantations and distilleries which by law are restricted to this area. Along the Gulf Coast tastes swing to rum or *agua ardiente* (a local liquor made from sugar-cane), while in the Yucatán peninsula the regional drink is based on honey fortified with the bark of the *balché* tree.

Production To make pulque, 10- to 12-year-old maguey hearts are punctured over a period of six months to yield a liquid which is transferred to the vats of the processing plant. Yeast speeds up the natural fermentation agents and within seven to 14 days the frothy, milky pulque is ready for the market. Perfect timing is essential as over-fermentation turns it sour.

Mescal and tequila production involves more complex processes. The pulpy spikes of the maguey are hacked off to obtain the solid *piña* (pineapple-type heart) which is then cooked in huge steam ovens before it is shredded and the juice is extracted. Sugars are added and the mixture is fermented for four days, followed by two distillations. Average (and rough) tequilas are colourless, while smoother, matured *tequila añejo* turns a golden colour after up to seven years of ageing.

TEQUILA ACCESSORIES
Often found at the bottom of a bottle of tequila or mescal is a *gusano de maguey*, the worm which inhabits the maguey and is added for good measure. It is sometimes reduced to a powder, mixed with salt and wrapped in a packet, attached to the bottle. More familiar is the ritual which accompanies tequila-drinking: salt is sprinkled on the hand, licked and then the juice of a lime squeezed on the tongue – followed by a shot of tequila. Another alternative involves a chaser, *sangrita* – a spicy cocktail of chillies, tomato and orange juice), which should be alternated with each shot of tequila.

TEQUILA GOES GLOBAL
Since 1940, the first year that tequila exports were of any consequence, business has multiplied 2,000-fold. Some 40 countries have acquired a taste for it, with 87 per cent of exports going directly to the US, followed, in order of consumption, by Germany, Belgium and France. Forecasts for future production indicate an annual production of 83 million litres, offering a rosy future to the 32 registered factories in Jalisco.

Enjoying a glass of tequila

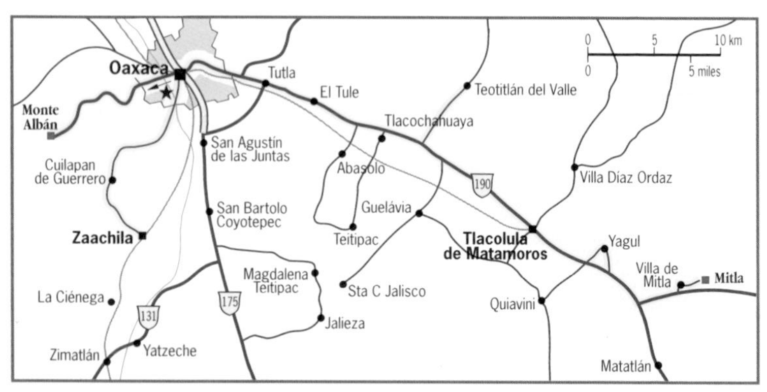

Oaxaca's valleys and Zapotec sites

El Tule, a giant ahueheute *tree outside Mitla, is said to be the Americas' widest tree and may be over 2,000 years old*

From Oaxaca, roads radiate through the valleys but do not connect. This drive follows several spokes but requires back-tracking through Oaxaca to drive east to Mitla. Allow a full day.

Drive south out of town following signs to Mexico DF until you reach MEX 175, where signs indicate Monte Albán. Cross a railway track and follow a winding road for 10km to the hilltop site of **Monte Albán** (see pages 198–9) , exceptional in the clear early-morning light. Allow two hours to explore the site. Retrace your route to the railway track, after which turn right immediately towards Zaachila. Ten kilometres further the road passes **Cuilapan de Guerrero**, a rare Mixtec town in this predominantly Zapotec area. Unmistakable are the roadside ruins of a beautiful 16th-century **Dominican church** and **monastery**, part of which stands open to the elements, although the two-storey Renaissance-style cloister has been restored. Here some rare murals survive, and the roofless colonnaded **chapel** is a marvel of graceful proportions.

Continue for 5km through flat farmlands to **Zaachila**, the last capital of the Zapotec empire and now a sleepy market town with a good selection of restaurants serving traditional Oaxacan dishes. Its busiest market day is Thursday, although villagers bring produce daily on mules. The town's main historic interest lies up the road behind the pink and yellow church in its *zona arqueológica*. Here stand the grassy tombs of ancient Mixtec royalty. From Zaachila drive back to Oaxaca's ring-road, keep to the central lane and follow signs to Istmo or Tehuantepec, which lead through the outskirts to link up with MEX 190, the main road east.

The first stop here is at **El Tule** (see page 194) to see what is claimed to be the world's largest tree, easily visible from the road, right in front of the church. Seven kilometres beyond is a turn-off to the right to **Tlacochahuaya**, a small village in undulating pastures. Follow the main road through the village and turn left at the end to reach a magnificent 16th-century **church**. This important Dominican monastery complex is notable for the church interior, entirely decorated in vivid floral murals by local artists and including an ornately painted 16th-century organ and a portrait of San Jerónimo by Juan de Arrué.

Back on the main road continue east to a turn-off on the left to **Teotitlán del Valle**, the oldest village in the Oaxaca valley and famous for its woollen rugs, woven on domestic handlooms. This is also the beginning of a lofty sierra that follows the road to Mitla and beyond. Another stop can be made at **Tlacolula**, known for its mescal, a few kilometres further on the right of MEX 190. Turn off at the Pemex station and drive straight on as far as the market area. Behind walls on the left stands a superb 1531 **church**, its side chapel rich in early baroque carvings, with a unique wrought-iron pulpit. From here return to the main road and continue to Mitla (see page 195), an arresting sight, with its impressive Zapotec structures merging into the church precinct (now joined by a crafts market). This lies uphill at the back of the village; the **Frissell Museum** is beside the main square on the road in. The end of this drive should take you back 10km on the road to Oaxaca to the little-visited Zapotec site of **Yagul**, magnificent in the late afternoon light on its strategic hilltop position with 360-degree views over the Tlacolula valley. Explore the large ball-court, palace patios, fortress and temple ruins in their verdant and panoramic setting of cacti before returning to Oaxaca on MEX 190.

Guatemalan imports at Mitla's local market

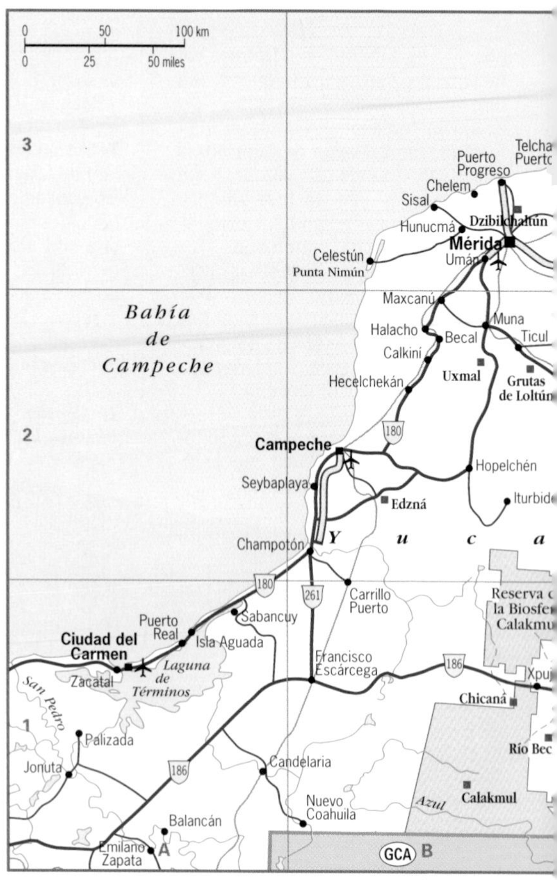

Below: monument on the waterfront at Chetumal, in Quintana Roo, on the border with Belize
Opposite: the Pyramid of Kukulcán, Chichén Itzá, also known as the Castillo, has nine terraces and a square temple on the top

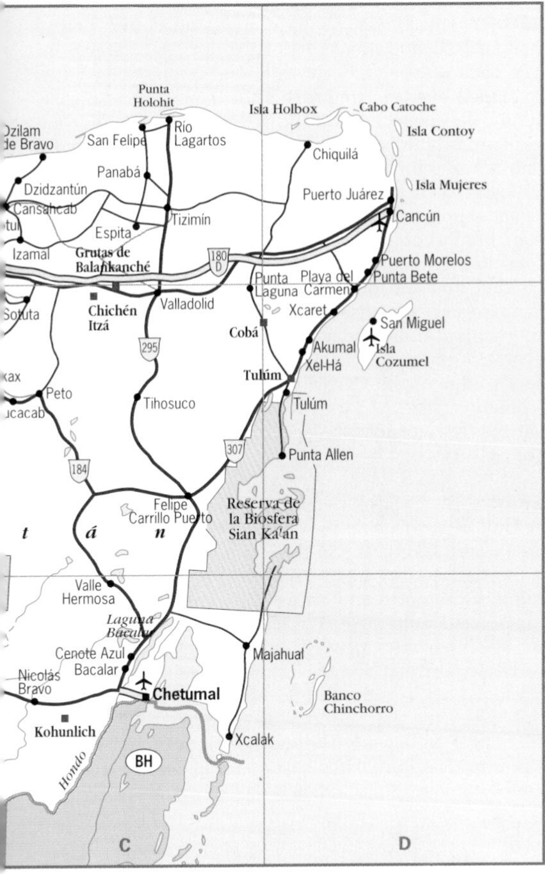

The Yucatán

▶▶▶ REGION HIGHLIGHTS

THE YUCATÁN Sun, sea and sand: this is why most visitors come to the Yucatán peninsula. Then there are the ancient Maya sites and the *cenotes* (sinkholes). The main port of call, though, is Cancún, a high-rise resort that sits beside the Caribbean in the north-east. Most of the visitors who flock here annually only venture south along the Cancún-Tulúm Corridor (now more exotically renamed the Maya Riviera), or across the sea to Cozumel and Isla Mujeres. This leaves a large part of the peninsula blissfully unspoiled. Of the three states that occupy the peninsula, Quintana Roo (the eastern slice) is by far the most tourist-oriented. Some 18 new developments are projected between Sian Ka'an and Xcalak, an area that until now remained attractively wild. This Costa Maya project will cash in on the Chichorro coral reef and should vastly improve communications with Chetumal, the state capital.

And the rest of the peninsula? Nestling in its flat, jungle-shrouded terrain are spectacular Mayan sites, sleepy villages and wildlife reserves that should not be by-passed. Rent a car and head inland to discover the real land of the Maya.

WATER, WATER NOWHERE
'The peninsula of Yucatán… is a vast plain. The soil and atmosphere are extremely dry; along the whole coast, from Campeachy to Cape Catoche, there is not a single stream or spring of fresh water. The interior is equally destitute and water is the most valuable possession in the whole country. During the season of rains, from April to October, there is a superabundant supply, but the scorching sun of the next six months dries up the earth, and unless water were preserved man and beast would perish, and the country be depopulated.'
John Lloyd Stephens: *Incidents of Travel*, 1841.

HISTORY The Mayan civilisation extended into Belize, Guatemala, Honduras and El Salvador, and dates from over 2,500 years ago. Great cities and ceremonial centres developed over the centuries until they suffered a cataclysmic decline in the 10th and 11th centuries. By the time the Spaniards arrived, the Maya had abandoned the main centres and returned to subsistence farming, but this did not lessen their resistance. In 1528 Francisco de Montejo began a prolonged and difficult campaign to subdue them, finally completed by his son, 'El Mozo', in 1542. As a result Mérida, then Campeche and Valladolid were founded and the once proud and independent Maya became mere *peons* (serfs) at the mercy of the Spanish landowners. Independence in 1821 sparked Yucatecan separatist moves and, more iniquitous, the long and bloody War of the Castes (1847), which decimated the population. The Mexican Revolution brought reforms that finally returned the land to its Maya inhabitants – four centuries on.

TERRAIN The Yucatán peninsula, which juts out between the Gulf of Mexico and the Caribbean Sea, is divided into three states: Campeche in the south-west, Quintana Roo in the east and Yucatán itself, which occupies a good chunk of the north and centre. For centuries this region was isolated from the rest of Mexico by dense jungle and vast swamps, only opening up in the 1950s with rail and road links. Formed by a flat limestone shelf, which is honeycombed with underground rivers, caves and *cenotes* (sinkholes), the dry countryside is covered with savannah, jungle and agave. The soil here is poor and there is little rain. The Puuc Hills, just south of Mérida, provide the only topographical relief.

Timeless traditions in the Yucatán

Fresh produce for sale at the local market

TRADING IN THE PAST
The Maya traded jade, salt, feathers, obsidian, cotton and pottery in an area extending from central Mexico to Costa Rica, with cacao (cocoa) beans used as currency. Under Spanish rule, the Yucatán was divided into vast creole *haciendas*. By the late 19th century they were profiting from the boom in world demand for *henequén* (sisal – used for ropes) before a decline set in after the invention of synthetic materials in the 1920s. Some of these once glorious, now decaying, partly derelict *haciendas* can be visited: San Bernardo (near Maxcanú off Highway 180), Yáxcopoil (south of Umán on Highway 261) and Teya (12km east of Mérida on Highway 180).

SOPHISTICATION OR NOT Those seeking an upbeat holiday should head for the coast of Quintana Roo, starting in the north with Isla Mujeres, continuing through artificial Cancún and down the so-called 'corridor', a coastal highway which ends at Tulúm. Originally a magnet for divers who came for the limpid Caribbean waters, thick with coral reefs and wrecked galleons, this stretch has been transformed by developers, exemplified by the high-rise horizon and international airport of the island of Cozumel. But all is not lost. Wildlife and biosphere reserves at Isla Contoy, Sian Ka'an, Río Lagartos and Calakmul preserve the last jaguars, toucans and tropical forest. The perfect base for exploring this region is Mérida, a handsome colonial city which cleverly mixes culture with pleasure.

SITES Virtually every Mayan village has a crumbling pyramid looming behind a colonial church, but the obvious archaeological sites to visit in the Yucatán are those of Chichén Itzá, Uxmal, Tulúm, Cobá, Edzná and the smaller excavated ruins in the Puuc hills (see pages 250–1). The Río Bec group between Chicaná and Kohunlich, together with Calakmul, are the latest draws for Maya *aficionados*. Hundreds still await excavation, while villages of thatched Mayan huts dot the interior, a reminder that today's inhabitants have not forgotten their illustrious and still mysterious forebears.

The sparkling turquoise waters off Akumal beach

SWASHBUCKLING
Sixteenth-century Campeche became the principal port on the Yucatán peninsula as shiploads of timber and *chicle* (gum) were sent back to Spain, along with vast quantities of silver, gold and other precious minerals. Such wealth attracted the covetous attention of pirates, who started attacking the city only six years after it was founded in 1540. Swash-buckling buccaneers included such infamous characters as Laurent Graff, El Brasileño, Diego the Mulatto, John Hawkins and peg-legged Pato de Palo. In 1663 the pirates united for a particularly murderous attack on Campeche, slaughtering the citizens and sacking the city. This inspired the building of the famous city ramparts.

►► Akumal *221D2*

Akumal, 'The Place of the Turtles', lies some 35km north of Tulúm. From May to August, loggerhead, green and hawksbill turtles lay their eggs on the powdery sands, and divers and snorkellers are drawn year-round to the outstanding coral formations of Akumal reef and a sunken Spanish galleon. Low-rise hotels and exclusive guesthouses nestle in the protected bays, but those with a less flexible budget can indulge in the marine offerings at the superb lagoon of Yalkú, just over 1km north.

►► Campeche *220B2*

The revamped state capital of Campeche on the west coast of the Yucatán peninsula combines a modern port with an unusual colonial history, reflected in its elegant architecture. Encircling the old town are the remains of a sturdy 2.5km wall, built between 1668 and 1704, and reinforced by *baluartes* (bastions) to protect the population from deadly pirate attacks. Seven of the original eight forts remain, best seen by following Avenida Circuito Baluartes. Overlooking the reclaimed sea-front area on one side and the Plaza Principal on the other are the ramparts of the **Baluarte de Soledad**, which houses the **Museo de Estelas Mayas►►** (*Open* Tue–Sun 8–8), displaying rare carved slabs from the region. Opposite, on the main square, stands the Yucatán's first church, the **Catedral de la Concepción**, dating from the 1540s, with a tourist office next door. Two blocks down Calle 8 is the **Baluarte San Carlos►**, with cannons, a small history museum and a network of tunnels. At the northern end of Calle 8 the courtyard of the **Baluarte de Santiago** is ablaze with the lush tropical plants of the **Jardín Botánico Xmuch Haltún►►** (*Open* Mon–Sat 9–2, 6–8, Sun 9–1). Beyond the walls to the south-east is the church of **San Francisco►**, built on the site where the first Mexican mass was held. Four kilometres south is the striking hilltop **Fuerte San Miguel►►** (*Open* Tue–Sun 8.30–1, 2.15–7), exhibiting remarkable jade masks and pottery from Calakmul.

Gate in the old town walls of Campeche, a target for pirates

► Cancún *221D3*

This artificially planned resort, designed by computer in the early 1970s, is the ultimate in a Mexican mega-resort.

Glitzy high-rise hotels tower over the Caribbean from the shores of a 23km-long sandspit that is connected to the mainland at both ends by bridges, creating a vast lagoon (Laguna Nichupté). This strip, the **Zona Hotelera**, along Boulevard Kukulcan, caters for every hedonistic need – from theme park to golf course, deep-sea fishing, parasailing or diving – and the luxury hotels battle to outdo each other. Cancún's latest brainchild is Puerto Cancún, a luxury marina development north of the Zona Hotelera including low-rise hotels and condominiums.

One of the resort's principal attractions is that it provides a convenient base for visiting many of the area's outstanding archaeological sites – Tulúm, Cobá and Chichén Itzá – as well as the islands of Mujeres and Holbox. Cancún's own Maya ruins include the **Ruinas del Rey▶** (*Open* daily 8–5), Boulevard Kukulcan, opposite Cancún's only public beach, Playa Delfines. Iguanas are usually the only visitors, slithering over a series of post-Classic temples. Other, smaller structures are **San Miguelito** and **Yamil Lu'um**, both squeezed between the hotel precincts.

The mainland **Ciudad Cancún** (Cancún City) is home to 250,000 residents, mainly immigrant workers and is also where hotels and restaurants offer almost normal Mexican prices. Dissecting the town, Avenida Tulúm leads to Puerto Juárez in the north and the Cancún–Tulúm 'corridor' to the south. With the relaxation of foreign trade agreements US investment has poured in, spawning recreation centres, hotel chains and giant shopping-malls. Over 25,000 hotel rooms cater for nearly 3 million annual visitors, generating 20 per cent of Mexico's total tourist revenue.

CRUISING CANCUN

What it lacks in authenticity, Cancún attempts to make up for in entertainment. At the Hyatt Regency Hotel the Tradicion Mestiza stages a folkloric ballet nightly (except Sunday) at 8.15pm, to be enjoyed while indulging in a buffet dinner. Or visitors can slip into pirate gear and cruise to 'Treasure Island' on a galleon, dining, dancing and drinking all the way – boats leave the dock at Playa Langosta at 6pm. Sunset cruises, which throw in a lobster dinner, leave from the pier at the Royal Mayan Marina daily at 4pm and 7.30pm. However, first prize for virtual reality goes to *The Sub Sea Explorer*, which offers a hermetic, air-conditioned submarine trip around Cancún's offshore reefs.

Cancún's hotels line the beach overlooking the Caribbean

Flocks of flamboyant pink-feathered flamingos adorn the shores of the Yucatán peninsula. The birds are a brilliant spectacle; from a distance, they create the impression that the water itself is a blushing, rosy liquid.

FLIGHTY FLAMINGOS
Four species of flamingo exist in the world, most common being the greater flamingo, the Caribbean race of which occurs in Mexico. All have elongated, webbed feet and sinuous necks and obtain food by filtering plankton through their beaks. Known for their powerful flight and preference for warm climes, they choose to live in India, Africa, South America, the Caribbean and the South of France.

EDEN
The extreme north-east corner of the Yucatán peninsula is now protected as an ecological reserve, El Eden. Río Lagartos, Isla Contoy and the Yum Balam reserve together offer diverse ecosystems, trails and basic facilities. Contact the Reserve office in Cancún, tel/fax: 98-80-50-32 or Mexico City, tel/fax: 553 2698.

Four hours from Cancún, on the north coast of the Yucatán, lies the 320sq km nature reserve of Río Lagartos, nesting and breeding ground for thousands of pink flamingos. Named by Spanish explorers after the alligators which infested the area, it is not a river but an area of eight ecosystems where salty coastal waters have eaten into flat marshes to create a network of estuaries and lagoons. Alligators can still be tracked down by the more adventurous (although hunting has greatly reduced their population), but the outstanding natural feature is the sheer number of pink flamingos drawn to the macrobiotic algae and aquatic life of the lagoon. From April to early July they join 270 other bird species (ducks, egrets, herons, ibises, storks, cormorants, pelicans and plovers), which in winter include migratory birds from the north. Among the latter are sandpipers, scarlet tanagers, black and white warblers and ovenbirds – best spotted in the early morning.

Nesting An estimated 15,000 flamingos nest in the muddy shallows of estuaries that extend west from Río Lagartos to beyond San Felipe and east past El Cayo. Official rangers patrol the area during the breeding season to ensure that visitors do not disturb the flamingos, and the only way to see anything more than a distant pink haze is to board a boat for a trip of five to six hours. This will bring you to their favourite nesting-haunts deep in the marshlands, although however isolated they are, flamingos are fast to take flight. Outside this season the best place to spot these graceful creatures is in the fish-laden lagoon of Celestún, south-west of Mérida on the Gulf of Mexico, where they spend the winter months.

Caribbean flamingo

►► Celestún 220B3

The small fishing port of Celestún, 92km west of Mérida, and its nature reserve are famous for flamingos. Birdwatching is best in the winter season when migratory birds wing in from North America to this mild corner. Boats make a two-hour tour of the mangrove-edged lagoon and there are plenty of sandy (though windy) beaches with seafood restaurants. The *bosque petrificado* is a spectacular area of partly submerged petrified trees. A handful of budget hotels and a new resort-hotel are clustered around the jetty.

►► Cenote Azul 221C1

The flat limestone terrain of the north and central areas of the peninsula is criss-crossed by labyrinthine caves and *cenotes* (freshwater sinkholes caused by the collapse of cavern roofs). Cenote Azul, on the south-western shore of Laguna Bacalar (see page 241), 36km north of Chetumal, is estimated to be 90m deep. Its brilliant blue water teems with fish and invites swimming, snorkelling and diving. The less energetic can admire the colours from a *palapa*-roofed restaurant.

► Chetumal 221C1

Relaxed, but with a mounting crime rate, Quintana Roo's state capital is tucked away in the south-east corner on the Belize border, isolated from the main Yucatán masses. It is a frequent victim of hurricanes, and has become a mainly modern port of wide avenues interspersed with a more Caribbean-style of beaten-up clapboard houses. The main cultural sight is the **Museo de la Cultura Maya►►** (*Open* Tue–Thu 9–7, Fri–Sat 9–8, Sun 9–2), where interactive displays explain Mayan history. The adjoining market attracts a transient population of Belizeans on shopping sprees, while a string of cheap bars and related amusements caters for the regular influx of sailors. The *malecón* (Boulevard Bahía) runs 6km north to Calderitas, a palm-fringed fishing village edged by a rocky beach. Just before this is **Punta Maya** where boat-trips leave for the manatee sanctuary further into the bay. At Muelle Fiscal (the main jetty in the town centre), ferries leave for Xcalak's wild beaches and coral reefs (see page 252).

DARK DAYS

After conquering northern Yucatán in the 1540s, Francisco de Montejo's son – 'El Mozo' – sent an expedition south under Lieutenant Gaspar Pacheco. Men and women were pressed into service as the Spanish advanced burning abandoned settlements and countering any guerrilla resistance with instant death. Prisoners were garrotted or dismembered by dogs and women were thrown into lagoons with weights attached to them. During the march Mayan porters were chained together by their necks and those who slackened were simply removed by decapitation. By 1544 resistance around Chetumal had collapsed and Pacheco had established a provincial capital on Laguna Bacalar.

Pelican, Chetumal

The Mexican–Belize border crossing, near Chetumal

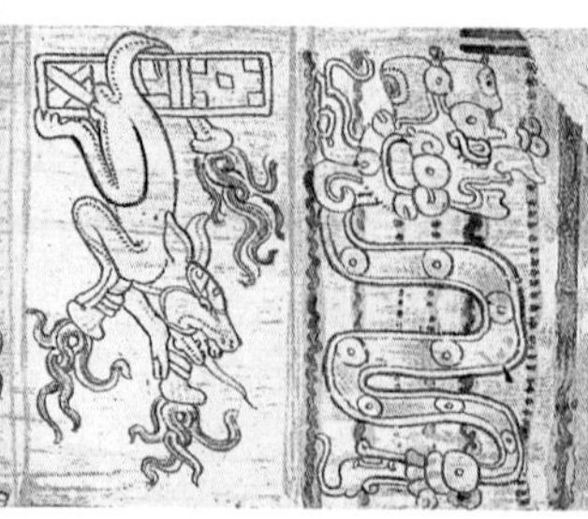

Brilliant pre-Hispanic mathematicians created a calendar that was more accurate than our Western Gregorian version. The obsession with planetary movements governed not only religious rituals and mythology but also daily life. Understanding the complexities of Mayan numerological achievements has become a pre-occupation of Mayanists, bent on uncovering the truth about this advanced civilisation.

CHRONOLOGICAL COERCION
According to American Mayanist Sylvanus Morley, Mayan belief in the repetitive nature of their almanacs was such that they underwent 'chronological coercion'. At the end of each cycle of 13 *katuns* (256.5 of our years) they 'went beneath the trees, beneath the bushes, beneath the vines, to their misfortune' as the books of *Chilam Balam* put it. For example the Itzá Maya claimed to have founded Chichén Itzá in the 5th to 6th centuries, before being driven out and settling elsewhere a century or so later. Precisely 256.5 years later they claim to have returned to Chichén, possibly bringing with them Kukulcán and other Toltec influences.

To assure their place in the cosmos, pre-Columbian Americans developed elaborate rituals based on their observations of the sun, the moon and the stars. Perceived as personifications of the divine powers, planetary movements were carefully observed with the naked eye, usually by trained shamans or priests who built up detailed records over the generations. Time and space were considered a unity. The earth was conceived as a disc divided between the four cardinal points, each quarter defined by its own colour, deity and associations, and representative of 13 years. Predictions such as forecasting the rainy season, the declaration of wars or dates for kingship rituals were all based on precise astronomical records.

Archaeoastronomy Cities were laid out, pyramids were built and openings were positioned in precise relation to planetary or astral positions: at the point where the Pleiades set behind the mountain of Cerro Colorado, as in Teotihuacán, or, as in the cave-shaft at Xochicalco, oriented to receive the sun's rays at its first passage through the zenith, or, as with the Governor's House at Uxmal, aligned to face the southern rising of Venus as the morning star. Interest in this domain has stimulated an emerging field of study named archaeoastronomy, which brings together astronomers, archaeologists and anthropologists.

Mayan calendars Mayan codices (ancient manuscripts) and sites offer a wealth of confusing sources of information on the subject. The Classic Maya calendar was based on the Long Count, starting, according to the most accepted correlation, on 12 August, 3113 BC. This was the beginning of a huge cycle of 13 *baktuns* (394.5 years), totalling 5,125 years and ending on 24 December 2011, with the destruction of the world. The Initial Series dates, found on inscriptions begin with the Long Count and are followed by the Calendar Round date, consisting of two calendars which existed throughout Mesoamerica. The ritual almanac (*Tzol kin*), made up of the numbers one to 13 times 20 named days (totalling 260), was meshed with the *Haab*, a 365 'vague year' of 18 months of 20 days, plus 5 unlucky days at the end. Dates in the 260-day count had symbolic and prophetic meaning, perhaps because of their equivalence to the interval between Venus' manifestation as evening and morning star. The start of a new Calendar Round, every 52 years, was a date of great

importance for the Mesoamericans, and often coincided with new pyramid construction. The post-Classic Maya of the 10th century abandoned the Long Count for the Short Count, which was based on 13 *katuns* of 256.5 years. It had an emphasis on the cyclical repetition of events, that confused prophecy and history in the written records.

Venus and the sun Mayan legend recounts the story of twin heroes, Hunahpu and Xbalanque, who, after overcoming countless obstacles in the underworld, finally emerged as gods themselves. Echoing the astronomical progress of Venus – which, in fraternal harmony, precedes the sun at dawn or sets later at dusk – Hunahpu became Venus and Xbalanque the sun, creating a partnership common in Mesoamerican celestial society (see pages 180–1). The complete orbit of Venus takes 584 days: multiply 584 by five and 365 by eight and you have the same total. The eight-year almanac, constructed to interlock the Venus-sun cycles, is thought to have served to determine propitious dates for ritual combat, sacrifice or war, since for the Maya this planetary god represented warfare and blood. More important still was the passage of the sun, whether at the spring and autumn equinox (21 March and 23 September) or at the summer or winter solstice (22 June and 22 December). The most celebrated indication of this is at Chichén Itzá's Pirámide de Kukulcán at the spring or autumn solstice, when the sun's rays descend, the pyramid is mounted by a serpentine shadow – a homage to Kukulcán, the Mayan plumed serpent, or mere chance?

OBSERVATORIES
Chichén Itzá's observatory (or Caracol) is a unique example of the significance of astronomy for the Maya. It was built with the sole purpose of tracking celestial movements. The circular construction stands on a platform at the top of a wide stairway and encloses an inner spiral staircase. The windows of the upper chamber (not open to the public) are aligned with the positions of the setting sun at the equinox and the solstice, while others indicate the four cardinal points. Alignments between other doorways and openings have been analysed as related to the cycles of the moon and Venus.

Chichén Itzá's Observatory, known as El Caracol *(The Snail) because of its spiral staircase*

RESERVA DE LA BIOSFERA CALAKMUL
A 723,000-hectare area to the north and south of Chicaná has now been established by Unesco as a biosphere reserve in order to save what remains of the Petén rainforest. Calakmul's jungle, the densest on the peninsula, is rich in flora and fauna, with 300 species of birds, rare orchids and jaguars, howler monkeys and tapirs still prowling through the undergrowth. To the south the reserve joins Guatemala's Maya Biosphere Reserve (north of Tikal) and to the west Belize's Río Bravo conservation area. Visits can be made with tour agents from Campeche.

► Chicaná 220B1

Open: daily 8–5

Chicaná is one of 45 archaeological sites lying along Highway 186 between Escárcega and Chetumal, the last being Kohunlich (see page 241). Still under excavation and surrounded by Quintana Roo's tropical forest, these little-visited Mayan sites offer the rare chance of being alone with time. Their regional style of architecture is characterised by giant serpents' mouths as doorways. Chicaná itself, built in a combination of the Puuc and Río Bec styles, reached its peak in the late 7th century when the eight-roomed palace – the main structure – was probably built. Its central serpentine entrance represents the open mouth of the rain god Chac.

Becán (once encircled by a moat) and Xpujil (famous for a lattice-towered pyramid) are also easy to reach from the road, but **Río Bec►►** lies down 16km of unpaved road. The undisputed queen of this area is **Calakmul►►** (*Open daily 8–5*), reached by a 64km road through the biosphere reserve. This site is now considered to have been one of the most important Mayan cities, which at its zenith in the 6th century covered over 25sq km. Extensive restoration continues on its many structures and inscribed stelae (stone slabs).

►►► Chichén Itzá 221C2

Open: daily 8–5

Overwhelming in its scale, architectural beauty and history of violence, Chichén Itzá is the most visited of the Yucatán peninsula's Mayan sites. The ruins are composed of three distinct zones, spread across a plain 120km east of Mérida. To visit them in relative peace it is advisable to stay at one of the many hotels near by and arrive early. The ceremonial centre was founded in AD 514 by a priest, and experienced two peaks: from 600 to around 900 and again from the late 10th century till 1196. Subsequently there was almost three centuries of civil wars and cultural stagnation before Chichén finally collapsed in 1441. When the Spanish arrived, they named the abandoned buildings arbitrarily, as their functions were not always known.

Temple of the Warriors with the Court of the Thousand Columns below. At the top of the stairs sits the famous chacmool

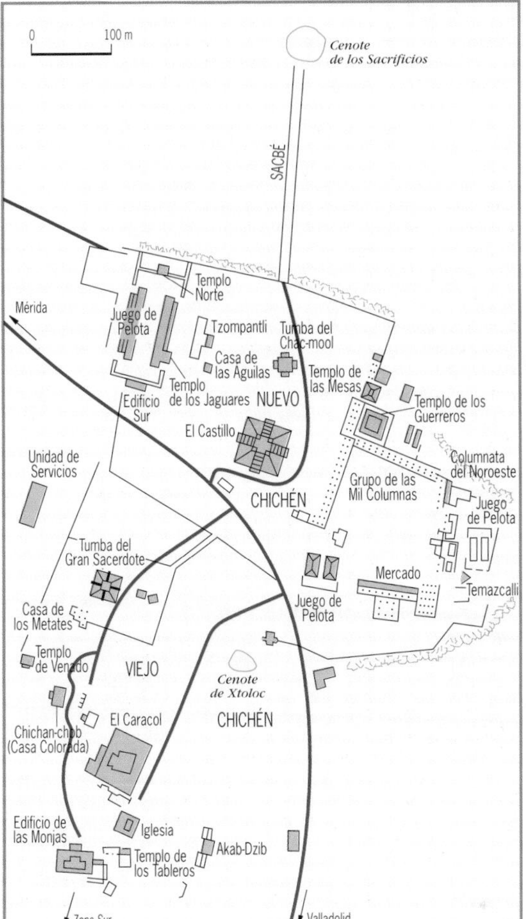

CHICHÉN EXTRAS
Services at Chichén Itzá comprise an excellent museum, bookshop, restaurant and auditorium, all at the main entrance. A sound-and-light show provides a 45-minute re-enactment of Chichén's historic highpoint. This is held in summer at 8pm in Spanish, and at 9pm in English; in winter the Spanish show shifts to 7 pm. However, conoisseurs of Mayan archaeological sites maintain that the show at Uxmal (see page 248) is far superior in quality and drama.

Chichén Nuevo (New Chichén) Soaring over the central plaza is **El Castillo** (or Temple of Kukulcán – the Mayan feathered serpent), which embodies the solar year in the total number of steps (365) and in the 52 panels lining each side of its base; twice a year, at the spring and autumn equinoxes, serpentine shadows are cast down the north staircase to join the carved snake heads at the bottom. In the northern flank a narrow stairway leads inside to a dank **tomb** (*Open* 11–3, 4–5), which contains a *chac-mool* (a reclining statue used to receive sacrificial offerings) and a red jaguar throne studded with jade and shell. To the north-west of the pyramid a group of temples is clustered around the **Juego de Pelota** (Ball Court), the largest yet discovered in Mexico, whose walls are lined with reliefs of ball-players. Overlooking this is the **Templo de los Jaguares** (Temple of the Jaguars), its walls carved with eagles and jaguars devouring hearts in Maya-Toltec style, as well as an image of Quetzalcóatl. Immediately east stands the macabre **Tzompantli** (Platform of Skulls), which once served as a display-case for the heads of sacrificial victims.

Detail on the façade of the Temple of the Warriors

CENOTE DE LOS SACRIFICIOS
Chichén's largest *cenote*, the Cenote de los Sacrificios, lies about 300m to the north of the plaza along a *sacbé* (sacred Mayan path – see page 232). Over 40m deep and with a diameter approaching 60m, this perfectly circular sinkhole probably served as a sacrifical site. Soon after the foundation of the city, around 650, offerings to the rain god Chac consisted of objects – statues, vessels, gold discs, jade or incense – but later human sacrifice was introduced. Victims were first purified in an adjacent steam-bath, then richly dressed before being cast into the well from a platform on its southern edge.

Towering over the opposite side of the plaza is the **Templo de los Guerreros** (Temple of the Warriors), a stepped structure built around the older Templo del Chacmool, named after the *chacmool* that surveys the site from its summit. Serpentine columns, Atlantean pillars and an extensive colonnade – the **Grupo de las Mil Columnas** (Court of the Thousand Columns) now roofless, are among the controversial elements below recalling Toltec Tula. South-east of here are the less spectacular ruins of steam-baths, a market place and smaller ball-courts.

Chichén Viejo (Old Chichén) From the main plaza a path winds south to another, older cluster of monuments: the **Tomb of the High Priest, Chichan-chob** (Red House) and **El Caracol**, an elevated, circular building which was used for astronomical observations. Facing this to the south is the imposing palace complex, the **Edificio de las Monjas** (Nunnery), its façades decorated with cut stone forming a Puuc-style mosaic. Between the two is the **Iglesia**, remarkable for its roofcomb and frieze adorned with masks of the rain god Chac and mythological creatures. A path from behind the nunnery leads off to the largely unrestored **Zona Sur** (South Zone), whose structures are best understood with the help of a guide.

▶ Ciudad del Carmen *220A1*

This fishing and oil town sits on the western tip of Isla del Carmen, joined to the mainland by causeways and enclosing the large Laguna de Términos. It is the Gulf of Mexico's chief shrimp fishing port and an expanding oil centre. During the 17th century it was a major pirates' base, vying with Isla Mujeres, on the Yucatán's Caribbean coast, for notoriety. Well off the main tourist circuit, the town makes a peaceful stop-off, with its palm-shaded plazas, good beaches and excellent seafood restaurants. However, it suffered considerable damage from hurricanes in 1995.

▶▶▶ Cobá *221C2*

Open: daily 8–5

Situated about 40km inland from Tulúm along a good road, Cobá (meaning 'wind-ruffled waters') is an easily accessible site that remains refreshingly unexploited. Its pretty lakeside setting encirled by jungle has spawned just a few hotels, restaurants and craft shops, and if you visit after Chichén Itzá or Tulúm the atmosphere is decidedly low-key. Excavations began in the

Deep in the jungle, Cobá was never discovered by the Spaniards: La Iglesia – one of the many structures found at the site

Cobá's Nohuch Mul, at 42m, is the tallest pyramid in the northern part of the Yucatán peninsula

SACBEOB

The longest known *sacbé* in the Mayan world begins at the base of Cobá's Nohoch Mul and runs for nearly 100km to Yaxuná near Chichén Itzá. The function of these numerous 'white roads', built of limestone and surfaced with cement, is debatable: they could have been used for transportation or for ceremonial purposes. Maya legend recounts *sacbé* construction ... The devout King Ucan unrolled the roads like a ribbon from a stone on his shoulder until one day a beautiful princess appeared. Refusing her advances, he turned away, only to be repeatedly blocked by her. At last he dropped his stone and made love to her. His magic power vanished and he could no longer pick up his stone!

1970s, and to date only a tiny percentage of this enormous Mayan city has been uncovered. Distances between each ruin are great – so come prepared with good shoes, water and insect repellent. Covering a total area of over 80sq km, Cobá flourished between 600 and 900 when thousands of homes huddled around the forested shores of five lakes. Its monumental structures were built in a style that curiously resembled Guatemala's Tikal rather than other northern Mayan sites. A further enigma is presented by the 45 wide *sacbeob* (plural), thought to be ceremonial avenues, which radiate from Cobá for distances of nearly 100km to other ancient settlements.

To the right of the main path is the **Grupo de Cobá**, whose narrow but steep pyramid rises 24m above the tree-tops to give a fabulous view south towards Lago Macanxoc and east to Nohoch Mul – the great pyramid. At its base is a vaulted tunnel with traces of murals and beyond here tracks lead through the jungle, past countless unexcavated structures, underground Mayan homes and tunnels to reach the lake. Back on the main path is a recently restored ball-court. The next turn-off leads to the **Conjunto de Las Pinturas** (Temple of the Painted Lintels), where a four-tiered temple displays badly deteriorated murals. Close by are some beautifully carved stelae (stone slabs) and circular altars known as the **Grupo Macanxoc**.

All Cobá's *sacbeob* converge on *Nohoch Mul*, an easy, but hot, kilometre's walk from Las Pinturas. Tapirs, butterflies, snakes, fire-ants and the occasional toucan will make the going more interesting. Towering 42m high, Cobá's great pyramid provides sweeping vistas over the surrounding jungle from a small temple decorated with descending god figures. Thought to be connected with the God of Honey, they stress Cobá's vital role as a trading centre for cocoa and honey.

Mayan carving at Cobá

Browsing in the shops lining Cozumel's pedestrianised main street is a favourite occupation with visitors

►► Cozumel *221D2*

Cozumel incorporates both extremes of the Yucatán's moods. Just 19km off Playa del Carmen and only 48km south of Cancún, it has become a prime target for cruise-ships, island-hoppers and beach fanatics. However, it was discovered by divers, drawn to its shores to follow in the wake of Jacques Cousteau, who filmed the fabulous Palancar Reef in 1961. Teetering on the shelf of a mighty 1,000m drop-off that teems with brilliantly coloured fish and incredible black coral formations, the reef is considered one of the world's top diving destinations. Altogether there are more than 13km of reefs lying in the limpid waters off Cozumel's west coast, all of which have been protected as a marine reserve since 1972.

The island Seventeen kilometres wide and 45km long, Cozumel boasts one road (the Transversal), which circles the southern half of the island, leaving the north to scattered ruins and much of the east coast to rocky headlands, rare hotels and dangerous surf. Ferries from Playa del Carmen and Puerto Morelos dock on the west coast at **San Miguel**, a pedestrianised, commercialised town entirely governed by tourism. Cruise-ships land their passengers a few kilometres south of town and international flights do the same at the airport to the north. Cozumel is certainly not the destination for lovers of unadulterated atmosphere or for those on a budget, although the latter can escape to the wilder east coast.

Reefs and beaches Cozumel is a paradise for divers: San Miguel's dive-shops outnumber the reefs, but those with less experience can also enjoy themselves. Ten kilometres south of San Miguel is **Laguna Chankanab►** where botanic gardens, a small museum, restaurants and a man-made beach line a bay which offers prime snorkelling – as well as gear for rent. In 1998 a dolphin centre was added where visitors swim with these extraordinary creatures. Avoid the middle of the day when cruise passengers pour in and access to the water becomes nightmarish. Five

PRE-DIVING DAYS
For the early Maya, Cozumel was a pilgrimage destination favoured by women who visited the shrine dedicated to Ixchel, the goddess of the moon and fertility. When the Spanish ships captained by Juan de Grijalva arrived on the horizon from Cuba in 1518, the reception was timid and Cozumel was left in peace. The following year, along came Cortés and a very different sort of encounter. In Bernal Díaz's words: 'It seems that a number of idols of most hideous shapes were kept in a prayer-house in Cozumel to which the natives of the country habitually offered sacrifices at that season.' Cozumel's shrines were soon destroyed and replaced with crucifixes.

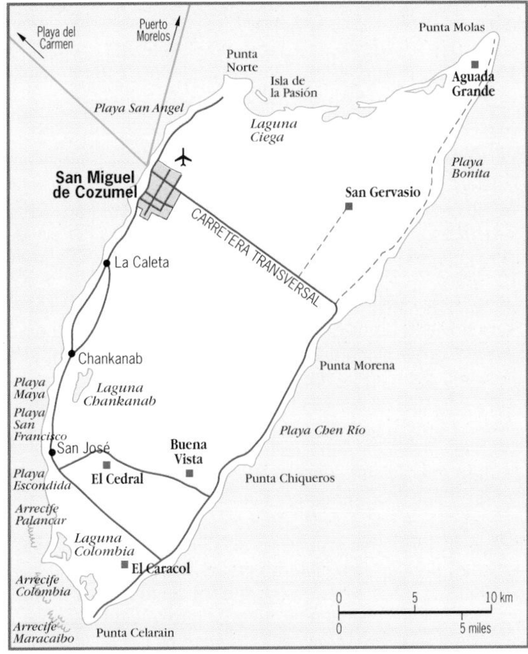

BEST DIVES
Divers head off in droves for the reefs of Palancar, Paradise, Santa Rosa, Colombia and Tormentos, where average visibility ranges from 35 to 50m. Silver bait fish, eels, angelfish, grouper, technicolour parrot-fish, sergeant majors and four-eyed butterfly fish are among the residents here. Experienced divers should head for the reefs bordering the southern point of the island (Colombia and Maracaibo), requiring an hour's boat-trip from San Miguel. These offer spectacular natural environments. The famed wall of Maracaibo is formed by coral-covered tunnels which descend to depths of 40m, while in the 20m shallows there is a dazzling wealth of reef and marine life.

kilometres further, **Playa Maya** is a quieter, sandy beach backed by jungle. This is beaten in the popularity stakes by the seemingly endless **Playa San Francisco▶▶**, where *palapa* restaurants, bars and pleasure-seeking sun-lovers set the tone. Next along the coast is the lovely **Playa Escondida▶▶**, reached via a rough turn-off from the main road about 19km south of San Miguel. At the southern tip is a lighthouse, **El Caracol**, a Mayan temple, and a restaurant. Cozumel's east coast beaches include **Punta Chiqueros**, a beautiful beach protected by a headland; the small cove of **Chen Río**, and **Punta Morena**, a rocky beach with beach-cabins to rent and a restaurant.

Fundación de Parques y Museos de Cozumel, A. C.
Parque CHANKANAAB
Cozumel, Q. Roo, México
R.F.C. FPM-870331-Q13
ADMISSION
CHANKANAAB
$12,000.00
N$ 12.00
Nº 352286

Rest of the island From Punta Morena a 24km sandy track, only navigable with four-wheel drive or motor-bike, winds north past minor Mayan ruins to **Punta Molas**, where a lighthouse and the ruins of **Aguada Grande** announce the northern tip of Cozumel. Better restored but not particularly enthralling is the site of **San Gervasio**, reached along a road off the east–west Transversal. Much of the rest of the island is swathed in jungle or edged by mangrove swamps and can only be reached on foot. This is in high contrast to the Manhattan-type skyline extending north from San Miguel along Playa San Angel.

The reef off Palancar Beach is excellent for fishing and diving

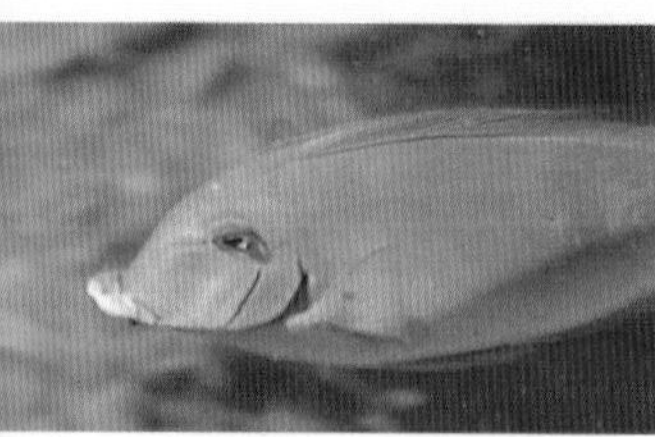

Colourful algae, sponges, striking coral formations and shoals of technicolour fish are not the only visions that await you in the waters of Yucatán's Caribbean coast. Sunken galleons add to the deep-sea thrills, while an inland network of underwater caves and cenotes offers an enthralling world of sculptural rock formations.

BEYOND THE YUCATÁN
Mexico's diving delights are not monopolised by the Yucatán. Although much of the Gulf of Mexico is polluted, Veracruz claims a sunken vessel at Isla Verde and, south of town, off the coast from Anton Lizardo, the protected reef of La Blanquilla where shelves and grottos descend to 50m and teem with marine life. Another spectacular sea is the Mar de Cortés, where deep underwater trenches reach depths of 3,000m. On the southern tip of Baja California, Los Cabos makes a fabulous destination for over 800 species of reef fish (including the unique Cortés angelfish, Clarion angelfish and Cortés rainbow wrasse) and is famous for its underwater sandfalls.

Tropical fish in the clear waters of Xel-Há, Quintana Roo

From tiny Isla Contoy, off Yucatán's northern tip, to the port of Chetumal on the Belize border, stretch 700km of the world's second largest barrier reef. Divers have flocked to the area since the 1960s after oceanographer Jacques Cousteau revealed the glories of the now legendary Palancar Reef. With the creation of Cancún, parts of this delicate underworld ecosystem have suffered and more time and money are now necessary to reach pristine coral reefs. Cruise ships pose another threat: in 1997 one ground up 80 per cent of a reef between Cancún and Isla Mujeres. Parallel to this popularity comes a new sport, that of closed-water diving through *cenotes* (sinkholes) to underground rivers and caverns that riddle the limestone shelf of the peninsula.

Reef diving Hard-bitten divers head for the remote promontory that ends at Xcalak, from where trips can be made to the fabulous Banco Chinchorro, a ring of islands edged with reefs about 25km offshore. The coastline between Cancún and Punta Allen is far easier to reach: Akumal, Puerto Aventuras and Xel-Há all offer numerous opportunities to experience sub-aquatic delights, including sunken galleons and night-dives.

Off Cancún itself good beginners' dive spots include the underwater garden of Punta Nizuc, Los Cuevones and the shallow Chitales Reef. Experienced divers head for open-sea sites such as El Tunel, San Toribio and San Miguel, where depths range from 15 to 20m and strong currents may bring with them dolphins, sea-turtles or sleeping sharks. These lethargic and normally dangerous creatures (bull, black-tip, lemon or nurse sharks), overdosing on oxygen bubbles from fresh-water undersea springs, favour, above all, the isolated Sleeping Shark Caves north of Isla Mujeres. Close by lies the 1980 wreck of *El Frío* (*Ultrafreeze*), now a refuge for stingrays, green morays, giant jewfish and brilliant yellowjacks. Between Isla Mujeres and Cancún, the elongated reef of La Bandera (averaging depths of 13m) is topped with elkhorn coral and slashed with ledges and overhangs. Schools of barracuda and pompano swarm over it, while clustered beneath the overhangs are large crabs, spotted moray eels and lobsters. Los Manchones is the other reef highlight.

Thirty kilometres of marine park make Cozumel the third most popular dive destination in the world. Exceptionally clear and nutrient-filled currents have nourished spectacular coral formations (including black coral) and abundant marine life, and maintain an unmatched underwater

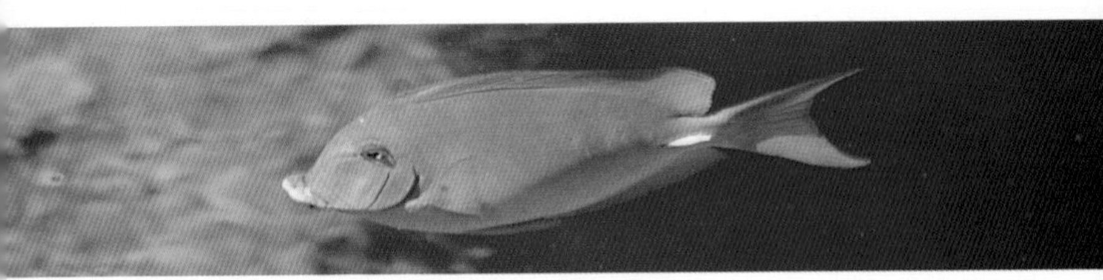

Snorkelling at Xel-Há – come early or late to avoid the crowds

visibility. Fifteen dive spots with depths of 15 to 40m are scattered across the massive southeastern reefs of Palancar, Santa Rosa and Colombia, while at the majestic Maracaibo Reef (off the southern point) coral-covered tunnels descending to over 45m swarm with grouper and yellowjack.

Cave diving Only developed in the Yucatán in the last decade, cave diving is a highly specialised and dangerous sport that has already claimed hundreds of lives. Over 80 cave systems have so far been registered along the Cancún–Tulúm Corridor, of which Nohoch (just southwest of Akumal) is the father of them all, its 18km of interconnected underwater passages and caverns making it the longest underwater cave system in the world. Huge waterfilled limestone caves, resplendent with gnarled columns, stalagmites, stalactites and radiating tunnels, were sealed by rising water some 10,000 years ago at the end of the Ice Age and now offer a dramatic environment for advanced divers. Aquatic life consists mainly of crustaceans, occasionally joined by blind-fish and eels. For snorkellers and inexperienced divers, the *cenote* entrances to these networks (notably at Nohoch, Xcaret and Dos Ojos) provide unique glimpses of these recently discovered underworlds.

CAR-WASH
No, this is not an enterprising Maya initiative but the name of one of many *cenotes* along the Tulum-Cobá road. Like most *cenotes* of the Yucatán, it is much used by local inhabitants as a fresh water source – and in some cases for a quick car-wash. The immense natural pool of clear water is an open invitation to snorkellers, swimmers and divers.

PUNTA XPU-HA
Ideal for snorkellers, the cenote of Xpu-há is one of the most extensive of the Akumal region, with a length of 500m and depths never exceeding 6m. It is between Akumal and Puerto Aventuras, and can be reached on foot from the beaches of Xpu-há or Rancho Viejo. A few kilometres south lies another superlative underwater spot around the inlets of Xaac and Xaac Chico, still relatively secluded due to their inaccessibility from the highway. With depths of up to 40m and easily reached from the shore, the coral reefs here offer brilliant formations and fluorescent fish.

CASTE WAR
Mexico's independence from Spain, signed and sealed in 1821, did not mean relief for the Maya, most of whom were enslaved by mounting debts to the great landowners. However, the Yucatán's wealthy ruling classes, aspiring to their own independence from Mexico, began arming their *peons*. This was a great mistake as the Maya soon turned against their masters, initiating the War of the Castes in Valladolid in 1847. Rebelling against centuries of oppression, they pillaged and murdered, their cause spreading throughout the peninsula. Suddenly, when all seemed lost for the whites, the rebels turned tail and fled to their fields – the sowing season had arrived and everything else took second place. White vengeance was terrible – between 1848 and 1855 the Mayan population was halved.

►► Dzibilchaltún 220B3

Open: site and museum daily 8–5

Dzibilchaltún is no longer the glorious Mayan city which was occupied continuously from 500 BC until the Conquest. North of Mérida, just off the road to Progreso, the site starts at the modern **Museo del Pueblo Maya**, that covers the general history of the peninsula and Mayan people. From here a path leads to the *sacbé* (sacred Mayan road). This runs east to the main restored structure, the **Templo de las Siete Muñecas** (Temple of the Seven Dolls), which has an unusual pyramidal roofcomb and is decorated with masks of Chac. Clay dolls were found at its altar, each with a different physical deformity, and are now exhibited at the museum. Due west along the *sacbé* stands the colonial Capilla Abierta, oppsite Structure 44, a 128m-long stepped platform. Other unexcavated buildings hide beneath the surrounding vegetation and the Cenote Xlacah, when dredged by archaeologists, yielded up numerous offerings.

►► Edzná 220B2

Open: daily 8–5

The most fully restored site in the state of Campeche lies 65km east of the state capital off Highway 261 and has far fewer visitors than others further north. Edzná ('The House of Gestures' in Mayan) was settled in 600 BC and reached its zenith between AD 550 and 810. It incorporates Puuc stone mosaic friezes into buildings of classic proportions. The main plaza is dominated by the

Dzibilchaltún's 'Temple of the Seven Dolls' draws hundreds at equinox when a shaft of light illuminates a mask of the rain god Chac

Templo de los Cinco Pisos (Temple of Five Levels), a tiered platform with rooms at each level, once faced in stucco and paint but now revealing only carved serpent and jaguar heads. Flanking this is the **Casa de la Luna** (Temple of the Moon). The entire site is riddled with a network of tunnels believed to have been used for irrigation.

►► Grutas de Balankanché *221C3*

Open: daily 9–5 (museum); guided tours at 9, 12, 2 and 4 (Spanish); 11, 1 and 3 (English)

This impressive network of caves was once the site for Mayan ceremonies honouring the rain god Tláloc, the Toltec version of Chac. Narrow passageways lead to three of the seven cave chambers, revealing stunning stalagmites and stalactites which in one case have mysteriously formed the shape of a *ceiba*, the sacred Mayan tree. Around the chamber are numerous *metates* (maize-grinding stones) and 1,000-year-old clay vessels, while another cavern is filled with a glassy pool. A small museum adjoins a botanic garden at the entrance, and visits include a 'sound and light' guided tour.

►►► Grutas de Loltún *220B2*

Open: guided tours at 9.30, 11, 12.30, 2 and 3

Even more impressive than Balankanché are the vast caves of Loltún, which lie in the heart of the pastoral Puuc Hills, just over 100km south of Mérida and 18km east of Labná. Stumbled upon in 1888 by the American consul, Edward H Thompson, they were not charted until 1959, when the giant 'Loltún head', reminiscent of the Olmecs, was discovered. Carbon-dating has confirmed that the caves were inhabited over 2,500 years ago and possibly much earlier. Apart from the extraordinary natural formations of this 2km network, the caves have revealed rock-carvings, wall-paintings, ceremonial and pottery-making areas and hollow stalactites which create musical notes, natural air vents providing fresh, cooled air and natural cisterns of filtered rainwater. The largest chamber – the **Cathedral** – soars 45m high. The tunnels here were used during the Caste War of the mid-19th century by rebellious Mayas seeking refuge from Creole landowners.

►► Isla Holbox (Yum Balam Reserve) *221D3*

This tiny island off the north-eastern point of the Yucatán was declared a biological reserve in 1994. Access is by ferry from the village of Chiquilá. The fishing village offers few services, but its endless sandy beaches attract campers and those seeking unadulterated nature. Shells are abundant along the shore, the water is clean and calm, and ocelots, flamingos and crocodiles hide out between the mangroves and jungle. Plans are afoot for a new hotel, so Holbox's character may change.

ISLA CONTOY
Another island off the northern point of the peninsula, between Isla Holbox and Isla Mujeres, provides rich rewards for birdwatchers. Protected as a wildlife sanctuary, the miniscule Isla Contoy is inhabited by over 100 species of birds, including brown pelicans, snowy egrets, boobies, cormorants, frigatebirds, flamingos and spoonbills. Its exquisite white beaches attract day-trippers from Cancún, Isla Mujeres and Cozumel and the surrounding waters are also great snorkelling territory. Count on two hours by boat.

ECOTOURISM
The following are recognised agencies:
Ecoturismo Yucatán, Mérida, tel: (99) 202772, fax: (99) 250947, e-mail: ecoyuc@minter.cieamer.conacyt.mx
Maya Ecotours, Mérida, (tel: 99 272510, fax: 99 278954, e-mail: yucatan-peon@pibil.finred.com. mx
Pan American Holidays, Cancún, tel: (98) 849063, fax: (98) 870894, e-mail: panamhol@cancun.rce.com.mx
Ecocolors, Cancún, (tel/fax: (98) 849589, e-mail: ecoco@cancun.rce.com.mx

The coral reef is close to the fine white-sand beach at El Garrafón, Isla Mujeres

A rare chance to see nature close up – shark at Isla Mujeres

▶▶ Isla Mujeres 221D3

Just 11km north of Cancún, Isla Mujeres has a decidedly different rhythm: more laid back, more Caribbean, in keeping with its pirate past. Less than a kilometre wide and barely 8km long, it is a typical palm-fringed tropical retreat, discovered in the 1950s when Cozumel and Cancún were mere figments of developers' imaginations. Today it is still a favourite destination for relaxed travellers and serious divers, though it is increasingly frequented by day-trippers from Cancún.

Ferries from Puerto Juárez and express boats from Cancún dock at the main village, its harbour dotted with colourful fishing boats and its sandy lanes lined with a jumble of shops, outdoor cafés and restaurants. Golf carts or bicycles are the most common forms of transport and are easily rented. Immediately north lies Isla's best beach, **Playa Los Cocos▶▶**. Calm, aqua-jade waters, gently sloping sands, watersports and a few *palapa* restaurants make it a popular haunt. **El Garrafón National Park▶** (*Open* daily 9–4) on the southern tip, is an underwater paradise for snorkellers, although most of the coral is now dead. Equipment can be hired here and facilities include an aquarium and panoramic, cliff-top restaurant. Avoid it in the middle of the day when the water swarms with Cancunites. Experienced divers can head further out to sunken wrecks, the reefs of Los Manchones or the 'Sleeping Sharks Caves' with diving trips organised from the port dive shops.

Escape the hordes by walking from El Garrafón up a rocky, windswept point to the ruins of a **Mayan temple▶** dedicated to Ixchel (the Mayan goddess of fertility) and a lighthouse, both of which have fabulous sea views. In the centre of the island is the derelict and overgrown **Hacienda Mundaca**, imbued with legends. On the west coast beside the Laguna Macax are various animal-related activities: visitors can swim with sharks or dolphins or visit the turtle farm.

▶▶ Izamal 221C3

Izamal is a striking, brilliant yellow market town 70km east of Mérida, which combines crumbling Mayan pyramids with the gigantic **Convento de San Antonio▶▶**

(*Open* daily 7am–8pm). Incorporating Mexico's largest atrium and built with the stones of a Mayan temple, this huge structure dates from 1553, although the church was rebuilt in 1795. A corridor and staircase to the left of the church leads to an inner sanctuary, where a statue of the

Virgin of Izamal (the patron saint of the Yucatán) is wheeled in and out of the front altar on rails. The Franciscan monastery still functions and Mass is celebrated in the church. The relaxed atmosphere of the town is heightened by horse-drawn buggies and the market on the main square below the monastery.

►► Kohunlich *221C1*

Open: daily 8–5

Kohunlich lies deep in tropical forest about 60km west of Chetumal. These little-visited ruins stand in an immense grove of *cohune* palms (sacred Maya trees that give the site its name). Two hundred or so mounds mainly dating from the 6th century were partially excavated and restored in 1992–4, revealing 8 main structures. Two large plazas are surrounded by a palace; an acropolis, a ball-court and, above all, the Edifico de los Mascarones (Building of the Masks). The central stairway of this pyramid is flanked by carved stucco masks depicting the sun god, Kinich Ahau: they are unique in Yucatán for their prominent features and height. The seven-stepped structure at the far southern end of the site has sweeping views.

► Laguna Bacalar *221C1*

About 40km north-west of Chetumal, Highway 307 runs past this brilliant palette of blues, a lake sometimes referred to as the 'lagoon of seven colours', the result of a mixture of freshwater and sea water. The lagoon's attractions lie in its *balneario* (bathing resort) and the imposing **Fuerte San Felipe Bacalar**, a stone fort erected in 1729 against pirate attacks, which now houses a small, rather dull museum (*Open* Tue–Sun 10–5). The shore has swimming areas, hotels, open-air restaurants and private villas.

WHAT'S IN A NAME?

Theories abound about the origin of the name Isla Mujeres, the 'Island of Women'. Some say it came from the pirates who left their women here while they plundered the high seas. Others say that the island was a sanctuary for sacred Mayan virgins. The most probable explanation is that it was given the name by the Spanish *conquistadores* who, on landing on the island in 1519, found sculptures of female figures in the temple dedicated to Ixchel, the goddess of fertility.

Left: monastery, Izamal
Below: Kohunlich

ISLA LEGEND

Isla Mujeres' Hacienda Mundaca was built in the early 1800s by the Spanish pirate and slave-trader Fermín Mundaca after he had fallen hopelessly in love with an island girl. Renouncing his lawless occupations, he set about creating the *hacienda* and an impressive tomb. But she spurned him for a younger and poorer island man, much to the chagrin of Mundaca, who spent the rest of his heartbroken days in Mérida, where he eventually died. The epitaph on his tombstone reads: 'What I am, you shall be; what you are, I was.'

CULTURAL AGENDA
Mérida's authorities ensure that tourists are never short of free entertainment. The following are held regularly at 9pm:
Monday – regional Vaquería with dances and costumes harking back to *hacienda* days, Palacio Municipal.
Tuesday – 1940s big-band music and dance in Parque Santiago, Calle 59 and 72.
Thursday – lively Yucatán dances and music at the Parque Santa Lucía, Calle 60 and 55.
Friday – students' serenade in the courtyard of the Universidad de Yucatán, Calle 60 and 57.
Sunday – food and handicrafts market on main square, Parque Hidalgo and Parque Santa Lucia (9am–9pm).

▶▶▶ Mérida 220B3

Mérida, the capital of the state of Yucatán, with a population approaching 1½ million, makes a relaxed base for exploring the surrounding Mayan sites and villages, as well as having plenty of charm and interest itself. Mérida emerged from a decaying Mayan city called T'ho, whose stones were used to build a grand colonial 'white city'. By the early 20th century it was the hub of a burgeoning sisal industry, attracting French investors who bequeathed a *belle époque* architectural legacy. Geographically isolated from their compatriots, Mérida's inhabitants had more contact with the US, Cuba and Europe, and also attracted Syrian and Lebanese settlers. This independent, cosmopolitan flavour only changed in the 1950s, when road and rail links were finally established with Mexico City.

Historical sights Founded by Francisco de Montejo in 1542, Mérida soon saw the south side of Plaza Mayor lined with the *conquistadore's* residence, the **Casa Montejo▶▶▶** (1542). Until recently this magnificent Plateresque building, with sculpted busts decorating the façade, was still inhabited by descendants of the Montejo family, but it is now a branch of Banamex, the National Bank of Mexico. Soon after, Mérida's massive **Catedral▶▶** (1556–99) was built with the stones of dismantled T'ho. The beautifully proportioned interior was stripped during the 1915 Revolution but this gives it a striking purity and reinforces the impact of a 7m statue of Christ. Across the large plaza stands the elegant **Palacio Municipal▶** (1735) and, on the northern flank, the **Palacio**

The Palacio Cantón Paseo de Montejo

de Gobierno▶ (1892), whose interior contains 27 paintings, mostly by Fernando Castro Pacheco, depicting the complex history of the Maya, Spaniards and Mexicans.

Calle 60, the main road north from Plaza Mayor, continues the parade of Mérida's history at the **Parque Hidalgo**, a social hub dominated by the **Iglesia de la Tercera Orden▶▶** (1618). Rising beyond this Jesuit church is the grandiose **Teatro Peón Contreras▶▶** (1900), a wildly ornate building with a Carrara marble staircase, rococo boxes and a frescoed dome. The city tourist office is in its south-western corner. Passing the Universidad de Yucatán, Calle 60 continues to the arcaded **Parque Santa Lucía**, site of a Sunday morning crafts market and a stirring folk dance performance every Thursday evening, before reaching **Parque Santa Ana**, four blocks further.

Paseo de Montejo One block east of Parque Santa Ana is the broad, tree-lined Paseo de Montejo, Mérida's answer to the Champs Elysées. Built by the wealthy *henequen* (sisal) *hacienda* owners of the late 19th century, the palatial homes (and a few modern intrusions) are now the focus for Mérida's banks, hotels, nightclubs and restaurants. At the corner of Calle 43 stands the Palacio Cantón – built between 1909 and 1911 at the behest of the state governor by the Italian architect responsible for the Teatro Peón – which now houses the **Museo de Anthropología e Historia▶▶** (*Open* Tue–Sat 9–8, Sun 8–2). In an interior of marble, Doric columns, chandeliers, and decorative stuccowork, the state archaeological collection runs the risk of fading into insignificance. However, it provides a clearly laid-out history of the Yucatán, its Mayan sites and culture, juxtaposing panels and photographs with artefacts that include a rare display of carved jade offerings recovered from the *cenote* (sinkhole) of Chichén Itzá.

South of Plaza Mayor Despite Mérida's large number of itinerant hammock-hawkers, strolling round the sprawling municipal **market** on Calle 56 and Calle 67 is essential. *Guayaberas* (men's tucked white shirts), *huipils* (embroidered tunics), Panama hats, hammocks of every size and colour, baskets, belts and much more are sold in tiny stalls or rambling stores, in between the chillies, limes, *tamales* and chickens. For an idea of high-quality handicrafts and fixed prices check out the official **Casa de Artesanías** (*Open* Tue–Sat 9–8), in the same building as a music museum on Calle 63, between 64 and 66.

OF HAMMOCKS...
Hammocks are compulsory purchases for visitors to the Yucatán, and Mérida is by far the best place to buy them. The finely threaded, colourful cotton webs made locally are the coolest way to have a siesta or even to spend the night on the beach, but the quality varies considerably. Make sure you get the right size: *sencillo* (single), *doble* (double), *matrimonial* (large double) or *matrimonial especial* (kingsize). Impress the street vendor by counting the knots at each end – 90 should be the minimum and threads should be triple. La Poblana, Calle 65 No 492 is recommended.

An easy way to see the sights of Mérida is to take a calesa *(horse-drawn carriage)*

Playa del Carmen's best beaches lie north of town

YUCATECAN CUISINE
One of the Yucatán's great pleasures, after the tribulations of northern *tortilla* diets, is its imaginative food, partly due to long isolation from the rest of Mexico and close contact with Europe (especially France), New Orleans and Cuba. Common dishes include *sopa de lima*, a delicious chicken broth cooked with shredded chicken, *tortilla* and lime juice; *pollo* or *cochinita pibil*, chicken or pork marinaded in spices and sour orange juice then baked in banana leaves; and *poc-chuc*, pork fillet marinaded in sour orange juice and served with pickled onions. A common ingredient is wild turkey (*pavo*), which can be shredded, wrapped in *tortillas* (*salbutes*), pickled (*escabeche*) or stewed in soups.

►► Playa del Carmen *221D2*

For years Playa del Carmen, opposite the island of Cozumel, was merely a launching-pad for the ferry across to the island. Today it has become a booming resort town with a grid of pedestrian streets around Quinta Avenida entirely devoted to visitors. Only 68km south of Cancún and 30 minutes by ferry from Cozumel, it attracts day-trippers for its wide, powdery beaches and lively atmosphere. Playa's palm-fringed sands extend north around a point to a wide, empty beach with clean waters and gentle waves much favoured by the topless brigade. Hotels are creeping in here, too. South of the jetty and airstrip a gigantic new development of hotel, marina, shops, condominiums and golf-course, collectively known as Playacar, offers a more structured setting. However, there are still some atmospheric *cabañas* (cabins) along the seafront or down side streets in the main town. Fishermen work off the beaches and at dusk a fleet of *triciclos* (tricycles) takes hundreds of crates of fresh eggs to be ferried across to Cozumel for divers' breakfasts. Mellow and fun-loving, its beach bars blasting 1970s rock music and mixing endless *Margaritas*, Playa makes an easy stop-off on the Caribbean trail.

► Puerto Morelos *221D3*

Just over 30km south of Cancún on Highway 307, this small fishing village is mainly frequented for its car-ferry service to Cozumel. So far Puerto Morelos has escaped the coastal development that continues elsewhere along the Cancún–Tulúm Corridor, and retains a low-key atmosphere with seafood restaurants, limited accommodation and uncrowded beaches, as well as an enticing offshore reef for snorkellers and divers. Near the highway turn-off leading to Puerto Morelos are the **Palancar Aquarium**, with exhibits on the area's marine environment, **Croco Cun**, a crocodile farm and zoo (*Open* daily 8.30–5.30) and, further south, the **Jardín Botánico Dr Alfredo Barrera Marín▶**, a delightful park featuring local flora, a nature trail and a small archaeological site.

▶ Puerto Progreso *220B3*

Progreso, 33km due north of Mérida, is a sprawling port town periodically invaded by Yucatecans looking for sea and seafood. Its main features are marinas, a jetty jutting 6km out into the Gulf of Mexico and a gently sloping sandy beach. Seafood is prepared in abundance in the cheap open stalls and the pricier, air-conditioned restaurants, and the constant sea breeze makes a welcome change from the interior.

However, the buildings lining its *malecón* are mainly charmless and there is no pressing reason to stay here rather than in Mérida – only 20 minutes or so away by bus. Eat and swim, then head on! More attractive beaches lie less than 8km west and east at **Chelem** and **Chicxulub** respectively. Both offer hotels and seafood restaurants.

▶▶ Punta Bete *221D3*

Isolated from the main resort 'corridor' by a rough 5km dirt road winding through tangled jungle and banana palms, Punta Bete makes an idyllic get-away only 52km south of Cancún. Four kilometres of palm-fringed sands beside typically transparent water once offered little apart from camping, hammocking or a handful of beach *cabañas* and relaxed *palapa* restaurants. Inevitably, progress now looms on the northern horizon in the shape of a large condo resort.

▶▶ Reserva de la Biosfera Sian Ka'an *221D3*

South of Tulúm and away from the Beetle-driving crowds, this vast 530,000-hectare wildlife reserve stretches south of Tulúm to Bahía del Espíritu Santo. Patchy tropical forest, mangrove swamps, grassy savannah and the world's second-longest ocean reef form a protected environment for the remaining fauna of Quintana Roo: jaguars and pumas, white-tail deer, crocodiles, howler monkeys and an astonishing 345 species of birds. About 1,000 inhabitants in the reserve live off fishing. All-day treks, which include a three-hour boat-trip, can be arranged through the Amigos de Sian Ka'an (which in Mayan means 'Where the Sky is Born') in Cancún, tel: 84 95 83, fax: 87 30 80.

▶▶ Río Lagartos *221C3*

This swampy lagoon area 103km north of Valladolid is an ornotholigical haven,

OF PANAMA HATS...
These famous hats are woven from *jipijapa* palm leaves. The Yucatán's centre of production is at Bécal, a small town on Highway 180, 85km south of Mérida. The best quality hats are the finest in fibre and weave. If made under optimum, humidified conditions, they obtain their springy resilience and can be rolled up, stashed away then reopened to their former glory. Not exactly the ultimate in fashion, but a practical, cool necessity in a Yucatecan wardrobe. Buy the real thing in Becal at Mario Farfan Herrera, Calle 30 No 210, tel: (943) 14046.

UNILATERAL ECOLOGY
Situated in semi-evergreen forest, menaced by logging concerns, Punta Laguna is a rare exercise in village self-determination.The villagers took the initiative of declaring their surroundings an ecological reserve. Spider monkeys and an abundant birdlife are what the tiny Maya community is trying to protect, and visitors are welcome to observe the wildlife. Contact Serapio Canul in the village, the man responsible for the movement, or the ecology group Pronatura Yucatán in Mérida, which advises the community (tel: 99 44 22 90).

counting over 250 resident and migratory species that revel in the varied ecosystem. It is known above all for its colonies of pink flamingos, which build their mud nests in the lagoons on their return from Celestún (see page 227) in the first part of the year. The 36,000-hectare wildlife refuge offers plenty of other sights, from spider monkeys to white-tail deer, a rare type of alligator and turtles.

Boat trips through the wetlands are easily arranged in the fishing village and can take you as far as Orilla Emal, the flamingos' nesting area, between April and July. Other abundant birdlife can be spotted around the lobster-fishing village of San Felipe, 10km west, or at Punta Holohit, just across the estuary from Río Lagartos. Basic accommodation is available.

►► Tulúm *221D2*

Open: daily 8–5

Magnificently situated, teetering on a craggy cliff overlooking the Caribbean, the walled ruins of Tulúm have become the crossroads for sun-worshippers and archaeological enthusiasts. From the clifftop site a path winds down to an idyllic beach; other coves that dot this stretch of coastline make it a favourite day-tripping target. The approach from Highway 307 leads into a giant car park with a sprawling shopping complex. From here you can take a toy train or walk to the site. A second turn-off nearer the village leads to the Zona Hotelera along the coast as far as Punta Allen: be warned, this road is badly pot-holed.

Thought to have been settled during the post-Classic period (AD 900–1500), when Mayan civilisation was on the decline, Tulúm was an important trading port and its fortress was still occupied when the Spaniards arrived in 1518. Fortified walls enclose palaces and temples with the sheer cliff face creating the fourth side. From the entrance, walking towards the Castillo on the cliff edge, you pass the ruins of a small royal palace before arriving at the **Templo de los Frescos►►►** (Temple of the Frescos) to the right. The façade of the palace is

The walled city of Tulúm overlooks the dazzling turquoise waters of the Caribbean from its magnificent clifftop vantage

decorated with carved reliefs of the descending god, a winged figure plunging earthwards (also depicted at Cobá and thought to be the god of honey). Faded murals in the interior of the temple depict the three levels of the Mayan universe and include one god astride a horse – evidence that the Maya had already had contact with the Spanish *conquistadores*.

The next complex is that of **El Castillo▶▶▶**, Tulúm's watch-tower landmark, fronted by serpent columns, which was built in several stages. Climb to the top for superb views both seawards and landwards. To the left stands the **Templo del Dios Descendente** (Temple of the Diving or Descending God), decorated with a stucco carving of the god above its entrance and mural fragments inside. There are several other ruined structures on this small site but its main interest is the dramatic coastal setting.

FOUR-LEGGED MYTH

One of the reasons for the success of the Spanish *conquistadores* was their beast of burden – the horse, completely unknown to the indigenous people. The mere sight of these powerful creatures convinced them of the Spaniards' god-like superiority. Only 16 were brought by Cortés' first expedition but the vision of mounted soldiers gave rise to a belief that man and animal were firmly one, a mythical four-legged beast with a man's torso.

Left: Valladolid's 18th-century church of San Servacio replaced an earlier one dating from 1545

The entrance to Cenote Zací, on the outskirts of Valladolid

▶▶▶ **Uxmal** see pages 248–9

▶▶ Valladolid *221C2*

Often treated as a halfway stage between Mérida, Chichén Itzá and Cancún or Tulúm, the town of Valladolid itself merits attention. Founded in the mid-16th century, it has an aristocratic old centre dotted with Spanish mansions and churches as well as two impressive *cenotes* (natural wells). Scene of the bloody massacre of its white élite by the Maya during the 1847 War of the Castes, Valladolid now enjoys a pleasant, provincial atmosphere. Of the many churches, the oldest is the **Iglesia de San Bernardino de Siena▶**, attached to the **Ex-Convento de Sisal**, four blocks south of the *zócalo* on Calle 41. Built in 1552 and set behind thick fortified walls, it was twice a target for attack by Maya; as a result its interior is bare apart from a statue of the Virgin of Guadalupe. Of the two *cenotes*, **Dzitnup▶▶▶** (*Open* daily 7–6) is the more beautiful and less visited; 7km south-west of town. In a cultural park off the town centre, the vast **Cenote Zací▶▶** (Calle 36, between 37 and 39), inside a large limestone cave, is a spectacular, stalactite-studded sight, but the algae-coated water is less inviting.

Uxmal's structures combine masterful stonework with a dramatic setting

cultur
22 OCT 1993
UXMAL
ESTACIONAMIENTO
VEHICULOS
Nº 011516
N$ 3.40

UXMAL'S DWARF-KING
Legend has it that Uxmal was erected by a dwarf with magical powers. Hatched from the egg of a sorceress, the young boy one day struck a forbidden gong, thus alluding to a prophesy which said that when the gong rang the ruler would be replaced by a boy 'not born of woman'. The ruler wanted the boy dead but he was offered a reprieve if he could accomplish three seemingly impossible tasks, one of which was building the Pyramid of the Magician in a single night. This he achieved but the ruler still demanded his execution. After a trial of strength, the ruler was killed and so the dwarf boy came to govern Uxmal.

▶▶▶ Uxmal 220B2

Open: daily 8–5

Uxmal means 'Three Times Built', and was developed in stages from around AD 600. Its fine Puuc architecture (named after the surrounding hills) makes it superior to Chichén Itzá in the eyes of some experts, although the layout lacks Chichén's impact. Occupying a broad plateau in the Puuc Hills, 80km south of Mérida on Highway 261, Uxmal was at one point one of the largest Mayan cities of the Yucatán, with 25,000 inhabitants. By 900, however, it had been abandoned, due either to drought or the magnetism of Chichén Itzá. It was first excavated by Frans Blom in 1929 and much of the site has now been restored. A museum with tourist facilities stands at the entrance. Excellent sound and light shows are held in Spanish at 7pm and in English at 9pm.

Main structures The first and largest monument is the **Pirámide del Adivino** (Pyramid of the Magician), a smooth, elliptically shaped structure which rises 35m, making a steep but rewarding climb. Composed of five successive temples, it has a western entrance formed by the mouth of a gigantic mask of Chac, a relic from the fourth temple. Immediately west of the pyramid lies the extraordinary **Cuadránglo de las Monjas** (Nunnery), whose elaborately crafted inlaid stonework exemplifies pure Puuc tradition but whose original function remains a mystery. Chac reappears constantly on the façades of four multi-roomed edifices facing inwards on to a central courtyard. Intertwined snakes (possibly forerunners of the plumed serpent), jaguars, seated figures and stylised thatched Mayan huts can be distinguished on the façades. The south building is embellished with a remarkable lattice design and corbelled arches.

To the south, beyond a ball-court, lies an elevated complex dominated by the superb 100m-long **Palacio del Gobernador** (Governor's Palace), considered the zenith of the Puuc style. Its upper façade boasts a remarkable frieze of intricate stone mosaic, creating geometric patterns interspersed with over 200 stylised faces of Chac and glyphs of the planet Venus. Arched entrances lead into 24 rooms.

On the north-western corner of this platform the **Casa de las Tortugas** (House of the Turtles) is adorned with carved turtles whose tears were believed to bring rain during periods of drought. On the other side of the palace is the partly excavated **Gran Pirámide**, which faces **El Palomar** (The Dovecot), a beautiful, crumbling structure crowned by nine roofcombs.

Other structures From the Governor's Palace, a path leads south-west to two edifices that can only be visited with guides: the **Casa de la Vieja** (House of the Old Woman) and, further still, the **Templo de los Falos** (Temple of the Phalli). The latter is named after its sculpted phalluses, some of which served as rainwater spouts, indicating a phallic cult otherwise unknown among the Maya. In the northern section of the site, the **Grupo del Cementerio** (Cemetery Group) is decorated with skulls, a rare reference to death in Uxmal, unlike the more militaristic Chichén Itzá.

STEPHENS AND CATHERWOOD
Images of the Mayan world burst into public consciousness in the mid-19th century when American archaeologist John Lloyd Stephens and British illustrator Frederick Catherwood published their remarkable *Incidents of Travel*. Their first trip to Central America in 1839 followed in the footsteps of Count de Waldeck to Palenque but the local climate and insects proved such an endurance test that, having finally reached Uxmal, the men beat a retreat to New York. Eighteen months later they valiantly returned and Catherwood produced his masterpiece, a highly detailed, panoramic drawing of the Governor's Palace.

Masks of the rain god Chac adorn the Pyramid of the Magician

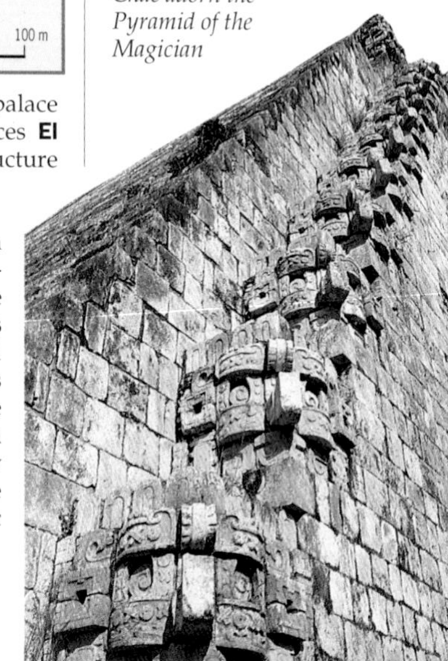

Drive

Haciendas, Mayan villages and sites in the Puuc Hills

South of Mérida lies the Yucatán's only hilly region, home to idyllic Mayan villages and lesser archaeological sites. For a better insight into today's Mayan traditions, it is advisable to spend the night on the way, although most of the route can be covered in a long day.

From **Mérida** drive west out of the centre to the ring-road and follow signs to Campeche on MEX 180. At Umán the road branches: follow MEX 261 to Muna, stopping for a short visit to the 16th-century domed **Church of San Francisco de Asis**. About 12km further stands the atmospheric *hacienda* of **Yaxcopoil**, once an important hemp factory, which is still equipped with original family furniture and machinery that was functioning as recently as 1987. Drive due south through a flat, green landscape, hiding a wealth of *cenotes* (sinkholes), to Muna, where the Puuc Hills start.

Follow signs to **Uxmal**, 16km further, one of the largest and most well preserved Mayan sites in the peninsula (see pages 248–9) and well

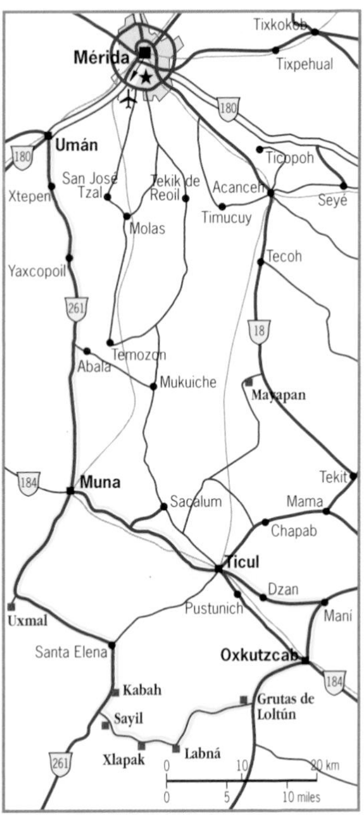

Mérida's colourful market, in the Yucatán

frequented by tourist buses from Mérida. From here the road winds south through **Santa Elena** (known for its hand-embroidery) to the site of **Kabah**, a Mayan ceremonial centre whose main structure, the **Codz Pop** (which in Mayan means 'Rolled Straw Sleeping-Mat'), is adorned with masks of the rain god Chac. The **Casa de la Bruja** and the **Templo de las Columnas** complete the excavated areas to the east of the road, but walk west to see an important arch structure in a huge unexcavated area.

Five kilometres further south follow the left-hand branch off MEX 261 leading to **Sayil**. Here, in a clearing, stands an outstanding palace structure on three levels, finely carved in the Puuc style, which once contained 100 rooms. The next archaeological stop, 5km further, is at the small site of **Xlapak**, where a relatively modest edifice with carved masks of Chac stands in pretty woods back from the road. Last on this Puuc loop is **Labná**, 4km beyond, where an elegant arch marks the limits of a ceremonial area once inhabited solely by priests and other high ranks. El Palacio and El Mirador are the most important structures in this complex.

Some 18km east, along often surprisingly straight roads, lie the fantastic **Grutas de Loltún** (see page 239), which can only be visited with a guide (aim for the 3pm tour). There is also a small restaurant at the caves' site. A further, sometimes potholed 10km leads to the important market town of **Oxkutzcab** ('Land Rich in Turkeys'). The church façade displays an interesting representation of the sun and moon and inside a valuable altarpiece is flanked by ridged columns. The market, indoors and out, is the centre of town activity, full of Mayan women in embroidered *huipiles* (tunics) and the Mayan taxi – the *triciclo*, a form of trishaw. From here, depending on the time of day, drive to the pretty town of **Mani**, which claims a *cenote*, and the 16th-century San Miguel Arcángel, with an open-roofed chapel. If time is short take MEX 184 (from behind the market) directly to **Ticul**, a small town with hotels and other services, mainly known for its shoe industry. At Muna the road rejoins MEX 261 which leads north to Mérida. If staying overnight at Ticul return to Mérida through the picturesque Mayan villages of **Chapab**, **Mama**, **Tekit**, **Tecoh** and **Acanceh**.

The Nun's Quadrangle, Uxmal, decorated with carvings of Chac

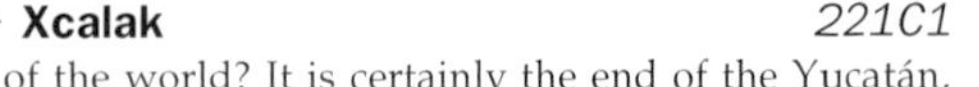

DIANA'S BATHING-PLACE
'What a *cenote* was we had no idea ... I came to a large opening in the ground, with a broad flight of more than fifty steps; descending which, I saw unexpectedly a spectacle of extraordinary beauty ... It was a large cavern or grotto, with a roof of broken, overhanging rock, high enough to give an air of wilderness and grandeur, impenetrable at midday to the sun's rays, and at the bottom water pure as crystal, still and deep, resting upon a bed of white limestone rock. It was the very creation of romance; a bathing-place for Diana and her nymphs. Grecian poet never imagined so beautiful a scene.'
John Lloyd Stephens: *Incidents of Travel*, 1841.

Xel-Há's warm, transparent waters

▶▶ Xcalak *221C1*

End of the world? It is certainly the end of the Yucatán, before Belize takes over. At the southern point of a desolate 64km peninsula traversed by dirt road, Xcalak, along with **Majahual**, 56km to the north, are being earmarked for development as the Costa Maya. Airstrips are in place and a ferry service connects Xcalak to Chetumal. Xcalak is known to divers for its proximity to the fabulous **Banco Chinchorro▶▶▶** an island-rimmed reef 26km offshore, where the sea floor is littered with wrecks. Diving facilities are provided by a few rustic *cabañas* hotels on deserted white-sand beaches edging the crystalline waters of the Caribbean.

▶ Xcaret *221D2*

Open: summer, Mon–Sat 8.30am–10pm, Sun 8.30–6. Winter, Mon–Sat 8.30–8.30, Sun 8.30–5

Seventy-two kilometres south of Cancún, a short distance from Playa del Carmen, this pricey leisure park has been developed around what was once a Mayan ceremonial centre and seaport. Its structured environment is announced by a giant fake Maya pyramid on Highway 307. Xcaret's main geographic feature is spectacular: over 500m of underground river wind through *cenotes*, caves and tunnels lit by natural light shafts. Children's attractions include scale models of Mayan sites, an aviary, a butterfly pavillion, botanical garden and aquarium. Activities include swimming with dolphins and horse-riding.

▶ Xel-Há *221D2*

Open: daily 8–6

This natural aquarium is a national park, but being only 10km north of Tulúm, its restaurants, gift shops and cafés are firmly geared towards tourists. Landscaped grounds edge a pretty lagoon that is fed simultaneously by subterranean springs and by the salty Caribbean, providing a perfect environment for a fabulous variety of exotic tropical fish. Snorkelling is allowed in specified areas – aim to come early or late to avoid the crowds. Some rather undistinguished ruins lie across the main road and a small marine museum displays items from off-shore wrecks.

Travel Facts

Arriving

By air American travellers flying to Mexico have a wide choice of direct flights to the following airports: Acapulco, Cancún, Cozumel, Guadalajara, Huatulco, Ixtapa/Zihuatanejo, Los Cabos, Manzanillo, Mazatlán, Mérida, Mexico City, Puerto Escondido and Puerto Vallarta. Europeans are, for the moment, limited to Mexico City, Cancún and Puerto Vallarta, however, Mexico City's Benito Juárez airport offers transfers on to domestic flights which leave from the same terminal. To reach the city centre either take the metro (station: Terminal Aerea) or buy a prepaid taxi voucher in the terminal. Most resort airports run collective taxi services (*transporte terrestre*), so watch out for their signs in the arrival terminals. All international airports have car-rental offices, duty-free and money-changing facilities.

By sea Cruise ships regularly stop off at Mexico's ports, from Cozumel to Acapulco or Puerto Vallarta: contact your local travel agent for schedules and itineraries. For ferries between Baja California and the mainland see page 260.

By rail There are no direct trains crossing from the US into Mexico. However, Amtrak serves two American border towns which offer easy on-going connections: from Laredo, Texas, cross to Nuevo Laredo where *The Aztec Eagle* departs every evening, arriving in Mexico City about 25 hours later; from El Paso, Texas, cross to Ciudad Juárez for the night-train to Mexico City (24 hours). From Mexicali and Nogales there are two trains daily along the main Pacific coast railroad to Guadalajara. In general, the bus service is far better than the train.

By car Make the best of Mexico by travelling by car or camper – but insure yourself at the border. No other national insurance is valid within Mexico, so before entering sign up with one of the many 24-hour insurance offices at main border towns. Proof of car ownership, current

The booking hall of Mexico City's Terminal Norte bus station

Off Cabo San Lucas – a popular Pacific destination for cruise ships

registration documents and a valid driver's licence are needed to obtain a 90-day vehicle entry permit (for a small fee). You cannot get out of Mexico again without the permit, so in the case of an accident make sure you have a police report/declaration to show at the border. US and Canadian drivers' licences are recognised but any other nationality should bring an international licence. Unleaded petrol (*magna sin*) is widely available.

By bus From some US border towns there are direct bus services into Mexico, but this costs more than the Mexican bus lines which start from across the border. From Guatemala there are bus connections between Guatemala City and destinations in Chiapas as well as between Flores and Chetumal (Yucatán peninsula). Frequent buses connect Belize City with Chetumal.

Customs regulations

Incoming travellers are allowed to bring personal photographic, radio and sports equipment and other goods up to a value of $300, three litres of liquor, 200 cigarettes and unlimited foreign currency. After submitting a customs declaration form, you push a button. If the red light flashes you will be searched; if it is green, you are clear.

Travel insurance

Take out a reliable travel insurance policy before leaving home: check the travel clauses carefully if you are considering sports such as rafting or diving. Travel agents usually offer reliable policies and some credit cards give partial coverage if tickets are purchased with them.

Visas and tourist cards

Citizens of the US, Canada, Australia, New Zealand and the UK do not need visas. Check with your local Mexican embassy for other national requirements. All non-visa holders need a tourist card, issued free of charge by Mexican consulates and air-lines or at border towns. This tourist card is validated on entry and must be kept throughout your visit to surrender again on exit. They are issued for 90-day or 180-day periods; if visiting Guatemala and Belize, ask for a multiple-entry card. Visits of less than 72 hours to border towns and the north of Baja California do not require tourist cards.

Departing

Tourists must surrender their cards and vehicle permits on leaving Mexico – do not overstay your time limit. Reconfirm your flight. An airport tax (payable in US $ or *pesos*) is required from air passengers but is usually included in the ticket.

Essentials

Climate

Mexico's climate is as diverse as its many latitudes and altitudes. Generally speaking the rainy season lasts from June to October, peaking in July and August, although Baja California has more rain during the winter months and flash floods all year round.

In the central highlands and plateaux the climate is temperate, while the arid northern plains experience extremes of stifling hot summers and cool winters.

Move towards the Pacific, Gulf and Yucatán coasts and you enter tropical zones where temperatures and humidity are permanently high and summer rains diluvial.

Complete contrasts can be found in the north-west Sierra Tarahumara and the Chiapas highlands of the south, where it remains cool and damp all year round except in late spring. A final factor is the coastal hurricane season, which starts in June but favours September.

The best time to visit is in the dry season, November to May, when you should encounter pleasant temperatures in most areas.

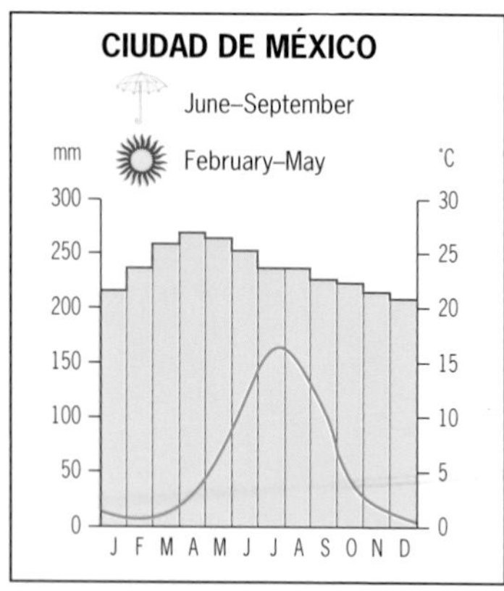

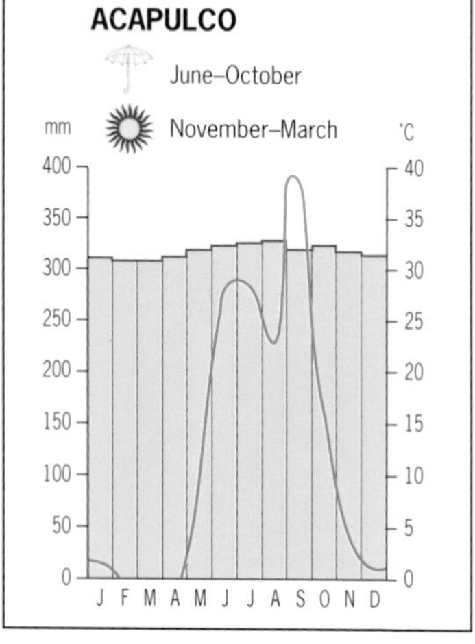

National holidays

Mexico's public holidays are legion but minimal in comparison to countless local *fiestas*. The following are celebrated nationally:

1 January	**New Year's Day**
6 January	**Epiphany (Day of the Three Kings)**
5 February	**Constitution Day**
21 March	**Benito Juárez Day**
March/April	**Easter (Maundy Thursday, Good Friday, Easter Sunday)**
1 May	**Labour Day**
5 May	**Battle of Puebla**
16 September	**Independence Day**
12 October	**Day of the Race (Columbus Day)**
2 November	**All Saints Day (Day of the Dead)**
20 November	**Revolution Day**
12 December	**Festival of the Virgin of Guadalupe**
25 December	**Christmas Day**

Time differences

Mexico has three time zones. Most of the country is on Central Standard Time (Greenwich Mean Time minus 6 hours); the northern states of Sinaloa, Sonora, Baja California Sur and parts of Nayarit are on Mountain Standard Time (GMT minus 7 hours), while Baja California Norte is on US Pacific Standard Time (GMT minus 8 hours). In line with California and British Columbia, this region also observes Daylight Saving in the summer months (GMT minus 7 hours). Quintana Roo, in the Yucatán peninsula, is one hour ahead of Central Standard Time.

Opening times

Archaeological sites are generally open daily from 8–5. National museums close on Mondays and occasionally Sunday afternoons. Their opening hours are generally 9–6, with closures for siesta usually from 2–4pm, although these are being abandoned in major towns where times are 10–5.

Government offices are open Monday to Friday 8–2, banks 9–1.30 and post offices 8–6. Shops open 9–8 Monday to Saturday, with siestas from 2–4 outside Mexico City.

Money matters

Mexico's currency is the *peso*, divided into 100 *centavos*. After devaluation in January 1993 new coins and notes marked *nuevo peso* (new *peso*) were issued. The new peso was written as N$ but in 1996 currency reverted to the peso, written as $ – not to be confused with the dollar. Coins are in denominations that range from 5¢ to $20 and notes $10 to $500: it is advisable to always hoard small change for taxis, buses and tips.

Foreign currency and travellers' cheques can be changed at banks but this can take a long time. Rates offered by more efficient *casas de cambio* (exchange bureaux, open Monday to Saturday 9–5) in large towns are generally equivalent to banks, so make use of them whenever possible. Avoid hotels and tourist stores as they offer the worst rates.

Credit cards are widely accepted in mid- to top-range restaurants and hotels: make sure you fill in the propina (tip) and 'total' sections on the voucher to avoid subsequent surprises! Cash can be withdrawn with MasterCard and Visa at automatic dispensers outside Banamex and Bancomer banks.

Tips are expected in hotels and restaurants – from $10 (10 *pesos*) for a porter to 15 per cent for waiters. Remember chambermaids, too. Taxi drivers do not expect tips, unless they have been particularly helpful.

Tipping in restaurants is customary

Getting around

Public transport

Air Price wars are hotting up between Aeromexico, Mexicana and Taesa, all now private companies vying for the domestic market. Travel agents are well informed about special offers and generally find you the best deal between the airlines. Subsidiary airlines operate short-hop flights: the south is covered by Aerocaribe and Aviacsa, the centre by Aeromar and Aeromorelos and the north by Aerocalifornia and Aerolitoral. For longer flights Aeromexico remains the most reliable and generally most expensive, operating over 40 domestic routes. Prices fluctuate, depending on the competition, but Mexicana offers savings with a 'Mexipass' or 'Mayapass', covering the Maya archaeology trail or colonial cities. These must be booked and paid for outside Mexico and flights cannot be changed. An airport tax is charged for every flight: this is added to tickets bought in Mexico.

Buses By far the best way of getting around most regions economically is by bus. Mexico has over 700 private companies, which offer a bewildering choice of routes and timetables, making time spent in the *Central Camionera* (bus terminal) an integral part of your journey. Prices, classes of bus and time-tables are posted up behind each bus-company counter: it is up to you to compare and choose. Bus stations are increasingly modern and efficient: all have left-luggage facilities, toilets, snack-bars, shops and long-distance phones. As terminals are often on the distant outskirts of town, check onward bus schedules when you arrive to save time. In some cases there is no *Central Camionera* so you need to trek around terminals or make phone enquiries.

Avoid *segunda* (second-class) buses except for short trips as they can be slow, bone-shaking and crowded. *Primera* (first-class) buses remain the standard, reliable and economical way of covering hundreds of kilometres in relative comfort. All have air-conditioning, toilets, videos and sometimes drinks. *Directo* first-class buses make very few stops. Luggage is usually checked into the outside lockers – keep the receipt to collect it on reaching your destination and keep your valuables on you. Videos are a permanent, noisy fixture.

At the top of the league are the luxury buses (*de lujo*) which compete with airlines for comfort, but plush reclining seats, hostesses and 'in-flight' magazines all boost the price to almost twice that of first-class.

Bus services deteriorate rapidly in the south. For any trip over five or six hours or during public holidays it is advisable to book a day or so in advance – refunds are given for cancellations made at least three hours before departure. A central bus booking agency in Mexico City is **Ticket Bus** (tel: 133-2424).

Rail Some 24,000km of railroad connect Mexico's major cities but this is neither a popular nor a recommended method of travelling. Trains are slow and not particularly safe, and are only worthwhile for overnight journeys in sleeping-cars (Mexico City to Veracruz, Guadalajara, Zacatecas, Monterrey or the US border towns). Trains in the south (Chiapas and Yucatán) are notorious for thefts and delays and are best avoided.

Segunda clase (second-class) travel is often dirty, dangerous and uncomfortable; *primera general* (regular first-class) is one step up and sometimes air-conditioned, while at the top, in *primera especial*, you have reserved reclining seats, air-conditioning and relative security. Sleeping-car supplements are charged on top of the first-class ticket (obligatory reservations) and can be for a *camarín* (small private berth with basin and WC), the roomier *alcoba* (for two adults) or *cama* (a simple curtained-off bunk). Tickets can be purchased in Mexico City at the Estación Buenavista from 6am–9pm, tel: (5) 547 1084/1097.

Taxis Every city has its own system but meters are rarely used. There is usually a flat rate but fares can be negotiated beforehand. Short town trips are generally cheap but airport rides become steep. For out-of-town destinations check on *colectivos* (often VW vans seating up to 14 people plus

Rail travel is the cheapest form of transport in Mexico, but it is often slow and unreliable

the odd animal) which cover set routes, usually scrawled in white paint on their windscreen. Modest fares are set for each route and the ground is covered much faster than in a normal urban bus.(See page 76 for essential advice on Mexico City taxis).

Flag down a taxi or call from a sitio (radio-taxi service)

Ferries Three car ferries ply the Mar de Cortés between Baja California and Mexico's west coast. Phone Festival Tours, (01-800 696 9600), for toll-free for schedules and prices. Daily overnight services run between Mazatlán and La Paz with first-class (private cabin and bath), salon and tourist classes. In Mazatlán contact the ferry terminal, tel: (69) 817020; in La Paz tel: (112) 53833.

Between Guaymas and Santa Rosalía, ferries leave Tuesday and Friday 11am and arrive at 6pm and Sunday and Wednesday leaving at 8am, arriving 3pm, in both directions: tourist and salon classes are available. Contact the Muelle Fiscal in Guaymas, tel: (622) 23390 and in Santa Rosalía, tel: (115) 20013. The Topolobampo–La Paz route leaves La Paz daily at 11am, arriving at 7pm; from Topolobampo it leaves at 10pm and arrives at 8am. In Topolobampo (Los Mochis) contact the Muelle Fiscal, tel: (686) 20141, in La Paz tel: (112) 53833. On the Caribbean coast there are frequent ferries to Cozumel from Puerto Morelos or Playa del Carmen and to Isla Mujeres from Puerto Juárez or Punta Sam. A new car ferry connects Chetumal with Xcalak.

Car rental

The only possible way to get around some of Mexico's more obscure and more rewarding places is by car. Car rental costs are particularly competitive in Mexico City but elsewhere rates are higher than in North America or Europe. Special offers occasionally crop up and it is always worth bargaining. You could try to get them to reduce their monstrous drop-off rates for example. Very often it is more advantageous to book and pay for car rental through your travel agent at home.

The basic VW Beetle is excellent for rough terrain and heavy rain as it is high off the ground and remarkably resilient. Before accepting a car, check all the lights, windows, brakes, windscreen-wipers, spare tyre and tools, and make sure every existing dent is noted on the contract. You need to be over 25, have a valid driver's licence and a major credit card.

Mexico City head offices of international car rental companies with branches all over Mexico include:

Avis, tel: 588 8880; toll-free: 01-800 70777.
Budget, tel: 271 4322.
Dollar Rent-a-Car, tel: 207 3838/4060.
Hertz, tel: 592 2867/9; toll-free: 01-800 7095 5000.
National, tel: 785 9330; toll-free: 01-800 90186.

Driving tips

Driving in Mexico requires constant alertness as dangers come not only from the road itself (cavernous potholes) but also from unexpected hazards – drunks and cattle figure prominently.

At night, unlit breakdowns, oncoming vehicles without headlights and invisible pedestrians and bicycles add further hazards. In poorer, rural regions there is also the threat of *bandidos* (bandits), who favour the curtain of darkness, so always be sure to reach your destination before sunset.

Never stop unless you are confronted with what seems a genuine accident: in this case do not touch any injured passengers as you may be liable for prosecution. Instead, drive straight to the nearest police station to report the accident.

Speed bumps are another Mexican speciality to watch out for. The ubiquitous *topes* or *vibradores* strategically lie across the road before every village or town and impose radically reduced speeds. Very 'awake' policemen make occasional spot-checks: be polite and produce all the car documents plus your passport. If for some reason a fine is demanded ask for a *recibo* (receipt): if this is not forthcoming a little *mordida* (unofficial tip) may speed you on your way.

Avoid street parking at night and always use locked hotel or private car parks.

Driving in Mexico City is not recommended. Fortunately the city is well provided with public transport

On a brighter front, Mexico possesses a unique road service, the Green Angels (*Angeles Verdes*) (tel: 5 250 8221), who patrol major highways in search of stranded tourists. This service, manned by English-speaking mechanics, can provide emergency assistance, administer first aid and carry spare parts, petrol and oil charged at cost price. Many new highways operate with tolls (cuota) that are extremely expensive.

Student and youth travel

There is little available in the way of student discounts for those not enrolled in a Mexican educational institution. Domestic flights offer 33 per cent reductions for children under 12.

Communications

Newspapers Mexico has a burgeoning local and national press as well as two English-language dailies, the *Mexico City Times* and the *News*. News coverage is US-orientated but both include good articles on Mexican affairs and the *News* publishes useful listings for the capital's cultural activities. The *New York Times*, *USA Today* and the *International Herald Tribune* are available in large cities and the *Miami Herald* in and around Cancún. Of the many local national dailies *El Universal* and *Excelsior* offer mainstream news and opinions, *El Financiero* business news, while *La Jornada* represents a more independent left-wing intellectual viewpoint.

Television and radio Despite the extreme poverty of the majority of the population, 60 per cent of households possess a TV. Targeting this mass audience, Televisa's four channels churn out vacuous entertainment – largely the seemingly endless *telenovelas* (soap operas). More worthwhile are the independents: TV Azteca's Channel 13, Channel 11 and the culturally rich Channel 22, with a good programme of foreign films. All large hotels have satellite television.

Radio stations are privately owned and generally operate on a regional basis. Mexico City's Radio XEVIP (AM 1560) broadcasts in English all day and major resort towns always include a few hours of English-language programmes. American radio stations can be picked up on medium wave (AM) in some regions, and BBC World Service can be found on 11.75 MHz.

Post offices Although no longer functioning by mule-back, the Mexican postal service is notoriously slow, but it is reasonably reliable. Allow at least 10 days for airmail post to the US and three flexible weeks for Europe. Always post mail at a central post office (*agencia de correo*). For anything vital use a private courier service (DHL, Federal Express etc.) or Mexpost, which operates from within post offices. Stamps can also be bought at hotels. Post boxes (*buzones*) are painted red.

Telephone and fax At last in the throes of modernisation, the newly privatised Mexican phone service (Telmex) is gradually improving services in the face of competition from AT&T and other rival American servers. Pay-phones dominate the provinces, although phone-card booths are replacing them in large towns. For these you need to buy a phone-card (*tarjeta de teléfono*).

Some new Ladatel phones function with international credit cards. Ladatel (*larga distancia*/long-distance) booths are found in bus stations, airports, railway stations and city centres and offer direct-dial service worldwide.

International and long-distance calls are phenomenally expensive and should be avoided in hotels: surcharges and taxes are added on. National calls are discounted after 8pm, North American calls after 7pm and European calls after 6pm. The cheapest method is, of course, a collect call (*llamada por cobrar*) made through the operator.

Prefixes: 01 for long-distance calls in Mexico; 020 (national operator-assisted calls); 090 (international operator-assisted calls); 001 for USA and Canada automatic calls and 00 for other international automatic calls.

Fax machines are easy to find in most public places (post offices, bus stations, airports) as well as in private fax offices in all towns. Internet cafés are still a rarity in Mexico though e-mail addresses are very common for businesses and individuals.

Where's the exit? A few words of Spanish are useful

Language

It will make a vast difference to your visit if you can speak some Spanish. In resort towns English is widely spoken, but the moment you enter small-town Mexico it is essential, and courteous, to communicate in Spanish, however limited. These are a few basic phrases for survival:

buenos días	**good morning**
buenas tardes	**good afternoon**
buenas noches	**good evening/ night**
adiós	**goodbye**
(muchas) gracias	**thank you (very much)**
por favor	**please**
si/no	**yes/no**
perdone	**sorry/excuse me**
como está/están?	**how are you? (singular/plural)**
muy bien gracias	**very well thank you**
cuánto vale ...?	**how much is ...?**
quiero/quisiera	**I want/I would like**
tiene ...?	**do you have...?**
hay ...?	**is/are there ...?**
no entiendo	**I don't understand**
habla inglés?	**do you speak English?**
no hablo español	**I don't speak Spanish**
donde está ...?	**where is ...?**
el central camionera	**bus station**
la gasolinera	**petrol station**
el sanitario/baño	**toilet**
la taquilla	**ticket office**
la casa de cambio	**money exchange office**
á qué distancia está ...?	**how far is ...?**
cuánto tiempo se necesita?	**how long does it take?**
tiene una habitación sencillo/doble?	**do you have a single/double room?**
con baño	**with bathroom**
con cama matrimonial	**with a double bed**
con dos camas	**with twin beds**
con aire acondicionado	**with air-conditioning**
con ventilador	**with fan**
puede hacer un descuento?	**can you give a discount?**
qué hora es?	**what time is it?**
hoy	**today**
mañana	**tomorrow**
mañana por la mañana	**tomorrow morning**
por la tarde	**in the afternoon**
por la noche	**in the evening**
me voy ...	**I'm leaving ...**
salida	**exit**

Emergencies

Crime and police

As in most countries, take care on public transport and in markets, Mexico City being the worst spot. Always stay vigilant, don't flaunt cameras, jewellery etc, avoid carrying large amounts of money and never leave your vehicle parked overnight in the street.

Pickpocketing is the most common crime that affects visitors, although taxi muggings are on the increase in Mexico City and in the south knife-attacks have been known: be careful about walking in remote areas, and stick to central and well-lit places for walking in the evenings.

Mexican police are not known for their helpfulness and have a penchant for *mordidas* (small bribes), so unless you need a theft report for insurance purposes, there is little point in contacting them. Drugs, although widely cultivated in Mexico, are illegal, so should be given a wide berth.

Embassies and consulates

- **Australia**: Ruben Dario 55, Polanco, Mexico City tel: (5) 531 5225
- **Canada**: Avenida Schiller 529, Colonia Polanco,11550 México DF tel: (5) 724 7900
- **New Zealand**: Lagrange 103, Colonia Los Morales, Mexico City tel: (5) 281 5486
- **UK**: Río Lerma 71, Colonia Cuauhtémoc, 06500 México DF tel: (5) 207 2089/2149
- **US**: Paseo de la Reforma 305, 06500 México DF tel: (5) 211 0042.

The US State Department operates a Citizens' Emergency hotline for information on health, political unrest or for locating travellers abroad in emergencies tel: (202) 647 5225.

Emergency phone numbers

Police/Fire/Ambulance 080
Angeles Verdes (Green Angels tourist patrol) (5) 250 8221
24-hour tourist hotline (5) 250 0123; toll-free: 01-800 90392
Missing persons (5) 658 1111
American British Cowdray Hospital (ABC) for emergencies (5) 230 8000
Medical emergencies (5) 271 2222
Radio Police Patrol 060 or (5) 250 0606

Lost property

If you lose essential items such as passport or traveller's cheques, report them to your embassy and to the

Traffic policeman on duty, Mexico City

issuing bank (always keep cheque numbers separate).

Other losses – cameras, jewellery etc. – can be reported to the local police station for insurance purposes, but you will need to speak good Spanish. If lost items are returned to you, it is common courtesy to give a token reward.

Vaccinations, health and pharmacies

Vaccinations There are no health requirements for entering Mexico unless you have been in a yellow fever, smallpox or cholera-infected country, in which case you need proof of these inoculations. For your own benefit, make sure your typhoid, polio and tetanus vaccinations are up to date. Cholera jabs are no longer effective. A vaccination against Hepatitis A (Havrix) replaces the old gamma-globulin: this requires two injections spaced over two weeks before departure, followed by two boosters a year later. Newer still is a vaccination against Hepatitis A and B (Twinrix). Consult your doctor about this.

Health hazards Mexico's main health hazards come from its polluted water: never drink tap water (unless in up-market hotels which have their own filtering systems) and in restaurants or street stalls always stick to *agua mineral/purificada*. Ice cubes should be avoided unless made from *agua purificada* (purified water).

Much is said about *turista*, also known as 'Moctezuma's Revenge' or more universally as diarrhoea, but this need not be inevitable. Don't eat fruit, salads or uncooked vegetables that are not peelable and avoid *ceviche* (marinated raw fish) in dubious-looking restaurants or hotels. Make liberal use of the lime slices served with most dishes – they apparently discourage bacteria. If you do undergo the dreaded Aztec revenge, drink lots of fluids (purified water with squeezed lime, weak tea and even Coca Cola) and eat only dry toast and bananas until it clears.

Malaria is not a major danger in Mexico, but if you intend to trek through southern rainforests it is advisable to take preventive treatment. Mosquitoes are omnipresent throughout the country and a good repellent is essential.

Dehydration and sunburn are the least obvious hazards but can be debilitating: the Mexican sun is powerful so take sensible precautions especially in deceptive sea breezes. Always drink plenty of non-alcoholic liquids and use total sun-blocks at least for the first few days. When visiting archaeological sites, take a large bottle of *agua purificada* and wear a hat.

Pharmacies *Farmacias* can be found in every small town and will supply all basic medication. Many prescription items are sold over the counter here. Every town has a clinic or hospital for emergency treatment but doctors vary considerably in their expertise. For anything serious contact your embassy, which will put you in touch with a reliable, English-speaking doctor.

Other information

Camping

Organised campsites are rare in Mexico but no permits are required for camping in nature parks or on beaches. Be careful of where you pitch your tent in terms of safety: it could be an easy target for thefts. Trailer parks are legion in Baja California and down the Pacific coast and, although not the most picturesque of settings, offer safe, low-cost havens with facilities. In some coastal areas you can rent a hammock and sleep under a *palapa* (an open, thatched hut).

Visitors with disabilities

Mexico is not particularly geared to travellers with disabilities but is improving. Some hotels are adapted for their needs and inbound tour operators, such as Grey Line Tours, Londres 166, Zona Rosa, Mexico City (tel: (5) 208 1163), can provide wheelchair tours on request, although the quality of their services cannot be guaranteed. Suitable destinations include Guadalajara, where the city centre abounds with ramps, museums and the Centro Historico of the capital, and the centre of Oaxaca.

Places of worship

There is no shortage of Catholic churches with regular daily masses in Spanish. Services in English are only held in cosmopolitan cities such as Mexico City, Guadalajara, Cuernavaca, Acapulco and Monterrey. The *News* lists times of services in its Friday edition. The following offer English-language services in the capital:

- Beth Israel Synagogue, Boulevard Virreyes 1140, Lomas de Virreyes.
- Capital City Baptist Church, Bondojito and Calle Sur 138, Las Americas.
- Christ Church Episcopal, Montes Escandinavos 405, Lomas de Chapultepec.
- Christian Science Church, Dante 21, Colonia Anzures.
- Lutheran Church, Palmas 1910, Lomas Barrilaco.
- St Patrick's Roman Catholic Church, Bondojito 248, Tacubaya.

CONVERSION CHARTS

FROM	TO	MULTIPLY BY
Inches	Centimetres	2.54
Centimetres	Inches	0.3937
Feet	Metres	0.3048
Metres	Feet	3.2810
Yards	Metres	0.9144
Metres	Yards	1.0940
Miles	Kilometres	1.6090
Kilometres	Miles	0.6214
Acres	Hectares	0.4047
Hectares	Acres	2.4710
Gallons	Litres	4.5460
Litres	Gallons	0.2200
Ounces	Grams	28.35
Grams	Ounces	0.0353
Pounds	Grams	453.6
Grams	Pounds	0.0022
Pounds	Kilograms	0.4536
Kilograms	Pounds	2.205
Tons	Tonnes	1.0160
Tonnes	Tons	0.9842

MEN'S SUITS

UK	36	38	40	42	44	46	48
Rest of Europe	46	48	50	52	54	56	58
US	36	38	40	42	44	46	48

DRESS SIZES

UK	8	10	12	14	16	18
France	36	38	40	42	44	46
Italy	38	40	42	44	46	48
Rest of Europe	34	36	38	40	42	44
US	6	8	10	12	14	16

MEN'S SHIRTS

UK	14	14.5	15	15.5	16	16.5	17
Rest of Europe	36	37	38	39/40	41	42	43
US	14	14.5	15	15.5	16	16.5	17

MEN'S SHOES

UK	7	7.5	8.5	9.5	10.5	11
Rest of Europe	41	42	43	44	45	46
US	8	8.5	9.5	10.5	11.5	12

WOMEN'S SHOES

UK	4.5	5	5.5	6	6.5	7
Rest of Europe	38	38	39	39	40	41
US	6	6.5	7	7.5	8	8.5

• Union Evangelical Church (interdenominational), Reforma 1870, Lomas de Chapultepec.

Toilets
Public toilets (variously described as *baños*, *sanitarios* or *servicios*) can be found in all restaurants, bus stations, airports, large archaeological sites and – usually the cleanest – in museums. Keep your own supply of paper and follow signs for *damas* (ladies) or *caballeros* (gentlemen).

Photography
Colour-print film is commonly sold in camera shops, pharmacies and hotels all over the country, but slide film is harder to find and there is rarely a choice of ASA or make. Prices are significantly higher than the US and slightly more than in Europe, so if you're a keen photographer it's worth bringing rolls of your preferred film with you. When buying film in Mexico, always check the expiry date. Should your trip involve several domestic flights, carry exposed and unexposed film separately to avoid excessive passages through X-ray security machines.

Electricity
110 volts, 60 cycles AC. From Europe you will need an adaptor for two-pin flat plugs, US-style.

Etiquette and local customs
Mexicans are, on the whole, a formal, conservative race, generally courteous and helpful. *Para servirle* (at your service) is a little phrase that will follow you around whenever you utter *gracias* even if the next most common phrase is ah*orita* (meaning 'in a short while' which is not necessarily the truth of the matter). The most sensitive area in terms of etiquette is in churches: don't interrupt worshippers, and show respect in the way you dress (no shorts or mini-skirts). When a sign says 'no flash', observe it and if, as in the churches of the Chiapas Highlands, photography is forbidden, observe that, too. Indigenous Mexicans are not always happy about being photographed, so be sensitive to their feelings, and ask first. Topless sunbathing is unheard of except on specific Yucatán and Oaxacan beaches.

Women travellers
Women travelling alone in Mexico will find traditionally *macho* Mexicans ever ready to help out, not always welcome but sometimes useful in explaining the complexities of internal travel. It is always advisable to have some command of Spanish in order to avoid difficult situations.

Precautions
Attacks on tourists (both male and female) do happen and rural walks or treks should only be undertaken in a large group or with a guide. Nocturnal wandering in large cities is not a good idea.

Tourist offices

Outside Mexico

Canada

Montreal: 1 Place Ville Marie, Suite 2409, Montreal, Quebec H3B 2B5 tel: (514) 871 1052), fax: 871 3825.
Toronto: 2 Bloor Street W, Suite 1801, Toronto, Ontario M4W 3E2 tel: (416) 925 2753, fax: 925 6061.
Vancouver: 999 West Hastings, Suite 1610, Vancouver BC, V6 C2 W2 tel: (604) 669 2845, fax: 669 3498.

UK

60–1 Trafalgar Square, London WC2N 5DS tel: (0171) 734 1058, fax: 930 9202, information line: 0891 600230.

US

Chicago: 300 North Michigan Ave, 4th Floor, Chicago, ILL 60601 (tel: (312) 606 9252, fax: 606 9012.
Houston: 1440 West Office Drive, Houston TEX 77042 tel: (713) 780 8362, fax: 780 8362.
Los Angeles: 1801 Century Park East, Suite 1080, CA 90067 tel: (213) 351 2075, fax: 351 2074.
Miami: 2333 Poce de Leon Boulevard, Suite 710, Coralglabes, FL 33134 tel: (305) 443 9160, fax: 443 1186.
New York: 405 Park Avenue, Suite 1401, New York, NY 10022 tel: (212) 838 1270/421 6655, fax: 753 2874, information line: 1-800-446 3942.

State tourist offices

Aguascalientes: Avenida Universidad 1001, 8th floor, 20000 Aguascalientes (tel: 49 123511).
Baja California Norte: Edificio Plaza Patria, 3rd Floor, Boulevard Díaz Ordáz s/n, 22000 Tijuana (tel: 66 819492).
Baja California Sur: Carretera Norte Km 5, Edificio Fidepaz, 23000 La Paz (tel: 112 40103/40199).
Campeche: Plaza Moch Couoh, Avenida 16 de Septiembre, Campeche (tel: 981 66767).
Chiapas: Boulevard Belisario Domínguez 950, 29000 Tuxtla Gutiérrez (tel: 961 39396/25509).
Chihuahua: Calle Libertad 1300, 1st Floor, CP 31000 Chihuahua (tel: 14 293300).
Coahuila: Boulevard Echeverria Alvarez 1560, 11th floor, 25000 Saltillo (tel: 84 152162/151714).
Colima: Portal Hidalgo 20, 28000 Colima (tel: 331 24360).
Distrito Federal: Amberes 54, 06600 México DF (tel: 5 525 9386).
Durango: Hidalgo 408 Sur, 34000 Durango (tel: 18 112139/119677).
Guanajuato: Plaza de la Paz 14, 36000 Guanajuato (tel: 473 21982/21574).
Guerrero: Costera Miguel Alemán 187, 35359 Acapulco (tel: 74 869171/67).
Hidalgo: Carr México-Pachuca Km 93.5, 42000 Pachuca (tel: 771 13806).
Jalisco: Morelos 102 Plaza Tapatía, 44100 Guadalajara (tel: 3 6131196).
Michoacán: Nigromante 79 Palacio Clavijero, 58000 Morelia (tel: 43 125244/127289).
Morelos: Avenida Morelos Sur 802, 62050 Cuernavaca (tel: 73 143709/1434654).
Nayarit: Avenida de la Cultura 72, 63000 Tepic (tel: 32 148071/72).
Nuevo León: Zaragoza 1300 Sur, Edificio Kalos Nivel A-1, 64000 Monterrey (tel: 8 344 4343/340 1080).
Oaxaca: Independencia esq García Vigil, 68000 Oaxaca (tel: 951 60717).
Puebla: 5 Oriente 3, 72000 Puebla (tel: 22 462044).
Querétaro: Pasteur Norte No 4, 76000 Querétaro (tel: 42 121412).
Quintana Roo: Carretera a Calderitas 622, 77010 Chetumal (tel: 983 25073).
San Luis Potosí: Alvaro Obregon 520, 78000 San Luis Potosí (tel: 48 129906).
Sinaloa: Paseo Olas Altas 1300, 82000 Mazatlán (tel: 69 165160/5).
Sonora: Centro Estatal de Gobierno, 83000 Hermosillo (tel: 62 170044/60).
Tabasco: Edificio Administrativo, Paseo Tabasco 1504, 86000 Villahermosa (tel: 93 163633).
Tamaulipas: 16 Rosales 272, 87000 Ciudad Victoria (tel: 131 21057).
Tlaxcala: Avenida Juárez 18 esq Lardizabal, 90000 Tlaxcala (tel: 246 22787).
Veracruz: Boulevard Cristobal Colon No 5, Torre Animas, 91000 Jalapa (tel: 28 128500).
Yucatán: Calle 59 No 514 X 62 y 64, 97000 Mérida (tel: 99 248386).
Zacatecas: Prol G Ortega, Edificio Marzes s/n, 98600 Zacatecas (tel: 492 40552).

Hotels & Restaurants

ACCOMMODATION

The hotels listed below have been divided into three price categories:

- budget (£): a double room in a simple adequate hotel within the £12–24 range;
- moderate (££): a double room in a well-appointed hotel with good facilities in the £25–45 range;
- expensive (£££): a double room in a luxury hotel offering top amenities and comfort costing upwards of £45.

For telephoning inside Mexico but from outside the province, dial 01 first.

MEXICO CITY

Best Western Hotel de Cortés (££) Hidalgo 85 (tel: 5 518 2181/2). This national monument, an 18th-century former hospice, makes a good choice to soak up colonial atmosphere. Pretty dining patio used for Saturday night *fiestas*. Rooms can be dark and/or noisy but the location is excellent.

Camino Real (£££) Mariano Escobedo 700 (tel: 5 203 2121). A 1960s architectural landmark belonging to a chain of luxury modern hotels. No fewer than 10 restaurants, 720 rooms.

La Casona (£££) Durango 280, Col. Roma (tel/fax: 5 211 0871). Elegantly converted mansion convenient for centre. Attentive service, friendly, small-scale.

Emporio (££) Paseo de la Reforma 124 (tel: 5 546 3062). Well-located 146-room hotel with restaurant, bar and car park.

Hotel Antillas (£) Belisario Domínguez 34 (tel: 5 526 5674). Friendly, basic 100-room hotel in lively neighbourhood north-west of the *zócalo*. TV and bathroom.

Hotel Canada (££) Avenida 5 de Mayo 47 (tel: 5 518 2106). Modern, spacious, clean rooms in a central location.

Hotel Catedral (£) Donceles 95 (tel: 5 518 5232). Some rooms actually have views of the cathedral in this 140-room hotel in heart of Centro Historico. Simple, modernised rooms and suites.

Hotel Gillow (£) Isabel La Catolica 17 (tel: 518 1440; fax: 512 2078). A 100-room hotel in the heart of the Centro Historic. Decent, modernised rooms and suites.

Hotel Majestic (££) Madero 73 (tel: 5 521 8800). Colonial-style hotel with panoramic terrace restaurant and attractive rooms. Unbeatable central location overlooking the *zócalo*.

Hotel Marco Polo (£££) Amberes 27, Zona Rosa (tel: 5 566 9688). Well located, catering to a business clientele. Large, well-appointed rooms, all air-conditioned, and good service.

Hotel Marquis Reforma (£££) Paseo de la Reforma 465 (tel: 5 211 0577). With good views of Chapultepec Park, this deluxe modern hotel offers good business facilities and art deco-inspired rooms.

Hotel Monte Carlo (£/££) Uruguay 69 (tel: 5 521 2559). Legendary for having housed D H Lawrence, this former monastery, now a 60-room hotel, offers a wide price range, depending on facilities. Great location near the *zócalo*, but choose rooms on the interior patio to avoid noise.

Hotel New York (£) Edison 45 (tel: 5 566 9700). Small, unpretentious hotel a few blocks north-west of Alameda and Reforma. Basic, clean rooms, small restaurant, and garage.

Howard Johnson Gran Hotel (££) Avenida 16 de Septiembre 82 (tel: 5 510 4042/4040; fax: 572 2085). Art-nouveau splendour and central location just off the *zócalo* makes this 125-room hotel a classic.

María Cristina (££) Río Lerma 31 (tel: 5 566 9688). A favourite with budget-conscious romantics, this charming 156-room colonial hotel offers gardens, patio, piano bar, a reasonable restaurant and plenty of atmosphere. Book well ahead.

Park Villa (££/£££) Gomez Pedraza 68, Polanco (tel: 5 515 5245). Tucked away in an attractive residential area. A modern, colonial-style hotel with 45 stylish rooms and a garden restaurant.

Vasco de Quiroga (££) Londres 15 (tel: 5 566 0701, fax: 592 7302). Friendly family hotel on less action-packed east side of the Zona Rosa, with 50 well-furnished, colonial-style rooms, restaurant.

Westin Galeria Plaza (£££) Hamburgo 195, Zona Rosa (tel: 5 211 0014). A quiet and well-appointed place with a popular nightclub and international restaurants.

BAJA CALIFORNIA AND THE NORTH

Barranca del Cobre/Copper Canyon

Casa Margarita (£) Avenida López Mateos 11, Creel (tel: 145 60045). Creel's back-packing institution, with rooms and dormitories in family-run guesthouse on main square. Now runs a smarter hotel near by, tel/fax: 145 60245. Organises tours.

Hotel Divisadero Barrancas (£££) Mirador 4516, Col. Residential Campestre (tel: 14 151199; fax: 156575). 50 rustic rooms on edge of Copper Canyon with fabulous views. Full board only. Family hotel with all amenities.

Hotel Paraiso del Oso (£) Cerocahui (tel/fax: 14 146811). Primitive log cabins often without electricity in spectacular canyon setting, 12km from Bahuichivo station. Tours available.

Parador de la Montaña (££) Avenida López Mateos 41, Creel (tel: 145 60075; fax: 60085). Well-appointed hotel on Creel's main street. International restaurant/bar, local tours, off-season discounts.

Pension Creel (£) Avenida López Mateos 61, Creel (tel: 145 60071/62). Rustic wood cabins and stone house (once Pancho Villa's HQ) located on the edge of town overlooking a pine forest.

Rancho Posada Barrancas (££) Cañon del Cobre (tel: 68 187046; fax: 68 120046). Close to station. Mexican ranch-style hotel with 35 rooms. Horse-riding, tours.

Cabo San Lucas

Hotel Casa Blanca (£) Revolucion/Vicario y Moreles (tel: 114 30000; fax: 30590). Reasonable, centrally located 30-room hotel offering boat trips.
Hotel Finisterra (£££) Boulevard Marina (tel: 114 33333). Perched high on a cliff overlooking the Pacific with 200 well-appointed rooms, bars, pools, restaurant, spectacular views.
Hotel Mar de Cortés (££) Cárdenas y Guerrero (tel: 114 30032). US bookings tel: 800 347 8821. Intimate colonial-style hotel just a short walk from the marina. Restaurant and bar.

Chihuahua

Hotel Apolo (£) Avenida Juárez 907 (tel: 14 161101/2). Astonishing 1900s hotel with original ornate lobby, but most rooms are in modern, upstairs extension. Well-appointed, central, car park.
Hotel San Francisco (£££) Victoria 409 (tel: 14 167770). Modern 140-room hotel behind the cathedral. All top hotel amenities, bar, restaurant, car park.

Durango

Hotel Plaza Vizcaya (£££) Ginez Vazquez del Mercado 806 (tel: 18 175322). 100-room hotel with numerous services, air-conditioning, cable TV, restaurants, gym, shops.
Hotel Posada Durán (£) Avenida 20 de Noviembre 506 (tel: 18 112412). Atmospheric old colonial mansion just off the *zócalo*. Reasonably comfortable.

Ensenada

El Cid Motor Hotel (££) Avenida López Mateos 993 (tel: 617 82401). Small hotel close to the bay with a strong accent on Mexican crafts and flamenco music. Restaurant, bar.
Hotel Bahía (££) Avenida López Mateos (tel: 617 82101/02). Popular, well-established place with large pool, great bay views, bar, restaurant.

Guaymas

Hotel Rubi (£) Avenida Serdán y Calle 29 (tel: 622 40169). Clean, pleasant air-conditioned rooms in centre near the harbour.
Playa de Cortés (£££) Bahía Bacochibampo (tel: 622 11047; fax:622 10135). Ten minutes out of town, Guaymas' original luxury resort built in discreet colonial style around a patio. Pool, restaurant, bar, tennis, trailer park.

Hermosillo

Calinda Hermosillo Quality Inn (£££) Avenida Rosales y Morelia (tel: 62 172417). Well-appointed modern hotel in central location. Pool, bar, restaurant.

Hotel Kino (£) Pino Suarez Sur 151, Centro (tel: 62 133131; fax: 133852). Modern 144-room hotel with pool, car-park.

La Paz

Hotel Los Arcos (£££) Pasco Obregón 498 (tel: 112 22744). Up-market, 190-room hotel overlooking the bay with *cabañas*, pools, fishing facilities, restaurant.
Hotel Marina (£££) Carretera Pichilingue (tel: 122 16254; fax: 16177). Large, modern hotel overlooking marina. Italian restaurant, diving, fishing, yacht rental.
Hotel Perla (££) Avenida Alvaro Obregón 1570 (tel: 112 20777). Pleasant, breezy central seafront location with well-kept rooms.

Loreto

Hotel Misión de Loreto (££) Boulevard López Mateos 1 (tel: 113 50048). Attractive, spacious, colonial-style hotel overlooking the seafront. Pretty patio/garden with pool and verandas, bar, restaurant.
Hotel Plaza Loreto (££) Paseo Hidalgo 2 (tel: 113 50280). Opposite the old mission and central plaza. Shady patio, cleanly designed with bar and restaurant. 32 rooms.

Los Mochis

El Dorado (££) Gabriel Leyva 525 Norte, Los Mochis (tel: 68 151111; fax: 120179). Standard or superior rooms. pool, restaurant, travel agent with tours to Copper Canyon.
Hacienda San Francisco (£) Obregon 201, El Fuerte (tel: 689 30242). 75km from Los Mochis on railway route. A friendly hotel with 18 rooms in a relaxing town.

Monterrey

Best Western Safi (££) Pino Suarez Sur 444 (tel: 8 399 7000/7004; fax: 8 399 7020). 115-room centrally located hotel with good amenities. Restaurant, bar, car park.
Gran Hotel Ancira Radisson Plaza (£££) Hidalgo y Escobedo (tel: 8 3451060). Grand old hotel dating from 1912: Pancho Villa once tethered his horse in the lobby. Pool, shops, live jazz bar. Rates drop at weekends.
Hotel Quinta Avenida (£) Madero Oriente 243 (tel: 8 3756565). Reasonable air-conditioned rooms with TV at moderate rates.

Mulegé

Hotel Las Casitas (£) Madero 50 (tel: 115 30019). Cheerful cabin-style rooms opening on to verdant patios. Restaurant, bar.
Punta Chivato Resort (££) Apartido Postal 18 (tel: 115 30188). Fabulous, isolated location on the headland north of Mulegé. Pool, restaurant, fishing and diving facilities.
Vieja Hacienda (£) Calle Romero Rubio (tel: 115 30021). Historic, atmospheric *hacienda* with a superb courtyard where John Wayne once sipped *margaritas*. Bar, pool, restaurant, inspired tours around the region.
Vista Hermosa (£) Camino al Puerto (tel: 155 30222). *Hacienda*-style hotel with 23 rooms overlooking river. Pool, restaurant, bar, fishing.

Saltillo

Hotel Plaza Urdinola (£) Victoria Poniente 427 (tel: 84 140940; fax: 140993). Eccentrically decorated, friendly hotel uphill from Plaza Acuña. Spacious, clean rooms round a courtyard. Good amenities.
Imperial del Norte (££) Boulevard V Carranza 3800 (tel: 84 150011; fax: 167543). A 100-room motor hotel and trailer park with restaurant, bar and pool.

San Felipe

El Capitán (££) Avenida Mar de Cortés 298 (tel/fax: 657 71303). This 42-roomed hotel has a pool, bar and car-park.

San José del Cabo

Hotel Ceci (£) Zaragoza 22 (114 20051). A last outpost budget dinosaur in developing luxury San José. Simple rooms with fan and bathroom at rock-bottom rates.
Posada Real (£££) Malecón (tel: 114 20155). US bookings tel: 800 528 1234. Low-rise 150-room hotel superbly sited in cactus garden leading to beach. Excellent sports and fishing facilities.

Tijuana

Camino Real (£££) Paseo de los Heroes 10305 (tel: 66 334000; fax: 334001). Large, 235-room luxury hotel with unique style and endless amenitites. Good service.
Howard Johnson El Conquistador (££) Boulevard Agua Caliente 10750 (tel: 66 817955). Colonial-style, 110-room hotel with good facilities, gardens, pool. South of town near the racetrack.

PACIFIC COAST

Acapulco

Boca Chica (££) Privada de Calotilla (tel: 74 836741). Superb secluded location on Playa Caletilla. Somewhat dilapidated but warm atmosphere. Restaurant with Japanese and Mexican dishes, very popular with locals. Pool.
Camino Real Acapulco Diamante (£££) Carretera Escencia Km 14 (tel: 52 74 661010; fax: 52 74 661111). Full-service luxury hotel, 156 rooms, each with terrace, many with bay views. Three pools, facilities for golf, tennis, water sports. Selection of restaurants.
Hotel Los Flamingos (££) Avenida Adolofo López Mateos (tel: 74 820690). Tranquil old 1930s hotel once favoured by Cary Grant, Errol Flynn etc. Fine garden, sea views, great food.
Hotel Misión (£) Felipe Valle 12 (tel: 74 822076/823643). A gem of an old hotel in downtown Acapulco. Spanish-style rooms overlooking verdant patio with restaurant.
Hotel Royal Elcano (£££) Avenida Costera Miguel Alemán 75 (tel: 74 841950). Well located opposite the golf course at the eastern end of Costera, overlooking the bay. Excellent restaurant, bars, pool, good service.
Las Brisas (£££) Carretera Escénica Clemente Merjia 5255 (tel: 74 841580). An established rendezvous for the rich and famous with 300 *casitas* (bungalows) dotted around the hillside offering superb bay views.

Barra de Navidad

Hotel Barra de Navidad (££) M López de Legazpi 250 (tel: 335 55122). Rooms with balconies overlooking the beach, slightly dilapidated pool.
Hotel Delfín (£) Morelos 23 (tel: 335 55068). Pretty, modestly scaled place on the lagoon side of town. Terrace breakfasts, German beer garden, pool.
Hotel Sand's (£) Morelos 24 (tel: 335 55018). Hotel in rustic style with patios and terraces overlooking the lagoon. Tropical garden, pool, parrots, monkeys.

Careyes

Club Med Playa Blanca (£££) Playa Blanca Cihuatlán (tel: 333 70734 or 800/CLUB MED). Self-contained resort in beautiful site for package deals only. Every possible amenity, sport and activity.
El Tecuan Hotel (££) Km 33.5, Highway 200 (tel: 335 15026). About 20km south of Careyes through mango plantations. Hilltop hotel overlooking the ocean, favoured by Mexican families. Pool, water-skiing on the lagoon.
Hotel Bel-Air Costa Careyes Resort (£££) Km 53.5 Careyes (tel: 335 10800). Huge, revamped villa resort on picturesque horse-shoe bay. All luxury amenities plus riding, watersports, spa.
Las Alamandas (£££) Quemaro, Valisco (tel: 328 55500; fax: 55027). Highly exclusive, romantic hotel on large estate. Tastefully decorated rooms and suites in four villas. Restaurant, beach-club, pool, tennis, gym, riding and private air-strip.

Colima

Hotel Ceballos (££) Portal Medellin 12 (tel: 331 24444). Historic 19th-century building, right on the *zócalo*, with 70 elegant, spacious air-conditioned rooms. Reasonable prices.

Ixtapa

Hotel Dorado Pacifico (£££) Boulevard Ixtapa (tel: 755 32025). Good beach location, spectacularly designed with spacious, landscaped gardens. All luxury facilities.
Posada Real Ixtapa (£££) Boulevard Ixtapa (tel: 755 31625). Pleasant, colonial-style, 110-room beach hotel with large pool, gardens and good fishing amenities. Slightly cheaper than other luxury choices.

Manzanillo

Las Hadas (£££) Avenida de los Riscos y Vista Hermosa s/n (tel: 333 40000). Now legendary Arabian Nights fantasy hotel with hanging gardens, cobblestone streets and marble-floored rooms.

La Posada (££) Lazaro Cardenas 201, Las Brisas peninsula (tel/fax: 333 31899). Friendly, American-run hotel on beach: 23 rooms, pool, restaurant.

Mazatlán

Costa de Oro (£££) Camarón Sábalo (tel: 69 135444, toll-free 800 342 2431). Design-conscious, oceanside hotel in Zona Dorada with rooms set round gardens and paths. Open-air restaurant, bar, pool, tennis.
Hotel Hacienda Mazatlan (££) Avenida del Mar, corner Flamingo (tel: 69 82700; fax: 827132). Opposite popular beach: 95 rooms in modern colonial style. Recreation centre with pool, tennis, water-slides.
Hotel Siesta (£) Paseo Olas Altas 11 (tel: 69 812640). Atmospheric tropical courtyard hotel in Old Mazatlán, above the famed Shrimp Bucket restaurant on cliff boulevard.
Playa Mazatlán (£££) Avenida Rodolfo T Loaiza 202 (tel: 69 134444/55). Semi-circular low structure with 424 rooms, right on the beach in the centre of Zona Dorada. Casual atmosphere and frequent fiestas.

Playa Azul

Hotel Delfín (£) Calle V Carranza (tel: 753 60007). Friendly small-scale hotel with comfortable rooms surrounding a small pool. Restaurant.
Hotel Playa Azul (££) Calle V Carranza (tel: 753 60024). The best place in town with a wide range of rates and trailer park. Pleasant patio restaurant beside pool.

Puerto Vallarta

Camino Real (£££) Playa Las Estacas (tel: 322 15000). One of Vallarta's most luxurious hotels (just five minutes south of the centre) monopolises an exquisite secluded cove. Beautiful pool, tropical gardens. All rooms have ocean views.
Hotel Rosita (£) Paseo Díaz Ordáz 901 (tel: 322 32000). Large 90-room 1950s hotel on the beach where the lively esplanade begins. Wide range of prices, fan or air-conditioned rooms, pool, restaurant. A bit worn at the edges but friendly and good value.
Los Cuatro Vientos (££) Matamoros 520 (tel: 322 20161). Peaceful retreat high up in the cobble-stoned streets of Old Vallarta. 16 rooms surround a flowery patio, with a small pool, excellent restaurant and great views from the rooftop bar.
Molino de Agua (££) Vallarta 130 (tel: 322 21957). Delightful tropical garden hotel centrally located by Río Cuale and the beach. Simple, air-conditioned bungalows or more luxurious ocean view suites. Pools, bar, restaurant, car park.
Playa Los Arcos (££) Olas Altas 380, Playa Los Muertos (tel: 322 21583). Large beach front hotel in lively area; 135 rooms, pool, restaurant.

San Blas

Hotel Garza Canela (££) Paredes Sur no. 106 (tel: 328 50307). Prettily designed 42-room hotel with gardens, pool, excellent restaurant. Comfortable, spacious rooms, well-screened against the local insect population. Close to the beach, car park.
Motel Posada del Rey (£) Campeche 10 (tel: 328 50123). Reasonable facilities, pool, restaurant and air-conditioned rooms.

Zihuatanejo

Hotel La Casa Que Canta (£££) Carmino Escenico Playa Ropa (tel: 755 42722; fax: 47040). Exclusive hideaway with 21 suites, each individually decorated in Mexican style. Two pools, restaurant with spectacular view.
Hotel Irma (££) La Mader (tel: 755 42105/43738). Good standard hotel with 75 rooms on main beach. Pool, tennis, restaurant, travel-desk.

CENTRAL HIGHLANDS

Aguascalientes

Hotel de Andrea Alameda (£££) Avenida Technologico (tel: 49 184417). Grand French turn-of-the-century-style hotel with 48 rooms. Restaurant, bar, pool, gym. Central location.
Hotel Francia (££) Avenida Madero y Plaza Principal (tel: 49 156080). An elegant 80-room establishment overlooking the main square, with restaurant, bar, and well-appointed rooms. Parking lot.

Guadalajara

Hotel Frances (££) Maestranza 35 (tel: 3 613 1190). Popular historic old hotel (1610) a few metres from Plaza de la Liberación. Inside patio, antique furniture, restaurant, bar, comfortable modernised rooms.
Hotel de Mendoza (££) Venustiano Carranza 16 (tel: 3 613 4646; fax: 613 7310). 104-room hotel in colonial style next to theatre. Heated pool. Parking, good restaurant.
Hotel Presidente Intercontinental (£££) López Mateos Sur y Moctezuma (tel: 3 678 1234/1270). Stunning glass pyramidal design for 346 deluxe rooms in the city's Zona Rosa, across from Plaza del Sol. All luxury amenities, lively bars, restaurants, pool, parking.
Hotel San Francisco (££) Degollado 267 (tel: 3 613 8954). Undergoing renovation and upgrading. A superb mansion with a large inner courtyard and fountain, on the edge of the historic centre.

Guanajuato

Hacienda de Cobos (£) Calle Padre Hidalgo 3 (tel: 473 20350). At the western end of Avenida Juárez, down a side alley. Bougainvillaea-shrouded courtyard with parking. 40 reasonable rooms. Restaurant.
Hosteria del Frayle (££) Sopeña 3 (tel: 473 21179). Atmospheric old hotel just east of the Jardín de la Unión. 37 spacious wood-beamed rooms at very reasonable rates.

Hotel San Diego (££) Jardín de la Unión 1 (tel: 473 21300; fax: 25626). Central location. Well-appointed, tasteful rooms, restaurant, roof terrace.

Posada Santa Fe (££) Plaza Principal 12 (tel: 473 20084; fax: 24653). An elegant 19th-century national monument on the lively main square, with colonial décor and antiques. Suitably stylish rooms. Excellent restaurant with outside tables.

Laguna de Chapala

La Nueva Posada (££) Donato Guerra 9, Ajijic (tel: 376 61444). Small colonial-style inn facing the lake with 16 spacious suites and pool. Restaurant and bar popular with local expatriates.

Real de Chapala (£££) Paseo del Prado 20, Ajijic (tel: 376 60007/14). Colonial-style, 85-room hotel set in lovely gardens overlooking the lake. Restaurant, piano bar, tennis, pool.

Morelia

Hotel Casino (££) Portal Hidalgo 229 (tel: 43 131003). On the *zócalo* overlooking the cathedral. Colonial architecture, good facilities and popular outdoor bar under arches.

Hotel de la Soledad (££) Zaragoza 90 (tel: 43 121888; fax: 122111). Beautiful converted monastery with flowery patio; 49 simple rooms, restaurant, bar.

Hotel Virrey de Mendoza (££) Avenida Madero 310 (tel: 43 124940). An 18th-century hotel on the *zócalo* with lofty atrium restored to former glory. Friendly service and comfortable rooms. Restaurant, bar, shops.

Pátzcuaro

Hotel Los Escudos (£) Portal Hidalgo 73 (tel: 434 20138/21290). Elegant colonial hotel on Plaza Vasco de Quiroga. Well-appointed rooms surround verdant patios. Popular restaurant.

Hotel Mansion Iturbe (£) Portal Morelos 59 (tel: 434 20368). Shadowy 17th-century mansion on Plaza Vasco de Quiroga. Parking, shop, restaurant.

Posada de la Basílica (£) Arciga 6 (tel: 434 21108). Small, old-fashioned hotel facing the Basilica, popular with pilgrims. Pretty, clean, spacious rooms. Excellent restaurant.

Posada de Don Vasco (££) Avenida Lazaro Cardenas 450 (tel: 434 20227; fax: 20262). Pátzcuaro's top hotel, just outside town on the highway. Best Western management, colonial décor, tennis, pool, restaurant, car park.

Querétaro

La Casa de la Marquesa (£££) Madero 41 (tel: 42 120092; fax: 120098). Mansion built in 1756, now converted in extravagent style into 25 luxury suites, each with different decoration. Good facilities, restaurant.

Hotel Impala (££) Colon 1 (tel: 42 122570). Modern 102-room block overlooking Parque Alameda. Well located with good, basic facilities. Avoid noisy front rooms.

Meson de Santa Rosa (££) Luis Pasteur 17 (tel: 42 242623/781). Magnificent converted colonial mansion on Plaza de la Independencia with 21 suites opening on to galleries above the courtyard. Excellent restaurant/bar inside and out.

San Luis Potosí

Hotel Maria Cristina (££) Juan Sarabia 110 (tel: 48 129408; fax: 128823). A 75-room, modern hotel with roof-top pool. Clean, comfortable. Restaurant, parking.

Quinta Real (£££) Real de Lomas 1000 (tel: 48 250200, fax: 250200). Modern luxury hotel built in style of local colonial architecture. Superb central courtyard with pools and garden. All possible amenities, 15 minutes from town centre.

San Miguel de Allende

Casa de Sierra Nevada (£££) Hospicio 35 (tel: 415 207040/888341 5998). Swiss-managed luxury hotel, discreetly located near main square in restored 1580s mansion, with 24 individually decorated suites, flowery patio, antiques, recommended gourmet restaurant.

Hotel Posada de San Francisco (££). Plaza Principal 2 (tel/fax: 415 20072). Rather small rooms but nice public areas in colonial style. Restaurant in front courtyard.

Hotel Sautto (£) Hernandez Macías 59 (tel: 415 20051/2). Rambling hotel in beautiful large garden with range of room prices. Discounts off-season and for long stays.

Posada Carmina (£) Cuna de Allende 7 (tel: 415 20458). Attractive converted colonial mansion beside Parroquia off main square. Pleasant, spacious rooms. Courtyard restaurant.

Posada de las Monjas (£/££) Calle Canal 37 (tel: 415 20171). Converted monastery with 65 rooms, restaurant, bar, roof terraces, car park. Comfortable rooms.

Sierra Gorda

Mésones de Queretaro (£) (tel: 42 143078/121241: fax: 143235). Four delightful hotels at Jalpan, Amealco, Conca, and Muralla. Lovely settings, clean simple rooms, pool, restuarant.

Uruapan

Hotel Plaza Uruapan (££) Ocampo 64 (tel: 452 33980). Relaxed, elegant 124-room hotel overlooking the zócalo. Inexpensive for its range of facilities and comfort. Restaurant, disco, car park.

Mansion del Cupatitzio (££) Parque Nacional s/n, Col Los Riyitos (tel: 452 32100). Magnificently sited 56-room hotel on the edge of the Parque Nacional Eduardo Ruíz. Colonial charm, large pool and garden, restaurant with views.

Xilitla

El Castillo (£££) O'Campo 105 (tel: 136 50038, fax: 136 50055). Converted village house mixing Mexican, Moorish and English styles. 17 comfortable rooms. Meals available.

Zacatecas

Hotel Posada de la Moneda (£) Avenida Hidalgo 413 (tel: 492 20881). Great location by the theatre and cathedral. Comfortable rooms, some with balconies. Restaurant.
Meson de Jobito (£££) Jardin Juarez 143 (tel/fax: 492 41722). Delightful 31-room hotel in renovated mansion. Antiques, satellite TV, excellent restaurant.
Quinta Real (£££) Rayón 434 (tel: 492 29104). Extraordinary, unique luxury hotel arranged around a 17th-century bullring with 50 suites. Generously scaled splendour, antiques, fine restaurant.

CENTRAL VALLEYS AND THE GULF

Cholula

Villa Arqueologica (££) Pirámide de Cholula (tel: 22 471966). Club Med hotel at the foot of great pyramid and views to Popocatépetl. Shops, restaurant, pool, tennis.

Cuautla

Hotel Hacienda Cocoyoc (£££) PO Box 300 (tel: 735 62211 or toll-free 800 537 8483). Beautiful 16th-century *hacienda* in landscaped grounds, with 300 rooms, pools, restaurants, tennis, golf, riding.

Cuernavaca

Hacienda de Cortés (££) Plaza Kennedy, Atlaco-mulco (tel: 73 158844). Historic hacienda built for Cortés in the 16th century, just outside Cuernavaca, with 22 deluxe rooms, lovely gardens, pool.
Hotel Casino de la Selva (££) Avenida Vicente Guerrero (tel: 73 124700). Sprawling 200-room hotel where Malcolm Lowry once hid out. Pools, riding, restaurant, disco. Popular with families.
Hotel Iberia (£) Rayón 9 (tel: 73 126040). Friendly old hotel in central location. Spartan but clean rooms with showers opening on to a terrace above a flowery courtyard.
Hotel Las Hortensias (£) Hidalgo 22 (tel: 73 185265). Centrally located. Modest but clean rooms opening on to a garden-courtyard.
Hotel Las Mañanitas (£££) Ricardo Linares 107 (tel: 73 124646). Lovely old converted mansion in well tended grounds with pool and peacocks. Excellent restaurant and garden bar.

Ixtapan de la Sal

Hotel Spa Ixtapan (£££) Plaza San Gaspar (tel: 714 30125 or toll-free 800-223 9832). Giant 250-room spa hotel with all-in facilities from diet menus to thermal pools, gym, golf, tennis, riding.

Jalapa

Hotel Salmones (£) Zaragoza 24 (tel: 28 175432/175431). Gloomy but atmospheric old hotel on the main street. Excellent value rooms with TV and phone, quieter on the garden side. Restaurant, bar.
Meson del Alfarez (££) Zaragoza y Sebastian Camacho (tel: 28 186351; fax: 149665). Converted 18th-century townhouse. Tasteful décor, rustic furniture, tiled bathrooms, TV, phone. Restaurant and bar.
Posada del Cafeto (£) Canovas 12 (tel: 28 170023). Prettily decorated little hotel down a peaceful side street. Cheerful, whitewashed rooms but service not so joyful.

Pachuca

Hotel Emily (£) Plaza Independencia (tel: 771 50868/50849). Good little hotel on *zócalo*, with views towards the hills; 35 rooms, some with balconies. Same owner as Hotel Ciro's, at the other end.

Papantla

Hotel Premier (££) Enríquez 103 (tel: 784 20080, fax: 21062). On the main square opposite the church. Comfortable hotel, air-conditioned throughout. Restaurant.
Hotel El Tajín (£) Calle José de Nuñez Domínguez 104 (tel: 784 20121, fax: 21062). Spacious old hotel near the main square. Clean, large rooms with TV, phone and balcony. Some with air-conditioning. Restaurant.

Puebla

Hotel Colonial (£) Calle 4 Sur No 105 (tel: 22 464612). Modernised colonial building in centre. Restaurant, bar, travel-desk.
Hotel Lastra (££) Calzada Los Fuertes 2633 (tel: 22 351501, fax: 351501). Well-appointed rooms, pretty garden, pool, restaurant, views.
Hotel Royalty (££) Portal Hidalgo 8 (tel: 22 420202, fax: 424740). Moderately sized, comfortable rooms in colonial-style hotel in plum *zócalo* location. Friendly service. Good restaurant/bar.
Meson Sacrista de la Compañia (£££) Calle 6 sur No. 304 (tel: 22 423554; fax: 32 4513). Exuberantly decorated mansion in heart of antiques and crafts area. Each room different but all with antiques and imagination. Fine patio restaurant.

San Juan del Río

Hotel Layseca (£) Avenida Juarez 9 Oriente (tel: 427 20110). Lovely old hotel on main street with rooms opening onto colonnaded garden. Parking. Excellent value, friendly.

Taxco

Hotel Agua Escondida (££) Plaza Borda 4 (tel: 762 20726/21166). Well-situated on the *zócalo* with terrace views of the cathedral. Colonial-style rooms, rooftop pool, good children's facilities, car park.

Hotel Montetaxco (££) Lomas de Taxco (tel: 762 21300). Sprawling 156-room resort hotel with fabulous views from the hilltop over the town and mountains. Popular with families, lots of sports facilities, restaurants.
Hotel Posada San Javier (£) Estacas 1/Ex-Rastro 4 (tel: 762 20231). Blissful palm-shaded garden with rustically furnished rooms with balconies. Small pool, car park, very central.
Posada de la Misión (£££) Cerro de la Mision 32 (tel: 762 20063). An attractive 150-room hotel at the bottom of the main slope, whose pool claims a mural by Juan O'Gorman. Average restaurant, bars, garden.

Tepoztlán
Albergue de la Loma ($) Guerrero 58 (tel: 246 20424). Spacious rooms, two blocks south of the zócalo. Parking.
Hotel Posada del Tepozteco (££) Paraiso 3 (tel: 739 50010). Beautifully sited *hacienda*-hotel with pools, gardens and terraces overlooking the valley. Exclusive atmosphere. Rates rise with private spa-baths.

Tlaxcala
Albergue de la Loma (£) Guerrero 58 (tel: 246 20424). Spacious, pleasant rooms, two blocks south of the *zócalo*. Parking.

Toluca
Hotel Plaza Morelos (£) Serdán 115 (tel: 72 159200). A reasonable, well-maintained hotel and restaurant. Convenient for central sights and action. Parking.

Veracruz
Hotel Colonial (£) Miguel Lerdo 117 (tel: 29 32 01 93; fax: 322465). Large, 182 room hotel on plaza. Recently revamped rooms, balconies, pool, outdoor café. Noisy but lively.
Hotel El Faro (£) 16 de Septiembre 223 (tel: 29 316538). Excellent family-run hotel a few streets back from the harbour. Clean rooms with TV and air-conditioning or fan.
Hotel Emporio (£££) Paseo del Malecón 244 (tel: 29 300222). Towering modern hotel facing the harbour, with 202 air-conditioned rooms and suites, three pools, tennis, restaurants, bars, roof garden.
Hotel Mocambo (££) Boulevard Ruíz Cortines (tel: 29 220333). Longstanding favourite on Mocambo Beach, about 10km south of town. Decent-sized rooms, some overlooking the gardens and beach beyond.
Hotel Ruíz Milán (££) Insurgentes Veracruzanos 432 (tel: 29 326707). Rather battered 'modern' hotel overlooking the harbour. Spacious air-conditioned rooms with TV, phone, balcony. Cheaper ones with fans. Convenient and relatively quiet location.

THE SOUTH

Catemaco
Hotel del Lago (£) Paseo del Malecón s/n (tel: 294 30160/30119). Reasonable air-conditioned rooms with TV, right on the town's lake-front. Modest pool, restaurant, tours, boats.

Comitan
Hotel Real Balún Canán (££) 1A Avenida Poniente Sur 7 (tel: 963 21094; fax: 20031). Central hotel with good facilities, restaurant, parking.

Huatulco
Hotel Flamboyant (££) La Crucecita (tel: 958 70105). On the main square of Huatulco's service town. Colonial-style hotel with 70 air-conditioned rooms, pool and restaurant.
Casa del Mar (£££) Balcones de Tangolunda (tel: 958 10203/5; toll-free 800 27751). Isolated spot on cliff-edge with superb views. 25 well-appointed suites, pool, restaurant, steps to private beach.
Hotel Marlin (££) Bahia de Santa Cruz (tel: 958 70055; fax: 70545). Pleasantly-scaled pink hotel with 28 spacious rooms. Efficient staff, pool.

Lagos de Montebello
Hotel Parador Museum Santa Maria (££) Carretera Lagos de Montebello (tel: 963 25116/21737). An extraordinary *hacienda* that combines history and nature in a remote setting 20km from the main road. Antiques abound.

Oaxaca
Camino Real (£££) Cinco de Mayo 300 (tel: 951 60611). Stunning 16th-century convent converted into a unique luxury hotel. Banquets and folk dance shows in a vaulted chapel. Excellent restaurant, pool, piano bar. Secluded gardens.
Casa Oaxaco (£££) Calle Garcia Vigil 407 (tel: 951 44173; fax: 64412). Exclusive guest-house in contemporary Mexican style. Patios, pool for only eight suites. Central, quiet.
Hostel La Noria (££) Hidalgo 918 (tel: 951 47844; fax: 63992). Attractively renovated mansion with excellent service and restaurant. Front rooms can be noisy but are very comfortable.
Hotel Antonios (£) Avenida Independencia 601 (tel: 951 67227). Medium-sized, well-located hotel just off the *zócalo*. Recently renovated rooms.
Hotel Principal (£) Cinco de Mayo 208 (tel: 951 62535). High-ceilinged, wood-beamed rooms, impeccably maintained, opening on to a lush courtyard. Four blocks north-east of the *zócalo*.

Parador del Dominico (££) Pino Suarez 410 (tel: 951 31812). Charming converted old mansion with central patio on east side of centre. Excellent amenities. Restaurant, car park, travel-desk.

Palenque

Chan-Kah Ruinas (£££) Km 3, Carretera Palenque Km 3 (tel: 934 51100). Beautifully sited bungalows in lush jungle grounds very close to the archaeolgical site. Good *palapa* restaurant, *cenote*-type pool, entertainment, tours.
Hotel la Cañada (££) Calle Merle Green 13 (tel: 934 50102). Legendary bungalow accommodation in jungle setting at the entrance to town. Air-conditioned or fan-cooled. Good, lively restaurant.
Plaza Palenque (££) Carretera Catazaja-Palenque, Km27 (tel: 934 50555; fax: 50395). New 98-rooms Best Western hotel in lush grounds with pool, playground, restaurant.

Puerto Ángel

Buena Vista (£) Aptdo Postal 48 (tel/fax: 958 43104). Best location on hillside, overlooking village and bay. Imaginatively designed, simple rooms, though with synthetic hammocks! Panoramic terrace restaurant.
Villa Serena Horencia (£) Virgilio Uribe (tel: 958 43044). Unpretentious, friendly, Mediterranean-style inn opposite fishermen's beach. Good simple rooms with air-conditioning or fan. Restaurant and sun-terrace.

Puerto Escondido

Hotel Arco Iris (£) Calle del Morro, Playa Zicatela (tel: 958 20432). Favourite surfers' haunt. Friendly 20-room hotel on beach. Clean rooms with fans, bathrooms and balconies.
Hotel Paraíso Escondido (££) Calle Unión 10 (tel: 958 20444). Lovely old whitewashed *hacienda*-style hotel, two blocks from the beach, with 20 air-conditioned rooms, pool, gardens, open-air restaurant.
Hotel Santa Fe (££) Calle del Morro (tel: 958 20170). Between Playa Zicatela and Marinero, a superbly designed hotel laid out around terraces, pool and gardens. Air-conditioned and/or fan-cooled rooms. Panoramic restaurant.
Posada Real (£££) Boulevard Benito Juárez (tel: 958 20133). A 100-room Best Western hotel perched above the ocean in magnificent gardens, offering useful tourist information, car rental, tours. Easy access to the beach.

San Andrés Tuxtla

Hotel De Los Perez (££) Rascón 2 (tel: 294 20777). Conveniently located just off the *zócalo*. Reasonable, clean air-conditioned rooms with TV. Restaurant.

San Cristóbal de las Casas

Casa Vieja (££) Maria Adelina Flores 27 (tel: 967 86868; fax: 86386). Attractive, rustic-style hotel in peaceful location three blocks from *zócalo*. Well-appointed rooms, good service, restaurant, parking.
Hotel Flamboyant Español (££) Calle 1 de Marzo 15 (tel: 967 80412/80045). Elegant colonial-style hotel in central location, with 50 well-appointed rooms with TV and fireplace off flowery patio. Restaurant, bar, solarium, gym.
Hotel Mansion del Valle (£) Diego de Mazariegos 39 (tel: 967 82582 fax: 82581). Central location, 48 well-appointed rooms, parking, restaurant.

Tapachula

Hotel Cabildos (££) 2A Avenida Norte 17 (tel: 962 66606). Central 29-room hotel with pool, air-conditioned rooms, cable TV, car rental, restaurant.
Hotel Don Miguel (£) Calle 1A Poniente 18 (tel: 962 61143). Bright, clean rooms with air-conditioning and TV. Restaurant.

Tehuantepec

Hotel Oasis (£) Melchor Ocampo 8 (tel: 971 50008). Friendly, 28-room hotel. Simple, clean, nice atmosphere.

Tuxtla Gutiérrez

Gran Hotel Humberto (£) Avenida Central Poniente 180 (tel: 961 22080). Well located near the *zócalo*. Spacious air-conditioned rooms with TV, though some a bit gloomy. 1950s-era restaurant.
Hotel Flamboyant (£££) Boulevard Belisario Domínguez Km 1081 (tel: 961 50888). Excellent facilities at reasonable rates in Moorish-inspired modern, 118-room hotel. Large pool, tennis, restaurants, live music.

Villahermosa

Hotel Don Carlos (£) Madero 418 (tel: 93 122499; fax: 124622). Central hotel near main plaza: 53 air-conditioned rooms, satellite TV, restaurant, parking.
Hotel Maya Tabasco (££) Avenida A Ruíz Cortines 907 (tel: 93 121111). 160-room Best Western hotel close to park and museums. Air-conditioned rooms with TV, pool, gym, tennis, disco, restaurants.

YUCATÁN

Calakmul

Chicanná EcoVillage (£££) Xpujil (tel: 981 62233; fax: 983 23304). Overpriced Ramada hotel near Chicanna ruins. Two-storey cottages with balconies, small pool, slow restaurant. Nice lush surroundings.
Hotel Calakmul (£) Xpujil (tel/fax: 983 29162). Family hotel and restaurant on main road. Clean, rather small rooms with fan.

Campeche

Hotel América (£) Calle 10 No 252 (tel: 981 64588). 52-room hotel converted from an old colonial mansion in the city centre. Spacious rooms with TV, phone, fan and bathroom.

Hotel del Paseo (£/££) Calle 8 No 215, San Roman (tel: 981 10100; fax: 10097). New hotel just south of centre. Good, air-conditioned rooms, parking, restaurant.

Cancún

Club Lagoon (££) Boulevard Kukulcán, Km 5.8, Zona Hoteleres (tel: 98 831111). Mediterranean-style architecture, patios, gardens facing Laguna de Nichupté, with 70 rooms and 19 suites. Pretty restaurant.

Hotel Hacienda Cancún (££) Avenida Sunyaxchén 39, Ciudad Cancún (tel: 98 843672, fax: 841208). Central location in the main town. Pleasant air-conditioned rooms with TV and bathroom, pretty patio and pool. Car park.

Hotel Margarita (££) Avenida Yaxchilán 41, Ciudad Cancún (tel: 98 849333). A 96-room hotel in the town centre, with restaurant, pool, beach-club. Air-conditioned rooms with TV, phone, large bathrooms, balconies. Baby-sitting, car rental.

Chetumal

Hotel El Dorado (£) Avenida 5 de Mayo 42 (tel: 983 20315). Good central location for 25 clean, spacious rooms with fan or air-conditioning, TV.

Hotel Los Cocos (££) Avenida Héroes 134 (tel: 983 20530). Modern 80-room hotel with pool, restaurant, bar and extensive facilities.

Chichén Itzá

Hotel Dolores Alba (£) Km 122, Carretera Cancún (tel: Mérida 992 85650). About 3km east of the ruins on the Cancún highway. Charming, family-run hotel, with small pool and reasonable restaurant.

Villa Arqueólogica (££) Chichén Itzá (tel: 985 62830). Two Club Med 'cultural' *hacienda*-style hotels, near the ruins, with air-conditioned rooms, good restaurant, pool, bar, disco, library, movies.

Ciudad del Carmen

Hotel Del Parque (££) Calle 33 No 1 (tel: 938 23076). Modest 24-room establishment with well-appointed rooms, restaurant, bar, pool.

Hotel Isla del Carmen (££) Calle 20A No 9 (tel: 938 22350). Reasonably priced modern hotel/restaurant. 96 rooms with air-conditioning, phone, TV.

Cobá

Villa Arqueólogica (££) Cobá (tel: 987 42090/42087). Hotel by Cobá's main lake, close to the ruins. Air-conditioned rooms, pool, good restaurant and excellent library for Maya-addicts.

Cozumel

Casa del Mar (££) Costera Sur Km. 4 (tel: 987 21900). Impressive 106-room hotel south of town on coast, with scuba facilities, restaurant/bar and own submarine.

Hotel Playa Azul (£££) Carretera San Juan Km 4 (tel: 987 20033; fax: 20110). Intimate 31-room hotel towards northern end of island. Rooms overlook secluded beach or gardens. French restaurant.

Hotel Suites Elizabeth (£) Calle Adolfo Rosado Salas 44 (tel: 987 20330). Close to the harbour, well-maintained self-catering suites. Hotel rooms too.

Isla Mujeres

Hotel Berny (££) Juárez y Abásolo (no phone). Simple rooms with fan or air-conditioning, TV and bathroom surrounding courtyard. Videobar and restaurant.

Na-Balam (£££) Playa Norte (tel: 987 70279). Lovely beach hotel in sophisticated *palapa* style. Tropical garden, yoga, pool, good bar and restaurant.

Posada del Mar (££) Calle Medina y Morelos (tel: 987 70044; fax: 70266). A delightful hotel with 41 comfortable rooms or bungalows north of the pier by a lighthouse. Sea views, pool, garden, restaurant, air-conditioning.

Laguna Bacalar

Hotel Laguna (£) Avenida Bugambillas 316, Chetumal (tel: 983 23517). Bright 36-room hotel on lake north of Chetumal. Fresh, simple rooms, some with balconies. Restaurant.

Mérida

Gran Hotel (££) Calle 60 No 496 (tel: 99 247730). Great location on Parque Hidalgo just off the *zócalo*. Magnificent 'grand hotel' with restaurant/bar in a verdant courtyard. Some very big rooms with air-conditioning or fan.

Hotel Casa del Balam (££) Calle 60 No 488 (tel: 99 242150). Large, stylish, central hotel, part 19th-century and part modern. Antiques, spacious atrium/bar, air-conditioned rooms. Car park, pool, travel agent. Good restaurant.

Hotel Posada Toledo (££) Calle 58 No 487 (tel: 99 231690; fax: 232256). Superb old family mansion recently converted leaving memorabilia intact. Ornate interior, particularly the very French-style suite but some rooms are dark, dingy and overpriced.

Hotel Trinidad (£) Calle 60 No 464 (tel: 99 232033). Rambling hotel filled with bric-à-brac and art. Wide range of basic but clean rooms around patios with fountains. Friendly and well-located. The smarter Hotel Trinidad Galeria (£) is at Calle 60 456 (tel: 99 232463) with slightly higher rates, pool, coffee-shop and similar eccentricity.

Montejo Palace (£££) Paseo de Montejo 483-C (tel: 99 247644). Modern hotel with colonial décor on Mérida's Champs Elysées.60 rooms, 30 suites, restaurants, bar, pool, nightclub. The rates are cheaper at its sister establishment across street, the Hotel Paseo de Montejo (££) (tel: 99 239033).

Playa del Carmen

Banana Cabañas (£) Avenida Quinta (tel: 987 30036). Clean, friendly place with selection of bungalows or fan-cooled rooms with

bathrooms in tropical garden on Playa's main pedestrian street, one block from the beach.
Blue Parrot Inn (££) Calle 12 (tel: 987 30083). Hip hotel in Playa on the beach to the north of the centre. Rooms or thatched *cabañas*, some with small kitchens. Beach bar and restaurant. Relaxed, fun atmosphere.
Posada Sian-Ka'an (£) Avenida Quinta (tel: 987 30202). Oldish building in the central Playa. Fan-cooled rooms with sea views, bungalows in garden.
Shangri-La Caribe (££) Km 69.5 Carretera Tulum (tel: 987 22888). 50 beachfront bungalows at the secluded northern end of the beach, accessible by separate turn-off from corridor highway. All fan-cooled or air-conditioned, with terrace. Restaurant, bar, pool. Diving.

Progreso
Sian Ka'an Suites (££) Calle 19 s/n (tel/fax: 993 54017). Small beachfront hotel with 11 suites. Pool, restaurant, bar.

Tulum
Cabañas Ana y Vosé (££) Carretero Boca Paila Km 7 (tel: 98 806121; fax: 806022). *Palapa*-roofed cottages on tranquil beach. Good restaurant, diving, snorkelling and mountain-bikes.
Hotel Boca Paila (££) Laguna Boca Paila (tel: 800 245 1950). Well-appointed 12-room hotel in the Sian Ka'an reserve, next to empty beaches and lagoon. Fishing and diving trips, bar/restaurant.
Pierdra Escondida (££/£££) Carretera Tulum-Boca Paila, Km5 (tel: 987 12092/local fax for messages). Comfortable, small-scale beachfront hotel. Excellent French-run restaurant. Snorkelling and diving tours.
Sian Ka'an Osho Oasis (££) Carretera Tulum-Boca Paila, Km5 (fax: 987 12094). At the edge of the biosphere reserve on the coastal road. New Age spirited group of cabañas with vegetarian restaurant. Well-equipped dive shop, reef and cenote trips. Morning meditation sessions on beach.

Uxmal
Hacienda Uxmal (£££) (tel: 99 280840; fax: 280840). Lovely *hacienda* in gardens near ruins. 80 rooms with veranda, pool, good restaurant.
Villas Arquealógicas (££) (tel/fax: 99 280644). A well-run, 40 room hotel at the entrance to the archaelogical site. Simple but comfortable rooms, pool, library, and restaurant.

Valladolid
Hotel María de la Luz (£) Plaza Principal (tel/fax: 985 62071). Pleasant 1970s hotel built around pool.Good rooms with fan or air-conditioning. Excellent, cheap restaurant, parking.
Hotel Mesón del Marqués (£/££) Calle 39 No 203 (tel: 985 62073). Valladolid's top hotel, a part colonial mansion on the main plaza. Tastefully decorated, reasonably priced for its setting. Air-conditioned rooms with TV and phone. Good restaurant, pool, car park.

Xcalak
Costa de Cocos (££) Carretera Xcalak (tel: 983 80478). Up-market palapa-roofed cabañas literally at the end of the road, about 50km south of Majahual. American-Mexican owners assure all basic comforts. Divers' haven as spectacular reefs lie only 10 minutes away.

RESTAURANTS

In smaller towns the best restaurants are often found in hotels. Refer to the hotel listings for these. Other establishments listed below have been divided into the following categories:
- budget (£)
- moderate (££)
- expensive (£££)

MEXICO CITY

Bar Jorongo (££) Maria Isable Sheraton, Paseo de la Reforma 325, Zona Rosa (tel: 5 207 3933). Although the menu is very limited, this is the perfect place to experience the lively Mexico City scene. Go for a late supper and enjoy the *mariachi* music.
Bar l'Opéra (££) 5 de Mayo 10 (tel: 5 512 8959). Ornate *belle époque* institution. Average food but a fabulous setting close to Bellas Artes. Go just for a drink.
Café El Parnaso (£) Felipe Carrillo 2 (tel: 5 554 2225). Best people-watching spot on Coyoacán's Jardín Centenario. Bookshop and café for whiling away weekend hours.
Café de Tacuba (££) Tacuba 28 (tel: 5 518 4950). Famous old Mexican restaurant. Endless *enchiladas*, *chiles rellenos* (stuffed peppers) and *mole* dishes. Lively, with entertainment on Friday and Saturday nights.
Caffé Milano (£) Amberes 27 (tel: 5 207 0119). An established Zona Rosa favourite for authentic Italian cuisine: pasta, fish or meat. Sidewalk tables. Open daily till 2am.
Carrousel Internacional (££) Nizza 33 (tel: 5 208 1280). Bar/pub/restaurant spiced up by vociferous *mariachis*. Drinks and copious snacks served noon till 2am daily.
Champs-Elysées (£££) Paseo de la Reforma 316 (tel: 5 514 0450). Parisian-style restaurant with five dining-rooms and a roof garden overlooking the city's grand boulevard. French cuisine. Reservations essential. Weekdays only.
Cicero (£££) Republica de Cuba 79, Centro Historico (tel: 521 7866). Over-the-top baroque and glamour for drinks, dinner and song. Also in the Zona Rosa at Londres 195 (tel: 533 3800) with an equally dramatic setting and fine Mexican cuisine.
El Bajio (££) Cuitláhuac Avenida, Col Obrero Popular, Azcapotzalco (tel: 525 341 9889). A little off the beaten path, but well worth the trip. The mother and daughter chef team serve regional food from Oaxaca and Veracruz in a beautiful, casual setting. Some of the best Mexican food in the city.

El Hijo del Cuervo (££) Jardín Centenario 17 (tel: 5 658 5306). Lively evening watering-hole on Coyoacán's main square. Wide range of drinks and snacks. Closed Monday.
Focolare (££) Hamburg 87, Zona Rosa (tel: 5 207 8055). Cheery place complete with a rooster overseeing the dining room. Extremely tasty regional Mexican cuisine with specialities from Oaxaca and Veracruz.
Fonda Don Chon (££) Regina 159 (tel: 5 522 1070). An exceptional place near La Merced - market, specialising in pre-Hispanic dishes (maguey worms, iguana, grasshoppers, vipers, ant-soup!). Friendly, popular, unpretentious with wide price range.
Fonda El Refugio (££) Liverpool 166, Zona Rosa (tel: 5 207 2732). Award-winning Mexican restaurant, reservations advisable. Fun atmosphere, excellent traditional dishes. Closed Sunday.
Fonda San Ángel (££) Plaza San Jacinto 3 (tel: 5 548 7568). A few steps from San Ángel's Bazar Sabado. Traditional Mexican dishes in relaxed setting. Closed Sunday.
Hacienda de Las Morales (£££) Vazquez de Mella 525 (tel: 5 281 4554). The setting, a 16th-century *hacienda*, makes this one of the most celebrated, and romantic eating places in Mexico City. The menu is composed of elegant Mexican classics, with French influence.
Hosteria Santa Caterina (£) Jardín Sta Caterina 6 (tel: 544 0513). Rustic old restaurant in Coyoacán, right next to small theatre. Great weekend buzz, friendly. Good range of typical Mexican dishes: try the excellent *nopales* (cactus-leaf) salad.
Lago Chapultepec (£££) Lago Mayor, Bosque Chapultepec (tel: 5 515 9585/6). Reservations and ties essential at this formal lakeside restaurant. Spectacular setting, outstanding wine list, French cuisine, smoochy music and dancing in the evenings. Good Sunday brunches.
Les Moustaches (£££) Río Sena 88 (tel: 5 533 3393). Pretentious restaurant off Reforma in a beautiful restored mansion. European cuisine includes snails, sea bass with almonds, pepper steak and lavish desserts. Jacket and tie. Weekdays only.
Los Danzantes (££) Plaza Jardin Centenaria 12 (tel: 658 6451). Opened in 1996, this has been praised as the best restaurant in the city. The dining room overlooks the Plaza de Coyoacan and there is an outdoor patio. The cuisine is Mexican: creative and refined dishes.
Los Girasoles (££) Tacuba 8/10 (tel: 5 510 0630). Exquisite Mexican nouvelle cuisine, inspired by pre-Hispanic recipes and ingredients. Good service, bar and *mariachis*.
Los Irabiens (££) Avenida de la Paz 45 (tel: 5 660 2382). Piano music, smart Mexican fittings, and antiques. San Angel's most inventive menu and discreet service, much favoured by the upwardly mobile.
Prendes (££) 16 de Septiembre 10 (tel: 5 521 5404/1878). Crowded lunchtime place in historic centre, more memorable for its murals and atmosphere than its menu. Seafood specialities and good Sunday paella. Closes daily at 6pm. Another branch at Frontón México, **Plaza de la República** (tel: 512 7517) is open till midnight.
San Ángel Inn (£££) Diego Rivera 50, Altavista (tel: 5 616 2222). Fabulous restored 18th-century mansion, an institution in San Ángel. Patio or indoor dining for international or Mexican food.
Sanborns de los Azulejos (£) Calle Madero 4 (tel: 5 512 2300). Eat in Moorish-style palatial splendour at the Casa de los Azulejos, close to Alameda. Average food but pleasant.
T'Cla (£) Durango 186A (tel: 5 525 4920). A good address for sampling Mexican *nouvelle cuisine* in the increasingly fashionable Colonia Roma – try the *fettucine con Mole Poblano*.
Tenampa (£) Plaza Garibaldi (tel: 5 526 6176). Touristy but still amusing for soaking up *tequila* and *mariachi* music. Open daily till 3am.

BAJA CALIFORNIA AND THE NORTH

Cabo San Lucas
Da Giorgio (£££) Km 25, Highway 1, Misiones del Cabo (tel: 114 31105). A superb Italian restaurant with fabulous ocean views, offering home-made pasta, *focaccia* bread and pizzas baked in a wood-fired oven. Open daily till midnight.
El Delfin (££) Playa del Medano (tel: 114 30011). A glassed-in *palapa* restaurant on the main town beach, serving large portions of Sonora beef, lobster and ultra-fresh fish. Open all day.
Mi Casa (££) Serdán y Lázaro Cárdenas (tel: 114 31933). A rare authentic Mexican restaurant on the main square behind the marina. Colourful; wide choice of typical dishes. Open till 10pm.

Ensenada
El Rey Sol (£££) Avenida López Mateos 1000 (tel: 617 81733). Seafood restaurant serving French Provençal and Mexican dishes. Elegant, colonial-style setting.

Loreto
Caesar's (££) Emiliano Zapata y Benito Juárez (tel: 113 30203). Top seafood restaurant founded over 20 years ago. Mega-portions of delicious lobster, red snapper and much more. Friendly service.

Monterrey
El Tío (££) Avenida Hidalgo 1746 Poniente (tel: 8 3460291). Landmark establishment over 60 years old in downtown area. Roast kid and steaks with lively indoor bullfight-theme (or in calmer garden patio).

La Paz
Bismark II (££) Degollado and Altamirano (tel: 122 24854) Relaxed surroundings and fresh seafood, prepared with a Mexican flair. The staff are extremely accommodating, and the

food, which ranges from simple to lavish, is always excellent.
La Costa La Paz (££) Navarro y Bahía de La Paz (tel: 112 28808). On the seafront with good bay views. Imperial shrimp, fish and grilled meats.

San José del Cabo

Café Fiesta (£) Boulevard Mijares 14 (tel: 114 22908). Good breakfast café with tables under shady trees on the plaza. More expensive.
Damiana (££) Boulevard Mijares 8 (tel: 114 20499). Elegant little restaurant tucked away beside San José's main square in an old town house. Romantic patio dining. Excellent seafood – giant prawns, abalone, lobster, shrimp, steak or châteaubriand.

Tijuana

Tía Juana Tilly's (££) Avenida Revolución y Calle 7 (tel: 66 856024). The most popular *gringo* hang-out in Tijuana, next to the Jai Alai stadium. Mexican specialities. Another branch across street called Tilly's Fifth Avenue.

PACIFIC

Acapulco

Bambuco's (££) Hotel Elcano, Costera Aleman 75 (tel: 74 841950). Wonderful, fresh seafood and sounds of the surf make this an attractive choice for a relaxed dinner. Also a good choice for breakfast.
Carlos 'n Charlie (££) Costera M Alemán 112 (tel: 74 840039/841285). Another of the Anderson's chain and one of Acapulco's 'in' places. Old photos, loud rock and queues for seafood and meat dishes.
El Amigo Miguel (£) Juarez 31 (tel: 74 83 6981). A local favourite, serving interesting seafood dishes. It may be crowded, but it's definitely worth the wait.
La Granja del Pingüe (£) Benito Juárez 10 (tel: 74 835339). Also known as the Fat Farm. Friendly, relaxed place offering good breakfasts, snacks, pasta, salads and pastries all day. Cool patio setting in an old farmhouse a few blocks west of the *zócalo.*
Restaurant Miramar (£££) Plaza La Vista, Carretera Escéncia (tel: 74 847874). A classically elegant dining experience, with a beautiful view of the bay. The menu has French dishes as well as Mexican. Definitely a place for a special occasion.
Tio Alex (££) Avenida Costera Miguel Alemán 111 (tel: 74 843656). In the thick of the beachfront action overlooking Playa Condesa. Open-air dining, cheerful service. Seafood, steaks and soups with booming rock music from the next-door Taboo bar.

Manzaillo

El Vaquero Campestre (££) Km 11.5, Salahua (tel: 333 30475). Just outside of town, this picnic-like spot specialises in tasty Sonora beef, prepared in a wide variety of ways. Definitely worth the trip, and especially fun for a large group.
Willy's (££) Crucero Las Brisas (tel: 333 31794). Highly reputed French-owned restaurant with a lovely beach view. Dinners only – get there early for a table.

Mazatlán

Copa de Leche (££) Olas Altas 33S (tel: 69 82 5753). Overlooking the ocean, Copa de Leche seems to have been there forever. Simple Mexican food and a nautical theme.
El Shrimp Bucket (££) Olas Altas 11 (tel: 69 816350). The original Anderson chain restaurant, open all day but more fun with the evening marimba band. Good seafood in picturesque courtyard.
Señor Frog's (££) Avenida del Mar 225 (tel: 69 851110). Heavily marketed chain of young, lively restaurants. Barbecued ribs or Madrazo oysters. Open till 1am.

Puerto Vallarta

Café San Cristóbal (£) Corona 172 (tel: 322 32551). A wonderful place for a coffee and a light snack; a relaxed Puerta Vallarta institution. The pastries and sandwiches are delicious, and the excellent coffee is also sold by the pound.
Chez Elena (££) Matamoros 520 (tel: 322 20161). Intimate, colonial-style, established in the 1950s, offering European menu. Views over the city.
Le Bistro Jazz Café (££) Isla Río Cuale (tel: 322 20283). Lush, riverside setting with cool jazz to escape Vallarta's tropical heat. Open all day for crêpes, *tampiqueña* (marinaded beef), seafood. Elegant but informal, indoor and outdoor eating.
Mr Gallo (£) Basílio Badillo y Pino Suárez (no phone). Normal Mexican prices in an area that is rapidly turning into Old Vallarta's gastronomic HQ . Lofty *palapa*-roofed place serving excellent barbecued meat or fish. Open till 11pm.
Restaurant Argentine Los Pibes (£££) Badillo 261 (tel: 322 2 1557). Opened in 1994. Specialises in authentic Argentine grilled meats. In addition to beef you can sample baby pig and home-made sausages. The Mexican and Argentinian accompaniments are also delicious.

Zihuatanejo

Casa Elvira (£) Paseo del Pescador 16 (tel: 755 42061). Facing the beach near the pier. Quaint interior, good seafood and authentic Mexican dishes.

CENTRAL HIGHLANDS

Guadalajara

El Abajeño (££) Minerva, Avenida Vallarta 2802 (tel: 3 630 0307). Smart courtyard bar/restaurant at the city's western end. Traditional Mexican fare, friendly service and *mariachis.*

La Fragata Azteca (££) López Cortilla 2120. Favourite long-lunching, bustling, place in giant tent-like structure. Good fish and meat dishes or local *mariachis*.
Portal San Angel (£) Edificio Progreso 102 (tel: 3 617 8199). Breezy café/restaurant with outside tables. Typical Mexican snacks. Open till 8.30pm.

Guanajuato

Casa del Conde de la Valencia (£££) Km 5, opposite La Valenciana Church (tel: 473 23550). Housed in the former home of the Count of Valencia. The menu features classic Mexican dishes. There is a lovely porch for serene outdoor dining.
El Trujo (£) Calle del Trujo 7 (tel: 473 28374). Design-conscious café/bar/restaurant in a side-street behind the cathedral. Lively; good background music. Open till midnight.
Restaurant 4 Ranas (£) Plazuela San Fernando 24 (tel: 473 20301). Simple Spanish-style place on beautiful, shady square. Breakfasts, snacks and late-night Mexican food are available. Open till 1am.

San Miguel de Allende

La Fragua (££) Cuna de Allende 3 (tel: 415 21144). Courtyard restaurant just off main square. Good atmosphere, live music.
Mamma Mía (££) Umarán 8 (tel: 415 22063). Popular courtyard restaurant with good all-round menu and copious breakfasts. Live music in evenings, open till midnight.

Zacatecas

Acropolis (£) Avenida Hidalgo y Tacuba (tel: 492 21284). Lofty old café-restaurant adjacent to the cathedral. Favourite Zacatecan meeting-place for *quesadillas*, ice-creams, cakes, coffee and juices.
El Mesonero (££) Jardin Juarez 143 (tel: 492 41722). Elegant, 19th-century setting near cathedral in Mesón de Jobito hotel. International dishes and regional cuisine.

CENTRAL VALLEYS AND GULF

Cuernavaca

La India Bonita (££) Morrow 106B (tel: 73 186967/125021). In the former residence of US Ambassador Dwight Morrow. Traditional Mexican setting and food including some pre-Hispanic dishes and grilled meats.
La Strada (££) Salazar 3 Centro (tel: 73 186085). Secluded, verdant patio with fountain and pomegranate tree, candle-lit at night. Copious Italian pasta, pizza, fish or meat dishes. Next to Palacio de Cortés.

Jalapa

La Casona del Beaterio (££) Zaragoza 20 (tel: 28 182119). Restaurant/coffeehouse of great character. Tasteful rooms thick with old photos, patio, good breakfasts and lengthy lunch or dinner menu.
Restaurant Casino Español (£) Gutiérrez Zamora 14 (tel: 28 175593). A budget-traveller's delight. Vast, echoing old restaurant serving delicious *corrida comida* in faded theatrical splendour.

Puebla

Fonda Santa Clara (££) Avenida 3 Poniente 307 (tel: 22 422659). Rather over-rated but still as popular with locals as with tourists. Friendly service and long menu of Pueblan specialities.
Restaurant El Cortijo (££) 16 de Septiembre 506 (tel: 22 420503). Designed in Spanish style with heavy wood beams; just south of the cathedral. Excellent *mole* and other Pueblan specialities.

Taxco

Paco's Bar Grill (££) Plaza Borda 12 (tel: 762 20064). The outdoor terrace is a great vantage point opposite the cathedral. Try to get there early for a good table and *queso cilantro*.
Restaurant Santa Fe (£) Miguel Hidalgo 2 (tel: 762 21170). Friendly family-run place with fish and chicken dishes.

Tepotzlan

La Sandia Azul (£) Avenida Revolucion 9 (tel: 739 50296). Pretty patio right beside the church walls, best at night. Family cooking, good grills, bar.

Veracruz

Gran Café de la Parroquia (£) Independencia 105 (no phone). One of Mexico's most famous cafés, founded in 1810. Always bustling and full, the place to linger and people-watch. Good, basic dishes served from 6am till midnight.
La Paella (£) Zamora 138 (tel: 29 320322). On the quiet side of the zócalo, a small, attractive place serving good seafood.
Pardiños (££) Zamora 40, Boca del Rio. Enormous and well-frequented by locals, particularly for Sunday lunch. Try the *vuelve a la vida* (return to life) seafood cocktail.

THE SOUTH

Oaxaca

Antijitos Regionales (£) Alcala 301 (no phone). Delicious *quesadillas, tamales* and *molotes*. Assorted tables in plant-filled courtyard, much frequented by local families. Open till 11pm.
La Casa de la Abuela (££) Aveinda Hidalgo 616 (tel: 951 63544). Excellent regional specialities, served at a quaint hideaway. Adventurous eaters will be eager to sample the fried grasshoppers; the more timid can stick to basic Mexican fare.

El Topil (££)Plazuela Labastida 104 (tel: 951 416617). Family-run; serving generous portions. Service is slow but warm and welcoming. Good Oaxaqueño fare.
Restaurant Catedral (££) García Vigil 105 (tel: 951 63285). Smart but relaxed place a block from the *zócalo*. Rooms lead off an open patio where live music is played nightly. Oaxacan meat specialities.
Restaurant Del Vitral (£££) Guerrero 201 (tel: 951 63124). Elegant mansion only two blocks from the zócalo. Serving sophisticated Oaxacan dishes combined with international cuisine.
Restaurant Tlaminalli (££) Aveinda Juárez 39 (tel: 952 44157). About 25 minutes from the centre of Oaxaca, but worth the trip. Run by six Zapotec sisters. The traditional Oaxacan food is skillfully prepared: *mole* and *pulque* sauces are superb.

Puerto Escondido

El Dorado (££) Marina Nacional (no phone). Slightly ageing open-air restaurant with the best view in Puerto over the bay. Friendly, erratic service, excellent breakfasts and seafood.

San Cristóbal de las Casas

El Fogon de Jovel (££) 16 de Septiembre 11 (tel: 967 81153). Chiapan cuisine and decoration; lively atmosphere. The menu features delicious specialities such as corn soup and chicken adobo.
El Puente (£) Calle Real de Guadalupe 55 (tel: 967 82250). New multi-activity centre, cheap coffee shop and restaurant, bookshop, workshops, tours etc.
La Galería (£) Hidalgo 3. Rambling bar/café/restaurant in tastefully converted mansion off the *zócalo*. Plants, paintings and live Latino music. Inventive fresh salads and chicken dishes.
Na Bolom (£) Avenida Vicente Guerrero 33 (tel: 967 81418). For a cultural lunch or dinner with researchers, students or anthropologists. Large communal table and stimulating conversation assured.

YUCATÁN

Campeche

Restaurant Miramar (££) Calles 8 y 61 (tel: 981 62883). One of Campeche's many excellent seafood restaurants in the central zone near the port. Copious seafood platters.

Cancún

Carlos 'n Charlie's (££) Paseo Kukulcán, Km 5.5 (tel: 98 830846). Cheerful service in sprawling lagoonside restaurant. Adjoining disco-bar in the marina complex.
La Dolce Vita (£££) Avenida Cobá 87 (tel: 98 840461/841384). Candle-lit Italian romance, with delightful pergola patio in main town. Fresh pasta and seafood, discreet service.

Chetumal

Restaurant La Ostra (££) Calle Efraim Aguilar 162 (tel: 983 20452). Air-conditioned dining room; just off Avenida de los Heroes. Serves typical Mexican dishes along with hearty breakfasts.

Cozumel

Café del Puerto (££) Avenida Rafael Melgar (tel: 987 20316). Upstairs harbour-front location with wide windows on both sides. Lobster, snail, crab, prime rib and soup specialities. Live guitar and piano music. Dinner only.
Casa Denis (£££) Calle Primera Sur (tel: 987 20067). Popular, intimate setting in converted old residence. Menus change daily and feature seafood and/or delicious Yucatecan cuisine. Dinner only, reservations essential.
La Choza (£) Avenida 10 Norte y Calle Salas (tel: 987 20958). Simple, family-run *palapa* serving traditional Yucatecan cooking.

Isla Mujeres

Restaurant Gomar (££) Calle Hidalgo (fax: 988 70142). Touristy but colourful *hacienda*-style restaurant with a choice of indoor and outdoor dining. Fresh seafood and meat dishes.
Restaurant Miramar (£) Avenida Rueda Medina Sur. Right beside ferry pier, a popular local spot for grilled fish, *sopa de lima* and fish *tacos*.

Mérida

Amaro (£) Calle 59 No 507 (tel: 99 282451). Cool courtyard vegetarian restaurant in birthplace of poet Andres Quintana Roo. Try the emerald-green *chaya* soup. Open all day till 11pm.
La Bella Epoca (££) Parque Hidalgo, Calle 60 No. 497 (tel: 99 247844/281928). Delightful *fin-de-siècle* setting overlooking the square. International, Mexican and Lebanese dishes with attentive service.
Los Alamendros (££) Calle 50 No 492, Mérida (tel: 99 285459). Highly recomm-ended for authentic regional cuisine. Pleasant staff and surroundings.
El Portico del Pelegrino (££) Calle 57501 between 60 & 62 (tel: 99 286163). Charming intimate patio or indoor air-conditioned dining. Yucatecan specialities and international cuisine. Excellent service.
Restaurant La Casona (££) Calle 60 No 434 (tel: 99 238348). Italian cuisine in a fine old Mérida mansion: elegant interior or leafy patio. Fresh pasta, seafood, grilled meats. Open till midnight.

Ticul

Los Almendros (££) Calle Principal 23, no 207 (tel: 997 20021). Rustic, slightly beaten-up setting acclaimed for some of the Yucatán's best traditional dishes.

Index

M

O

Q

R

S

T

Picture Credits

The Automobile Association would like to thank the following photographers and libraries for their assistance in the prepartion of this book:

JAMES DAVIS TRAVEL PHOTOGRAPHY F/Cover (c) Chac-Mool statue and base. **FIONA DUNLOP** 15 Crafts, Tzintzuntzán, 41 Mitla church, 86, 87a Chihuahua, 87b Cañon del Cobre, 88, 101b Sierra Tarahumara, 130 Guadalajara, 136b Templo de la Compania de Jésus, 155a Independence Day, Zacatecas, 170a Papantla, 222 Mayan village, 223 Yucatán village, 241a Izamal monastery. **MARY EVANS PICTURE LIBRARY** 29b Hernando Cortés, 39 Moctezuma II, 43 Maximilian, 44 Porfirio Díaz, 45 Juárez 1911, 228/9 Mayan script. **RONALD GRANT ARCHIVES** 90a Cantinflas 'Pepe', 90b 'The Exterminating Angel', 91 Cantinflas & Janet Leigh. **THE IMAGE BANK** F/Cover (a) Siesta. **ADI KRAUS** 11 dancers, Zócalo, 23 car restriction sign, 51 Mexico City, 60b Mexican Museum of Anthropolgy, 144b displays for the Day of the Dead, 196 flora. **NATURE PHOTOGRAPHERS LTD** 226b Caribbean flamingo (PR Sterry), 236b lemon-peel angel fish (SC Bisserott). **R NOWACKI** 100a, 100c, 101 Tarahumara Indians, 209a Man, 246 Tulúm, 250 Mérida market. **PICTURES COLOUR LIBRARY** 138b Mariachis **PLANET EARTH PICTURES/SEAPHOT LTD** 93b gray whale. **REX FEATURES LTD** 24 Carlos Salinas de Gortari **SPECTRUM COLOUR LIBRARY** 238 Mayan temple, Yucatán. **F SPOONER PICTURES LTD** 46 Carlos Salinas de Gortari **TONY STONE IMAGES** F/Cover (b) Tamahumara Indian woman.

The remaining photographs are held in the Automobile Association's own photo library (AA PHOTO LIBRARY) and were taken by Rick Strange, with the exception of pages 2, 6/7, 18/9, 20/1. 20, 24/5, 26, 27, 40/1, 78, 80a, 80b, 81, 82, 84a, 85a, 85b, 89b, 92b, 93a, 95a, 96, 98a, 98b, 102a, 102b, 103, 104, 105a, 105b, 118a, 119a, 255, 259b, which were taken by R Holmes, and pages 3, 7, 83, 84b, 92a, 94, 99, 135, 143, 167, 169, 183, 206, 232, 247a, 251, which were taken by P Wilson.

The author would like to thank the following for their help and advice: the Secretaria de Turismo in Mexico City, in particular Mirentxu Barreneche, Sedetur in Oaxaca and Chiapas, Lupita Ayala at the Mexican Ministry of Tourism in London, Mexicana Airlines, Linda Ambrosie of Tourimex and, not least, Jessica Johnson.

Contributors

Original copy editor: Karen Bird Revision verifier: Fiona Dunlop
Revision copy editor: Nia Williams